WHOSE

BLUES

?

WHOSE

Adam Gussow

BLUES

?

THE
UNIVERSITY
OF NORTH
CAROLINA
PRESS

Chapel Hill

Facing Up
to Race and
the Future of
the Music

Publication of this book was supported in part
by a generous gift from Cyndy and John O'Hara.

Designed by Jamison Cockerham
Set in Arno, Scala Sans, Poplar, Irby, and Saga
by Tseng Information Systems, Inc.

Cover photograph: © Tom Copi

Manufactured in the United States of America

The University of North Carolina Press has been a member
of the Green Press Initiative since 2003.

LIBRARY OF CONGRESS CATALOGING-IN-PUBLICATION DATA
Names: Gussow, Adam, author.
Title: Whose blues? : Facing up to race and the future of the music / Adam Gussow.
Description: Chapel Hill : The University of North Carolina Press,
2020. | Includes bibliographical references and index.
Identifiers: LCCN 2020015417 | ISBN 9781469660356 (cloth : alk.paper) |
ISBN 9781469660363 (paperback : alk.paper) | ISBN 9781469660370 (ebook)
Subjects: LCSH: Blues (Music) — History and criticism. | Music and race — United
States. | African Americans — United States — Music — History and criticism.
Classification: LCC ML3521 .G95 2020 | DDC 781.64309 — dc23
LC record available at https://lccn.loc.gov/2020015417

Previous versions of Bars 4, 5, 6, 9, 10, and 11 appeared, respectively, as Adam
Gussow, "I Will Be Free, I Will Be Me: Rethinking Blues Origins, 'Bluesmen,' and
Blues Feelings in the Age of #blacklivesmatter," *Arkansas Review* 48, no. 2 (2017):
83–98; Adam Gussow, "Blues Expressiveness and the Blues Ethos," *Study the South*,
January 24, 2018, https://southernstudies.olemiss.edu/study-the-south/blues
-expressiveness-and-the-blues-ethos; Adam Gussow, "W. C. Handy and the 'Birth'
of the Blues," *Southern Cultures* 24, no. 4 (2018): 42–68; Adam Gussow, "'Fingering
the Jagged Grain': Ellison's Wright and the Southern Blues Violences," *boundary 2*
30, no. 2 (2003): 137–55; Adam Gussow, "If Bessie Smith Had Killed Some White
People: The Blues Revival and the Black Arts Movement," in *New Thoughts on the
Black Arts Movement*, ed. Margo Natalie Crawford and Lisa Gail Collins (New
Brunswick, N.J.: Rutgers University Press, 2006), 227–52; and Adam Gussow, "Giving
It All Away: Race, Locale, and the Transformation of Blues Harmonica Education
in the Digital Age," *Journal of Popular Music Education* 1, no. 2 (2017): 215–32.

For

NAT RIDDLES

CONTENTS

ILLUSTRATIONS

WHOSE BLUES?

part 1

Introduction

Some people are born with a feeling for the blues, and it has
nothing to do with color. I know black kids who love the blues
and want to play it, but they have no feeling for it. I've also heard
white guys play the blues so deep it makes you want to cry.

Lonnie Brooks, Chicago blues musician (1990)

It's too bad that blacks are drifting away from the blues; it's one of
their greatest contributions to American culture. But let's face it:
If it weren't for whites, this music might be dead right now.

Howard Stovall, director, the Blues Foundation (1997)

These blues are not of you or for you, though some are about you.
These blues are in spite of you, Mr. Charlie. These blues are mine
and my children's as they were my grandfather's and his father's.

Sugar Blue, Chicago blues musician (2012)

There's no essential race to a genre of music. It's a
fabrication. It's been even painstakingly calculated.
Which means that it doesn't belong inherently to
anyone. So what if I'm an Asian guy playing blues?

Dr. Ken "Sugar Brown" Kawashima, PhD,
Chicago blues musician (2019)

1

THE BLUES WORLD—the contemporary American mainstream scene and its discussants—has a race problem. It's a problem with a long prehistory, one that first surged into view when the Black Arts Movement confronted the Blues Revival in the 1960s, then went dormant for several decades. The problem reemerged briefly in the mid-1990s, smoldered underground for a while, then burst into flames in Chicago between 2011 and 2012, the same time period in which an African American teenager, Trayvon Martin, was killed with one endlessly debated shot by George Zimmerman, a "white Hispanic," in a Florida housing development. One goal of *Whose Blues?* is to address that problem, the blues-and-race problem, by staging an imaginative encounter between the two sides and then complicating the dialogue at every turn, so that a more thoughtful and productive conversation begins to emerge. (Blues literature is a help in this endeavor, which is why a secondary goal of this book is introducing fans of blues music to canonical works by W. C. Handy, Langston Hughes, Zora Neale Hurston, and other blues literary pioneers.)

Many decades ago, fresh out of college, I spent a few months working as a paralegal at a labor law firm in San Francisco. It was there that I first heard the term "bad facts." Bad facts are facts that work against the case you're trying to make. They are part of what the court invokes as "the truth, the whole truth, and nothing but the truth" when witnesses swear in: uncomfortable, incontrovertible realities that the other side will surely ride hard, and that your side wishes did not exist. But they do exist. Lucky for you, the other side also has its share of bad facts.

In *Whose Blues?* I do my best to highlight bad facts about the blues, the better to undercut a pair of ideologies that, considered individually, don't fully account for the music, the histories and experiential realities that lie behind it, the people who have made and continue to make it, and the lived worlds in which the music currently dwells. I term these ideologies "black bluesism" and "blues universalism." Each ideology has a partial purchase on the truth. (The first ideology has a proportionally greater purchase on the truth, as this book will make clear.) Each comes with a ready-made slogan:

Blues is black music!
No black. No white. Just the blues.

The first slogan, a sentiment of long duration but uncertain provenance, became a battle cry in May 2015 as the title of a new blog by Corey Harris, a Colorado-born African American blues artist and MacArthur Fellowship winner of aggressively pan-Africanist leanings. Harris precipitated an uproar

Corey Harris
(courtesy of the John D. and Catharine T. MacArthur Foundation)

among white blues aficionados and musicians with an inaugural post titled "Can White People Play the Blues?"[1]

The second slogan, a familiar T-shirt meme on Beale Street in Memphis in the mid-1990s, was picked up and repurposed by Rick Looser, an advertising executive born in Alabama and based in Jackson, Mississippi—a southern white man, yes—who in 2005 decided to spend $300,000 of his own money on a campaign called "Mississippi, Believe It." Hoping to upgrade the state's racially retrograde image in the American imagination, Looser created a poster, headlined by the slogan and featuring photographs of B. B. King, Muddy Waters, and five other black male blues legends born in or associated with the state. "Some see the world in black and white," begins the ad copy. "Others see varying shades of gray. But, Mississippi taught the world to see . . . and hear . . . the Blues."[2] The slogan, if not the ad campaign, has survived and prospered; several years ago I saw it on the wall of a visitor's welcome center on I-20 in Vicksburg. A mural featuring the phrase has held pride of place for almost a decade at F. Jones Corner, a late-night blues club in downtown Jackson with a notably diverse clientele.[3] It can still be found on many T-shirts.

Seductive as they are in this Facebook-shareable, meme-besotted age, slogans are a bad way to get at what TV commentator Van Jones calls "the messy truth." But a conversation between slogans is something else. *Whose Blues?* strives to honor the passions, histories, and lived experience that inform both black bluesism and blues universalism, even while thinking critically about the way these ideologies enable their proponents to evade certain inconvenient truths. In this tribalist moment, I am seeking common ground for the blues tribe, my tribe.

Whose Blues? first took shape in an unlikely form: a series of twelve improvised one-hour lectures, roughly one a day, that I delivered to a videocam from the front seat of my car in December 2012 and released shortly thereafter on YouTube. The outpouring was unplanned. I had recently handed in my grades for the fall term at the University of Mississippi, where I'd been teaching for the previous decade. The spirit of liberation produced by that lull in the academic calendar led me to think back over the undergraduate course I'd just taught on the blues literary and cultural tradition—a course I'd debuted at the New School back in 1999 and had offered half a dozen times on three different campuses since then. On any other occasion, I would have quickly turned aside from the term's work. But on this particular mid-December day, I was possessed. I grabbed a handful of books and lecture notes off a filing cabinet in my campus office, jumped in my car, and drove to an empty parking lot near the soccer field—an isolated spot where, on several previous occasions, I had filmed instructional videos for my Modern Blues Harmonica channel.

I was propelled by a range of motives. In the previous five years I had uploaded several hundred video tutorials in which I did my best to teach all comers, not just Americans but a world audience, how to play blues harmonica. But I had thus far said almost nothing about the other side of the blues—the side that passionately concerned me as a scholar of blues literature and of African American history and culture more broadly. I'd offered my students the fruits, but I hadn't pulled them down into the roots, hadn't shown them the branches or sketched the lay of the land. I wanted to give them a free-form seminar on the texts and authors I'd been teaching and writing about—the Handy/Hughes/Hurston triumvirate, for example— and show them how that sort of journey could deepen and enrich their understanding of blues and blues people. Recent blues scholarship had revised many of our conventional understandings about the music and its evolution; I wanted to guide them through those developments, too, translating academic insights and disputes into the conversational voice I'd developed as a YouTube harp guy. While I was at it, why not introduce them to some of the concepts I'd been using in the classroom—the blues ethos, for example—and some of the local Mississippi blues musicians, like Bill "Howl-N-Madd" Perry, who had visited my class and whose stories had brilliantly illustrated those ideas?

All of these intentions were simmering when I flipped open my videocam and began talking on that cold gray December day. Driving the process, however, was a roiling mixture of less altruistic, more combative feelings: deep frustration, a sense of personal betrayal, the edgy mix of exhilaration and defensiveness one feels in the presence of somebody else's harsh truths, and a desire to speak much more frankly than I had ever spoken in any public venue about the troubled cultural politics of the contemporary blues scene.

What set those other juices flowing was a YouTube video I had just stumbled across with the title "Opening Plenary: Blues Summit on the State of the Music Today," filmed the previous May at the "Blues and the Spirit" symposium at Dominican University, just outside Chicago.[4] I knew Janice Monti, the organizer; she had attended "Blues Today," an annual symposium I'd put on at Ole Miss between 2003 and 2005 that staged public dialogues between a cross-section of blues people—scholars, journalists, musicians, DJs, poets, many of them African American—and she had expressed a desire to create similar dialogues within Chicago's blues community. I knew four of the panel's participants. Three of them, Sugar Blue, Billy Branch, and Matthew Skoller, were harmonica players. In 2010, when I had staged the inaugural Hill Country Harmonica, a new workshop-and-festival event near Oxford designed to highlight African American players, Branch, a peerless teacher and performer, was the first call I'd made. In 2011, Sugar Blue, a blazingly original modernist whom I'd been championing for years, was our headliner. We'd brought Branch back to headline again in 2012, along with his Chicago-based Sons of Blues band and three other African American harp players: Phil Wiggins, Robert "Dr. Feelgood" Potts, and Brandon Bailey.

The plenary session, more than ninety minutes long, was an aggrieved indictment of the contemporary blues scene, on racial grounds. The ten panelists, six black and four white, described a wide range of offenses. Many of them centered on the idea that so-called heritage blues musicians, which is to say black blues performers, had been displaced by white blues performers—from blues festivals, from club gigs, from the Grammys and the Blues Music Awards. Even the BMAs themselves, formerly the W. C. Handy Awards, had been renamed in a way that erased their black namesake, W. C.

Samantha Fish
(courtesy of the photographer, Fally Afani)

Handy. The charges rained down. Singer Sharon Lewis, Texas native and longtime Chicagoan, complained about "talent buyers, festival promoters, club owners, who continue to overlook us as females because we don't play amplified guitars," a veiled reference to Samantha Fish, Sue Foley, Ana Popovic, and other white female singer/guitarists in tight-fitting dresses who were, and are, popular festival attractions. There were complaints about white blues fans who patronized and disrespected older black blues players; about white blues singers who used black dialect; about blues societies run by whites that actively tried to limit African American participation; about black performers being given less stage time than white artists at the Blues Music Awards show; and about a frank but tactless comment made in a widely discussed 2011 interview by Bruce Iglauer, founder and head of Chicago-based Alligator Records, the largest independent blues label, that struck many black Chicago blues players and their white allies as racist, hurtful, and ill-informed.[5]

The specific phrase "Blues is black music" was invoked by only one black panelist: Lincoln T. "Chicago Beau" Beauchamp, poet and publisher of the *Original Chicago Blues Annual* (1989–95), an important blues periodical with deep community roots. "I'm so happy to hear what I'm hearing here," said Beauchamp, "because I remember 15 years ago . . . if you said around some white folks, 'Blues is black music,' everybody be scared they wouldn't get no gigs." But black bluesist sentiment, a fierce desire to reclaim what was felt to be an expropriated racial legacy, dominated the proceedings. After insisting that his blues were "paid for in the blood that whips, guns, knives, chains and branding irons ripped from the bodies of my ancestors," Sugar Blue called out the white blues world in a calm, determined voice. "These Blues are not of you or for you, though some are about you. These Blues are in spite of you, Mr. Charlie. These Blues are mine and my children's as they were my grandfather's and his father's." "Black music is intrinsically African American," agreed Skoller. "Black folks owns the blues," insisted Wayne Baker Brooks. "How is it that the very musicians who carry this music in their bloodlines," Monti asked, "are no longer considered as relevant or worthy of respect and recognition? How is it that those who have no clear understanding of the roots and legacy of this music have somehow come to define the state of the Blues in 2012?"

I watched the video in a state of fascinated agitation. I was torn between frustration at the torpedoing of my own conception of contemporary blues culture as a scene of equitable, convivial interracial endeavor, a conception grounded in my twenty-five-year partnership with Mississippi-born guitarist Sterling "Mr. Satan" Magee; admiration for the full-frontal candor of the indictment; and fervent approval of the idea that a "clear understanding of the roots and legacy" of the blues was essential and that top-of-the-line working musicians like Sugar Blue and Billy Branch deserved all the recognition we could give them. It was precisely for that reason that I had created Hill Country Harmonica and brought Blue and Branch down to Mississippi. I had insisted, from the beginning, in prioritizing black artists. Was I the only white blues promoter striving to do the right thing? Were there really *no* countervailing dynamics in the contemporary blues scene—nothing positive worth acknowledging in a survey of "the state of the music today"?

At that point, suddenly curious, I scrolled back to the beginning of the video and saw the date stamp. And then, as I put two and two together, I got angry. May 18, 2012: That was the day Branch sat on the panel and complained about "the disproportionate number of artists, black artists versus white artists that appear at blues festivals. Now we have blues festivals that have no black artists. That's insane. That is crazy. None. I mean zero." The following day, May 19, he and his band got in a van and drove 600 miles from Chicago to Foxfire Ranch, a black-owned-and-operated venue in Waterford, Mississippi, where he basked in the admiration of our 100+ registrants, signed autographs, sold CDs, watched Brandon Bailey and Robert "Dr. Feel-

Sugar Blue
(photograph by Peter Amft, courtesy of Alligator Records)

good" Potts do their thing, and praised the event we had created, as he had two years earlier when we first invited him down. The following evening, after Phil Wiggins's performance, Branch and the Sons of Blues were our headliners, playing for a hefty fee negotiated by his manager, who insisted that Branch, now a Grammy nominee, be paid top dollar for his services. Wincing at the cost, we had agreed, and paid.

If he wanted to, Branch could have spoken to the Dominican University audience about Hill Country Harmonica. He could have talked about an event where four out of eight blues harp performers were African American; where the house band, led by Bill "Howl-N-Madd" Perry and featuring his son Bill Jr. and daughter Shy, was all black; where the venue itself was owned and run by an African American couple, Bill and Annie Hollowell. To do so, however, would have complicated the recitation of grievance in a way that undercut the political efficacy of the moment. So he said nothing about his weekend plans and the way he would soon be profiting from, and praising, our event. And the litany of white malfeasance rolled on: an old, old story of exploitation, disrespect, and control, but also a new story of displacement from the very grounds of expression—blues—that black folk had created to unburden themselves.

What really bothered me, in light of what felt like Branch's evasion, was the fact that he had called me up and yelled at me for *not* bringing him back after 2010's inaugural event. My partner Jeff Silverman and I had made him a quick, "Of course we will!" promise at the tail end of that year's festivities, then decided late that summer, on reflection, that we wanted Sugar Blue to headline in 2011. Jeff gave Billy the news, but he tracked me down regardless to express his personal dissatisfaction. "Dammit, Adam," he shouted into the phone. "I really thought you were doing something good down there in Mississippi! And now this! You're stabbing me in the back!" Cringing, I tried to explain that it was nothing personal; that Jeff and I loved his 2010 performance and his lecture on "Juke" but felt we needed to switch up headliners the second time around in order to retain audience interest. He wasn't interested in the sorts of calculations that blues promoters, especially novices trying to find their way, are forced to make. He just knew that I had personally betrayed him. And he let me have it. It was a baptism in the blues. It hurt for a long time. It stung. We ended up bringing Sugar Blue and his band down for 2011, and it was the right decision. He slayed our crowd. And when the time came to book a headliner for the 2012 event, I held no grudges. Billy was still the best teacher/performer in the business. We booked him *and* his band—we couldn't afford the band first time around, but that's what he wanted and that's what we gave him—and he and they did a fantastic job. We grabbed hands and shoulder-bumped when he showed up. No hard feelings. Until now.

I looked at the date-stamp on the Plenary Session video. I thought about the choice that Branch had made to say nothing to his Chicago blues peers about our event. I thought about Sugar Blue's silence on that same issue, combined with his slurs against the Mr. Charlies of the blues world: any whites whose investments in the music struck him as compromising his own impassioned heritage claims. I was forced to wonder in retrospect how both men felt about the teaching component of Hill Country Harmonica. If they were carrying such bitterness in connection with the blues-is-black-music idea, what sort of spiritual commitment were they bringing to the project of sharing their hard-won wisdom and their technical expertise with the audience I'd put in front of them: more than 100 blues harmonica students, the overwhelming majority of whom were white? Were they freely sharing their knowledge, or holding something back? Did they truly want to help my registrants become excellent players — gigging players, recording artists, people in whom the blues tradition was fully invested? At bare minimum, the evidence seemed to suggest that they and their black peers were deeply conflicted: glad to have the work and be celebrated as the superior talents they were, unhappy with the general direction of culture transmission in the contemporary blues world, hoping secretly for more black faces in the student/audience cohort even while trying not to treat the rest of us like stepchildren, infuriated by what felt like a steady drip of racist slights and white cluelessness.

I didn't know how they really felt. But I was forced for the first time to entertain such thoughts. And that was a good thing. I'm grateful for the wakeup call, in fact. I don't want contemporary blues culture to feel like a zero-sum competition, much less a net loss for some people, and I certainly don't want to see my fellow blues people disrespected, on the bandstand or anywhere else. As it turned out, much of the critique leveled by Billy and his fellow panelists was substantially true, and much of my own pique at the time was misplaced, even petty — an immature response to an urgently needed call for justice, one that deserves a thoughtful critical assessment. It took years for me to understand that. I had to write this book to understand it.

So I'd like to apologize in advance, especially to Billy, for the aggressive candor with which I've set this particular conversation in motion. I have dumped everything on the table in the hope not just of bodying forth our collective angst as a blues community but of moving us down the road toward a more just and equitable future.

We can get there. But we need to have this conversation.

———————————————————————————

Perhaps none of us, by ourselves, have the tools needed to make ethically consistent sense of the weird and unprecedented situation into which the blues, a music we love and a legacy we're struggling to honor, has gotten itself. A substantially African American creation with a century-long history of white participation and an irreplaceable pantheon of black stylistic originators and stars that transformed itself during the Blues Revival of the 1960s into a mass white phenomenon even as an entire generation of young black people lost interest; an American music that has spread around the world, spawning not just fans but players on all continents—players who, among other things, back up touring African American performers (including Branch, Blue, Lewis, and Chicago Beau) and flock to Memphis every January for the International Blues Challenge. What *is* this music? Even as white commentators cry, "Keep the blues alive!," even as Chicago's black blues stewards and Corey Harris cry, "Blues is black music!," an all-black world known as the soul blues scene remains vibrantly alive in the Deep South, essentially ignored by the white-and-black mainstream: the remains of the chitlin' circuit, featuring black stars, black audiences, black DJs, and black promoters.[6] That form of blues truly *is* black music; the people on that scene, lacking white competition on the bandstand and white fan-administrators offstage, never, as far as I know, feel the need to assert their music's inalienable blackness. That's taken for granted. Yet many whites and some blacks insist that soul blues isn't real blues—as though contemporary black Mississippians, who call the music blues and dance to it in the clubs, don't really know what they're talking about. The most curious irony of all: neither Harris nor the "Plenary Session" cohort have any name recognition on the soul blues circuit.[7] It is the mainstream blues audience, overwhelmingly white, to which they have plighted their troth, even as they seek to enforce their heritage claims and demands for more gigs and awards in the face of competition from their white blues-playing peers.

Sugar Blue and Billy Branch are superb blues musicians, and they remain heroes of mine. But they are also, like me, only human. We've all got fierce passions, and rough edges. Their statements on the "Blues and the Spirit" panel—not just what they said but what they chose not to say—were both enlightening and liberating. Some public settings are conducive to complaint; to the collective articulation of the blues' primal grievance, "You've done me wrong." But complaints—even well-founded, racially grounded complaints—are merely part of the blues dialectic, not the whole story. The truth is messier than that.

It was with that conviction in mind that I improvised the first "Blues Talk" lecture in December 2012. One lecture led to another, and another; the third eruption led me to write a list of twelve lecture titles—a twelve-bar blues—on the back of an envelope, then execute them in order, like a daily meditation, all in the front seat of my old Honda. Videocam rolling, I'd reach into the back seat and grab a book from the accumulating small library, page through, read a few lines, riff some commentary, toss it back, and keep rolling. Lightly edited, the videos were numbered and released on YouTube, two or three per week, over the first five weeks of 2013. I created a webpage on my instructional website, ModernBluesHarmonica.com, and linked the videos and supplementary materials, including syllabi for my blues lit course and a handout, "Teaching the Blues: A Few Useful Concepts for the Classroom," that I'd unpacked over the course of the first four videos. The webpage is still there for your perusal, as are all twelve videos.[8]

Although a desire to think critically about black bluesist ideology was one motivation for the lecture series, I was even more intent on forcing my white blues brethren to question their own resistance to race-talk, a resistance that takes solace in the "No black. No white. Just the blues" meme. There is a certain kind of white blues aficionado, I've discovered, who is actively offended when somebody tries to introduce race into conversations about the blues. This sort of aficionado—a man, more often than not—is almost always quick to assert his love for the music of Robert Johnson, B. B. King, Jimmy Reed, Little Walter, Muddy Waters, Howlin' Wolf: an illustrious pantheon of black male blues masters. (Most such men, I've discovered, tend to forget that blueswomen like Bessie Smith and Dinah Washington are part of the pantheon.) Few such aficionados would deny that the music they love was created, shaped, and given enduring models of excellence by African American artists. Yet explicitly to speak about race to such people, to frame the blues in a way that foregrounds the importance of racially inflected meanings, is often taken as an aggressive and unwanted intrusion. It's as though you've shown up with your race-talk just to spoil their party.

My goal in this book is to spoil the party for everybody concerned. Here I'll make a provocative claim: If you are white blues lover and you wish I would just let all that race stuff go, I think you're coming to the music with an unconscious investment in a pastoral idea of the blues. You want the blues to be the safe, inviting place that you can retreat to in order to get away from all that race stuff: Trayvon Martin, Michael Brown, Black Lives Matter. (This may be one reason why gear—guitars, harps, amps, mics—is such an all-absorbing obsession for your cohort. Gear is color-blind.) You want the blues to take you away from contemporary politics, from your job, just ... *away*.

There's nothing intrinsically wrong with wanting to escape from your troubles through music. A hunger to do this, in fact, gives you something in common with the black southerners who played and listened to the blues back in the 1920s, '30s, and '40s. They, too, wanted to get away from race, in a manner of speaking: from the problems conferred on them by their blackness in a world governed by the protocols of white supremacy. Race was there in the cotton and tobacco fields—in the hard, grinding stoop-labor that black people were expected to perform—and in the way that African Americans were held down by the sharecropping system. Race was there in the way that vagrancy laws and lynching corralled black people, especially men, and the presence of those threats made the juke joints a vitally important free space, a sort of after-hours refuge from the storm. If you're black in America, you're a minority in a country where your skin marks you as different, not just phenotypically but juridically. Your blackness helps determine the way laws and customs are applied to you, and it helps ensure that enduring legacies of violence, economic exploitation, and dehumanizing caricature shadow your every move. By the same token, one of the things that distinguishes being white in America from being black in America is that if you're white, you don't really have to think much about your race unless you choose to. This was truer seventy-five or a hundred years ago than it is in our own notably unsettled era, when the phrase "white supremacist terror" has reentered public discourse, but the racial differential remains true enough that it needs acknowledging, especially by white people who claim to love the blues.

How do we talk when we talk about the blues? In a surprising number of ways. That's partly a function of the music's creole origins, with Africa and the U.S. South high in the mix, but Europe (German-made harmonicas), Hawai'i (slide guitar), and even Native America (an exciting new vein of blues scholarship) audible as well.[9] Cultural politics plays a role, of course, but even more impactful has been the range of different academic disciplines that have brought their investigatory zeal to bear on the blues over the past six decades. There are many ways of talking about the blues; *Whose Blues?* ranges more widely than most studies, in part out of a deliberate desire to highlight the productive disarray of our contemporary moment.[10] We can talk about the blues, for example, the way that music historians or discographers do, as a musical form with discernable antecedents that first becomes audible and visible at certain places and times: a series of "firsts," with names, dates, and catalog numbers attached. We can talk about the blues like musicologists, focusing on characteristic chord structures, lyric forms, timbral attributes, and microtonal inclinations. Or we can talk like ethnomusicologists, describing the blues as a set of traditional musical and social practices elaborated within specific communities. We can talk about blues as a racial legacy—black music—with a deep sociohistorical and existential basis in suffering and oppression, and we can, if we want, supplement such talk with theological grounding, invoking a "Blues God," in Larry Neal's phrase, that was born during the Middle Passage and has accompanied, protected, and divinely inspired black Americans, especially musicians, at every point along their journey.[11] We can talk about the blues in more narrowly sociological terms, as a music enmeshed in a patchwork of local, regional, and national "scenes" within which individual musicians make alliances, uphold status hierarchies, create legends, and achieve or fail to achieve geographic and economic mobility. (Literary critic Vincent Leitch and sociologist David Grazian engage in this sort of theorized empirical description in "Blues Southwestern Style" and *Blue Chicago*, respectively.)[12] We can talk about the blues like literature scholars, as an array of blues texts that includes both lyrics (characterized by an AAB format, first-person declarative voice, signifying vernacular language, etc.) and literary texts (epigrams, poems, plays, stories, novels, autobiographies) that sometimes share structural and thematic elements with those lyrics. We can talk about the blues in biographical terms, focusing on the lived experience and life arcs of those who sing, play, and write blues music and blues books. Or we can talk about blues from a notably different perspective: as practitioners seeking to learn, or teach others, how to play blues on a specific instrument. I dwell frequently in this particular discursive world, thanks to my extracurricular life as a blues harmonica player and teacher. The practical, pedagogical language of blues instrumental and vocal performance is a vital component of the blues universe—but it, too, is merely one form of blues talk. *Whose Blues?* acknowledges the usefulness of all these discourses but refuses to certify any particular discourse as the one right way. In this respect, *Whose Blues?* is a profoundly antifundamentalist exercise. (Fundamentalism is the strident assertion of orthodoxy in a time of confusion.)

The first seven chapters of this book—Bars 2 through 8—roughly parallel the first seven Blues Talks, but the process of transforming improvised lectures into publishable prose was more challenging than I'd anticipated. The transcribed lectures ended up serving as road maps, caches of evidence and insight around which, after additional research, I spun denser and more substantial essays. In most cases, very little of the actual wording from the lectures has remained. But the improvisational zigzags are still there, along with a fondness for the bad facts that unsettle familiar morality plays.

Bar 2 frames contemporary disputes about the origins, meaning, and legacy of the blues as an ideological struggle between black bluesism and blues universalism. I urge white blues fans skeptical of black bluesist bitterness to flip the script, envisioning how Dr. Ralph Stanley—for example—might feel if the contemporary bluegrass scene were dominated by black players, fans, record labels, and magazines. This chapter draws on writings by August Wilson, B. B. King, Honeyboy Edwards, and others to explore a black southern blues condition marked by painful subjection to, and creative struggle against, white southern violence. The chapter advocates for both/and reasoning, rather than either/or reasoning, as a way of honoring the dialectical energy of the blues. The familiar sayings "I'm laughing just to keep from crying" and "You can't tell a book by looking at the cover" foreground such paradoxes, urging us to look beneath the surface, rethink our certainties, and avoid unilateral, reductive statements about the music and its creators.

Bars 3, 4, and 5 expand on themes raised in Bar 2 with the help of my "Teaching the Blues" handout. *Blues conditions*, I argue, provoke *blues feelings*, which in turn are expressed in *blues music*; all three elements function within a field of action governed by the *blues ethos*. This analytic framework, evolved as an aid to classroom instruction, is only one way among many to parse the weirdly unstable thing called blues—a phenomenon at once singular and plural. The blues is, or the blues are? Both are true, but context matters. Fleshing out those concepts with examples drawn from the blues literary and lyric tradition, and with insights provided by Mississippi blues elders Sterling "Mr. Satan" Magee and Bill "Howl-N-Madd" Perry, I also survey a range of recent revisionist blues scholarship by Elijah Wald, Paige McGinley, Karl Hagstrom Miller, and others. Wald asks us to attend to the way "bluesmen" (a problematic concept) were actually songsters, human jukeboxes whose economic survival depended on being able to play, and express themselves, through a much wider array of nonblues music than we might realize. This phenomenon, exemplified by the "polka hound" Robert Johnson, undercuts the idea—one I argued for in *Seems Like Murder Here* (2002), and one implicit in Sugar Blue's conception of the blues—that such musicians were essentially conduits of collective black pain. McGinley reassesses the so-called country blues from a feminist perspective, reminding us that the classic urban blueswomen of the 1920s *were* the blues. They weren't just naming and lending their theatricalized style to the new music as the race-records revolution took the country by storm but carrying the music into the Deep South cotton fields with their traveling road shows a decade earlier, when they were still termed "up-do-date coon shouters" rather than blues queens. Miller, seconding Wald's argument, reminds us that the terms "race music" and "hillbilly music" were inventions of a white-run recording industry intent on segregating southern musicians, black and white, whose performing repertoires overlapped to a considerable extent; racism, in that time and place, has left us with a mistaken impression that "black bluesmen" only played blues and that white artists had no real role in shaping the music.

Bars 6, 7, and 8 each focus on a founding member of the blues literary tradition: W. C. Handy, Langston Hughes, and Zora Neale Hurston. All three writers were members of the black intelligentsia; each found a different way of giving literary form to the bittersweet dynamism of the blues and the charismatic black working-class figures who made and used that music. Handy made his mark first, in two very different formats. As the blues' first superstar sheet-music composer, author of "St. Louis Blues" (1914) and inventor and claimant of the "World Famous Blue Note," he found a way of shoehorning minor-key inflections into major-key melodies, simplifying and commodifying the vocal improvisations of black southern blues singers and entrancing an international audience in the process. As the autobiographical subject of *Father of the Blues* (1941), he created a mythic landscape for the blues, one that featured Mississippi crossroads, "weird" music played by a "threadbare Negro," and other enduring tropes of Deep South authenticity, even as he asserted his own essential role as conduit and scribe.

Just as Handy, the conductor of a minstrel band in the 1890s, was scorned by an educated black elite that viewed blackface minstrelsy with disdain, Hughes was attacked viciously by the black press for daring to write poems that let black blues people express their passions with a vernacular bluntness and swagger in which sexual signifying and brooding violence played a visible role. Hughes boldly defended his creative liberty in "The Negro Artist and the Racial Mountain" (1926) before scandalizing the world with the poems of *Fine Clothes to the Jew* (1927), but it was his first and best-known blues poem, "The Weary Blues" (1925), that established a template later blues poets would follow, bisecting the three-line, AAB verse of sung blues to make a six-line stanza that he then incorporated into his moody, celebratory portrait of a stoic black piano man singing the blues in a Harlem dive.

Like Handy and Hughes, and long before it became common stock at blues clubs around the world, Zora Neale Hurston sampled the familiar three-line blues verse in her books. Like those two men, she was an explorer, one who encountered the blues not on record (although she did that, too, and bemoaned the degrading effects of recordings on black folk communities) but in the flesh. A Columbia-trained anthropologist, memoirist, and novelist, Hurston was the first investigator of any color to immerse herself in black southern juke joint life. In Bar 8, I explore that period of her career: an extended stay at a rural Florida turpentine camp that brought her into contact with a rough-and-tumble cohort of gambling men and knife-wielding women. Inadvertently allowing herself to be drawn into the heated sexual economy of the juke as she collected songs from her male informants, a jittery Hurston ends up fleeing for her life when one female antagonist tries to murder her. The entire episode, which she renders vividly in a folklore collection, *Mules and Men* (1935), and her autobiography, *Dust Tracks on a Road* (1942), offers a provocative meditation on the ethics of representation and the troubling scenes—the bad facts—that the imperatives of black cultural celebration might have led another writer to suppress. Why does Hurston tell *this* story, of all stories, about the Florida jukes? Why doesn't she smooth off the rough edges? And why does she revisit the juke in her best-known novel, *Their Eyes Were Watching God* (1937), and rework the earlier debacle with the help of a young bluesman named Tea Cake, to create a triumph for her fictional protagonist, Janie? I try to answer these questions with the help of tantalizing clues provided by Valerie Boyd's biography, *Wrapped in Rainbows: The Life of Zora Neale Hurston* (2003).

Bars 9, 10, and 11 of *Whose Blues?*, departing from the improvised lectures, consist of previously published essays, two of which predate those lectures and all of which have been substantially rewritten for this volume. Bar 9 explores the way three different sorts of violence—disciplinary, retributive, and intimate—show up in the blues tradition, helping us see more clearly what Wright and Ellison were doing in *Black Boy* and *Invisible Man*. Bar 10, focusing on the Black Arts Movement critique of the Blues Revival of the 1960s, provides essential context for contemporary disputes over who gets to play, manage, and speak for the blues. Bar 11 is a more recent meditation on a practical problem with profound implications: How did black blues harmonica players teach their protégés back in the day—I use Sonny Boy Williamson and Junior Wells as a test case—and how have the shifting racial dynamics of the blues world over the past sixty years transformed that pedagogical encounter?

White hipster Tony "Little Sun" Glover's book *Blues Harp* (1965), the leading instructional guide of that pivotal decade, pioneered blues harmonica education as distance education, divorced from the long-duration, face-to-face mentoring that had previously dominated the subculture. Here I draw on my own experience as a teenaged student of Glover's book and, in later years, an entrepreneurial pioneer in the field of downloadable instructional videos and tab sheets. Acknowledging the ethical dilemmas provoked by a white blues musician who makes the harmonica's esoteric techniques available to a worldwide audience, I also describe the way YouTube's "comments" section brought me together with Brandon Bailey, a young black harmonica player from Memphis. The mentoring relationship we forged, which helped him triumph in a "Star Search" competition and transformed both our careers in unanticipated ways, suggests that contemporary blues culture, despite the race problems explored in this book, is also, if unevenly, a transracial brotherhood—an "inescapable network of mutuality," in Martin Luther King Jr.'s phrase, in which a shared destiny is being worked out.

Finally, in the Turnaround, the twelfth and final "bar" of this book, I fan the deck of cards to offer a handful of thematic and anecdotal explorations: a prismatic view of the blues in the second decade of the third millennium. What happens when we add Asia—a sampling of younger bluesmen from Japan, China, and India—to our reckoning? Is the statistical disparity between African American and white blues performers in contemporary American blues festivals and awards ceremonies really a thing, as they say, and at what point does that disparity become objectionable? What might a white blues scholar have to learn by attending the all-black Jus' Blues Music Foundation's annual awards ceremony in Tunica, Mississippi? What sort of blues is being played and sung by the best younger African American bluesmen, teens and twenty-somethings, when they get together after hours at a picnic table in Cleveland, Mississippi—the town where W. C. Handy first had his revelation about the power of the blues more than a hundred years earlier? *Whose Blues?* ends with a capsule portrait of Akarsha "Aki" Kumar: a Silicon Valley bluesman from Mumbai and a former software engineer at Adobe who has reinvented himself in the age of Trump, blending jump blues grooves with Bollywood lyrics and costumes to heighten his ethnic self-presentation, calling out the U.S. president with signifying language rooted deeply in the African American blues tradition.

bar 2

Starting the Conversation

KEEP YOUR HANDS OFF MY BLUES

Speaking very broadly, people who have emotional investments in the blues—people who like, play, think about, talk about, and identify themselves with the blues—have two diametrically opposed ways of configuring the blues in ideological terms. An ideology is simply an idea-set: an intellectual orientation that governs the way one sees the world and thinks through the problems it presents. One way of ideologizing the blues is to say, "The blues are *black* music." They're a black thing. When you look at the history and cultural origins of the blues, when you look at who has a right to claim the social pain expressed through the blues—what you might call the "I've got the blues" element of the blues—and when you look at who the most powerful performers and great stylistic innovators have been, it's black people who have a profound, undeniable, and inalienable claim on blues in a way that whites just don't. The history, the feelings, the music: they're a black thing. And when whites get involved, as they always do, black people suffer.

This ideological position, a form of black cultural nationalism that I term "black bluesism," is expressed with great clarity and power by Roland L. Freeman, an African American photographer and cultural documentarian, in a poem titled "Don't Forget the Blues."[1] Freeman composed his poem in 1997 to mark the twentieth anniversary of the Mississippi Delta Blues and Heritage Festival—the oldest black-run blues festival in the country—and he read it out loud to the crowd. "Do you see 'em," the poem begins, "here they come":

> Easing into our communities
> In their big fancy cars,
> Looking like alien carpetbaggers

19

Straight from Mars.
They slide in from the East,
North, South and West,
And when they leave, You can bet they've taken the best.

Listen to me,

I've been drunk a long time
And I'm still drinking.
I take a bath every Saturday night,
But I'm still stinking.
This world's been whipping me upside my head,
But it hasn't stopped me from thinking.
I know they've been doing anything they choose,
I just want 'em to keep their darn hands off 'a my blues.

After directing a verse at his female lover and repeating the chorus, the poet continues his litany:

There they go, with our gold.

They drug us out of Africa
By our heels,
They slapped us down in their
Tobacco, rice and cotton fields.
They've fashioned our rhythm 'n blues
Into their rock 'n roll.
And now they have the nerve to come back
Looking for our souls.

The poet repeats the chorus, ending with the refrain, "I know they've been doing anything they choose, / I just want 'em to keep their darn hands off 'a my blues."

That aggrieved "I," demanding our attention, is an avatar of the blues, his blackness unmarked but evident, who refuses to say die: drunk and stinking, beaten down by the world, he is still "thinking," still conscious and resistant. The poem's omnipresent "they" is white people—more specifically, white blues tourists, fans, producers, musicians, anybody who seeks pleasure and profit from the music. "They" is the oppressive white world, an all-points barrage ("from the East / North, South and West") that surrounds, exploits, and unmakes black people ("us") and their ("our") world, body and soul. Playwright August Wilson evokes both worlds in his "Preface to Three Plays"

Starting the Conversation

(1991) when he talks about how the blues gave him "a world that contained my image, a world at once rich and varied, marked and marking, brutal and beautiful, and at crucial odds with the larger world that contained it and preyed and pressed it from every conceivable angle."[2]

Like Wilson, Freeman sees the blues as an art form that contains an image of his humanity, but, unlike Wilson, he sees *the blues themselves* as something that the white world has purloined and profited from, an expropriation anticipated by the earlier refashioning of rhythm 'n' blues into rock 'n' roll. "How can we stop 'em," he cries as the poem rolls on, "or will it ever end?":

> Mama's in the kitchen
> Humming her mournful song.
> Sister's moaning in the bedroom,
> Crying some man has done her wrong.
> Papa's in the backyard sipping on his corn-n-n-n . . . liquor,
> He's just screaming, hollering and yelling.
> And the old folks on the front porch keep saying,
> "There just ain't no telling
> How long it'll take 'em to leave us alone."
> They have taken our blues and gone.

"I know they've been doing anything they choose," he repeats one last time as the poem ends, "I just want 'em to keep their darn hands off 'a my blues."

"Don't Forget the Blues" speaks to the blues from a beleaguered black nationalist perspective. At the heart of the poem is a contemporary black folk community in crisis. There's mama, there's sister, there's papa and the old folks, and there's the poet himself; the family is a microcosm for Black America, and everybody is hurting. Freeman's black family *has* the blues at the very moment when the surrounding white world is consuming and capitalizing on the blues. That white world, these days, is populated by self-styled blues aficionados who claim to love the music and who shout things like "Keep the blues alive! Let's drive on down to Clarksdale, Mississippi, and listen to the *real* blues at Red's Lounge! Let's pay five thousand dollars and take a blues cruise to the Bahamas! Let's fly our Dutch blues band to Memphis and compete in the International Blues Challenge. Let's go to Adam Gussow's website, Modern Blues Harmonica, and purchase video lessons and tab sheets so we can learn how to play the blues." Freeman's poem articulates the pain created by the juxtaposition of, and the power differential between, two radically different blues worlds: an immiserated but tightly knit black community on the one hand and, on the other, a widely dispersed mainstream blues scene that takes pleasure and profit from the music. When Freeman cries, "There they go, with our gold," he is, at least implicitly and with prophetic foresight, taking aim at my viewers, my customers, and me—millions of blues harmonica players from 192 countries and territories around the world who enjoy the hundreds of free instructional videos I've uploaded to YouTube since 2007, a modest percentage of whom visit my website every year and sometimes buy my stuff.[3]

Freeman's poem speaks, in other words, to the transformations that mark our contemporary blues moment, even though it was composed in 1997, before the full extent of those transformations had become evident. It evokes the alarm felt by one particular black community advocate at the fact that blues music has moved outward from his community into the larger world, even while black people in those communities are still suffering, still hurting. Black people still *have* the blues. Young black kids may not particularly like or play blues music. But they and the old folks still have the blues. And something vitally important is being lost, Freeman's poem insists, as blues music floods outward into that surrounding (white) world. Not just lost: something is being taken away from black people in an old, familiar, hurtful way. "I know they've been doing anything they choose," he says repeatedly. "I just want them to keep their darn hands off of *my blues*."

This primal sense of expropriation, of something valuable being spirited away from you by the white folks, is an enduring trope of black economic and cultural life in America, one that links contemporary African American listeners back to those who were "drug . . . out of Africa" and enslaved. But for many in Freeman's audience, the most vivid and proximate source of such feelings would have been sharecropping in the cotton fields. (Freeman, a Washington, D.C., native who had spent considerable time documenting black life in Mississippi in the late 1960s and early 1970s, knew that world well.) Three or four generations of black Mississippians knew that you might work all year long for somebody, and at the end of the season, the cotton would be harvested, you'd give the white man half of your crop as agreed, and then he'd subtract from the proceeds for your half of the crop the cost (as he tallied it) of everything he had provided you over the winter and the long growing season: food, seed, miscellaneous supplies. He'd say, "You know what? You worked all summer long for me and you've come out only $100 behind. You didn't make any money this year, but you're $100 behind." You couldn't argue with him. If you argued with him, you could end up hurt or dead or forced to move to another town or state. Your labor power was being used to accumulate profit for somebody else. The white man owned you, in effect, and used you; he profited from the sweat of your brow. That seemingly inescapable historical situation was bad enough. But now, adding insult to injury at this late moment, the white man isn't just profiting from the song you were singing while you were laboring and sweating in his cotton fields, but he's singing his own corrupted version of the song, and profiting from that! That, in essence, is Roland L. Freeman's vision of the blues. It's one side of the contemporary blues conversation.

NO BLACK, NO WHITE

The black bluesist vision certainly has its virtues, and I'll explore them by and by. It is confronted, in any case, by a second and diametrically opposed way of ideologizing the blues, one that holds somewhat more sway in our contemporary moment, at least among denizens of the mainstream scene. I'll call this second orientation "blues universalism." The epitome of blues universalism is a phrase—a T-shirt meme—that the Mississippi Development Tourism Authority has put up in the waiting rooms of the welcome centers as you enter Mississippi: "No black. No white. Just the blues."

As problematic as that phrase is, I understand and appreciate the anti-racist message that it believes it is conveying. One nation under the sign of the blues! No segregation, no overt disrespect, no "If you're black, stay back." All that race-madness is behind us now. Blues can be a place—or so the slogan suggests—where blacks and whites and, by implication, a whole bunch of different people, come together. Gay and straight. Men and women. Working-class and middle-class. Americans and foreigners. That's a good thing, right? Certainly it is a huge improvement over the bad old Mississippi of the Jim Crow era, a place known over the years as "the lynching state" and "the closed society," where blues was "nigger music" and got no respect whatsoever from white people. Now, an irritable black bluesist might point out that since an overwhelming majority of the greatest Mississippi blues performers, historically speaking, have been African American, and since Mississippi's contemporary blues tourism industry is anchored in the reputations of those celebrated performers, there's something disingenuous about welcoming blues tourists to your state with a slogan like "No black. No white. Just the blues." Doesn't that formulation tend to underplay the hugely disproportionate black contribution to the blues—the very reason, in fact, why so many white blues tourists flock to Mississippi in the first place? Wouldn't a phrase like "Welcome, white blues tourist, to the home of real black blues" be more accurate? But at least the welcome mat has been thrown out, and at least Mississippi's blues are being celebrated in Mississippi. That's a good thing, isn't it?

Before addressing those questions, I want to talk about a Mississippi blues performer who visited my blues literature class at the University of Mississippi several years ago. His name — his stage name — is Muleman. He's from Clarksdale, a Delta town that, like Memphis, St. Louis, and Chicago, styles itself as a "birthplace" or "home" of the blues. He frequently plays Red's Lounge, the same juke joint where Ike Turner used to play. And he's a heck of a player. He's got the groove, the sound, and the attitude.

His family grew up on the edge of the cotton fields. Muleman's father used to hang out in the Delta juke joints, and Muleman spent time learning his trade at Junior Kimbrough's old juke in Chulahoma, up in the hills. He was attracted to the blues in part because his family situation was so unstable. His brother was a junkie; at one point, trying to defend himself, Muleman shot his brother three times with a pistol. The police gave him a break and let him go because they knew he was from a troubled family. Then he got busted for dealing pot and the system had no mercy. He was tried, sentenced, and thrown into the Mississippi State Penitentiary at Parchman. A young Mississippian, Parchman Farm. It's a familiar blues story. What makes it almost surreally perfect is that Muleman actually began singing and playing the blues, on guitar, while he was in prison. He joined the prison band, in fact. He ended up serving four years, and it was the blues — the feelings inside of him and the music he made out of them — that got him through. He was released nineteen years ago and he's still singing and playing his blues. He runs a wheels-and-tires shop in Senatobia during the day and drives a huge old Cadillac limo; his debut album was called *Mississippi Lockdown*. Last time I saw him at Red's Lounge, his foot had been accidentally stomped on by one of his mules and he was sipping moonshine from a fruit jar in an effort to kill the pain.

What do he and I have in common? Nothing, you might think, except the music we both love and play. But we've got something else in common, and perhaps you've figured it out. He's a white guy. Mark "Muleman" Massey has an impeccable blues pedigree, but he's white, not black. The contemporary blues world is full of such paradoxes. One problem with viewing the blues through an ideological lens is that ideologies tend not to leave much breathing room for the human complexities and unlikely scenarios that often characterize contemporary blues lives.

Yet it is the ideologies, a potent and compelling pair of them, that currently hold sway. On one side of the divide: "Blues is *black* music." Blues, in this view, is an inalienably black cultural resource. Whites can't really play it, haven't lived it, don't understand it — yet they've somehow managed, as they always do, to weasel their way into a near monopoly of the means of production. They run the blues societies, book the festivals, and craft the historical narratives that make Joe Bonamassa, Eric Clapton, Bonnie Raitt, and Stevie Ray Vaughan seem like the natural inheritors of a tradition forged by Robert Johnson, Bessie Smith, Muddy Waters, and B. B. King. Even as they profit like thieves from the whole corrupt and exploitative cultural edifice they've created, they view themselves as saviors, crying "Keep the blues alive!" all the way to the bank. Or so the black bluesists would have us believe.

On the other side of the divide is blues universalism: "No black. No white. Just the blues." The Blues Foundation in Memphis, sponsor of the International Blues Challenge, the Blues Music Awards, and the Keeping the Blues Alive Awards, is a key placeholder for this ideological position. It has affiliate blues societies in virtually every U.S. state and more than twenty-five other countries. In the last ten years, although African American men such as Mr. Sipp and Selwyn Birchwood have triumphed in the band portion of the IBC, white winners and runners-up in various categories have come from Canada, Germany, Spain, France, and Australia.[4] Over the past decade or two, and with the help of the Blues Foundation, blues has become the world's most beloved and widespread roots music: a global American success story.

Why do so many different kinds of people around the world not only listen to blues but sing and play the music? Why is it so receptive to their embrace, so adaptable to infusions of local flavor, even while maintaining its identity *as* blues? Perhaps the music's distant African origins offer a clue. Many enslaved Africans in the antebellum South, especially in Louisiana, were brought from Senegal and Gambia. One thing that made that part of West Africa distinctive was the trade routes: a lot of Arab traders coming through, bringing along their Islamic religion and its melismatic vocal music. Melisma is a vocal technique that takes one word or cry and runs it through a long series of pitches; it often takes the form of what ethnomusicologists call a "descending vocal strain." Melismatic singing — also known as "riffing" in black cultural contexts — lies at the heart of the blues tradition, and black popular and religious music more generally. Field hollers are melismatic. B. B. King is a wonderfully evocative blues singer because he brought gospel melisma into the blues. In other words, one core element of the blues isn't African per se but Arabic: this is the argument made by German ethnomusi-

Mark "Muleman" Massey
(photograph by Ron Modra)

cologist Gerhard Kubik in *Africa and the Blues* (1999).[5] Senegalese musical culture made a space for Islamic melisma, absorbing and transforming that influence even while maintaining its core values. People who live on trade routes need to be quick on their feet, culturally speaking: taking what they like and mixing it into the local stew, even while maintaining that stew's brand identity. Senegalese culture, in turn, became the generative matrix of blues culture after the crucible of slavery brought Senegalese musicians to the southern United States.

One reason why blues music has such universal appeal, I suggest, is because it's got this Senegalese DNA. It has certain core elements that give it an immediately recognizable flavor—the three-chord harmonic structure and AAB verse form, the shuffle and breakdown grooves, the epic or dramatic black vernacular language tinged with hoodoo (mojo hands, black cat bones)—and beginners can learn the basics fairly quickly. But it is also uniquely adaptable to local conditions. I became aware of this when, for my book *Journeyman's Road* (2007), I interviewed a Brooklyn Jewish harmonica player named Scott Gold about his experience with the Guam Blues Scholars, a quartet based on that Micronesian island in which two of the players were native Guamanians, members of the Chamorro tribe. "Yeah," he said, "we do songs like Baby, Please Don't Go . . . Back to Tokyo" and "One Room

Coconut Shack." Gold and his bandmates season the African American stew with Guamanian spices.[6]

Are the Guam Blues Scholars, with their audible debt to Muddy Waters and Sonny Boy Williamson, their multicultural background, and their playful South Seas references, a laudable embodiment of the blues universalist message? Or are they, in the way they epitomize the promiscuous worldwide spread and ceaseless mutation of the blues, the crux of the problem evoked by Roland L. Freeman—cultural interlopers who need to be confronted head-on by the fierce black bluesist assertion, "Blues is *black* music"? Have they taken the blues and gone, in a way that merits criticism, or censure?

FLIPPING THE SCRIPT

One way of appreciating why Freeman might have felt the need to write his angry poem is to engage in a thought experiment that I call flipping the script. What would the present situation involving whites, blacks, and the blues look like if we picked a "white" folk music—bluegrass, say, rather than blues—and flip-flopped the races, so that blacks, suddenly an overwhelming numerical majority, were the larger world, in August Wilson's terms, that preyed and pressed on a beleaguered "white" folk-musical community from every conceivable angle?[7] What would that situation look like? It's a fanciful scenario, one that traffics in stereotypes and exaggerations in order to make a point, but I'd like to play it out, much the way that African American author George Schuyler envisioned the chaos wrought on America by a drug that could turn black people white overnight in his satirical novel *Black No More* (1931).

Imagine that you've got not just black Americans but also musicians and fans from all parts of Africa, trekking up to the mountains of Kentucky, wanting to hang out with bluegrass banjoist Ralph Stanley, Man of Constant Sorrow. This isn't Jon Spencer and a bunch of white punk rockers hanging out with bluesman R. L. Burnside in Mississippi, this is Jamal and Dewayne and Ibrahima heading up into the hills and hollers to hang out with Ralph—and Imani and Jada, too, all of them wanting to party with, and document, the mountain man. Imagine that over a fifty-year period, the situation had evolved from a few black folklorists and fans tracking down Ralph, Bill Monroe, and Flatt & Scruggs, to a situation in which hundreds of thousands of black kids are buying banjos, guitars, fiddles, and learning how to play bluegrass, to a point where now, at this late moment, black people actually have a monopoly, or near monopoly, on the means of production. The record labels — Motown and Boogie Down Productions — are up in the hills. They're doing field recordings of Ralph Stanley and his family, and the hard-core black bluegrass aficionados are publishing a magazine called *Keeping the Mountains Real*. It's the analogue to *Living Blues*, but instead of being written and published by whites, with lots of blues album reviews by white reviewers, it's written and published by an all-black staff, with lots of bluegrass reviews by black reviewers. *Keeping the Mountains Real* has a certain number of white subscribers; a handful of them even come from the Kentucky hills. But most subscribers are black urbanites, and, as aficionados, they engage in fierce debates about the music they love. Some of them, the "purists," argue that black bluegrass players just can't sing bluegrass with an authentic twang; this invariably produces cries of outrage from another cohort of black bluegrass lovers and performers who insist that it's not about color, it's about the high lonesome feeling in your heart. They've got a slogan: "No white or black, just some bomb-ass 'grass."

Imagine that this contemporary bluegrass scene has developed to a point where it's completely dominated, on every front, by black people. Their dominance isn't just numerical, it's institutional. There is a Mountain Music Foundation, for example, based in Hazard, Kentucky, and although a few local white musicians and businesspeople are invited to join the board of directors, most of the directors are black folks from Memphis, Chicago, New York, and L.A. They're promoters, DJs, scholars, and of course businesspeople — hustlers of every sort, but truly passionate about, as they say, "keeping the 'grass alive": growing and profiting from the worldwide audience for bluegrass among black people. They've got Keeping the Mountains Real Awards, of course. These often go to the few remaining celebrated white elders, but as those elders slowly die off, younger black urban recipients are starting to claim their share, a demographic shift that causes black aficionados in the purist camp a great deal of consternation.

Given this situation, do you think it's possible that Ralph Stanley and the white bluegrass players who still live in the mountains might occasionally decide to show up at a mountain music festival, shake their fists, and read angry poems that ask, "What in tarnation has happened to my bluegrass?"

The contemporary situation of the blues, as evoked by Freeman, is sort of like that. Of course this little thought experiment has an element of funhouse exaggeration, but only enough to make a point: something weird and unsettling has happened to the blues — at least when viewed from a certain kind of skeptical black community perspective.

I've already suggested a way I find myself, as purveyor of a popular blues harmonica instructional website, ethically implicated in the present discussion. But I'm interested in having the conversation for a different reason: as the interracially married father of a black/biracial son, I dwell in a family circle where there is no racial "they." There is only "we." At the age of thirteen, Shaun's musical talents have already made themselves vividly obvious—he plays trumpet and half a dozen other instruments—and I've taught him the rudiments of blues tonality, along with the heads for "Watermelon Man" and "Doozy." At some point in the future, if he realizes his promise, it is entirely possible that he will be able to tell an interviewer that he learned to play the blues from an old white man down in Mississippi. The marvelous absurdity of that statement makes me want to think these issues through. If I'm a member of a troubled, unsettled blues community—a white-and-black community, a world community—I want to understand where we are *as* a community. I don't see Freeman, with his black nationalist perspective, as a "they" who is stirring up trouble but as a member of my extended family, as it were, who is doing his best to speak the truth as he sees it. If there's no black and no white, just the blues, then I want to understand where we, as blues people, really are at this moment in history.

One of my allies in this process is playwright August Wilson. He and my son have something in common: both are the products of interracial marriages. August Wilson's father, Frederick August Kittel, was a German-born baker and pastry chef; his mother, Daisy Wilson, was an African American cleaning woman, a southern migrant who'd moved from North Carolina to the Hill District of Pittsburgh. His father abandoned the family when Wilson was a boy, a fact that caused the son great pain—as though his father had used his mother and then thrown her away. In 1965, the year his father died, after he'd dropped out of high school and moved from his mother's house into a rooming house, Wilson put on a record by Bessie Smith and found his life transformed by the sound of her voice and the world of meaning opened up by her song. What's curious about the song, a double-entendre blues titled "Nobody in Town Can Bake a Sweet Jelly Roll Like Mine," is that it signifies on his absent father's occupation, implicitly downgrading him and the culture he represents. The recording, in any case, precipitated a conversion experience: not simply a rejection of his white father but a whole-souled embrace of the black blues world that southern migrants like his mother had brought with them to Pittsburgh and other northern urban locales.[8] Wilson embarked soon after on a grand plan: he would write one play for each decade of the twentieth century, exploring the dreams, struggles, triumphs, and tragedies suffered by the black people he'd known in the Hill District and beyond.

One of his earliest plays, and his first big hit, was *Ma Rainey's Black Bottom* (1984). The play is set in a Chicago recording studio in 1927; its subject is Ma Rainey, one of the greatest African American blues singers from the so-called classic blues era when such women were culture heroes and pop stars. As the play begins, two white men—Sturdyvant, a record producer, and Irvin, Rainey's manager—are sitting in the recording studio engaged in an anxious conversation about Ma, who is overdue for her scheduled recording session. Where's Ma? That's the focus of Sturdyvant's concern. We need to get in, get out, and make the record, he says; let's get what we need from her, and quickly, before she has a chance to make trouble. Irvin, meanwhile, reassures Sturdyvant that he's got everything—and especially Ma—under control. So the *mise-en-scène* of the play, the given with which it begins, is white anxieties about how to control and extract profit from black blues people who are viewed as a kind of troublesome property. Sturdyvant and Irvin represent the greedy, exploitative white world that preys and presses on blues people from every conceivable angle.

After introducing these problematic white men, Wilson introduces Rainey's band: a quartet of black musicians named Toledo, Cutler, Slow Drag, and Levee. They are fully individuated characters, evoked with the help of Wilson's extraordinary ear for the intimate, jousting, self-dramatizing way that such musicians speak among themselves. Each of these men has a flaw, a weakness; each is less than fully self-actualized. Wilson makes this clear in his stage directions. But he also makes clear, lest we're inclined to judge them harshly, that their insufficiencies are as much social as personal: they're the unsurprising harvest reaped by African American men forced to grow up in racist America. One of these men, an older blues piano player named Toledo, is the play's organic intellectual: as a thinker, he's a product of the community, not somebody who has just parachuted in, and he's trying to make sense of the troubled, oppressed condition in which black people find themselves. Wilson tells us that Toledo's thoughts aren't perfectly formed. He has more ideas than he knows what to do with and they don't all fit together. But at least he's *trying* to be conscious. At one point, halfway through the play, he delivers a remarkable monologue, a down-home parable about African American history. He's trying to convince his bandmates that in order to make good choices about their lives, they need to see their actual historical

A scene from *Ma Rainey's Black Bottom* at the Mark Taper Forum, 2016
(© 2019 Craig Schwartz Photography)

situation as clearly as possible. The operative word is "leftovers." "That's what you is," he tells his bandmates, "that's what we all is. A leftover from history":

> Now, I'm gonna show you how this goes . . . where you just a leftover from history. Everybody come from different places in Africa, right? Come from different tribes and things. Soonawhile they began to make one big stew. You had the carrots, the peas, and potatoes, and whatnot over here. And over there you had the meat, the nuts, the okra, corn . . . and then you mix it up and let it cook right through to get the flavors flowing together . . . then you got one thing. You got a stew.
>
> Now you take and eat the stew, you take and make your history with that stew. All right. Now it's over. Your history's over and you done ate the stew, but you look around and you see some carrots over here, some potatoes over there. That stew's still there. You done made your history and it's still there. You can't eat it all. So what you got? You got some leftovers. That's what it is. You got leftovers and you can't do nothing with it. You already making you another history . . . cooking you another meal, and you don't need them leftovers no more. What to do?

See, we's the leftovers. The colored man is the leftovers. Now what's the colored man gonna do with himself? That's what we waiting to find out, but first we gotta know we the leftovers. Now, who knows that? You find me a nigger that knows that and I'll turn any whichaway you want me to. I'll bend over for you. You ain't gonna find that. And that's what the problem is. The problem ain't with the white man. The white man knows you just a leftover. 'Cause he the one who done the eating and he know what he done ate. But we don't know that we been took and made history out of. Done went and filled the white man's belly and now he's full and tired and wants you to get out the way and let him be by himself. Now, I know what I'm talking about and if you wanna find out, you just ask Mr. Irvin what he had for supper yesterday. And if he's an honest white man . . . which is asking for a whole heap of a lot . . . he'll tell you he done ate your black ass and if you please I'm full up with you . . . so go on and get off the plate and let me eat something else.[9]

When I teach Wilson's play in my blues lit classes, students love this speech. They understand immediately that Toledo is offering a parable about slavery and its aftermath. Three years after Wilson's play was first produced, a black scholar named Sterling Stuckey offered essentially the same vision in *Slave Culture: Nationalist Theory and the Foundations of Black America* (1987), arguing that black culture first begins to take shape on the slave ships and in early New World slave communities when African people from widely dispersed origin-points find themselves crammed together, forced to find common languages and discern common goals. "Everybody come from different places in Africa . . . different tribes and things . . . they began to make one big stew." The stew is Wilson's metaphor for slave culture, for early black culture, for a beleaguered black community in formation, one incapable of resisting exploitation and dazed by the horrible turn of events that has thrown them together.

When Toledo says, "You take and eat the stew," who is "you"? "You" is the white slavemaster and by extension the entire historical process—the slave trade and New World slavery—that he represents. "You" is the reason why people were enslaved and transported in the first place, which was to eat up, devour, their labor-power. Slave labor was needed to grow tobacco and cotton. Slavery organizes labor in a way that makes a lot of money for the people on the top and no money whatsoever for the people on the bottom. The people on the top own the people on the bottom; they buy and sell them, trade them — and then, when the Civil War is over and slavery has been outlawed, they say, "I'm tired of you. Go away." They don't say "Go away" right away; it takes a while for that process to work itself out with the help of the mechanical cotton harvester in the 1940s and '50s, but by the mid-1960s, white plantation owners in Mississippi were literally driving their black workers off of the land.[10] Many of those workers moved north to Chicago and Detroit; some moved into southern towns and did their best not to starve. That's the history of America. It's a history that black people feel deeply. And it's a history that Wilson, through the mouthpiece of Toledo, brilliantly sums up in a folksy little tale with deadly implications.

What does Toledo's parable of black history have to teach us about the blues? One thing to remember is that there were continuities between slavery and what came after slavery. In his autobiography, *The World Don't Owe Me Nothing* (1997), bluesman Honeyboy Edwards says, "They treated us like we was property," meaning the white people in Mississippi in the 1920s and '30s.[11] He talks about his grandmother, a former slave. She was sold like a mule from hand to hand, he says. So you may be a young black Mississippian growing up "free" in a world filled with blues music, but you know former slaves — they live in your house — and you yourself are out there, at a young age, sharecropping in the same fields that they used to slave in. You're not owned — you're not *legally* owned — but then again you're thoroughly trapped in a system designed to keep you working compliantly in the fields. There's lynch law, there's vagrancy law, there are all these things pressing down on you. So for some blues people, "freedom" felt like very much like an update of slavery, and the blues felt like an enduring, inescapable condition. John Lee Hooker claimed that the blues came "not only [from] what happened to you" but from "what happened to your foreparents and other people. And that's what makes the blues."[12]

As tempting as it is to insist that slavery is the origin point for the blues, there is a significant strain of thought within black intellectual circles that views blues as a novel, innovative music, one evoking a distinctively *post*-slavery, "leftovers" condition. "The blues ain't slave music," insists Kalamu ya Salaam, a poet and performance artist from New Orleans. "Didn't no slaves sing the blues. We," he continues, meaning African Americans,

> we didn't become blue until after reconstruction, after freedom day
> and the dashing of all hopes of receiving/attaining our promised
> 40acres&1mule. in essence, the blues aesthetic is the cultural
> manifestation of former slaves expelled from the land, promised

a new land, and ultimately and callously, turned into an easily exploitable surplus, unskilled and semi-skilled, migratory, landless, politically unenfranchised, labor pool. even when we left the plantations under what we thought was our own steam, it was really an expulsion from the slave/agrarian plantation society into the emerging urban/industrial society. our so-called great migration should be seen specifically for what it was: mass urbanization. this social process, this dispossession of the formerly possessed, set the stage for the two basic blues music forms, country and urban.[13]

Toledo's claim in *Ma Rainey's Black Bottom* that black people are leftovers is essentially identical with Salaam's claim here about the dispossession of the formerly possessed. When you become a surplus, when you realize that you are part of an easily exploitable labor pool—migratory, landless, politically powerless—then you've got the blues: that is Salaam's claim. Slaves weren't free to travel, after all, but sharecroppers were free to move at the end of the season if they thought they could find a better deal somewhere else, and bluesmen (and women) were defined by freedom of movement and a hunger for love. It's not hard to find blues songs that evoke this condition, often as a kind of profound loneliness or unwantedness. "I'm a poor boy, long long way from home." (If home is a dimly recalled African homeland, of course, this line evokes the shattering dislocations of the Middle Passage.)

The blues tradition arises in part out of the decision made by many African American men, musicians and nonmusicians alike, to ramble rather than remain tied to the cotton fields and subject to the will of their bossmen. The paradox of that rambler's freedom was that it brought them that much more quickly into conflict with a system that viewed rambling black men as wasted labor-power and potential rapists. "In the South, they had that vagrancy law," Honeyboy says,

> That hog law. I got pulled in for that a number of times. That means better have a job or don't be seen on the streets. The police pick you up on the street during the day when everybody's working. "What you doing walking around here? Get in the car." They carry you into jail and they give you four or five days and at that time, was spent out in the fields working the cotton. "Don't you know so and so out there? His cotton growed up with grass and he can't get nobody to work it."
>
> You could be out there working, but he didn't want to give

nobody but a dollar a day and nobody wanted to work all day in the hot sun for a dollar.[14]

Black people may have been leftovers, in Toledo's terms, but when the cotton needed to be chopped or harvested, white southerners still believed that a black man's duty was to labor in their fields. "They treated us like we was property," Honeyboy complained. "Come all through slavery time and they still wanted us to be slaves. If them farmers couldn't get nobody to chop their cotton, they'd have the police enforce that vagrancy law and get you to work for a few days."[15]

YOU'RE REALLY BLUESY THEN

At this point, if you're a certain sort of earnest white blues fan, you may be saying to yourself, Okay, I get it. Life was hard for black people in the South and the blues comes from that. You know what? Right on. I understand that, man. I get it. Blues is the voice of oppressed black people. It's all the bad shit that The Man threw down on them, especially in the Deep South. It's that pain and despair and hopelessness, put into musical form.

My answer is, Sort of. But it's much more complicated than that. And at least one blues scholar — I'll explore his views in Bar 4 — says that blues music isn't about that hardship stuff at all.

I won't criticize you, though, if you see the blues as the musical expression of the collective burden borne by African Americans, in the South and beyond. That is a familiar idea, it clearly has some validity, and it's an idea that I embraced wholeheartedly during my years as a graduate student. The first academic panel I ever put together, at the 1995 American Studies Association meeting, was called "Singing Black Pain, Birthing a Blue Nation." I'd had a conversion experience in a seminar the year before; I was just discovering the scourge of lynching suffered by black southerners between the 1890s and 1940s, and my shock and outrage led me to connect that violence with the emergence, development, and spread of blues music during that same period. Although I'd had a career as a touring blues performer by that point, following a five-year stint as a Harlem street musician, in some ways I was still an innocent white guy suddenly being confronted by vicious, ugly things that were old news to black people. But as I began to digest the bad news and let it reshape my understanding of the blues, I began to encounter resistance from some white blues lovers to the very idea that there might be a connection between lynching and other forms of white violence, on the one hand, and blues song, on the other hand. This was my first encounter with whites who held fiercely to what I've come to think of as a pastoral idea of the blues — the conviction that blues music, although it sang of "hard times," was really more about lusting after women, losing your lover, and rambling widely in the hope of hooking up. It certainly wasn't about politics or protest: white blues aficionados and a fair number of white blues scholars were sure of that.

I wasn't so sure. So I went looking for evidence. And I found dozens of examples — not just in blues song but even more pointedly in blues auto-biography — where black blues musicians talked about it lynchings they had witnessed or heard about and the way those events had hurt, scared, and scarred them.

The violence that preoccupied me, so-called spectacle lynching in front of large crowds, had emerged not during slavery but several decades after Emancipation. And this helped me understand a key distinction between the condition of a slave and the condition of a sharecropper. When you were a slave, somebody owned you. You were somebody's capital, somebody's in-vestment. Usually the owner was a white man, although there were black slave owners in Louisiana and a few Cherokee slave owners in North Caro-lina. But by and large slave owners were white men, along with a few white women. Although only 5 percent of white southerners actually owned slaves at the dawn of the Civil War, far more white people who didn't own slaves, particularly wives and children, lived in slaveholding households, and this was especially true in certain Deep South states. In 1860, for example, almost half of white Mississippians lived in slaveholding households.[16] And accord-ing to historian Walter Johnson in *Soul by Soul: Life inside the Antebellum Slave Market* (1999), many southern white men who didn't own slaves were hungry to get them.[17] Buying a slave was a big, expensive investment, like buying a new car. If you could scrape enough money together to buy a slave, you'd taken a big step up the social ladder. The key thing is, slaves were an investment. So most slave owners took at least minimal care of them, the way most people take care of their new cars. Just as important, no white man would think of killing another white man's slave. That would be like trashing somebody's car with an axe. It was a crime against property. So slaves, curi-ously enough, had a measure of protection against white violence, or at least violence administered by somebody other than their master.

Emancipation changed all that. Suddenly black people — black labor-ers — were free, not owned. White southerners found it extremely difficult to rid themselves of the reflexive need to control these ex-slaves and their children. Many white men were filled with rage at black property, so to speak, that had escaped from their control, and they did their damndest to reassert control, so that the bossman, although he didn't actually own you, quickly took on the role of master in the post-Emancipation world. As long as you lived and worked on his land, he had the power to command and punish you. Just as important, whatever value you'd once had as somebody's slave, whatever cash value had once been put on your body, had suddenly been erased by Emancipation. Now you were nobody's investment. You were simply the labor power you were capable of delivering. This meant that no white man was protecting you. Unless you were an extremely strong, capable, and productive worker, you were entirely expendable, vulnerable to violence at the hands of almost any white man who cared to cultivate a grievance against you. The criminal justice system in the South looked the other way when white men killed black men. "They had to have a license to kill everything but a nigger," Mississippi Delta juke joint owner Shelby "Poppa Jazz" Brown told folklorist William Ferris. "We was always in season."[18]

The "freedom" experienced by black southerners during the blues years, in other words, was in some ways worse than slavery. And the blues reflected this grievous condition, this open season on black men. B. B. King, for example, told an interviewer the following in 1968:

> Where I lived, a little place between Itta Bena and Indianola in Mississippi, the people are practically the same way today, they live practically the same way, and that is under the fear of the boss in a manner of speaking. Because so many Negroes down there have been killed many, many different types of ways if you said the wrong thing at the wrong time. . . . So when they use the word frustration, I don't think that really tells the whole story because a guy get to feeling a lot of times he's afraid, he's actually afraid. . . . If you live under that system for so long, then it don't bother you openly, but mentally, way back in your mind, it bugs you. . . . Later on you sometime will think about all this and you wonder why, so that's where your blues comes in, you're really bluesy then, y'see, because you are hurt deep down, believe me, I've lived through it, I know. I'm still trying to say what the blues is to me. So I sing about it. The next thing, which is relatively minor compared to living like I have, is your woman.[19]

Fear of the boss. Fear of the violence perpetrated by "that system." This, according to King, is where is his blues come from. Woman troubles are strictly secondary.

This is an astonishing claim. Most blues lovers I know would insist that woman troubles (and women's troubles with men) are *the* central theme of the blues. But no, King says. It's the deaths of fellow black people, and the possibility that something similar might happen to you, that produces the "deep down" hurt that you sing to get off your chest. This doesn't mean that you sing a song that is overtly about lynching, or fear of the boss — although such songs certainly exist. King never sang those sorts of songs. Still, he insists, that is the feeling that he was working off in his music. And it was this claim about the blues-generating capacity of white violence, more than any other single piece of testimony, that convinced me there was something worth pursuing here — some huge but hidden stream of blues feeling that white blues players, scholars, and fans like me had ignored at our own peril.

I made this argument linking blues and violence in my dissertation, and when I submitted it my book manuscript to the University of Chicago Press, one of the referees was a well-known professor of African American studies, Trudier Harris, author of a *Exorcising Blackness: Literary Lynching and Burning Rituals* (1984), a bracing, honest, scarifying study of the way black writers had responded to violence against black bodies in the South. Her book had helped shape my own vision of the situation, so she was in some ways an ideal reader. But while she generally approved of what I'd done, she offered one major critique. "Gussow," she wrote, "needs to find some way of denuding his manuscript of the sense that African Americans spent this [post-Reconstruction] time period in their songs, texts, and LIVES simply reacting to white folks. Certainly there is no denying that reaction is relevant, but must Gussow make black folks mere automatons to white folks' cruelty? There is at times a prevailing spiritual helplessness and despair . . . that overshadows almost everything else. That is not a view of African American life and culture that I can accept."[20] And she was right. In focusing so pointedly on black abjection, black fear and misery, I had significantly underplayed the way the blues tradition shows black people living, loving, and fighting among themselves without much regard for the white man's world. I took her critique seriously and revised my manuscript with that in mind.

I think it's important to get real if we're going to talk about the blues, doing everything we can to avoid myths, clichés, and polemics. Even that phrase — to "get real" — can become an affectation rather than a path to the truth. But there are pitfalls to be avoided: ways that even the most passionate and best-intentioned people get the blues thing wrong. That's why I began by sketching the black bluesist and blues universalist approaches. Each approach has something to offer — the claim "blues is black music," in particu-

Starting the Conversation

lar, has an undeniable baseline validity—but each is also an oversimplification grounded in an understandable yearning for clarity and justice. My own current approach to the blues highlights paradox; it takes pleasure in the two-sidedness of apparently clear-cut issues. I'd like to think that this approach, a kind of trickster's ethos, is itself grounded deeply in the blues tradition. "You can't tell a book by looking at the cover" might serve as my slogan, warning us as it does against leaping to conclusions based on surface appearances—including the skin color of the blues purveyor.

So here are two pitfalls for those who would speak truth about the blues. One mistake is to argue that blues music is nothing but African American social history. It's the accumulated pain that black people have felt when white people oppress them, given musical form. That's *all* it is, finally, and that's why white people can never really play the music, own it, or have a deep, creative, and enlivening relationship with it. If you're tempted to make this claim, please remember Mark "Muleman" Massey, the white blues musician from Mississippi who grew up in a shack next to the cotton fields. He shot his junkie brother, dealt drugs, spent time in Parchman penitentiary, learned how to play the blues as an inmate; he owns mules, sips moonshine, and plays juke joints. When he visited my class at Ole Miss, he spent the first twenty minutes testifying about the disaster-filled life he'd lived. "I'm gonna tell you guys," he said. "You don't *want* to play the blues. You don't *want* to live the life I've lived." But he survived that life, he paid his dues as a working musician, and he can indeed sing, and play, the blues.

By the same token—and here's the second pitfall—please don't imagine for one moment that the example of Muleman and the spread of blues music around the world means that race no longer matters when we're talking about the blues. Whether you're a player who wants to master the music or a fan who wants to appreciate it fully, it is your duty to educate yourself about the world in which the people who created the music actually lived. Become a student of African American culture and history; keep ideas about black oppression in constructive tension with ideas about black agency. Blues isn't just the "ouch!" that black people groan when white people do bad things to them: that was the point Trudier Harris impressed on me. Blues people made creative choices about how to respond to what oppressed them; one of the choices they made, especially after Emancipation, was not to spend every waking minute worrying about the White Man. "Who the hell wants to go hear something that reminds them of a lynching?" said Albert Murray, author of *Stomping the Blues* (1976), arguing that blues music and the culture that embraced it was far less concerned with protest than with pleasure, elegance, and purgation of bad vibes."[71] Yet Murray was not arguing that the blues were a pastoral retreat, an art form entirely divorced from the painful realities of black people's lives. Quite the reverse: the Saturday night blues ritual he celebrates was a fiercely energetic repudiation of all that sought to hold black spirits down. The slogan "No black. No white. Just the blues," laudable as it might seem, is far too quick to render the historical burdens and achievements of black blues people invisible. It also severely discounts the way the political economy of the contemporary blues scene, with whites dominating both the audience and the institutional superstructure, sometimes works against the interests of African American performers. Race still matters when you're talking about the blues. It matters in the same old way—and in brand new ways. The challenge of our postmodern moment is to discern and embrace the paradoxes rather than pretending they don't exist.

par 3

Blues Conditions

For more than two decades I've been teaching a college-level course called "The Blues Tradition in American Literature." At some point early on, I came up with a two-page handout headlined "Teaching the Blues: A Few Useful Concepts for the Classroom."[1] In the next several chapters, I'm going to explore those concepts, beginning with something I call "blues conditions." Before I do that, I'd like to reprise a little cultural history.

If there's one idea that can help us make sense of the current state of the blues, it is *aftermath*. (In this respect, we might take a cue from Toledo.) As American blues people, black and white, we are living in the long aftermath of slavery and segregation. Early in the new millennium, we're still working through the traumas that those related but distinct epochs inflicted on America's African American residents, and we're still conjuring with the African roots and creole contours of the blues' musical inheritance. But we're also living in the aftermath of a more recent series of changes that transformed blues music and blues audiences during the 1960s, especially in America. What happened during that decade still critically shapes the contemporary blues scene and the tensions that inform it.

Between 1920 and 1960, more or less, blues music was black popular music. This is true whether we're talking about blues queens like Bessie Smith and Dinah Washington, or urbane city bluesmen like Charles Brown, Leroy Carr, and B. B. King, or the Mississippi-to-Chicago axis that gives us Charley Patton, Jimmy Reed, and Muddy Waters, or R&B bandleaders like Wynonie Harris and Louis Jordan. In 1952, a Louisiana-born bluesman named Little Walter had a #1 R&B hit for eight weeks with "Juke," a harmonica instrumental. In 1952 blues was big. It was a music where young black men with talent and ambition like Walter, Jimmy Rogers, and Muddy Waters dreamed big dreams. The film *Cadillac Records* (2008) gives you some sense of what it was like to be a young Chicago blues performer in the early 1950s.

Then rock 'n' roll shows up. The rock revolution happens at Chess Records in the summer of 1955, when Bo Diddley and Chuck Berry have #1 hits with "Bo Diddley" and "Maybelline." The Chess brothers suddenly become much more interested in recording Bo and Chuck than Muddy and Walter.[2] The white kids are dancing to rock 'n' roll, and there's big money to be made if and when the Chess brothers' black artists cross over. The black kids, too, are quickly beginning to pivot from blues to rock 'n' roll. By the time we get to 1960, to judge from the #1 hits, blues is beginning to ebb as a black popular music, or certainly as *the* black popular music. It's beginning a downward arc, at least among black audiences. With white audiences, of course, exactly the opposite is happening. The British blues invasion hasn't happened yet, but by 1960 the folk revival is in full swing and white audiences, along with a few white musicians, are suddenly starting to get interested in something called "country blues." *The Country Blues* is the title of Samuel Charters's groundbreaking 1959 study of the music, a book whose deliberate romanticism helps stoke white fascination. The following year, British researcher Paul Oliver publishes *Blues Fell This Morning* (1960), a richly detailed study that interprets the lyrics of hundreds of blues songs in the context of African American social history to offer a panoramic view of black America's struggles and triumphs during the long dark night of Jim Crow. The books by Charters and Oliver hit the white audience hard, helping them hear the music as deeply connected with the freedom struggle of the ongoing civil rights movement. But those books also conjure up the blues people, with their forthright sexuality, restless ramblings, and vivid juke joint nightlife, as an irresistible locus of romance, guardians of down-home authenticity and preternatural vitality — and thus the antidote to the uptight world of middle-class white adulthood, the world of the Squares and Organization Men and feminine mystique that the counterculture is gearing up to demolish with an all-points assault later in the decade.

Now, it's important to acknowledge that there had always been *some* white audience for blues music. There was a white urban audience for blues queens like Bessie Smith and Ma Rainey in the 1920s, and there was a blues craze of sorts on Broadway during that decade, a time in which Tin Pan Alley songwriters wrote "blues" that don't really deserve that name. An example of this trend is Irving Berlin's "Shaking the Blues Away," a 1927 dance number at the Ziegfeld Follies featuring lines like "When they hold a revival way

Cover of sheet music for "Shaking the Blues Away"
(courtesy Rue Royale)

down south / Every darkie with care and trouble that day / Tries to shake it away."[3] Sophie Tucker, a Russian Jewish immigrant who took lessons in blues singing from African American star Ethel Waters, was billed as both a "coon shouter" and blues singer in the 1920s and given the moniker "Last of the Red Hot Mamas," paving the way for subsequent white torch singers like Janis Joplin, Bette Midler, and Mae West.[4] Elvis and Jerry Lee Lewis were singing hillbilly blues in the 1950s, as Jimmie Rogers was singing his "Blue Yodel" songs in the 1920s. White blues, to paraphrase Gil Scott Heron, ain't no new thing.

But those earlier developments are merely a prelude to what happens when white America's fitful fascination with the blues is powerfully reinvigorated at the beginning of the 1960s. With this white interest, not surprisingly, come misunderstandings and distortions. Given the worldwide stardom that B. B. King enjoyed for the last five decades of his life, it may be surprising to learn that he and Bobby "Blue" Bland were dismissed by many blues aficionados and commentators in the early 1960s as purveyors of a gaudy, commercialized, aesthetically impoverished variant of the "true" blues played by the country bluesmen. It wasn't until Charles Keil published *Urban Blues* (1966), one year after the British blues invasion and the Paul Butterfield Blues Band had launched a white blues revolution, that subcultural opinions about King began to change. Spurning country blues advocates as clueless "moldy figs," Keil made a cranky and convincing case for King and Bland as preacher-like figures in the black community, great blues artists who ministered to their black fans on Saturday night in a way that wasn't wholly different from what went on in church on Sunday mornings.[5] It didn't hurt that audible evidence for Keil's claims could be found on King's 1964 album, *Live at the Regal*—one of the greatest live blues albums ever recorded, chiefly because it registers the close and mutually sustaining relationship between King and his adoring black fans. But that album also registers something that was rapidly disappearing from the scene: an African American blues performer as black pop star.

By 1968 B. B. King is playing for the white flower children at the Fillmore West—he's suddenly a huge star with that audience—but young black people are turning away from him to embrace soul music. They think of his blues as backward, "country," the sound of slavery and submission that their parents and grandparents may have put up with but that they no longer will. The disrespect he suffers at the hands of younger black audiences brings him to tears on at least one occasion. Yet on the night he debuts at the Fillmore, the white kids give him such a warm reception that they, too, bring him to tears. "By the time I strapped on Lucille," he remembers in his autobiography "every single person in the place was standing up and cheering like crazy. For the first time in my career, I got a standing ovation *before* I played. Couldn't help but cry. With tears streaming down, I thought to myself, *These kids love me before I've hit a note. How can I repay them for this love?*"[6]

The first big blues festival, a white-run event featuring black blues artists playing for countercultural crowds, takes place in Ann Arbor, Michigan, in 1969 and repeats in 1970. The blues societies that will come to dominate mainstream blues life in the 1990s and beyond haven't yet happened—the first will be formed by Vietnam vets in Bucks County, Pennsylvania, in 1977—but by 1970 there's no question that the white blues revolution has arrived. In December 1969 there's a concert at Madison Square Garden featuring Janis Joplin and the Paul Butterfield Blues Band; one white rock journalist calls it "the greatest blues battle of recent years," even as black intellectuals fume at the hubris of it all.[7] Why and how did this upheaval take place? Where did these white blues audiences and white blues musicians come from? How did black people, the undisputed originators of the music, lose control of the music? What does this loss of control mean for the music? Don't the music and its social meanings change when it is taken up and used by people who hail from outside the music's culture of origin?

In order to answer these questions, we need to have some idea of what the music meant to the people who created it. We need to pause for the cause, return to the source, and explore the foundations. We need to do so with a sense of restraint and irony, precisely because that is so rarely how commentators approach the blues. Something about the blues encourages large generalizations, decisive pronouncements, and passionate investments, rather than nuanced claims, as though the music is the audible distillate of Black America's sufferings since the 1619 landing at Jamestown, or, alternately, a universal solvent that resonates in every corner of the world. Yet the blues' own epigrammatic tradition encourages restraint—or at least one portion of it does. When Bo Diddley tells us that "You can't judge a book by looking at the cover," he's warning us against jumping too quickly to conclusions about the content of someone's character, including their musical character, based on surface appearances. Are blues a black thing? Of course they are. How could they not be? Are they a white thing? Well, a whole lot of white folks (and Asian folks) these days sing and play something that they *call* the blues. If we're being empirical rather than prescriptive, shouldn't this matter? But the story of the blues isn't just the story of who is singing the song, or what they've suffered in order to sing it. The audience matters, too. Call-and-response, the reciprocal interplay between a performer and his or her community, is a foundational aesthetic principle of the blues. If B. B. King was so moved by the warm response he received from the white hippies at the Fillmore that he not only burst into tears but delivered what he calls "the best performance of my life," aren't the blues—contemporary blues—a black-and-white thing?

If our quest for enlightenment has to begins somewhere, it might begin with the following summary statement from my "Teaching the Blues" handout:

> The blues are relentlessly dialectical, foiling any attempt we make to crystallize their truths into one incontrovertible statement. This curious and under-remarked quality has something to do with the freedom needs and trickster sensibilities of the music's African American originators: a refusal to be either nameless or wholly known, a refusal to be held in place, defined downward by slander, quietly rubbed out.

To say that the blues are relentlessly dialectical means that when the blues show up, they almost always show up not as one thing—one feeling, one spiritual orientation, one musical element—but as two or more things in tension. The blues are country, they're down-home. But they're also big-citified, urban. They're Muddy Waters in Mississippi, driving a tractor through the cotton fields and playing guitar with a sawed-off bottleneck slide—but they're also Muddy getting off a train in Chicago and plugging his guitar into an amp. The blues are rough like Howlin' Wolf, but they're also as smooth and urbane as Dinah Washington. Blues are songs of sadness: I just can't keep from crying. But I'm also *smiling* just to keep from crying— smiling on the outside, even when I'm crying, or rage-filled, on the inside.

Blues are songs of sadness transfigured by rhythmic energy into a source of healing. Albert Murray made this point in *Stomping the Blues*. Stomping the blues doesn't just mean that we're going to jump up off the couch and dance our low-down blues away; it also means that we're going to stomp *on* those blues and give 'em a beat-down. We're going to rout them and drive them out the door. Janheinz Jahn made exactly the same point. Blues music, he argued, is designed to conjure up Nommo: "the spoken word, the sound of the drums, the laughter of the throat, the poem, and the song."[8] Blues song doesn't just reflect low-down blues feelings in a passive way; it summons Nommo, purges those feelings, and creates a mood of uplift. Blues music brings relief from the blues.

Blues feelings are despair backed by euphoria. "I may be down, but I won't be down always." But the blues are also euphoria shadowed by despair. Watch out! You may be sitting on top of the world at this particular moment, but one summer day your baby might just decide to go away. Then again, if you're a skillful blues navigator, you'll find a way of surviving that disaster, too. "But now she's gone . . . and I don't worry . . . Because I'm sitting on top of the world."

The blues are relentlessly dialectical. And this "curious and under-remarked quality" is connected with the "freedom needs and trickster sensibilities of the music's African American originators." When I make this claim, I'm speaking to a male tradition within the blues. I'm thinking once again about David Honeyboy Edwards and *The World Don't Owe Me Nothing*, a story of blues life in the Mississippi Delta of the 1920s and 1930s. Life in that time and place was dominated by cotton sharecropping. Young black men like Honeyboy were consigned to the cotton fields from the time they were nine or ten years old. Honeyboy got a taste of that life, working alongside his parents and siblings, until Big Joe Williams, an itinerant bluesman, wandered along. Fascinated by Big Joe's music, Honeyboy got his father's permission to head south with the older man. The two guitarists, master and apprentice, worked their way down to New Orleans. Williams showed Honeyboy how to "make it": how to play for tips in the street. At a certain point, when Big Joe got drunk and violent, Honeyboy took off; he worked his way back home, heartened by his newfound ability to handle the streets on his own. By the time he rejoined his family in Greenwood, his vision of life's possibilities had been transformed. Once he realized he could harvest spare change from the public by playing the music he loved, he resolved never to be a sucker again, picking cotton all day long in the hot sun for a dollar.[9]

What are the blues? They are a way of self-presencing, self-annunciating. They're a way of asserting your identity rather than remaining an exploited anonymous cog in a cotton-producing machine. They're a way of saying "I'm *here*, baby. I'm a Howlin' Wolf. I'm a crawling kingsnake and I'll crawl beneath your door." They're about renaming yourself in a bold way, declaring yourself powerfully present. Willie Dixon's great musical innovation is the stop-time riff that drives "Hoochie Coochie Man." Da DA-da-da DUH! "I'm the hoochie coochie man, everybody knows I'm here!" Self-presencing is important when you live in a world that has corralled you with vagrancy laws and terrorized you with lynch law, a world that sees you as a pair of hands that should be in the cotton field working hard all day for next to no money, without complaint.

Etched into the blues tradition is the fact that some people found a way out of that destiny. Honeyboy and other traveling musicians are the skilled tradesmen of the blues, men who honored their creative gifts by honing their skills and evolving a free-floating guild that stretched from New Orleans to Chicago. Blues songs tell the truth about this life. I'm going to leave this

David Honeyboy Edwards, 2008
(courtesy of the photographer, Bill Steber)

town, I'm going to catch the first mail-train I see—but if I head out into the great wide world, I'm risking the wrath of those vagrancy laws. I risk being accused of rape if I find myself in a town where there's no white boss to vouch for me. Living out your freedom demanded a trickster's sensibility. In other words, even as you're singing "I'm here!" and making a name for yourself, you're also finding ways of whispering "I'm *not* here" and dancing away from the disciplinary net that encircles you.

Honeyboy shrewdly gamed this element of the blues dialectic. As he roamed the Delta, busking for nickels and dimes, he'd spend the night with a series of different women—one in every town, more or less, and often somebody living on a plantation. He didn't want to get hooked up to a plow, he didn't want to sharecrop for a white boss, so he'd stay at a woman's house for a relatively brief period of time. She'd feed him with leftovers from the

Blues Conditions

white man's table, sleep with him, give him some money or clothes. As a black man present on a plantation during the work day, of course, he was still fair game — unless he fooled the boss. "The way to get by all that," he said, "[was to] stay in the house all day long. I was like a groundhog. Come 6:00 I'd take a bath, come out like I'd been in the field. They don't know whether you've been in the field or not then. That's the way I done."[10] In this manner, he evaded the white boss's proprietary gaze and retained self-ownership. He escaped what Houston A. Baker Jr. calls the carceral network, the network of laws, customs, people, and institutions that wanted to kill you, imprison you, or merely lock you in place as part of a compliant black labor force.[11]

Honeyboy's footloose lifestyle is a strategy of resistance, and it's organized around a paradox. I'm here, I'm here in a big way, I'm in your face, I'm the show. I'm Honeyboy, the ladies' man. But the next moment, I'm gone.

BLUES IS, BLUES ARE

The blues is, or are, a devilishly tricky thing to talk about, in part because of such paradoxes. Start with the sentence I've just uttered. Do we say "the blues *is*" or "the blues *are*"? Is the blues singular, or are the blues plural? It is a strange object of inquiry indeed that oscillates in such a way. Blues is, we might stipulate, a form of music that originates in African American communities in the southern United States. But the blues are also a range of emotions, not just a generalized sadness, and so there's an undeniable plurality to the blues as well. The blues is a mutable but durable music with a distinctive sound that takes a range of forms as it undergoes a modernizing process, a music that continually renegotiates its relationship with its own traditions.

One of the things that makes the blues powerful is precisely the fact that when we have them, or have very strong feelings about them, we're sure we know what they are. Yet when people have disagreements about what the blues is, or are, those disagreements often result from the fact that they are confusing or conflating several distinct facets of the blues.

So let's begin again, very carefully, with a four-part definition that has proven useful in undergraduate classrooms: *Blues conditions* lead to *blues feelings*, which are expressed as *blues music*; the feelings and the music are encompassed by, and the conditions are endured with the help of, the *blues ethos*.

Blues conditions, blues feelings, blues music, blues ethos. Four interrelated facets of the surprisingly complex social and aesthetic phenomenon known as the blues. Needless to say, most people who talk about the blues don't dissect the word, or concept, into component parts. Quite the reverse:

they tend to use the word expressively, assertively, in ways that blend or blur several elements. They drive on Mississippi's country roads, see a tumble-down sharecropper's shack, and say "Now *that* is the blues." What do they mean? In an English department, we might say that the material object — the shack — instantiates a specific conception of the blues. It exemplifies and expresses an idea of the blues as something connected with poverty, with beat-downness, with southernness, with blackness. If you live in a shack like that — well, if the weather is cold outside, you're going to be shivering inside. It's small and cramped, and since it's falling down, you obviously don't have the money to fix it. With a house like that, you'd just sit around in the evening after working all day and feel bad about being poor, or fume at being exploited. Or maybe you'd sit on the front porch, set some rhythm going on a guitar, and sing out those feelings. All those bluesy ideas somehow coalesce around a specific material object, that tumbledown shack.

The declarative statement, "Now *that* is the blues," fuses all those ideas about the blues. But we can, if we want, come along and begin to disentangle those ideas. We can talk about blues conditions: the shack itself, cold and dirty and collapsing. We can talk about blues feelings: how you'd feel if that was where you were forced to live. We can talk about blues music: the sort of music you might make if you lived in a shack like that. And we can talk about the blues ethos: a philosophical orientation toward life that might sustain you if you were the guitar-playing, blues-singing resident of that shack.

Let's begin with blues conditions. What are they? The first thing to be said is that many people conflate blues conditions and blues feelings. That's not entirely misguided — the two easily intermingle — but neither is it the best way of seeing clearly what is going on. Blues conditions are best defined relationally: they are *the material facts and social environment that together constitute the ground out of which blues feelings emerge.* Failed love is a classic blues condition. A man loves a woman, makes love to her, and then she leaves him for somebody else. The blues condition isn't the painful, rip-your-heart-out feelings that this situation tends to incite in such men, it's merely the fact that a love relationship has ended. Not every failed love, after all, produces rage, jealousy, and despair. I felt all those things when, as a much younger man, I lost my girlfriend of five years to a man I knew. The wounds were bone-deep and lasted for years. But fifteen years later, when a second five-year live-in relationship failed, I felt nothing except exhaustion, disdain, and a desire to move on. As a blues condition, in other words, failed love doesn't automatically produce a specific kind of feeling in those who suffer or merely experience it. Sometimes you hurt, sometimes you don't. The conditions and the feelings don't always coexist in predictable ways—which is why it's useful, for the sake of careful analysis, to distinguish them.

The blues condition of failed love is universal, a fact that some have used to explain the global popularity of blues music. By the same token, failed love has certain specific implications in black southern working-class contexts that deserve attention. In a place and time where black men were squeezed hard by both sharecropping economics and the daily indignities of Jim Crow, a beautiful and beloved wife or lover was a particularly valuable possession—the most charismatic possession, arguably, that a black working man might claim. The loss, or threatened loss, of such a prized possession took on outsized importance in such a context. Honeyboy Edwards, neither more nor less promiscuous than most traveling blues musicians, understood the danger that indiscriminate promiscuity could engender among jealous local men in the communities he was passing through. "You take some ordinary man that's working hard," Edwards insisted, "he's not a musician, and he's got a good-looking woman, he don't want to lose her. Because he figures he won't find another one like her, he'll kill you about her. He'd rather be dead than lose her. So I leave that woman alone. When I got older I learned that wasn't nothing but trouble and death. I learned to leave that alone."[12]

"He'd rather be dead than lose her." There's a world of feeling—fierce possessiveness, murderous jealousy, boundless despair—evoked in such a sentence. Honeyboy doesn't body forth the feeling in flowery language, he just acknowledges it, warily, as a blues one would be advised not to inflict, and steers clear. This world of feeling makes more sense if we appreciate the contours of the Deep South world in which Honeyboy and that "ordinary man" were living. The blues conditions they confronted were sociohistorical as well as personal, and the effects of this linkage were profound.

One way of understanding the blues is to say that it's a music created by people who were comprehensively unloved by the surrounding white world, wanted only for their labor power and the profits that labor power could produce. This was as true for slaves like Honeyboy's grandmother as it was for men his own age, but with a critical difference that I noted in the previous chapter. When you're a slave, somebody owns you; they have a material investment in your physical person. Anybody who hurts or kills you is damaging a white man's property, which puts a check on the violence that other white men other might do to you. After Emancipation, this check on white violence vanished. The apocryphal saying, "Kill a mule, buy another; kill a nigger, hire another," spoke to this condition of decapitalized worthlessness.[13]

Love, in such a context, gives a man respite from the killing fields. A lover's embrace creates a world for you. Failed love, by contrast, strips a man of that comfort and dangles him once again over the precipice. Failed love is indeed a universal blues condition, but it is shadowed, in Honeyboy's Mississippi, by larger and social ills.

Failed love is a representative blues condition, but my classroom handout lists several dozen others. *Unrequited love*: I love her, but she won't love me. And *a promiscuous lover*: a central theme of the blues, one that shows up in brags, laments, and everything in between. "Checkin' on My Baby," "Careless Love," "I Am the Devil," "Mustang Sally," "Bumble Bee." In *Blues Legacies and Black Feminism* (1998), a study of women's blues, Angela Davis attributes the prominence of sexuality as a blues theme to the changed situation in which southern black folk found themselves after Emancipation. A key thing distinguishing a slave from a freedperson is that when you're a slave, somebody else—your master—is determining who you're going to sleep with. There were, of course, slave marriages, but they were difficult to maintain. When slaves got married, they often ended up being forced to live on distant plantations rather than being able to live together, an arrangement known as "abroad marriages."[14] When freedom came, it manifested in various ways, including the right to marry and live with whomever one wanted and, alternately, the right to live out an unprecedented sexual license and mobility. The latter was especially true as one descended the social ladder into the places where blues were being played and danced to. The black middle class defined itself *as* middle class by hewing to standards of respectability that involved marital fidelity, regular attendance at church, chaste dress, abstinence from liquor, and polite conversation, but the blues people let all that go. There was a lot of promiscuity among juke joint folk. Promiscuity is exciting, dramatic. You may not have much money, but if you've got a little money, some flashy clothes, the requisite curves (if you were a woman), and a good rap (if you were a man)—well, you've got something to work with, and blues people worked what they had.

This gets us to the heart of a blues paradox. Angela Davis says the blues sing of sex because that was one of the principal ways the children and grandchildren of slaves experienced their freedom. But that source of freedom was also a source of pain. If I'm free and you're free, we're free to choose each other, and that enactment of our freedom can indeed be wonderful. But you're also free, if you wish, to play around behind my back. That enactment of your freedom creates emotional anguish for me—an anguish that many would consider a paradigmatic blues feeling.

But here again we've skipped ahead to blues feelings when what we were supposed to be inventorying was blues conditions: the interpersonal or behavioral situation within which feelings arise. The reason why we distinguish conditions from feelings is that a given blues condition doesn't automatically give rise to the expected blues feeling. A lover who cheats on you might lead you to feel an anguished, murderous rage, but you might also feel somewhat liberated; your lover's faithlessness might license your own misbehavior, your own resolve to get a little something on the side. Not infrequently, blues feelings manifest as a powerful, combustible mixture of negative *and* positive emotions, a sense of being uneasily suspended between conflicting imperatives. As Kalamu ya Salaam once famously wrote, speaking of blues people, "Life [for them] is not about good vs. evil, but about good and evil eaten off the same plate."[15] There are sweet blues as well as bitter blues, in other words, and bittersweet blues may be the bluesiest blues of all.

A terrific lover: now there's a blues condition! Many blues songs have been written from the standpoint of a man or woman who wants to sing the praises of the gal or guy who is driving them wild. Little Walter brags of his lover in "My Babe" that "once she's hot, there ain't no coolin'."

Unrequited love, failed love, a promiscuous lover, a terrific lover: all four situations are variants of one specific kind of blues condition: the charged atmosphere created by the dance between lovers. Here's another variant: *the arrival of Saturday night with all of its romantic possibilities*. Juke joints, dance halls, cabarets: the spaces of black leisure were critically important for working-class African Americans, both rural and urban and especially in the South, precisely because their laboring lives left them exploited, exhausted, and in need of spiritual regeneration and completion. Saturday night, which might easily last "all night long," was the week's one big chance to catch up — to drink, flirt, brag, dance, style and profile, and, with luck, score a lover. The blues tradition offers a number of songs that represent the heady freedoms of club life, from the boisterousness of Willie Dixon's "I'm Ready" and "Wang Dang Doodle" to Louis Jordan's "Saturday Night Fish Fry" and Matt "Guitar" Murphy's "Way Down South."

JIM CROW SOCIAL RELATIONS

My "Teaching the Blues" handout leaps from the category of love relationships to something that seemingly stands at the farthest remove from love: *Jim Crow social relations*. When I say Jim Crow, I mean southern segregation: the establishment and maintenance of the color line in the U.S. South; the enforced inferiority inflicted on black southerners through law and custom. In its own way, this is just as central a blues condition as those generated by troubled love; one might even argue that Jim Crow social relations are the ground on which all other blues conditions stand. The forty-year period from 1920 to 1960 in which blues was black popular music happens to correspond with the period in which segregation hardens into what white defenders were fond of calling the "southern way of life." Segregation doesn't begin in 1920, of course. It slowly emerges in the 1870s and 1880s as a piecework series of local statutes, and it is first formalized in 1890 with the introduction of the so-called Mississippi plan: a new Mississippi state constitution that disenfranchises the state's black voters, greatly diminishing the ability of black Mississippians to determine their own future at the ballot box. Other Deep South states follow Mississippi's lead. At the same time, those states begin to enact segregation statutes—back-of-the-bus laws—mandating separate accommodations in every place where black and white might actually come into social contact. This is the very moment when a generation of upwardly mobile middle-class black southerners are becoming doctors and lawyers and dressing in good Victorian fashion. But the white South says "Get back." The two worst years for lynching in the South are 1892 and 1893. The moment you prevent people from voting, you can do anything you want to them and they have no legal recourse. That's what segregation was and how it worked.

The mid-1890s, interestingly enough, are the moment when blues songs start to show up in the American South. One of the best-known witnesses to that moment is W. C. Handy, the self-styled Father of the Blues. I'll speak at length about Handy later; what deserves mention here is one particular song referenced by Handy, and later adapted by him: "Joe Turner Blues," with its curious talk about how the "long-chain man" has "come and gone." Joe Turner was actually Joe Turney, a Tennessee lawman whose job it was to transport prisoners, most of them black, from one prison to another back in the days before motorized transportation. He accomplished his task almost exactly the same way that his predecessors, the slave traders, would have marched slaves from back-country Virginia down to Mississippi in days gone by: on foot, with the prisoners in leg irons, chained together.[16] If you've read Douglas Blackmon's Pulitzer Prize–winning study, *Slavery by Another Name: The Re-enslavement of Black Americans from the Civil War to World War II* (2008), you know how frequently the African American men who ended up chained in those sorts of neoslave coffles were not criminals at all but victims of unscrupulous white men who'd arrested and imprisoned them on the flimsiest of pretexts, generally as "vagrants," then profited by selling their labor to other men who ran coal mines and cotton fields.

As a blues condition, in other words, the idea-set called "Jim Crow social relations" opens out into more than just separate-but-equal accommodations. It's a comprehensive set of oppressions that descended on black southerners, particularly men, in the period after 1890s. Suddenly, after being able to vote for several decades after the Civil War, you're told that you can't vote. Suddenly black men are being strung up, tortured, and burned publicly in so-called spectacle lynchings, and there is no legal recourse for the wives and families of the victims. If you're a man, you're forced to step off the curb in your small town every time a white woman passes. If you so much as look at her, or if she *says* you looked at her, that's potentially a lynching offense. Sociologist John Dollard spent the mid-1930s doing research in the Mississippi Delta; in *Caste and Class in a Southern Town* (1937), the study that emerged from that research, he described the sense of fear that this social tightrope instilled in the black men there:

> White people may or may not be very conscious of this threatening atmosphere in which negroes live, but negroes are extremely conscious of it. It is one of the major facts in the life of any negro in Southern town. I once asked a middle-class negro how he felt about coming back down South. He said it was like walking into a lion's den. The lions are chained, but if they should become enraged it is doubtful whether the chains would hold them, hence it is better to walk very carefully. Every negro in the South knows that he is under a sentence of death. He does not know when his turn will come. It may never come, but it may also be at any time. This fear tends to intimidate the negro man.[17]

I use the term "disciplinary violence" to convey this sense of overhanging threat, a key element of the segregated world in which southern bluesmen lived and worked. The teaching handout lists not just Jim Crow social relations but also *racism, the presence of lynching and vagrancy laws in the social field*, and *race-based disrespect*. All of these related phenomena are blues conditions. But so, too, is *disrespect from one's racial coevals*, which is to say, intraracial disrespect. It is hardly surprising that in a world structured by a comprehensive, legally sanctioned disrespect of blacks by whites, black men should be keenly attentive to perceived disrespect from their black peers. This phenomenon was exacerbated by the broad persistence, across the

South, of patterns of hands-on vengeance and justice, something that white men and black men actually had in common. When injured or offended in some way, southern men, regardless of race, have tended through the years to take the law into their own hands, seeking immediate retributive justice rather than waiting for the criminal justice system to restore equilibrium.

One of the most powerful evocations of this theme within the blues literary tradition shows up, again, in August Wilson's *Ma Rainey's Black Bottom* (1984), specifically in the figure of a southern-born trumpet player named Levee. The narrative present of the play, as I described in Bar 2, is a Chicago recording studio circa 1927. Levee is the youngest member of Ma Rainey's recording ensemble. He's young, he's restless, he's edgy; he's something like Little Walter in *Cadillac Records*. He's a flirt—he's trying to seduce Rainey's female lover—and he spends his money on fancy shoes. He thinks that his bandmate Toledo, the historian/philosopher who speaks of black people as "leftovers," is a fool. Levee is an impatient young hothead, basically, who doesn't respect anybody. When his bandmates start to rag on him about the way he's currying favor with Sturdyvant, the record label owner, he starts to get mad. They say, "You don't know how to handle the white man," and Levee suddenly fumes. "Levee got to be Levee! And he don't need nobody messing with him about the white man—cause you don't know nothing about me! You don't know Levee. You don't know nothing about what kind of blood I got! What kind of heart I got beating here!"[18]

Then he starts to tell a story, one that transports us from the Chicago recording studio back in time and southward to his boyhood in Mississippi. It's a story about a particular traumatic experience that has marked him irreparably. It's Levee's blues: the ground out of which his subsequent emotional and professional life has developed. "I was eight years old," he said,

> when I watched a gang of white mens come into my daddy's house
> and have do with my mama any way they wanted. We was living in
> Jefferson County, about eighty miles outside of Natchez. My daddy's
> name was Memphis . . . Memphis Lee Green . . . had him near fifty
> acres of good farming land. I'm talking about good land! Grow
> anything you want! He done gone off of shares and bought this land
> from Mr. Halley's widow woman after he done passed on. Folks
> called him an uppity nigger 'cause he done saved and borrowed to
> where he could buy this land and be independent. (68–69)

Honeyboy Edwards escapes the dead-end of sharecropping by grabbing a guitar and rambling widely, but Levee's father does it the hard way: he manages to scrimp and save enough to buy his own land and "go off shares." "It was coming on planting time," Levee continues,

> and my daddy went into Natchez to get him some seed and fertilizer. Called me, say, "Levee, you the man of the house now. Take care of your mama while I'm gone." I wasn't but a little boy, eight years old.
>
> My mama was frying up some chicken when them mens come in that house. Must have been eight or nine of them. She's standing there frying that chicken and them mens come and took hold of her just like you take hold of a mule and make him do what you want. There was my mama with a gang of white mens. She tried to fight them off, but I could see where it wasn't going to do her any good, I didn't know what they were doing to her . . . but I figured whatever it was they may as well do to me too. My daddy had a knife that he kept around there for hunting and working and whatnot. I knew where he kept it and I went and got it.
>
> I'm going to show you how spooked up I was by the white man. I tried my damndest to cut one of them's throat! I hit him on the shoulder with it. He reached back and grabbed hold of that knife and whacked me across the chest with it. (69)

Levee, Wilson tells us, "raises his shirt to show a long, ugly scar." It isn't just a bodily injury, it's the physical manifestation of a traumatic wound to his soul. (The original meaning of the word "trauma" is "wound.") "That's what made them stop," Levee continues.

> They was scared I was going to bleed to death. My mama wrapped a sheet around me and carried me two miles down to the Furlow place and they drove me up to Doc Albans. He was waiting on a calf to be born, and he say he ain't had time to see me. They carried me up to Ms. Etta, the midwife, and she fixed me up.
>
> My daddy came back and acted like he'd done accepted the facts of what happened. But he got the names of them mens from mama. He found out who they was and then we announced we was moving out of that county. Said goodbye to everybody . . . all the neighbors. My daddy went and smiled in the face of one of them crackers who had been with my mama. Smiled in his face and sold him our land. We moved over with relations in Caldwell. He got us settled in and then he took off one day. I ain't never seen him since. He sneaked back, hiding up in the woods, laying to get them eight or nine men.

He got four of them before they caught him, before they got him. They tracked him down in the woods, caught up with him and hung him and set him afire.

My daddy wasn't spooked up by the white man. Nosir! And that taught me how to handle them. I seen my daddy go up and grin in this cracker's face . . . smile in his face and sell him his land. All the while he's planning how he's gonna get him and what he's going to do to him. That taught me how to handle them. So you all just back up and leave Levee alone about the white man. I can smile and say yessir to whoever I please. I got time coming to me. You all just leave Levee alone about the white man. (70)

Wilson is evoking a deep and complicated blues here: a young Mississippi-born bluesman in Chicago demanding the respect of his black bandmates not just by baring his own wounds — a mother gang-raped while he watched, a father hung and burned — but by testifying to the spirit of retributive justice against white malfeasance that animated his father and continues to guide him. The southern scene of trauma is carried forward as a black migrant's fierce creed. But Levee has overestimated his achieved control over the situation. As the play draws to a close, Sturdyvant suddenly announces that he is unable to use the songs he has commissioned Levee to write. "I don't think I can use those songs," he says in effect. "I'll pay you $5 each, but I don't really think I can use them. I'll take them off your hands, though." Aghast, Levee suddenly discovers that he has been played.

The entire play has been constructed, in some sense, to produce the train wreck of blues conditions that now pour down on Levee, flooding him with an explosive mixture of dismay, rage, and humiliation. This is the moment when Toledo, crossing the studio, accidentally steps on his shoe. What should have been the smallest of inconveniences, easily soothed with a quick apology, becomes the last straw, the final insult. "All the weight of the world suddenly falls on Levee," reads the play's stage directions, "and he rushes at Toledo with his knife in his hand." When Levee stabs and kills Toledo, what is he killing? Not just his bandmate but also the black community's historian and conscience — which is to say, the possibility of full historical consciousness and critical analysis, both of which are desperately needed if the community is to survive and prosper. But black-on-black violence doesn't erupt out of nowhere, for no reason: that, too, is a lesson taught by Wilson's play. The southern world out of which these musicians emerge and the northern world in which they're presently striving to live full and authentic lives are both superintended, "managed," by predatory white men. Where Levee's father takes his time to inventory the injury to his family, make a getaway plan, and then exact suicidal vengeance on his white antagonists down in Mississippi, his son up in Chicago simply acts on his feelings, his blues—and slays his fellow black musician, pointlessly.

Blues music is left to bear witness. "The sound of a trumpet is heard," reads the play's concluding stage direction. "Levee's trumpet, a muted trumpet struggling for the highest of possibilities and blowing pain and warning" (111). *Ma Rainey's Black Bottom* evokes the blues not just as a poetry of aftermath but also as a lived condition of beleaguerment in which past exploitations and the feelings of rage and powerlessness they engendered in African American subjects continue to haunt the present. And they *do* haunt the present: not just the play's narrative present but also our own contemporary moment, one marked by both the Black Lives Matter movement and gang violence in Chicago. Blues conditions endure in black communities, even as the music has moved outward into the surrounding world.

bar 4

Blues Feelings and "Real Bluesmen"

By this point, I presume, you've got a working sense of the ideological struggle that governs contemporary blues talk and a somewhat more nuanced sense of the music's sociohistorical origins and aesthetic strategies. Before we move ahead into a counterstatement of sorts, I'd like very briefly to recapitulate. (The twelve-bar blues structure is characterized by both repetition and inflection points—i.e., chord changes. Bar 4, the first such inflection point, is always characterized by a feeling of incipient change.)

I began by framing contemporary blues talk as a struggle between two polarized positions. The first, black bluesism, insists that blues is, or should be, a black thing. White blues audiences are acceptable although not ideal; white blues performers (and especially singers) are deeply problematic, at once aesthetically inadequate and unconsciously beholden to blackface minstrelsy; whites who seek to profit from, speak with presumed authority about, or in any other way make possessive claims on the music are inflictors of the blues rather than legitimate claimants, and thus aligned with the slave owners, bossmen, and unscrupulous record label owners of yore.

The other position, blues universalism, acknowledges that a great preponderance, if not quite all, of the past masters of the music were black, but it also celebrates white inheritors, a select set of what might be called white blues greats. More important, it views blues music and contemporary blues culture as an inspiring democratic melting pot, a healing cauldron in which blacks and whites and everybody else who plays and grooves to the music is, or should be, judged not by the color of their skin but by the content of their musical character. Blues, in this case, becomes a shared subcultural endeavor with an antiracist sense of purpose.[1] The shared sense of purpose among black and white musicians is understood, moreover, to have a fugitive history tracing back to the days of Jim Crow. David Honeyboy Edwards speaks in his autobiography about Harmonica Frank Floyd, a white Mississippi-born blues musician with whom he traveled and worked in the 1920s and '30s. "Musicians was just musicians back then, it didn't have nothing to do with black or white," Honeyboy insisted. "We was all glad just to see each other. We made music together."[2] Blues universalism views black bluesist race-talk as hurtful, a needless stirring up of trouble in the face of so much good news.

One problem with the blues universalist position is that such scenes of musical brotherhood are situated within a political economy in which white people have more economic and institutional power.[3] This power differential was certainly operative in the early days of the race records industry, as Karl Hagstrom Miller argues in *Segregating Sound: Inventing Folk and Pop Music in the Age of Jim Crow* (2010), and as August Wilson dramatizes in the figures of Sturdyvant and Irvin, and in some ways it's even more noticeable today, in the aftermath of the white blues eruption of the 1960s. In Gramscian terms, whites have achieved something close to hegemony. With few exceptions, they run the festivals, record labels, clubs, museums, cruises, and booking agencies; they dominate the blues societies, radio shows, instructional web-sites, and audiences. Not surprisingly, white ideas about, and tastes in, blues tend to dominate the mainstream market—if not, importantly, the much smaller soul-blues market. African American artists know this. Some resent the situation; some make the necessary adjustments and profit from it.[4] A black bluesist might argue, for example, that Honeyboy's autobiographical cowriters, Janis Martinson and Michael Frank, are both white; that Frank was his longtime manager as well as harmonica accompanist at the time; that Honeyboy's contemporary audience is overwhelmingly white; and that his fond memories of Harmonica Frank Floyd may contain an element of calculated self-interest, abetted by the editorial interventions of his white handlers.

When cultural politics enter the picture, contemporary conversations about the music trend rather quickly toward either black bluesism or blues universalism. Both extremes tend to shy away from the paradoxes that would call their certainties into question. It would seem hard to argue, for example, with the claim that the blues, understood both historically and experientially, come *from* somewhere—specifically, the difficult material and social condi-tions that confronted working-class African American musicians in the Jim

Crow South. Yet even that "from" is, at least potentially, a bone of contention. Some commentators on the black bluesist side of the divide argue for a longer horizon; they view the blues as the audible residue of transgenerational black struggles that extend back beyond the Civil War into the slave past. Yet many black commentators, as I've noted, distinguish the pressured freedom of Jim Crow from the manifest unfreedom of slavery in an effort to explain the difference, the novelty, of blues song. Theologian James H. Cone argues for that position in *The Spirituals and the Blues*. "Despite the fact that the blues and the spirituals partake of the same black experience," he writes,

> there are important differences between them. The spirituals are
> slave songs, and they deal with historical realities that are pre–
> Civil War. They were created and sung by the group. The blues,
> while having some pre–Civil War roots, are essentially post–Civil
> War in consciousness. They reflect experiences that issued from
> Emancipation, the Reconstruction Period, and segregation laws. . . .
> Also, in contrast to the group singing of the spirituals, the blues are
> intensely personal and individualistic.[5]

Although Cone distinguishes the blues from slave songs both formally (i.e., solo singing versus group compositions) and experientially (i.e., post-Emancipation experience versus pre–Civil War experience), he also reinforces the idea that experience, *black* experience, is the key constitutive element of the music. Until recently, most people would have considered this claim uncontroversial, especially if what was being discussed was blues music created during the first half of the twentieth century. Aren't the blues, at bottom, a sort of collective black feeling of suffering, of beleaguerment, in the face of white racist violence and exploitation in the Deep South? When contemporary black commentators like Corey Harris insist, in the face of the white blues onslaught, that blues is *black* music, with that specific and audible emphasis on the word "black," their claim is founded, among other things, on a familiar declension: blues isn't just a musical form, a set of lyrics and sounds and instrumental techniques that anybody can master, and it isn't just a feeling. It's a specifically *racial* feeling, one grounded in the painful particulars of the black experience. Since whites don't share that experience, either historically or existentially (i.e., in the present day), they can't possibly play the music for real. They're just appropriating, mimicking, pretending.

Regardless of how far back one sources the music or what one thinks about white blues musicians as a group, it would seem hard to argue with the base-line claim that there's some connection between blues music and the multiple stresses of black life under Jim Crow. But that is precisely what Elijah Wald does in his paradigm-shifting study, *Escaping the Delta: Robert Johnson and the Invention of the Blues* (2004). Wald doesn't deny racism. He readily admits that the world in which blues music was popular was a world in which African Americans were terrifically oppressed. He just doesn't believe that that oppression had much to do with the reasons why black people sang, played, recorded, and—above all—purchased and listened to the blues. In this respect, he is arguing against one of the central claims I offered in my own academic study, *Seems Like Murder Here: Southern Violence and the Blues Tradition* (2002), which is that the blues tradition, both musical and literary, is marked in various ways by anxiety, grief, and rage bred by lynching and other forms of disciplinary violence.

Before digging more deeply into the debate, I should note that Wald and I are both white blues musicians who spent a lot of time working side by side with gifted and charismatic older African American performers, and our ideas about the music have been strongly inflected by that experience. My partner and guide was Sterling "Mr. Satan" Magee, a Harlem-based guitarist and singer who hailed from Mt. Olive, Mississippi. Wald worked with Howard "Louie Bluie" Armstrong, a string-band musician from Tennessee who played fiddle and mandolin. Many people would call Armstrong a songster, not a bluesman, somebody who played a wide range of folk, jazz, and popular material, and here it is worth pausing to clarify an issue that will become important in a moment.

When most people use the word "bluesman," they use it not just as a way of objectively describing the repertoire that a given musician performed and recorded but as a term of high praise, a marker of authenticity: a "real bluesman." The irony is that no term has less relevance to the lives that African American blues performers in the prewar South actually lived. The term "bluesman" is the creation not of black blues performers but of white folklorists and journalists. The term appears in print very sporadically prior to the early 1960s; the online *Oxford English Dictionary* offers two early journalistic uses of the unhyphenated "blues man," one each in 1930 and 1953, both of which refer to white jazz clarinetists (Ted Lewis and Mezz Mezzrow) and seem edged with gentle mockery, as though commenting on a fad.[6] In 1961, folklorist Mimi Clar and D. K. Wilgus, the record review editor of the *Journal of American Folklore*, use the terms "blues men" and "blues-men," respectively, when discussing recently issued recordings by African American blues performers.[7] The publication of foundational studies by Charters (1959) and Oliver (1960), along with the emergence of the folk revival and the rediscovery of older black southern recording artists, including Son House, Mississippi John Hurt, and Skip James, seems to have given currency to the term, but it also introduced a complication: by 1965, Wilgus is invoking "the new distinction between 'songster' and 'bluesman.'"[8] The distinction is an academic one, quite literally. Prior to the intervention of white folklorists, the word "songster," along with the words "musicianer" and "musical physicianer," were what people in black communities called traveling musicians who performed blues and other popular material; white journalists and record collectors tended to just call them blues singers. Folklorists, concerned with delineating and preserving black folk communities and disconcerted by the recent emergence of a white blues "thing," wanted to distinguish between what they took to be two different sorts of black male blues performers of acoustic or "country" blues: those whose repertoires, especially on record, seemed to consist primarily of blues songs, and those whose repertoires included a broad range of nonblues material, much of it oriented toward white audiences as well as black ones. They called the former bluesmen, the latter songsters. Son House was a bluesman; Mississippi John Hurt was a songster. The bluesmen, to these folklorists and the journalists who took cues from them, were the hardcore, defined by terms of critical approbation like "raw," "impassioned," and "authentic"; the songsters were . . . songsters. Hurt was "gentle," "soft-spoken," and "soothing."[9] Bluesmen were the presumptive carriers of race-wide pain—"the conscience of the Delta," in the words used by ethnomusicologist David Evans to describe Charley Patton.[10] Songsters were something less than that.

Bluesmen and songsters. It's a false distinction, based on a significant misunderstanding, and it's a falsehood that Wald skewers in a chapter in *Escaping the Delta* called "What the Records Missed." Our foundational error, according to Wald, is to imagine that we can accurately assess what blues performers like Honeyboy Edwards, Robert Johnson, and Muddy Waters played live by looking at their recorded repertoires. But we can't. The reason this assumption would be mistaken has something to do with racism in the music industry, a lot to do with racism in the Jim Crow South, and everything to do with the fact that juke boxes—which spun 78 rpm records and provided music without live musicians—didn't really enter the southern scene in a big way until the late 1930s. If you were a black folk musician who wanted to make a living prior to the jukebox era, and even after jukeboxes were introduced, you had to act like what we might now retroactively call a human jukebox. You needed a wide range of material that you could pull out of the hat on a moment's notice, whatever the public requested. You needed current hits, regardless of the idiom, along with old favorites, and you needed to minister to white as well as black audiences. That's how you made enough nickels and dimes to stay out of the white folks' fields. It turns out that Edwards, Johnson, Waters, and their peers had much broader performing repertoires than they were actually permitted to record. When Muddy was interviewed by Alan Lomax in the early 1940s, he listed a half-dozen Gene Autry songs in his repertoire.[11] Johnson, according to his traveling companion Johnny Shines, "did anything that he heard over the radio" but was especially fond of polkas. ("Polka hound" was Shines's term.)[12] "Overall," Wald writes of those players and others of their ilk, "it is probably true that no one outside vaudeville made a living during this period as purely a 'blues' player. All were dance players, party players, street-corner players — songsters and musicianers, if you will — who included blues because it was one of the hot sounds of their time."[13] As a consequence, the repertoires of these so-called bluesmen and their white peers in the South overlapped to a considerable degree, which is to say that both cohorts drew on a common stock of songs, both old and new. The black musicians didn't just play blues or "black music," in other words, and the hillbilly players didn't just play old-timey or "white music." The situation on the ground was much more hybrid than that.

But, as Miller articulates in *Segregating Sound*, racism in the recording industry worked hard to clarify — which to say, racialize — the situation. In essence, the industry put all southern musicians through a racial sorting process. Talent scouts told the black musicians, "You will be permitted to record race records," which meant blues. They told the hillbilly musicians, "You will be permitted to record old-timey, mountain, vaudeville, and novelty numbers." Some white musicians of the period, most notably Jimmie Rodgers, recorded blues as well ("Blue Yodel No. 1"), but they were sold as hillbilly records rather than race records. Just as important, gatekeepers to the blues recording industry like H. C. Spier of Jackson, Mississippi, insisted that the black musicians perform their own original tunes, not covers of current pop songs, in part to feed the "hot" race records market and in part to avoid paying the statutory royalties that pop covers would have required. Faced with this situation, songsters like Edwards, Johnson, and Waters set aside the full

spectrum of songs and idioms through which they'd been expressing them
selves and making a living—"ragtime, pop tunes, waltz numbers, polkas,"
in Johnson's case—and said, in effect, "Okay boss, since blues are what you
want, I'll give you blues." They narrowed their focus and remanufactured
themselves as bluesmen, although that specific term didn't exist at the time.

What has been handed down to us as a result is this idea that blues artists,
"real bluesmen," just play pure, dark, down-home blues in which the soul-
deep ache of an oppressed race finds expression. Nothing could be further
from the truth. Almost all of the prewar blues artists played, and expressed
themselves through, a much wider range of material than that—material
that spoke to a world of experience beyond the blues conditions and blues
feelings that I've been exploring thus far. If we know that Johnson's favorite
performance pieces, apart from polkas, included "Yes, Sir, That's My Baby,"
"My Blue Heaven," and "Tumbling Tumbleweeds," that tends to undercut
not just the idea of Johnson as a tortured genius obsessed with the devil but
also the larger idea of the black southern bluesman as a musical mechanism
for bodying forth the cry of an oppressed people.[14] The revisionist arguments
offered by Wald and Miller profoundly destabilize both ideas.

RETHINKING "REAL BLUES"

Wald's revisionism is enabled by a specific definitional decision that he introduces early in his study and that turns out to have enormous implications.
His working definition of blues, he says, will be "whatever the mass of black
record buyers called 'blues' in any period."[15] This seemingly innocuous move
accomplishes several things. One thing it does is completely separate blues
music from any necessary connection to oppressive conditions and bruised
feelings. Instead, it insists that blues is pop music: music that sells a lot, charts
well, and compels the interest of the widest possible swath (the "mass") of
the black record-buying public. A second thing that happens when you shift
the definitional focus from the harsh world out of which the music emerged
to the tastes of the black audience that helped determine the market for the
music is that the "deep blues" of Charley Patton, Son House, Robert Johnson, and other Delta legends is suddenly decentered in favor of . . . what?
Well, the recordings that a nationwide audience of black music consumers
actually purchased, rather than the Delta blues stuff that never caught their
fancy. W. C. Handy and his compositions, especially "St. Louis Blues," take
center stage in the 1910s, not Henry Sloan and other country blues precursors. Bessie Smith, Ma Rainey, and the other blues queens dominate the

1920s, since they were, as theater historian Paige McGinley argues in *Staging the Blues: From Tent Shows to Tourism* (2014), the first blues performers who actually became pop stars; they literally defined the word "blues" as an American show-business concept at a time when Patton and House were strictly local celebrities.[16] In the 1930s, crucially, an urbane singer and pianist named Leroy Carr becomes for Wald the paradigm of a blues recording star, waxing several hundred recordings, including "How Long, How Long Blues." Carr not only outsold Robert Johnson by a hundredfold or more, but he also was remembered decades later by aging black listeners who had no idea who Johnson was.

Why don't we—meaning contemporary blues fans, black and white alike—know as much about Carr as we know about Johnson? According to Wald, it's because the story of the blues has for a long time been told by white writers invested in what historians would call a presentist narrative line. Seeking a blues genealogy for aging rock-blues superstars like Eric Clapton, the Rolling Stones, and Led Zeppelin, the baby boomer blues story anchors itself in what it imagines to be the autochthonous brilliance and gothic atmospherics of a Delta primitive like Johnson, neglecting the fact that Johnson's recordings barely registered with the nation's black record-buying public. Carr and the blues women, by contrast, although immensely popular with black audiences during their lifetimes and beyond, offer no anchoring mythology for rock's grand narrative, no shared aesthetic strategies or thematic concerns—except perhaps when Janis Joplin is viewed as an update on Big Mama Thornton. When the blues story is told as essentially the run-in to rock, what gets erased is a radically different and in some ways much truer history in which the tastes of "the mass of black record buyers" are tracked from the 1910s right up into the present day, bypassing rock entirely to focus on black blues and soul-blues artists like Willie Clayton, Ms. Jody, Sir Charles Jones, Denise LaSalle, Bobby Rush, Johnnie Taylor, and Dinah Washington. In this respect, at least, Wald's intervention serves the black bluesist cause by forcing white blues lovers to acknowledge the self-serving way they've distorted the music's history even while pretending to honor it.

Wald isn't content, however, just to shift the center of gravity from what he sees as the overvalued stock of Robert Johnson to the undervalued stock of Leroy Carr. He insists, incredibly, that Johnson is irrelevant to the course of blues history—at least when blues is defined in terms of black pop-musical tastes. In the face of the mass of white blues musicians, journalists, scholars, and fans who consider Johnson to be a central figure, one who anchors the tradition, Wald suggests "that Johnson was nothing of the kind, and that as far as blues history goes, he was essentially a nonentity."[17] This is no more than a half-truth; if nothing else, Johnson remained an important influence on Muddy Waters, and Muddy had a fair number of hits on the R&B charts. But the half-truth it contains is potent: neither Johnson nor his songs achieved the slightest visibility, on a *national* level, with the black record-buying public of his time. Compared to a hundred other blues artists, from Leroy Carr to Bessie Smith, from Lonnie Johnson to Walter Davis, Robert Johnson was, in fact, a nonentity. He wasn't "hot." He wasn't even warm. His form of solo guitar-based blues wasn't at all what the black record-buying public wanted in the late 1930s. If we — today's imputed white blues-consuming public — think of Johnson as important, Wald argues, that's because he's important to Eric Clapton and Keith Richards and other boomers who were introduced to him on record in the early 1960s as a disembodied phantasm, a "legend" to whom few biographical facts were ascribed and whose Faustian myth and tragic death made him impossibly attractive as a precursor figure for a rock-blues lineage of bad boys.

There is something elegant, logical, and compelling about defining blues as "whatever the mass of black record buyers called 'blues' in any period." It certainly seems at first blush like a gesture designed to rescue the blues tradition from the distortions accrued during the decades of white ascendance. But Wald's revisionist move has unforeseen consequences. One problem surfaces when we imagine somebody making the same claim with regard to literature: that the really important and representative stuff, finally, is the stuff that shows up on the best-seller lists. The bestselling novels of 1930 were *Cimarron* by Edna Ferber and *Exile* by Warwick Deeping; a relative unknown named William Faulkner also published a novel that year.[18] *As I Lay Dying* sold poorly and was soon forgotten — until, fifteen years later, a literary critic named Malcolm Cowley published *The Portable Faulkner* and people began to pay attention. Today, Faulkner is the canonical figure, the conscience of his era, and Ferber and Deeping are all but forgotten. Isn't it possible that in recuperating and celebrating Robert Johnson, the white blues audience, like Cowley with Faulkner, rescued a neglected genius from the unwarranted obscurity to which mercurial black popular tastes had consigned him? Although mass popularity can be an index of what is on people's minds, the category of "unpopular" often turns out to contain artists — Henry David Thoreau and Herman Melville, for example — who are speaking complex, uncomfortable truths about their own historical moments that the popular audience isn't prepared to hear. Maybe "Hell Hound on My Trail" was too much of a downer for a black public that preferred lighter, more danceable fare. And maybe it's a good thing that Clapton and Richards were electrified by it.

There's no reason to assume, in other words, that the white blues audience's extraordinarily high valuation of Robert Johnson is misplaced. But Wald's claims might lead us to think twice before saying, in effect, "I'm going to anchor my ideas about the blues in a specific group of rural artists" — the Mississippi Delta bluesmen — "whose recordings sold very poorly to black consumers." Why *not* begin with the early blues artists whose recordings black consumers actually bought in large quantities? When you do this, you're forced to say, "Well, the women blues singers were really important." They sold really well in the 1920s, and their performances garnered infinitely more attention in the popular press than the Delta bluesmen. And here Wald confronts us with another paradox, one that pressures our residual desire, whoever we are, to locate the "real blues" in those black male bluesmen. We are inclined to think, because the story has so often been told this way, that the country blues predate the city blues — that the blues "come from the cotton fields," as the saying goes — and, consequently, that the country bluesmen inaugurate a rough-hewn tradition that the classic blueswomen appropriate, gussy up, theatricalize, and render less authentic. This story gains apparent explanatory power from several factors, including the fact that the classic blueswomen like Ma Rainey and Bessie Smith traveled in posh Pullman coaches rather than hitchhiking along gravel highways and the fact that Tin Pan Alley songwriters, ambitious and urbane black men, composed many of the songs these blueswomen performed and recorded. The bluesmen were rural primitives, the classic blueswomen were urban professionals; the latter capitalized on the music of the former. That's how the story goes. But the story, or at least the second half of the story, is wrong — or so Wald argues.

Although African American blueswomen first debuted on record in 1920, with Mamie Smith's epochal "Crazy Blues" (authored by Perry Bradford), it turns out that they had a significant prehistory in the Mississippi Delta during the preceding decade. This is the revelation offered by archival historians Lynn Abbott and Doug Seroff in *Ragged but Right: Black Traveling Shows, "Coon Songs," and the Dark Pathway to Blues and Jazz* (2007). The Delta, it turns out, was overrun at harvesttime with black minstrel troupes and tent shows featuring "Southern coon shouters" and "up-to-date coon shouters," the then-current terms of art for Rainey, Smith, Lizzie Miles, and other soon-to-be recorded blues stars. "Eighteen shows have made Clarksdale in the past month," wrote an entertainment reporter in 1917, as the cotton harvest came in. "And still they come to Mississippi."[19] The word "blues," we know, was just beginning to develop a pop-musical valence during those years in the aftermath of W. C. Handy's "St. Louis Blues" (1914) and "Hesitating Blues" (1915). Rainey and Smith weren't yet called blues singers, but they sang songs called blues — and they did so with a power and polish, backed by jazzy horn-and-rhythm ensembles, that mightily impressed the rural Mississippi audiences who had paid a nickel or a dime to see their show. Charley Patton, Son House, and other future legends of the Delta blues were a part of that audience, and, argues Wald, they were paying attention. Those men as yet had no name for the little cotton field ditties and "jump ups" they'd been evolving with the help of steel-stringed guitar and slides, but there is every reason to think — or so insists Wald — that the tent-show women, blues singers before the term existed, helped them shape and name their own new acoustic music. So if you thought that blues starts in the country and then migrates to the city: not so fast! The city — Bessie and Ma out of Chattanooga and Atlanta — came to the country, and the country took notes. After the tent shows had packed up and left the Delta for the winter, a musician who could flavor his guitar and vocal stylings in a way that evoked the blueswomen and their flashy repertoire stood a better chance of attracting a paying audience.

It is at this point, I suggest, that we might begin to glimpse common ground between Wald's blues-as-pop-music perspective and my own claims about the way the blues tradition is marked by anxieties about white mob violence and disciplinary encirclement. Why might have the Delta bluesmen, and Robert Johnson in particular, have been so interested in where the cutting edge was, stylistically speaking? Because the cotton fields were right there, offering their specter of hard, exploitative labor backed up by vagrancy law and lynch law, and that was your fate unless you found another way to get by. Any freedom worth having was premised on economic freedom; knowing how to satisfy your audience, knowing what was "hot" and getting at least a little of that into your repertoire, was the traveling musician's escape route. This is why the "bluesmen" weren't bluesmen at all but songsters, musicianers, jacks-of-all-trades. They were skilled musical artisans, rambling tradesmen with guitars. They aimed to please the people, by any means necessary. And the people were pleased. The women in particular, according to Honeyboy Edwards, were so pleased that a traveling musicianer could have his pick.[20]

Where, amid all this pleasure and careerism, is the suffering out of which the blues were supposedly born? A central paradox of the blues lies in the

Blues Feelings and "Real Bluesmen"

tension between what Wald rightly calls the "up-to-date power and promise" that attracted black listeners to the music and what he dismisses as the "folk-loric melancholy" lingering behind the music, the "heart-cry of a suffering people" that, he argues, just doesn't have much to do with why black record buyers made the choices they did.[21] That heart-cry, that blues feeling, is, for contemporary exponents of the black bluesist position such as Sugar Blue, the whole point. It's the transgenerational inheritance voiced by the music, a collective race memory that contemporary white investments in the music threaten to obliterate. "This is a part of my heritage in which I have great pride," Blue told a crowd of scholars, musicians, and aficionados at the 2012 "Blues and the Spirit" symposium at Dominican University near Chicago.

> Paid for in the blood that whips, guns, knives, chains and branding irons ripped from the bodies of my ancestors as they fought to survive the daily tyrannies in the land of the free, where some men were at liberty to murder, rape, and lay claim to all and any they desired. From this crucible, the blues was born, screaming to the heavens that I will be free, I will be me. You cannot and will not take this music, this tradition, this bequest, this cry of freedom and dignity from bloodied, unbowed heads without a struggle as fierce as the one that brought us in chains of iron beneath the putrid decks of wooden ships to toil in pain but not in vain.[22]

Sugar Blue (born James Whiting in Harlem, N.Y.) is uninterested in the sorts of arguments tendered by African American scholars such as Cone, Davis, and Salaam about why blues music stands apart, formally and the-matically, from the music of the slavery era. Instead, he sources the blues in a continuing narrative of brutally compelled black labor, one that at some indeterminate moment provoked the birth of a prophetic musical scream or cry—freedom-seeking, individualized, a mode of resistance that conferred personhood. The invidious "you" he indicts is, it would seem, the whole white blues "thing": not just his white musical peers (whom he may not even consider his peers, since the oppressive history he invokes isn't theirs to claim) and a million lesser talents but the white-dominated superstructure of the mainstream blues world—DJs, clubs, festivals, magazines, societies, museums, instructional websites, advocacy organizations, and awards cere-monies. Scholarship, too, perhaps.

Sugar Blue's conception of the blues as an ancestral inheritance, an in-alienable black cry tracing back to slavery, is echoed in a 2019 interview by Pulitzer Prize–winning black poet Tyehimba Jess, author of *leadbelly* (2005):

You're talking about a sound that came directly out of slavery getting directly transported from the continent, laboring under the duress of loss of language, not being able to speak your language upon punishment of death, not being able to learn how to spell or read and write in the language of your captor. Not being able to do that, and then not being able to own yourself or any of the things produced from your labor, or even the things you produced *from* yourself—your children. Or any of the things that produced you; your mother and father are taken away from you. The only thing you actually do have that they can't touch is what comes out of you—and that is the blues, that is the sound of the blues. So you sing the sound that is labored underneath all of that tension, has been shaped by that tension. . . . So when you're talking about the blues, that is what you're talking about.[23]

Perhaps because his forum is the literary world, where he has essentially no white peers seeking to fill the role of blues poet, rather than the mainstream blues scene, where any number of white blues harmonica players are jostling with Sugar Blue for available gigs, Jess's heritage claim is animated by far less frustration and aggression than Blue's. "[The blues] still manifests on the technical level in playing the instruments," Jess says, praising a recent performance by Billy Branch,

but I think, in a lot of ways, you want to talk about ownership by the people who created it. Literature is where you find the real ripple effect of the blues the strongest. The most impermeable. Because it's directly out of the black experience. . . . Other people will be able to practice the blues. But it generated from us, and the most direct experience of it is coming through other art forms. The one I know best is literature.[24]

The word "practice" signifies on and delegitimizes white (indeed, any non–African American) blues musical performance. But Jess also defends the black blues, as a larger project, by decentering blues music: insisting that the ancestral inheritance and its resonance in contemporary black experience can't be endangered, no matter how many whites play the music, because "the sound of the blues" lives on in the poems he writes.

Jess has a luxury, in a sense, that Blue, Branch, and other black blues musicians on the mainstream scene don't have: freedom from direct competition. This can help explain why the words "fierce" and "struggle" rip out through the belly of Blue's manifesto. Sidestepping the paradoxes and com-

Tyehimba Jess
(courtesy of the photographer, Keliy Anderson-Staley)

plexities of lived historical experience explored by Wald and others, including Robert Johnson's fondness for polkas and the wholesale abandonment of blues music in favor of soul music by black youth during the 1960s, Blue evokes the blues less as music than as the purest and most hard-won sort of feeling, a racial and ancestral feeling *carried* by the music, whose continuance is profoundly endangered by the present state of affairs.

Whatever objections one might raise, one is forced to say: here is a distinctly contemporary evocation of blues feeling, this mixture of pain, pride, and outrage felt by an African American musician seeking to reclaim a cherished inheritance from the predations of the contemporary blues world. One might go a step further than that, in fact, and view Blue's and Corey Harris's aggressive pushback against white-dominated blues-business-as-usual as a cultural development that parallels the political advocacy of Black Lives Matter: new black consciousness demanding, in no uncertain terms, that a palpably unjust situation—at least in the eyes of those who so adjudge it—be rectified in a way that acknowledges the continuing precarity of black life.

We have the grounds for a worthy debate here. Although I view Blue's totalizing claims as a kind of mythmaking rather than a properly historical argument, mythmaking—personalizing and enlarging grievance to epic dimensions—is an essential constituent of the blues tradition, as the names Howlin' Wolf and "the Devil's Son-in-Law" suggest. Blue's statement speaks powerfully, in any case, to two key concerns that animated African American blues performers in the Jim Crow South: economic exploitation and disciplinary violence, the latter enforcing the former. In actual practice, the desire to scream, "I will be free, I will be me," was mediated by a keen sense of self-preservation, since the same vigilante violence that bred terror and resentment could easily jump down on anybody foolish enough to complain about it directly. In 1946, folklorist Alan Lomax sat down with Big Bill Broonzy, Memphis Slim, and Sonny Boy Williamson in a New York City hotel room and got them to speak openly, into his Presto disc recorder, about such matters—a recording issued more than three decades later as *Blues in the Mississippi Night*. "Tell me what the blues are all about," he said. And they did. "Here, at last," he later wrote, "black working class men had talked frankly, sagaciously and with deep resentment about the inequities of the Southern system of racial segregation and exploitation." Broonzy and Slim both described the practice of signifying: men they knew who wanted to "cuss out the boss," but, fearful of reprisal, did that indirectly by cursing out a nearby mule or encoding the insults into a work song. "Signifying and getting his revenge through songs," Slim summed up: that was the southern black man's strategy. Yet after having unburdened themselves so frankly to Lomax, the three men were terrified when he played back the recording and they begged him never to share it with the public. "If these records came out on us," they told him, southern whites would "take it out on our folks down home; they'd burn them out and Lord knows what else."[25]

The violence was real, the feelings it produced in these bluesmen were urgent and real; both the violence and the feelings shaped the blues tradition in profound ways that dismissive phrases like "folkloric melancholy" don't do justice to. This is where I part company with Wald and his decision to ground claims about the blues in black popular taste. If Sugar Blue is too quick to totalize the blues, reducing the entire tradition to a freedom-scream paid for in blood, whips, guns, knives, chains, and branding irons, then Wald is too ready to write off any critical concern with the darker blues feelings as a species of white blues romanticism, a projection of an imagined "heart-cry of a suffering people" into a streamlined pop music characterized by professionalism, humor, "up-to-date power and promise." My own perspective has been shaped by the blues literary tradition, especially autobiographies by Mississippi musicians such as Willie Dixon, Honeyboy Edwards, B. B. King, and Henry Townsend. When I speak about the blues, I am speaking about not just the songs those men recorded but also the life stories they told about the Deep South world in which they came of age, including the emotional scars they bore as a result of that upbringing.

CONFESSING THE BLUES

One thing that became apparent to me as I began to investigate this material is that the autobiographical process offered these men a long-deferred chance to bear witness. The songs they'd recorded as younger men were one way of doing that, perhaps, but their late-life confessions gave them a chance to speak with considerably more frankness about southern blues life than their Jim Crow environs permitted them back in the day. Their confessions were enabled by their knowledge that they were no longer in danger of violent reprisal. Quite the opposite: they were bearing witness into the tape recorders of congenial white ghostwriters who were eager to help them shape those confessions into books that could be shared with an admiring white public of blues fans who, like Lomax, wanted to know where their blues came from.

I termed this form of retrospective witness-bearing "confessing the blues."[26] In Blues All around Me (1996), King offers a remarkable example of this phenomenon, one that supplements his somewhat more circumspect claim in 1986 about how "so many Negroes . . . had been killed many, many different ways if you said the wrong thing at the wrong time," that people in Mississippi lived under "fear of the boss," and that his blues—the blues he sang and played—were prompted by living under that threat of violence.[27] It's crucial to remember that King never directly addresses lynching and other forms of racial violence in his lyrics, with one notable exception: the second verse of "Why I Sing the Blues" (1969), with its invocation of slavery in a first-person voice that stands in for the collective subject of black history:

> When I first got the blues
> They brought me over on a ship
> Men were standing over me
> And a lot more with a whip
> And everybody wanna know
> Why I sing the blues
> Well, I've been around a long time
> Mm, I've really paid my dues

But lynching? King never sings of it. Very few blues performers did. There wasn't much of a market for it. But the musicians certainly knew about lynching, saw its after-effects, avoided its clutches as best they could. They felt it. Its presence in the social field was part of the emotional palette from which many of them were working. King makes this clear by describing his own encounter, as a preteen, with the aftermath of a lynching in Lexington, Mississippi—a legal lynching, in fact, where the body of a young black man who had been hung inside the jail was brought out front for all to see. It was a moment "of shock and pain," he recalls, "that can't be erased from my memory":

> A sunny Saturday afternoon and I'm walking to the part of Lexington
> with the stores and the main square. I'm running an errand for Mama
> King, feeling the summer heat along my skin, feeling halfway happy.
> At least there's no school today. I'm delivering a big basket of rich
> folks' clothes Mama King has washed and ironed. Suddenly I see
> there's a commotion around the courthouse. Something's happening
> that I don't understand. People crowded around. People creating
> a buzz. Mainly white folk. I'm curious and want to get closer, but
> my instinct has me staying away. From the far side of the square,
> I see them carrying a black body, a man's body, to the front of the
> courthouse. A half-dozen white guys are hoisting the body up on a
> rope hanging from a makeshift platform. Someone cheers. The black
> body is a dead body. The dead man is young, nineteen or twenty, and
> his mouth and his eyes are open, his face contorted. It's horrible to

look, but I look anyway. I sneak looks. I hear someone say something about the dead man touching a white woman and how he got what he deserves. Deep inside, I'm hurt, sad, and mad. But I stay silent.

What do I have to say, and who's going to listen to me? This is another secret matter; my anger is a secret that stays away from the light of day because the square is bright with the smiles of white people passing by as they view the dead man on display. I feel disgust and disgrace and rage and every emotion that makes me cry without tears and scream without sound. I don't make a sound.[28]

Here is B. B. King as a black boy in Mississippi, shocked into awareness of his own vulnerability. Even as he is suffused with the most intense sort of blues feeling, a mixture of disgust, disgrace, rage, and "every emotion" that might make a boy cry and scream, he's terrorized into silence by whiteness-as-violence.

If we can grant that what King feels here *is*, in fact, the blues, then we might reasonably ask, What happens to this feeling? Where does it go? It finds late-life expression as autobiographical confession, to be sure, but how does it shape King's musical production? In his earlier statement about living under "fear of the boss," he speaks about how he broods afterward on such moments and becomes "really bluesy" because he is "hurt deep down," and how he sings from that feeling as a way of "trying to say what the blues is to me." The next most important source of blues feeling, he insists, "which is relatively minor compared to living like I have, is your woman." Yet most of King's hit recordings are about women, and none of them openly address white racial violence. Quite a few of them, in fact, exemplify the up-to-date power and promise that black consumers, according to Wald, are far more compelled by than any sounding of folkloric melancholy. How do we make sense of this paradox?

We are left, I think, with no choice but to take King at his word about the sources of his art. And we are forced to modify Wald's claim in a way that allows blues music to speak from, and call to, currents of feeling—embodied individual sadness with collective resonance—that may not be immediately and universally discernable in the lyrics or stylistics of specific songs. In *Seems Like Murder Here*, I used the term "transcode," drawn from philosopher Paul Gilroy, to speak about the way a blues musician's meditations on racial violence might express themselves as narratives of romantic loss.[29] For all we know, for the black audience that made King a star, the appeal of King's music may have been his singular ability to fuse a forward-looking rhythm-and-blues aesthetic with a "cry" sourced in the feelings generated by his youthful wounding; his gift for transcoding individual and ancestral trauma into elegant and feelingful songs addressed to the "baby" who has done him wrong.

My "Teaching the Blues" handout offers a long catalog headlined "blues feelings." Blues feelings, the emotions that lead people to sing the blues and that are frequently referenced in the lyrics themselves, are more diverse and nuanced than they might first appear. Many of them are grounded in varieties of loss or lack or both; the "good" blues feelings often speak to moments when loss and lack have been alleviated, at least temporarily. Keeping Gilroy in mind, it may be possible to hear the deeper meanings that linger behind the blues' familiar invocations of loss and lack.

Loneliness, for example. Loneliness is one of the most primal feelings evoked in the blues. I'm a poor boy a long way from home. I ain't got nobody. We tend to hear such invocations as cries of romantic or familial despair: there's nobody around to hug and hold me, give me shelter, tell me I'm their special somebody. That's an entirely valid reading—one that enables blues universalism without foreclosing black bluesism. Black male blues performers back in the day traveled widely, often solo; few of them enjoyed a settled domestic life complete with home, hearth, spouse, and children. But the loneliness evoked in such lines has another, more pointedly racial dimension, one connected with vulnerability in Jim Crowed public space. Vagrancy laws had such rambling men as their prime targets; lynch law was markedly more suspicious of what it called "strange Negroes"—black men not on the plantation payroll and unknown to local whites. Honeyboy speaks in his autobiography of how important it was to have a white man around who could speak in your defense.[30] (He may not have wanted a boss, but he knew how helpful they could be.) In that sort of context, invocations of loneliness could speak to deeper kinds of vulnerability and unwantedness; they could transcode a yearning for protection from the storm, from that ever-present threat that could reach down out of the skies and carry you off.

Blues, as a dialectical art, often works on multiple levels simultaneously. A lover creates a world for you, distancing you psychologically from the harsh, unloving, potentially deadly world of southern segregation. The loss of a lover, in such a context, can be particularly devastating, because you are left alone with your fears, your isolation, and your exploitation. Lynch law has you in its sights if you head out onto the highway; the cotton fields are all you've got if you stay put. "Loneliness," in such a context, is a freighted term; it has a romantic dimension, to be sure, but it carries more weight than that.

James "Son" Thomas and Walter Liniger
(courtesy of Walter Liniger)

I've been speaking here not just about *loneliness* but also about *romantic abandonment*. James "Son" Thomas, a Mississippi Delta bluesman and gravedigger whom folklorist William Ferris once referred to as his guru, evokes that primal scene as well as anybody I know. "I get a feeling out of the blues," he told Ferris:

> That may be because I been worried a lot. After my first wife quit me, I had the blues. I was working in the field, and I come in one evening. I had bought a pack of cigarettes. I never will forget that. A little boy told me, "Your wife gone."
> And I got sick all at once. I said, "I know she gone."
> "She carried away all her clothes."
> I said, "Get on away from here, boy."

But that hurts you. After that, anytime you get lonesome, you gonner want to hear some blues.[31]

Romantic hopelessness is a third sort of blues feeling, one that enters the blues lyric tradition in several different ways. In Bessie Smith's "I Ain't Got Nobody" (1925), the singer's romantic hopelessness is accompanied by loneliness; both feelings follow on the heels of abandonment by a "lovin' man" who has "throwed [her] down." "I sings good songs all the time," Smith complains. "Won't some man be a pal of mine? / I ain't got nobody, nobody, ain't nobody cares for me." In Howlin' Wolf's "Killing Floor" (1964), by contrast, hopelessness isn't generated by abandonment but by mistreatment—and, crucially, by the singer's foolish willingness to endure that mistreatment. "I should have quit you . . . a long time ago," he sings, bemoaning the fact that, not having left her, he now finds himself "down on the killing floor," a reference to the location in a slaughterhouse where livestock is killed and butchered. Here again, death shadows love in a blues context.

Anger at romantic mistreatment or rejection: a familiar blues feeling. In psychiatrist Elisabeth Kubler-Ross's schema, anger is the second stage of grief precipitated by loss or threatened loss.[32] Honeyboy Edwards talks about the homicidal jealousy that he strove to steer clear of when he thought about messing around with beautiful women whose husbands or lovers might take it badly; this sort of rage, in a blues context, is as likely to lash out at the philandering beloved as at the meddling outsider: "If I can't have you, nobody else will."[33] The all-points dispossession that marks black southern blues lives, ameliorated by the joys of sexual love, becomes intolerable the moment love turns fickle and is withdrawn, especially when a third party is involved. This is the theme of Ma Rainey's canonical "See See Rider Blues" (1925):

> See, see, rider, see what you done done, Lord, Lord, Lord
> Made me love you, now your gal done come
> You made me love you, now your gal done come
>
> . . . .
>
> I'm gonna buy me a pistol, just as long as I am tall, Lord, Lord, Lord
> Gonna kill my man and catch the Cannonball
> If he don't have me, he won't have no gal at all.

Although this particular narrative of romantic mistreatment seems a straightforward story of jealousy and violence, black blues romance is always shadowed by the possibility of white malfeasance. When blues musicians wanted to curse out their bossman, they didn't just curse at the mule; they sang about the woman or "baby" who had mistreated them. When Mississippi-born pianist Eddie Boyd (1919–94) spoke to interviewers Jim O'Neal and Amy van Singel in 1977, he claimed to have narrowly evaded lynching on three occasions before he was twenty-three, simply because he refused to be disrespected or whipped by his white employers. "They were always beating some black man to death down there," he said. "I went through terrible experiences here in this country, man. Just because I didn't buck dance and scratch behind my head when I'm looking at a white man."[34] He fled for his life after the third dispute, moving first to Memphis, then Chicago, before eventually resettling in Europe. In "Five Long Years" (1952), he uses romantic mistreatment to signify on workplace mistreatment:

Have you ever been mistreated? You know
    just what I'm talking about.
Have you ever been mistreated? You know
    just what I'm talking about.
I worked five long years for one woman,
    she had the nerve to put me out.

I got a job in a steel mill, shucking steel like a slave.
Five long years, every Friday I come straight
    back home with all my pay.
Have you ever been mistreated? You know
    just what I'm talking about.
I worked five long years for one woman,
    she had the nerve to put me out.

"Put me out," in this context, signifies on the familiar mode of white reprisal against an insubordinate plantation hand: the bossman's nonnegotiable demand that the troublemaker pack up his belongings and "be off the place by sundown."

Homesickness is a blues feeling—the emotional obverse, in a sense, of the restlessness, rage at mistreatment, spirit of free enterprise, and urge to partake of the world's pleasures that leads so many blues performers to ramble. The blues tradition here takes its cue from American popular music, which has been mining the theme of yearning for the "southern home" at least since Stephen Foster's "Old Folks at Home" (1851). Even as they evoke a dozen different reasons for heading down the big road that speeds them away from mistreatment and north toward the promise of Chicago and New York, blues performers also pause to reflect on the changed circumstances into which migration has thrown them. In some cases they sing longingly of returning home, as in Roosevelt Sykes's "Southern Blues" (1948): "Chicago and Detroit. Folks have you heard the news? / Old Dixieland is jumping, I've got those southern blues. . . ."

Anxiety, often with an admixture of fear, is a quintessential blues feeling. Its sources are many and varied. Anxiety is a reasonable response—a suppressed flight-response—to racial terrorism, especially the threat of lynching, but it's also a reaction to the knowledge that one is being financially exploited for another's gain. Much more widespread in the blues tradition are the anxieties that result from troubled romance: the forward-projected yearnings that occur when you're opening yourself to a new lover and desperate for acknowledgement, and, on the other end, the pain that accompanies a bad fight or a breakup. Being anxious in this way isn't the same as being heartbroken, although it may accompany heartbreak. When I was twenty-six, my live-in girlfriend of five years left me for somebody I knew. I experienced the sort of lonely desolation that James "Son" Thomas evokes with such stark force, but I also came face to face with the anxiety I've sketched here. It struck me with the force of a revelation, an augury of mental breakdown, although the latter never quite took place. Knowing more or less where she was—at his apartment, twenty blocks away—I found it physically impossible, many nights, to sit by myself in what was now my, rather than "our," apartment. I was haunted by what was not there. It was during this period of my life that I began to frequent a blues club in the East Village, drinking and losing myself in the music, letting the grooves and songs, many of which suddenly took on profound meaning, comfort me as best they could. Albert Collins's "My Mind Is Trying to Leave Me" (1983) dug particularly deep: "I began to think about my baby / Aha, like a crazy fool would do / You see, my woman gone away an' left me / An' now my mind is tryin' to leave me too." On one occasion, literally shaking, I called a good friend from the club and begged him to let me sleep on the floor of his apartment because the thought of sleeping in my own bed, formerly "our" bed, filled me with dread. It sounds surreal now, but it was quite real then—that preternatural anxiety and the way blues music helped voice it and keep it at bay. No other available music, and certainly not the synth-pop of the mid-1980s, spoke to my condition and purged my anxiety the way blues did.

The fact that I, a white man, can offer this particular response to the blues call might stand as counterevidence for the black bluesist declaration, "Blues is black music." Although some white investments in the blues are

Blues Feelings and "Real Bluesmen"

surely invidious—profiteering, minstrelized, callow, touristic—others are deep and transformative. My baptism in the blues was the secular equivalent of a conversion experience, a spiritual rebirth; it led me into an apprenticeship with a Bronx-born black harmonica player, a five-year stint as a Harlem street musician, a lifelong partnership with the older black Mississippi-born guitarist I met there, an interracial marriage, an academic career devoted to blues literature and culture, and a decades-long blues harmonica teaching practice in which, among other things, half a dozen black men have sought me out for private lessons.[35] To dismiss those sorts of investments and relationships as essentially trivial, as Black Rock Coalition founder Greg Tate does in *Everything but the Burden: What White People Are Taking from Black Culture* (2003), is to misrepresent the true scope of the music's transformative powers, powers that are themselves a product of the music's long confrontation with the evilest of circumstances.[36] By the same token, it is vital that we attend to the specific ways blackness inflects blues subjectivity— marking the difference, for example, between my own anxious encounter with the blues occasioned by romantic loss and the encounter with "Mr. Blues" evoked by Little Brother Montgomery (and later covered by Buddy Guy) in "The First Time I Met You" (1936):

> The first time I met the blues, mama,
>   they came walking through the wood
> The first time I met the blues, baby,
>   they came walking through the wood
> They stopped at my house first, mama,
>   and done me all the harm they could
>
> Now the blues got at me, lord, and run me from tree to tree
> Now the blues got at me, and run me from tree to tree
> You should have heard me begging Mr. Blues, don't murder me

Blues songs rarely signify on lynching, but this one does, with startling directness. Every element of the ritual is named except the rope: the terrifying but unspecified mob-wrought tortures adumbrated by "all the harm they could"; the "tree" where such rituals frequently took place. "Blues," in this case, is the lynch mob itself, personified in the figure of Mr. Blues— "Mr." being the honorific that every white man in the South demanded, on pain of beating or death, from every black man. The song is aligned with Montgomery's own anxious, fearful temperament, to judge from the portrait offered by New Orleans banjoist Danny Barker:

Little Brother was a master at travelling through the south. I noticed that he never stopped at any place that was owned or operated by white folks. When he wanted to stop for food or drink he would ask some coloured person where there was a coloured place. He drove slowly and carefully when passing through a community. He watched the road like a hawk, but when we hit the outskirts he'd sigh and relax.[37]

The anxiety I felt in the aftermath of romantic loss, frightening as it was, was merely personal; the abject fear evoked in Montgomery's song and corroborated by Barker's recollections are personal soundings of a much broader social ill, the terror inflicted by whites and suffered by blacks under the reign of Jim Crow. Yet blues music speaks to and for both of us.

My "Teaching the Blues" sheet lists *anxiety* as part of a subset of blues feelings that includes *fear, restlessness, terror, fury*, and *bitterness*. Fury and bitterness, like the other emotions, manifest lyrically in both romantic and political contexts; they're directed not just toward lovers and competitors but also toward those who inflict a range of injustices, including racial ones. Another subset of negative blues feelings, directed inward rather than outward, includes *a sense of worthlessness, shame*, or *guilt*. Commentators such as Albert Murray, evoking blues music as a kind of sonic force field that drives away bad feelings and evinces a spirit of prideful resistance, tend to understate the degree to which some blues songs hold up the white flag of spiritual surrender. "It's my own fault, baby," B. B. King sings in "My Own Fault, Darlin'" (1952), "treat me the way you wanna do."

And then, because the blues are relentlessly dialectical, our catalog of blues feelings tacks suddenly in the direction of hope. *A sense of renewed possibility, hopefulness*, or *potency*: the sector of the blues lyric and performance tradition that speaks to the moment when, as in "Trouble in Mind," the clouds dissipate, the promised "some day" arrives, and the sun finally shines in your back door. A lot of people are under the mistaken impression that the blues, perhaps because it's been (rightly) associated with the burdens of black history, is uniformly a music of downheartedness and despair. But that's no more than a half-truth. The blues musician's role has always been to conjure good feelings out of bad, using lyrics, rhythm, and onstage stylistics — a sense of dramatic occasion and the right amount of swagger — as magic wands. Someone who has the blues may feel that the world has broken apart in the worst kind of way, or is merely a cross to be borne, but the right kind of song and groove, in the right hands, have the power to resusci-

Blues Feelings and "Real Bluesmen"

The Holmes Brothers
(© Joseph A. Rosen)

tate. Blues music can drive away your despair and put the swing back in your step. The community is a crucial part of this process. When I was suffering the blues actively as a newly single young man and couldn't abide my own apartment at night, I'd drive down to Dan Lynch, that East Village juke joint, where the Holmes Brothers, an African American trio of wise older men, were the house band presiding over the weekly jam sessions. I'd get a drink, or a few drinks, and sit at the bar listening to songs about the women who'd done them, and me, wrong; I'd lose myself in edgy guitar solos that tracked and voiced my pain, share in the yells of approval that the room gave back to the bandstand. I'd look around at the motley interracial brotherhood and decide that I'd found my place and that all was not lost. Later I'd stride out the swinging front doors, music vibrating through me, ready to call it a night. Feeling just fine, for the moment.

part 5

Blues Expressiveness and the Blues Ethos

For me the blues is the perpetual reckoning with what should be agony, but finding ways of making that reckoning pleasurable. The agony and the pleasure exist right up next to one another. The question is how do we most effectively hold ourselves together through the pain, through the suffering, and through the agony? My history in this country teaches me that you have to do it through art. That doesn't mean the art that gets sold. But the art of talking. The art of listening. The art of making sounds. The art of rhythmically manipulating repetition, which I think was really at the core of the blues.

Kiese Laymon (2019)

THE STANZAIC ACCUMULATION OF DISASTER

In the last several chapters I've been exploring blues conditions and blues feelings, the first two elements of a four-part schema on a handout called "Teaching the Blues: A Few Useful Concepts for the Classroom." Once again I'll offer an advisory: this analytic framework is merely one way among many of teasing the blues apart. Many blues fans, of course, would rather engage the blues on the level of groove-sponsored bodily pleasure, kicking back or boogying down with a shot of bourbon in hand, and that's fine, too. But critical reflection demands that we bracket such participatory pleasure, holding it in tension with a willingness to explore the inner workings of the form.

Even as we break the blues down into component parts, it's important to acknowledge that all four things—conditions, feelings, music, and ethos—

interpenetrate. They're bound up with each other; they're in dialogue; they work in concert. Many people think of the blues as a continuum in which the music, the feelings, the problems being sung about, and the swaggering (or stoic, or hyperemotive) persona all flow together, and this flow-zone theory of the blues has a certain basic validity. What blues music expresses, for example, isn't just feelings: most blues songs, from "Back Water Blues" and "Sweet Home Chicago" to "Sweet Rough Man" and "Mean Old World," spend considerable lyric energy representing the conditions—the challenging, despair-and/or-euphoria-inducing situations—that give rise to the feelings. Blues songs often state a problem, let it simmer and intensify, then pose a provisional solution. What generates the solution, as often as not, is the blues ethos: the blues philosophy of life. The blues ethos, as a concept, is multipronged, not unitary. It's a handful of attitudes and strategies for coping gracefully with the worst that life can throw at you. African American philosopher and social critic Cornell West defines the blues ethos in the form of a memorable rhetorical question: "How do you generate an elegance of earned self-togetherness, so that you have a stick-to-it-ness in the face of the catastrophic and the calamitous and the horrendous and the scandalous and the monstrous?"[1]

Blues poetry finds surprising ways of staging all four elements of my schema—as in "Bad Luck Card" by Langston Hughes:

> Cause you don't love me
> Is awful, awful hard.
> Gypsy done showed me
> My bad luck card.
>
> There ain't no good left
> In this world for me.
> Gypsy done tole me—
> Unlucky as can be.
>
> I don't know what
> Po' weary me can do.
> Gypsy says I'd kill my self
> If I was you.[2]

The blues condition undergirding the poem is failed or unrequited love: the "you" in the first line who does not love, or no longer loves, the poem's speaker. Superadded to that condition and reinforcing it in the speaker's mind is a more general condition of unluckiness, one affirmed by the gypsy's fortune-telling. Blues feelings here begin as the speaker's desolation in the face of doomed love, but they quickly enlarge themselves, in the second stanza, into a comprehensive sense of doom, in which the speaker, convinced that all "good" has vanished from the world, seems headed toward suicide. Blues expressiveness shows up in a range of ways, including the black vernacular language deployed by the speaker and the "autobiographical chronicle of personal catastrophe expressed lyrically" evoked in Ralph Ellison's famous definition.[3] Repetitions—the stanzaic accumulation of disaster through "me" and the gypsy—are one formal means through which that chronicle does its work. Finally, the blues ethos is visible here not as West's elegance of self-togetherness but rather as the poem's unexpected last couplet: a summary insult to the speaker's collapsing ego, one that wards off pain by precipitating harsh laughter. What might at first seem like egregious tactlessness on the gypsy's part can also be seen as a healer's shrewd attempt, with a wink and a nod, to puncture the speaker's maudlin and maladaptive response to bad news. Or perhaps the speaker, telling us his story of woe, is extrapolating from the fortune-telling situation, inventing the gypsy's final comment in an act of creative exaggeration. We cannot know, but the poem offers us a moment of enlightenment regardless; it lifts our spirits with a chuckle by conjuring up a blues figure who says, in effect, "You think *you've* got troubles? Ha!"

The emergence of blues literature, in fact, is partly the story of how poets like Hughes and Sterling Brown, novelists like Claude McKay, songwriters like W. C. Handy, and folklorists like Howard Odum rendered the "humble blues lyric" (Ellison's term) on the written page, translating and transforming it in the process. The fact that Hughes's poem consists of three stanzas might remind us of the debt that blues poetry owes to the tripartite, AAB structure that is blues music's best-known and most ubiquitous formal characteristic. It would behoove any blues scholar in training to become intimately familiar with the AAB verse form. That form happens to be lingua franca at blues jams around the world, but it's also one of African American music's signal contributions to American literature.

One of the things that characterizes early blues music is an unusual amount of repetition and a distinctive song form. American popular music in the first two decades of the twentieth century, the stuff of Tin Pan Alley, gravitated toward a thirty-two-bar format, so-called AABA form: two eight-bar verses followed by a bridge and a final eight-bar verse. Blues, by contrast, offered itself in a three-line, twelve-bar format, and without a bridge—except for Handy's "St. Louis Blues" (1914), a bridge-bearing blues and the exception that proves the rule. By the mid-1920s, with the advent of recording and especially with the popularity of Blind Lemon Jefferson as a recording star, the AAB verse form had become the accepted norm, as in Jefferson's "That Black Snake Moan" (1927), a memorable evocation of loneliness and lust in which the latter is figured as a phallic "black snake" with a will of its own:

> I . . . I ain't got no mama now
> I . . . I ain't got no mama now
> She told me late last night, "You don't need no mama no how"
>
> Mmm, mmm, black snake crawlin' in my room
> Mmm, mmm, black snake crawlin' in my room
> Some pretty mama better come and get this black snake soon.

The AAB verse form, when performed by blues singers, is characterized by a specific sort of repetition-with-variation: the A line, when repeated, is sung over a different chord (the subdominant or IV chord) than the first time around, and singers frequently embroider or "worry" the repeated line in a series of microtonal adjustments, sometimes with lyric elisions or embellishments, that highlight this chord change in subtle but important ways. The difference between the two iterations of the A line is just substantial enough that scholars sometimes refer to the second A line as the A-prime line. The B line, by contrast, is an answering line rather than an echoing line; it almost always rhymes with the A line (although eye-rhymes and nonrhymes occasionally show up), and it sometimes puts an unexpected spin on the theme or emotion or question that was set in motion by the AA pair. In a philosophical sense, it's almost as though what blues song does is try out a statement, one that proposes an emotional or stylistic orientation toward life's bad news, then reprises or repeats that statement in a way that suggests either a possible variant on the initial stance or, by contrast, an *intensification* of the initial stance. The B line, in any case, puts a cap on it—or in it—and sends you hurtling into the next verse.

The repetition-with-variation-as-intensification dynamic, so crucial to the language and formal structure of the blues, is one that feels uncannily familiar to those who have suffered on the field of battle that is failed love:

> I hate you
> I *hate* you
> Take the goddamn house, and your little dog, too.

The rage that fuels a divorce, rendered this nakedly and with an unintended lagniappe of comic deflation, is not blues lyricism, but it may have something to teach us about where the music's magic is sourced: in an urgently felt need to unburden an aching heart, and in the way that a certain kind of immediately repeated complaint may facilitate that unburdening. Repeating their indictments in this way, blues songs harden romantic rage with metaphors that exaggerate to produce bitter laughter. New Orleans blues guitarist Lonnie Johnson ended his seven-year common-law marriage to blues singer Mary Smith in 1932 — she had borne him six children during that period — and the acrimony that powered that breakup is audible in "She's Making Whoopee in Hell Tonight" (1930):

> Baby, you've been gone all day baby . . . set to make whoopee tonight
> You've been gone all day . . . set to make whoopee tonight
> I'm gonna take my razor and cut your late hours
>   . . . I will be serving you right

> The undertaker's been here and gone, I gave him your height and size
> Undertaker's been here and gone, I gave him your height and size
> You'll be making whoopee with the devil in hell tomorrow night

> You made me love you . . . just got me for your slave
> You made me love you . . . just got me for your slave
> And from now on you'll be making whoopee in your lonesome grave.

The AAB form is now so ubiquitous as to seem both natural and inevitable, but blues scholars are still not precisely sure where it came from. In *I'd Rather Be the Devil*, a study of Skip James, Stephen Calt argues that the AAB pattern ultimately derives from "Roll Jordan," a spiritual penned by Charles Wesley (1707–88) that showed up at camp meetings in the 1820s and became an anthem of the second Great Revival, the religious movement that made Christian converts of many black southern slaves.[4] In *Africa and the Blues*, Gerhard Kubik argues for possible Yoruba origins of the AAB stanza, while Harriet Ottenheimer argues for East African origins in the Comoros, an island chain between Mozambique and Madagascar.[5] Even as we chase down such distant sourcing, it's worth remembering that early blues songs manifested a range of stanzaic forms. When Handy encountered a "lean, loose-jointed Negro" playing slide guitar with a knife and singing at the Tutwiler, Mississippi, train station in 1903 or 1904, a celebrated moment of first contact evoked in *Father of the Blues*, the man repeated the line "Goin' where the

Blues Expressiveness and the Blues Ethos

Southern cross' the Dog" three times—an AAA verse, and a form that still raises its head from time to time.[6]

VICTORY OVER THE BAD THINGS

The AAB stanza, so broadly and variously utilized by blues poets and worked into the tissue of prose works, including Handy's autobiography, is merely one of the formal elements that constitute what I am calling blues expressiveness. A second element is *call-and-response* or antiphony: the idea that a given blues text, like a blues performance involving a musician and an audience (or a musician who is his own audience), stages a sort of dialogue or conversation between two voices or ideas or energies. Two things are calling back and forth to each other—reinforcing, versioning, outdoing, and/or signifying on each other. Each is dynamically adjusting itself to the other, so that each response in turn becomes a call that provokes further response. Call-and-response, as an organizational principle, shows up not just in the blues tradition but in jazz, soul, work songs, slave seculars, and the black religious tradition: church choirs, quartets, anywhere that gospel and the spirituals are sung. It's one of the givens of African American music. Its deep origins arguably lie with the drum-and-dance dialogue that animates many kinds of West African music—an inheritance from slavery, once again—and it has deep philosophical implications for the blues.

Early blues is distinguished from slave music, among other things, by the fact that it is individualistic rather than collective: it features a lone guitarist singing as he picks and strums (Handy's Tutwiler musician), or a lone female singer backed up by a jazz orchestra. It's not choral music. It's very different in that respect from the raised hymns that one finds in the Gullah churches of coastal Georgia, where a series of voices chime in, double each other, and toss the ball back and forth between a leader and followers. And yet, if one listens closely to the solitary bluesman with his guitar, or the blues queen and her orchestra, one realizes that the call-and-response conversation, the antiphony, has been preserved. In the case of the solitary guitarist, the vocal lines are the calls; the fills, little two-bar snatches of slide guitar riffs *between* the vocal lines, are the responses. If the guitarist is playing duo style with a harmonica player, the harmonica responds to the vocal "calls" in similar fashion. In the case of the blues queen, the orchestra provides not just rhythmic and harmonic background to her vocals but also solo instruments that surface in the spaces between her vocal lines; their instrumental commentary becomes the response to her calls.

Call-and-response knits the blues community together. In philosophical terms, call-and-response says, "Yes, you are suffering and I am suffering. *We* are suffering. And you hear my suffering, and respond to it, as I hear your suffering and respond to it. We get the feeling out, we give it a ritual public airing. We give it form—a powerful, elegant, shapely expressive form. And in so doing, we earn ourselves a victory over the bad things that have happened to us. The music we make together is more powerful than the *thing* they're trying to make of us." This philosophical victory takes a slightly different shape when a blues queen like Bessie Smith is fronting her orchestra before a packed house than it takes when Belton Sutherland, a little-known Mississippi guitarist, is communing with his guitar alone at home, but the underlying principle is the same. Rather than one person suffering quietly and alone, there's a conversation going on, one that manifests dialectical energy and human creativity. A deep cultural form tracing back to Africa is being worked with, animated, put in service. I am dealing with the loneliness that I feel by creating a call-and-response dialogue between me and my guitar, or my orchestra. If I've got an audience, the dialogue I'm staging may in turn provoke a second-order conversation in which you, my congregation, respond to what I'm offering you with your own running commentary, your shouts of approval and affirmation. Then, as they say, we are really cooking with gas.

Call-and-response procedure, in short, bodies forth a core value of the blues: the idea that pain needs to be externalized and shared rather than suffered alone, along with the idea that there is something ennobling and healing about this process. As with many elements of the blues, this value first takes shape during the slavery era. In *Slavery and Social Death: A Comparative Study* (1982), historian Orlando Patterson explores the way slavery was, in fact, a kind of comprehensive social death, one that left the enslaved person not just powerless and without honor but also alienated from his natal rights—that is, shorn of all familial connections and ancestral claims, including his own name. The Dred Scott decision (1857) affirmed social death when it argued that all blacks were "beings of an inferior order" and, as such, "had no rights which the white man was bound to respect." The African American response to this situation in the antebellum South was the so-called invisible institution of the black church: hush harbor meetings out of sight and hearing of whites within which wounded spirits could be salved by a shared unburdening that was sustained by mutual recognition and respect. In the decades after Emancipation, black churches were a visible and proliferating source of pride for the communities they served. Titles, honorifics, and a high sense of ritual purpose helped heal the comprehensive disrespect

Blues Expressiveness and the Blues Ethos

that enforced social death. During those same post-Emancipation decades, as Katrina Hazzard-Gordon reminds us in *Jookin'* (1990), juke joints were also beginning to emerge across the South, offering a similar kind of healing to the blues communities that circulated through and within them.[7] In *The Spirituals and the Blues* (1972), black theologian Cone calls the blues "a secular spiritual" as a way of getting at this dynamic.[8] The juke joint is the place where performers and their congregations stage a sacred ritual of unburdening. The most skilled and powerful performers, those who fulfill the call-and-response mission in the most cathartic way, literally create names for themselves in the process.

Along with AAB structure and call-and-response procedure, we might add a third item to our survey of blues expressiveness: *vocalizations*. What makes blues music instantly identifiable—not the lyrics but the music itself—isn't just the twelve-bar harmonic structure, or the instruments (slide guitar, harmonica), or even the microtonality of the blues scale that finds useful pitches between the white and black keys of the piano. It's also, and more specifically, the way blues players—especially guitar and harmonica, but also saxes, trumpets, and other brass—model elements of their playing on what blues singers do. They make their instruments yelp, hoot, curse, scream, and cry. Talk, in a word. Salty Holmes's "I Want My Mama" (1933) and Sonny Terry's "Talking Harmonica Blues" (1959) offer vivid examples of harmonica players doing this; Albert Collins and Luther Allison were masters of the talking-guitar technique, sliding their fingers up and down the strings to create the illusion of utterances like "No, I won't!" or "Ohhh, noooo!" In "Luther's Blues" (1974), Allison stages an agitated dialogue between himself and his woman—the guitar "talks" her part—so that call-and-response procedure and vocalizations work synergistically, but the idea of talking through an instrument has a deeper meaning than merely signifying on human speech.

Talking drums were a significant element of musical life in the part of West Africa preyed upon by the Atlantic slave trade. The deep historical origins of the virtuosic vocalizations of musicians like Holmes, Terry, Collins, and Allison lie in the pitch-tone language being instrumentally mimicked by the talking drum of Africa. That language, and that conception of drumming, was a part of the cultural material that slavery ended up depositing in the southern United States. After drums were banned in South Carolina and then across the South in the aftermath of the Stono Rebellion of 1741—a slave rebellion orchestrated, whites insisted, by talking drums—drum language and rhythmic fluency were preserved for more than a century as the slapping-the-body practice known as patting juba. Black people in the South found ways of keeping the drum alive, despite white proscriptions. Drums flourished in the post-Emancipation world of black minstrelsy, brass bands, and jazz, of course, but the blues was one of the places where the broader drum-function created by the earlier ban remained in play: in Charley Patton's habit of beating rhythms on the wooden body of his guitar, in the way Bukka White snaps and pops the strings on his National Steel resonator guitar, in the heavy front-porch foot of Belton Sutherland and other solo guitarists looking to entertain a dance crowd, in phrases like "Spank dat ole pe-anner" shouted by Zora Neale Hurston's Florida juke joint informants in *Mules and Men.*[9]

SIGNIFYING, SUBTERFUGE, AND SEXUALITY

So *vocalizations* are an important element of blues expressiveness, along with AAB structure and call-and-response procedure. A fourth aspect of blues expressiveness is *blues idiomatic language*: the rich linguistic stew in which members of the blues subculture—musicians, audiences, and assorted hangers-on—conduct their daily lives, on and off the bandstand. There are two superb recent books about this subject: Debra DeSalvo's *The Language of the Blues: From Alcorub to Zuzu* (2006) and Stephen Calt's *Barrelhouse Words: A Blues Dialect Dictionary* (2009). African retentions show up in blues language, as DeSalvo notes—the words "hip" and "cat" both have Wolof origins—but even more important is the "freewheeling all-American lingo" of the underground economy that helped folks on the receiving end of Jim Crow survive and occasionally prosper. "Blues artists," she writes, "—looking to steal from the best, like all songwriters—nicked words and phrases from the numbers runners, hookers, drag queens, thieves, junkies, pimps, moonshiners, hoodoo doctors, dealers, rounders, and con artists who made up the street set."[10]

The language of blues expressiveness is a rowdy, street-level American vernacular rooted in the language of the black southern folk. Anybody who has read Hurston's *Mules and Men* (1935) and *Their Eyes Were Watching God* (1937), anybody familiar with her evocations of Sop de Bottom, Big Sweet, and Tea Cake, knows how much boastful, playful, threatening, self-annunciating energy the language of blues people contains. The blues underworld that generated that language was, among other things, a place where flesh—sexual attractions, sexual potency—was an important currency. The prominence of sexuality in blues discourse is what academics call overdeter-

Blues Expressiveness and the Blues Ethos

mined: it has multiple sources, not one source. The red-light-district environs within which early blues performances often took place were a breeding ground for such language; the harsh, labor-centered daylight lives of black blues audience members made bodily pleasures an enticing theme. The world of touring blues shows and, later, R&B shows, as historian Tyina Steptoe has noted, not only facilitated expressions of queer sexuality by performers such as Ma Rainey, Big Mama Thornton, and Little Richard, but also, when such shows rolled into town, helped "queer people from small southern locales like Ariton, Alabama or Macon, Georgia [to encounter] one another." (The earliest version of "Tutti Frutti" championed anal sex: "Tutti Frutti, good booty / If it don't fit, don't force it / You can grease it, make it easy.")[11] Commercial considerations, too, incentivized titillating blues songs. Once Tin Pan Alley jumped on the blues bandwagon in the 1920s, the "clean and racy . . . folk speech" of early blues singers, according to Harlem Renaissance spokesman Alain Locke, was transformed into "the mawkish sentimentality and concocted lascivity of the contemporary cabaret songs and dances." "The one," he insisted, "is primitively erotic; the other, decadently neurotic. Gradually the Negro singers and musicians succumbed to the vogue of the artificial and decadent variety of song, music, dance which their folk-stuff started, and spawned a plague, profitable but profligate, that has done more moral harm than artistic good."[12]

The distinction between good-sexy ("racy," folk-originated) and bad-sexy ("decadent," commercial, modern) blues songs is difficult to uphold. What both sorts of songs have in common, in any case, is a familiar rhetorical move that remains alive and well in our own day: *signifying.*

Signifying plays a key role in African American expressive culture; it's as much a church thing as a blues thing, and it's actually a range of related things, not one thing. At heart, signifying is *saying one thing but meaning another,* where the thing that is said often takes on a figural energy of its own, even as the interest and importance of the "meant" thing, by being partly or wholly masked, is highlighted for an audience hip enough to get the wordplay. Signifying, in folklorist Roger D. Abrahams's words, is a "style-focused message" in which "styling . . . is foregrounded by the devices of making a point by indirection and wit."[13] In a church context, signifying shows up in the spirituals, where a phrase like "crossing over" may gesture toward a range of real-world referents, from fleeing slavery's clutches across the Mason-Dixon line to any yearned-for political development, such as the election of President Barack Obama, that represents a prophetic realization of black freedom-dreams. In a blues context, the most familiar form of signifying is sex talk: finding a thousand and one ways of boasting, preening, and configuring a sexual come-on, or complaining about a lover's faithlessness.

Sexual signifying is a foundational element of blues expressiveness. The most familiar lyric of this sort might be, "If you don't want my peaches . . . please don't shake my tree." That line first enters the tradition, surprisingly, in a 1914 composition by Irving Berlin, the dean of Tin Pan Alley, but Berlin had almost certainly taken it — as an overheard phrase — from black oral tradition, and it shows up, along with its many variants, in songs by everybody from Bessie and Trixie Smith to Elmore James and the Mississippi Sheiks.[14] In "Peach Orchard Mama" (1929), Blind Lemon Jefferson sings of his errant lover's fondness for robbing the cradle: "you swore nobody'd pick your fruit but me / I found three kid-men shaking down your peaches free." Sexual signifying in blues lyrics achieves several things. If we remember, as theater scholar Paige McGinley urges us to, that the great African American blues queens used every expressive technique at their disposal to dramatize their songs onstage, then we can appreciate the way such lyrics open up an enlivening participatory conversation between the statuesque female performer, gesturing at her own curves, and her appreciative audience.[15] Men appreciate the curves; women appreciate the ethical point, which in our own vernacular might be voiced as: Don't play me. If you want all this — the glory of my womanhood — then don't just arouse my interest long enough to steal my sex and hurt my feelings. Follow through. Show me your love and make me your woman.

Sexual signifying offers blues song a way of creating pleasure through heavily freighted indirection: plays on words that gesture forcefully at sexualized bodies and the sex acts they engage in without actually using the four-letter Anglo-Saxon equivalents. In "Empty Bed Blues" (1928), composed by J. C. Johnson, Bessie Smith sings of being deserted by a new lover, celebrating with vivid suggestiveness his hip-powered prowess and endurance:

> Bought me a coffee grinder, got the best one I could find
> Bought me a coffee grinder, got the best one I could find
> So he could grind my coffee cause he has a new grind.
>
> He's a deep sea diver with a stroke that can't go wrong
> He's a deep sea diver with a stroke that can't go wrong
> He can touch the bottom and his wind holds out so long.

The origins of signifying lie in the antebellum South, when enslaved African Americans had a pressing need to communicate sensitive information

Blues Expressiveness and the Blues Ethos

Bessie Smith, 1936
(photograph by Carl Van Vechten, courtesy of the Library of Congress)

with each other in public spaces on the plantation—an impending escape attempt, for example—in a way that evaded detection by the master. Sexuality wasn't part of the signifying equation at that point, but it takes center stage in the blues during the post-Emancipation period because, according to Angela Y. Davis, sexuality, along with travel, "was one of the most tangible domains in which emancipation was acted upon and through which its meanings were expressed."[16] In other words, sexual signifying plays such a central role in blues expressiveness because the right to flirt with, chase, romance, couple with, and ravish the lover (or lovers) of one's choosing was a key way freeborn black southerners lived out, *knew*, their freedom. No longer did the slavemaster have the right to select your mate and keep you down on the farm. It's all about me and you, baby: the crawling kingsnake and the fine brown hen. The blues lyric tradition signifies endlessly on this point.

A BRUTALLY HONEST RECOGNITION OF REALITY

Thus far I have been talking about a range of topics that can be subsumed within the category of *blues expressiveness*—the AAB verse form, call-and-response, vocalizations, blues idiomatic language, and signifying. I'd like to turn now to the fourth global concept on my handout: the blues ethos. What is it and why does it matter?

Like blues expressiveness, the blues ethos is several things, not just one thing. When most people offer definitions of the blues, they tend to neglect the blues ethos. It's easier to invoke the distinctive three-line stanzas, or major/minor tonalities, or the multiple oppressions of black life in the rural South, and say, "*That* is the blues." Yet the blues ethos—an attitudinal orientation toward experience, a sustaining philosophy of life—may be the most important ingredient of all.

My first exposure to the blues ethos came long before I had encountered the concept by name. In 1986, shortly after I began playing harmonica on the streets of Harlem with a Mississippi-born guitarist known as Mr. Satan, one of his sidewalk fans told me that his real name was Sterling Magee. When I expressed curiosity about the name-change, a story soon emerged. I was told he'd had a very beautiful wife—curvy, sexy—and she'd gotten cancer. He stayed right by her bedside, nursing her. When she died, he fell off the deep end. He dragged himself back home to Mississippi, drunk and inconsolable; months later, when he returned to Harlem, he was calling himself by the new name and demanding that everybody else do the same. That was five years before I came along. The Mr. Satan I knew was the opposite of despairing: he was a ring-tailed roarer animated by phenomenal talent and energy, joyous and irrepressible. We would talk about women from time to time, as musicians do, and I'd confess my own fury at the live-in girlfriend who had cuckolded and deserted me a couple of years earlier. He'd respond by decrying the worthless temptation represented by women and their "smelly little behinds." When I would speak of my lingering pain, he'd vigorously push

Blues Expressiveness and the Blues Ethos

The author and Sterling "Mr. Satan" Magee, 1989
(photograph by Cory Pearson, in author's collection)

back. "Hell," he'd say with a harsh laugh, "I had so many women die on me, I was thinking of opening a funeral parlor." How could I not chuckle along with him? How—knowing what I knew of his own encounter not just with romantic tragedy but with death—could I not put aside my self-pity and get back to the business of living?

That was my baptism into the blues ethos: that harsh laugh, and the exaggeration that accompanied it, transforming pain into life force. I had not yet encountered the writings of Albert Murray or Kalamu ya Salaam, but the experience helped me appreciate their insights when I finally did. "What is ultimately at stake," writes Murray of black blues life in *Stomping the Blues*, "is morale, which is to say the will to persevere, the disposition to persist and perhaps prevail; and what must be avoided by all means is a failure of nerve."[17] Stoic persistence, a refusal to give up, lies at the core of the blues ethos. And a certain kind of reality-based, fantasy-assisted humor, according to Salaam, is a tool with which blues people have managed to enable such persistence. "Rather than an escape from reality," he argues in his essay,

> when we fantasize, it is based on a brutally honest recognition of
> reality, a reality albeit clothed in metaphorical grace. This grace
> includes, but is not overcome by, a profound recognition of the
> economic inequality and political racism of America. Thus, we laugh

loud and heartily when every rational expectation suggests we should be crying in despair. The combination of exaggeration and conscious recognition of the brutal facts of life is the basis for the humor of blues people, which is real black humor.[18]

Mr. Satan's joke about dead wives and funeral parlors, exaggerating and ridiculing heartbreak in order to swat it away, epitomizes the blues ethos. There's a spiritual wisdom in it. How *should* you deal with bad news? Black southern blues people, given the economic and social challenges arrayed against them, figured out pretty quickly that wallowing in despair—whining—just wasn't an effective long-term strategy. They complain, to be sure, but they do so in a context that facilitates a spirit of creative resistance. The blues ethos acknowledges the power generated when emotional pain is annealed with a self-mockery that wards off descent into outright, immobilizing depression. The sadness of the blues, according to Langston Hughes, "is not softened with tears but hardened with laughter," and that word "hardened" is important. Spiritual toughness is part of the blues ethos.[19] Never, ever, ever, *ever* give up. Even when you give up, do so only as long as you need to. Then pick yourself up and get cracking.

Don't, in other words, spend any more time in that state of given-upness than you need to. To do so bespeaks spiritual immaturity: an unwise insistence on reifying the miseries of the present moment. To say, like a pouting child, "Because I am down now, I will always be down," is to blind oneself to the possibilities for escape and future triumph that are always present, at least potentially, in even the most unpromising of circumstances. This is the wisdom contained in the blues standard "Trouble in Mind":

Trouble in mind . . . lord I'm blue
But I won't be blue always
You know the sun's gonna shine in
. . . my back door someday.

"Trouble in Mind" is sung from a condition of deep sadness, but it demands that we reframe that sadness in a way that looks ahead, with prophetic wisdom, to the possibility of a better life. The long arc of black history, bringing African slaves to Jamestown in 1619 and an African American president to the White House in 2008, energizes both poles of the dialectic. When all else fails, insists the blues ethos, look down that road. Take the long view. Stay loose. Keep things moving. Give your luck a chance to change.

Blues Expressiveness and the Blues Ethos

When Bill "Howl-N-Madd" Perry, a Lafayette County bluesman, visited my undergraduate blues class at the University of Mississippi in 2012, he had to be helped to his seat by his daughter, Shy, who travels and plays keyboards with him. Several months earlier, Bill had had a minor stroke and lost 90 percent of his vision. Yet his spirits were undimmed, even ebullient. When I described the blues ethos, a concept we'd been working with, and asked him what he thought, he smiled and said, "I'll tell you a story about that."

Many years ago, he said, he'd played guitar in Little Richard's band. They were based in Chicago—he'd migrated from Mississippi to Chicago as a young man—but they traveled a lot, and on this particular trip they were in Los Angeles. That's where Little Richard fired him. "When I came down in the morning from my hotel room," he said, "they were gone."

"What do you . . . that's how they fired you?" I asked.

"They were gone." He chuckled. "They were just gone. The whole band."

"What did you do?"

"Well," he said slowly, leaning back in his chair, "I didn't feel too good." The class laughed.

"But what was your next step?"

"Well, the band was gone, and I had a dollar in my pocket."

"What did you do?"

"I spent ninety cents on some breakfast."

More laughter. He was grinning now.

"What did you do after that?"

"I got out on the road and started walking with my guitar. And somebody came along who knew me—we'd been in town for a few days and somebody drove by and they knew me, they'd come to one of our shows, and they picked me up and brought me to their place. I stayed there for a week, played a few pickup gigs, and made enough money to get back to Chicago."

There's a kind of wisdom here that deserves our attention. Bill could have retreated his hotel room in shock. He could have drowned in his own fury and self-pity. But his response to the sudden appearance of blues conditions—loss of a job and housing, incipient poverty, sudden stranding a long way from home—was to remain loose and forward-looking rather than giving in to shame, fear, and despair. He got out on the road and gave the world a chance to rectify the situation. And it did. That sort of quick reversal rarely happens, of course. But it's guaranteed not to happen unless you put yourself in a position where it *can* happen. The blues ethos knows all this. Those who embody the blues ethos have the wisdom and resilience, the

Shy Perry and Bill "Howl-N-Madd" Perry
(courtesy of the photographer, Joshua Branning)

strength of character, to respond to bad luck by setting transformative possibilities in motion.

YOU'LL LIVE THROUGH IT

I came to a deeper understanding of the blues ethos after Mr. Satan and I left
the streets of Harlem in the early 1990s and began to tour, putting in some
serious road-miles. He was a feelingful man but an unsentimental one, disinclined to coddle or be coddled. He'd spent a fair bit of time picking cotton
in the Mississippi Delta as a boy; he was a hard worker, not a complainer,
and he expected the same from me. One night when I picked him up at his
apartment for a downtown gig, he had a bloody bandage wrapped around his
hand. "What happened?" I asked. "I cut myself on a piece of wood," he said,
making a sour face. "I'll live through it." The cut turned out to be a deep gash
in one of the heavily callused fingers on his fretting hand. Any other guitar
player would have canceled the gig. That wasn't his way. He played the five-
hour gig, wincing occasionally but never complaining. Make the gig: that
was his philosophy. The blues ethos in action.

"You'll live through it" was Mr. Satan's all-purpose rejoinder whenever I'd complain about something. The phrase began to make sense when I thought about the sorts of challenges he'd encountered growing up black and male in rural Mississippi in the 1930s and '40s. Living through it, whatever "it" was, couldn't be taken for granted—which was precisely why he'd evolved that saying. It put things in perspective. It reframed them in a useful way. It didn't say, "Things are easy." It said, "They're bearable, compared with the worst-case scenario, and they'll get easier by and by." When disasters threatened out on the road, or even just modest inconveniences, Mr. Satan was ready. "We'll live through it." And we always did.

Several summers ago I drew on the blues ethos in a way that showed me the practical efficacy of the concept. With the help of some friends, I had organized a weeklong one-man-band tour that was going to take me from Oxford, Mississippi, up through Columbia, Missouri, to Mankato and St. Paul, Minnesota, back down through Chicago, and then home. Two club dates, a festival, and a guest slot in a blues harmonica workshop. Decent money and some professional recognition on my own terms, not as part of a duo. Two thousand miles, there and back.

The night before I was supposed to take off, I came down with a fever. The road is hard enough when you're well, but a solo tour when sick not something I wanted to do. I woke the next morning—I hadn't yet loaded up the car—and the fever was still there. When I hobbled outside to do a quick walk-around, I discovered that the worn-out rear tires I'd been nursing for months had suddenly developed the sort of bubbled sidewalls that precede a blowout. I sat there on the sofa at 7:30 in the morning, feverish and thoroughly demoralized, with the entire tour hanging on a thin string. If I stayed put for a few hours, giving the fever a chance to subside, I'd miss that evening's gig in Columbia, 450 miles away. If I blew off the Columbia gig and left for Mankato the next morning, I'd have 900 miles to drive in one day. That wouldn't happen and the tour would collapse. I thought about the young harp guys who had helped set up those two gigs, each of whom was opening for me, and asked myself whether my fever could justify disappointing them.

Then I thought back, suddenly, to a tour that Mr. Satan and I had taken in 1997—a trip to Australia, our first. I'd developed a big, ugly fever blister on the way over, during the fourteen-hour flight from Los Angeles. Once we landed, we'd be playing two shows a day for seven straight days, starting the day we arrived. When I showed the blister to Sterling, frustrated and depressed, he just shrugged and said, "You'll live through it." Then he added, "We're *playing* those gigs, mister." And we did, and I did. It wasn't pretty—I'd wiped some blood off my mouth for the first couple of nights—but the pain was bearable. I'd settled in after a couple of days, I'd drunk a fair bit of booze to smooth off the rough edges, and we'd made the gig. That's what blues players do. You want to play this music, white boy? Toughen the fuck up.

I sat on the sofa, thinking about all this. Then, for no good reason, something inside me reached down into a layer of cussedness lurking just below the feverish negativity. "Here's what you're gonna do," I said to myself, as though lecturing somebody else. "You're going take a shower and load up the car, you're going to drive over to Batesville and buy some tires, and you're going to head north. If the fever gets worse and you can't make Columbia, you can pull off the road and crash for the night, and at least you'll know you tried. If you have to, you can cancel the rest of the tour first thing tomorrow and drive home. But if you don't leave now, bad as you feel, you'll blow the whole tour before it starts. Too many people worked too hard to let that happen."

Thinking about others, reorienting myself toward the blues community, was a part of the cure. But toughness of spirit, a decision to move forward regardless, was also required. As it turned out, everything worked out. I bought the new tires and rolled north; the fever gradually subsided. By the time I hung a left past St. Louis, late that afternoon, I was fine. The weather was hot—over a hundred degrees—but I couldn't complain. The tour went off as planned.

Buddhists talk about the difference between pain and suffering. Pain, they teach, is an inevitable part of embodied life. Suffering, however, is a mental construct—all the feelings of disappointment, negativity, apprehension, and despair with which we routinely surround, and heighten, pain. Blues songs traffic in suffering; they "finger the jagged grain," in Ellison's words. But the blues ethos prefers to acknowledge pain in order to evade suffering, whenever possible. See it, say it, sing it, share it. Get it out, by all means. Don't deny the pain, or hide from it. But don't wallow in it, either. Kick it away with harsh humor. Use stoic persistence to push past it. With luck, you'll leave it in your rearview mirror.

Blues Expressiveness and the Blues Ethos

bar 6

W. C. Handy and the "Birth" of the Blues

CRAZY, LONG LOST, AND ORIGINAL

Where do the blues come from, and when do they come into being? I've suggested a range of answers in the preceding chapters, but I haven't once spoken about the blues being "born." Chalk that up to scholarly reflex, or a writerly distaste for cliché. There is, in any case, something uncanny about the tenacity with which the birth-of-the-blues metaphor endures. Many people through the years have found it almost impossible to think about the music's origins without invoking it. Sophie Tucker's recording of Harold Dixon's "Stay Out of the South" (1928), for example, cycles through every careworn cliché of the pastoral South, including "darkies humming" and "banjos strumming," before noting that the region "gave the blues the[ir] birth." In _Dutchman_ (1964), playwright LeRoi Jones (Amiri Baraka) satirized this tendency by having white female provocateuse/seductress, Lula, repeat the phrase "And that's how the blues was born" four times in quick succession, emptying it of all content except her desire to mock those—above all, Clay, the younger black protagonist—who would take the music seriously. Clay finally slaps her across the mouth and shouts, "Now shut up and let me talk, you liberated whore!" before offering his own furious sourcing of the music's origins in sublimated black rage, Bessie Smith's frustrated desire to kill white people.[1] Yet the birth-of-the-blues cliché, despite such critique, remains seductive—especially in the world of contemporary blues tourism.

"A cousin of gospel, soul, and rock 'n' roll," proclaims Visittheusa.com, "the blues were born in a thousand sharecroppers' fields, humble shacks and rural juke joints." Clarksdale, Mississippi, brands itself bluntly on Clarksdaletourism.com as "Where the blues were born."[2] In directing our attention toward locales where blues music and its iconic old-school performers were first heard, seen, "discovered," which histories does the birth metaphor privilege—and profit from—and which does it conceal? It may be an easier sell, for example, to talk about how the blues sprang from the cotton fields surrounding Muddy Waters's log cabin on Stovall Plantation than to provide a fully loaded cost accounting of slavery, segregation, convict lease, the panoply of long-term oppressions inflicted on black southern blues people. Sometimes, to be sure, the metaphor is animated by a desire to sound those oppressions. In a video produced by the B. B. King Museum in Indianola, Mississippi, called "The Blues Were Born," the Reverend David Matthews, who worked with King on the Johnson Barrett plantation in the 1940s, evokes a familiar catalog of oppressions—poverty, the bossman, romantic disappointment—and declares, "Under those conditions, blues were *born* and not written."[3]

Metaphors of blues-birth beget metaphors of blues paternity and maternity. A shrewd self-mythologizer, songwriter, and bandleader, W. C. Handy titled his 1941 autobiography *Father of the Blues*, but as early as 1919 he was already being called "daddy of the blues" by the African American press, a nod to the popularity of his compositional "children," "Memphis Blues" (1912), "St. Louis Blues" (1914), "Hesitating Blues" (1915), and "Beale St. Blues" (1917). Gertrude "Ma" Rainey (born Gertrude Pridgett) was similarly known as the "Mother of the Blues." "The blues," writes blues scholar Chris Albertson, "claim no predecessor to this extraordinary woman."[4] But that's not quite right, because Rainey herself told musicologist John W. Work Jr. in the late 1930s that she remembered first hearing the blues in a small town in Missouri in 1902, when "a girl from the town" came to her tent show and "began to sing about the 'man' who had left her." "The song," according to Work, "was so strange and poignant that it attracted much attention. 'Ma' Rainey became so interested that she learned the song from the visitor, and used it soon afterwards in her 'act' as an encore. The song elicited such response from the audience that it won a special place in her act. Many times she was asked what kind of song it was, and one day she replied, in a moment of inspiration, 'It's the *Blues*.'"[5]

Albertson's claim that Rainey had no predecessors falters not just in the face of Rainey's own testimony about the unnamed blues-singing "girl," but in light of recent scholarship by Lynn Abbott and Doug Seroff, whose archival research into early black southern vaudeville offers insight into the process through which Rainey achieved primacy as a blues origin figure. Work's "soon afterwards," for example, has no basis in fact. As late as 1910, Abbott and Seroff establish, Rainey was singing what were then termed "up-to-date coon songs" and performing comedy routines with her husband, but they find no evidence that she was showcasing blues songs until a 1913 performance in Chicago drew notice in the black press.[6] As for Rainey's sobriquet: the singer had been known as "Ma" since 1913, Abbott and Seroff claim, but the title "Mother of the Blues" was "a 1924 advertising invention" in the *Chicago Defender* that had "no historical basis."[7] Yet Rainey was, for all that, a preeminent female blues star of the 1920s, and one of the most prolifically recorded (ninety-four sides between 1923 and 1928). She, like Handy, provides the blues tradition with plausible biographical anchoring, at least for those who care about such things and don't mind facts leavened with myth. The father and mother were there for, and responsible for, the birth of the blues. Or so the story goes.

I'm going to speak in a moment about the role Handy played in the blues emergence process as songwriter, autobiographer-historian, and crafter of myth. But I want to do so with an awareness of the way those who attempt to narrate the genesis of the blues find themselves suspended between two conflicting imperatives, neither of which is fully honored by the birth-of-the-blues cliché. On one side stands Sugar Blue — Clay's inheritor — who demands that we look to the slave past for existential anchoring and remember that the blues was "paid for in the blood that whips, guns, knives, chains and branding irons ripped from the bodies of [his] ancestors."[8] Blue's evocation of the traumatic black past depends on sensationalized language, but there's no denying the deeper truth he articulates: for some contemporary black performers and advocates, the blues are a site of memory for the grievous losses wrought by slavery and Jim Crow. On the other side stand the positivists, blues scholars — especially discographers, virtually all of them white — who traffic in the names of performers and towns, recording titles, and dates, as though the real history of the blues is to be found there. Blues history, told in this latter fashion, is filled with firsts: first documented sightings and hearings of the music, first sheet music, first recordings. Yet one thing that blues scholarship consistently demonstrates is that even the firmest of such dates turn out to be much less firm than we thought, so that mythology reenters the picture in the form of critical consensus.

A good example is Mamie Smith's "Crazy Blues" (1920), the first blues recording by an African American performer with an all-black band, which sold tens of thousands of copies and — or so it is argued — almost single-handedly established a market for race records. There's a general understanding among blues scholars that Smith's hit was preceded by roughly a decade of blues-themed sheet music authored by whites as well as blacks, but the surprising number of white blues singers who made records during that decade is often left out of the story. "What should be clear from the discussion of [Sophie] Tucker and [Marion] Harris," concludes musicologist David Brackett, "is that the idea of a (white) woman singing blues, jazz, or ragtime had been well established by 1920."[9] Harris recorded a handful of vaudeville blues in the three years before "Crazy Blues," including "I Ain't Got Nobody Much" (1916), a composition by the interracial team of Roger Graham (lyrics) and Spencer Williams (music). As a blues singer, Harris is no Bessie Smith (who later covered the song as "I Ain't Got Nobody") but she's certainly Mamie's equal. W. C. Handy, whose "St. Louis Blues" Harris recorded four months before "Crazy Blues" and also made a hit in 1920, said that the "celebrated white blues singer . . . sang blues so well that people hearing her records sometimes thought that [she] was colored."[10] But for scholars and advocates looking to anchor the blues tradition firmly in African American culture, "Crazy Blues," authored by black songwriter Perry Bradford without white assistance, offers a cleaner and more satisfying narrative line than "I Ain't Got Nobody Much," even though the earlier song and its singer were part of the cultural fabric out of which "Crazy Blues" emerged.

Yet as it turns out, this particular debate about the early days of the popular blues market is itself badly in need of revision. In *Long Lost Blues: Popular Blues in America, 1850–1920* (2010), music historian Peter C. Muir argues for a radically extended foreground to that market, a move that heightens our attention to early white creative investments in the music. Although the core of his book is a detailed examination of more than 450 different blues compositions by white and African American songwriters published between 1912 and 1920, Muir extends his gaze backward to explore an archive he terms "proto blues": songs displaying one or two elements that would later coalesce into the familiar twelve-bar, AAB form. Since the condition of having the blues, a pop cultural trope, predates the emergence of blues music per se, and since more than four-fifths of popular blues compositions in the 1912–20 period used some version of the phrase "I've got the blues," Muir searches for the earliest such usage and finds "I Have Got the Blues To Day!" (1850), by Gustave Blessner, a composer of waltzes and polkas, and Sarah M. Graham, about whom nothing is known. Judging from the sheet music, the song sounds nothing like the blues we know, but it tells the familiar blues story of a male singer-narrator deserted by his female lover. Next comes "Oh, Ain't I Got the Blues!" (1871) by A. A. Chapman, a sentimental parlor song with strongly comic flavor that was performed by a blackface

W. C. Handy and the "Birth" of the Blues

Cover of sheet music for an early ukulele adaptation of "The Saint Louis Blues,"
with image of Marion Harris and reminder of her popular 1920 recording.
Composed by W. C. Handy, 1914. Published by Handy Bros. Music Co.
(photography © New-York Historical Society)

minstrel troupe. By the late 1870s, according to Muir, white society was beginning to medicalize the blues by calling it "neurasthenia," a condition of sustained melancholy that could, it was believed, be cured by music. One of Muir's proto blues shows up at this point: "Billy's Request" (1879), a pop song by white composers who performed in a blackface minstrel troupe that announced itself on the published title pages as "A Cure for the Blues"—the earliest such song making that particular claim, but by no means the last.[11]

Muir's revisionist study has recently been supplemented by Abbott and Seroff's *The Original Blues: The Emergence of the Blues in African American Vaudeville* (2017). They focus not on early white investments in the blues lyric tradition but on the world of black southern vaudeville performance that generated its own storehouse of such material—especially the male stage performers, virtually all of them unrecorded, who fall into a historiographic black hole between guitar-wielding country bluesmen and female blues queens. Anybody looking for blues origins would do well, they argue, to celebrate the career of Butler "String Beans" May, an Alabama-born African American singer, dancer, piano player, and risqué comedian who was, they insist, the very first blues star. May achieved early fame in 1910 with "Elgin Movements," a double-entendre song about hip action that ended up providing the blues lyric tradition with a widely adapted metaphor, one that shows up in Robert Johnson's "Walking Blues" (1936) and a host of other recordings. He went on to spend much of the next seven years touring with his wife, Sweetie, as the team of May and May, bringing down houses with a mixture of raw comedy, brilliant pianism, and blues songs such as "Kitchen Mechanic," "Alabama Blues," "Hesitation Blues," and "Gimme a Piece of What You're Settin' On." May was the "blues master piano player of the world" whose "work talks for itself," wrote one black journalist in 1916. "His blues say something definite. They moan and weep and cry, setting up kindred emotions in the listeners. . . . I am not much on blues; don't think much of any variety of them. But if they are anything, Beans has got them."

Announcing himself as the "commander-in-chief . . . of the real blues," Butler May was the first nationally celebrated blues performer, one whose far-reaching influence was occluded by his premature death in 1917, and by the fact that he never recorded. But he had quite a few black male peers, and almost none of them made records, either—although one, Alabama-born pianist Baby Seals, published several compositions that similarly echo through the blues lyric tradition, including a "crap-shooting ragtime-cum-blues song" called "You Got to Shake, Rattle and Roll" (1909) and "Baby Seals Blues" (1912), "arguably the earliest known commercial sheet music

W. C. Handy and the "Birth" of the Blues

Sweetie May and Butler "String Beans" May, 1915 (courtesy Archives & Special Collections, J. D. Williams Library, University of Mississippi)

publication of a vocal blues" and a composition whose tag-lines show up in later recordings by Sara Martin, Ida Cox, Blind Lemon Jefferson, Memphis Slim, and a host of others. Seals, too, died prematurely, in 1916. "Had [he] not died so early," Abbott and Seroff argue, "he might have been a contender for the title 'Father of the Blues.'"[12]

What can we take away from this brief excursion into the earliest days of blues-in-formation? A skepticism toward those who speak with supreme confidence about where the blues come from, and from whom, might be a good idea. In 1991, with his eye on the sort of sheet music evidence Muir will later explore and with Butler "String Beans" May and other early black vaudevillians still consigned to scholarly obscurity, anthropologist Charles Keil argued that "blues music as such"—rather than the blues as an imputed racial-ancestral inheritance—might have begun in the first decade or two of the twentieth century "as a displacement of white moods, hurts, needs onto black oral tradition."[13] One need not push revisionism that far, however, to appreciate that the conventional blues origin story, rooted in rural black southernness and a panoply of oppressions, occludes an awkward truth: white folks didn't just waltz into the world of the blues for the first time with the folk and blues revivals of the 1959–65 period. White songwriters and performers played varied and important roles in shaping blues music from the very beginning, at least when it took the form of sheet music and recordings. White audiences were there as well, according to Abbott and Seroff, not just as consumers of race records but also—and especially in the South—at "midnight frolics," late-night shows featuring regular casts of black vaudevillians and blues singers performing for whites-only crowds.[14] At these shows, theater owners upheld the letter of Jim Crow while profiting from white hunger for the music. If blues, as pretty much all commentators agree, is a music shaped by call-and-response aesthetics that represent a core Afrodiasporic inheritance, then white blues people have participated in both sides of the dialogue for far longer than the conventional story allows.

DELTA AND HEARTLAND

"The white thing," as Black Arts spokesman Larry Neal once termed it, is hard to escape.[15] But suppose that we sidestep the question of early white influence—all the (presumptively) ersatz, sentimental, minstrel-flavored published and recorded white blues, plus any shaping input from white audiences. We're betraying the complexities of history when we do that, but black history, too, has its imperatives. Suppose we're interested only in black oral tradition. What, then, do we know for certain about the early days of the blues—not black vaudeville, important as it was, but music from the country precincts?

Perhaps because histories of the blues tend to privilege the same set of very early Mississippi sightings (Peabody, Handy) and the Henry Sloan / Charley Patton story set at Dockery Farm, or perhaps because Mississippi's blues tourism boosters have waged a successful propaganda campaign, many blues aficionados are under the impression that the statement "Blues originates in the Mississippi Delta" is settled scholarly consensus.[16] The atmospherics of rural black existence in what James Cobb famously called "the most southern place on earth" contributes to this impression—the inescapable cotton fields, the harshness and poverty of the sharecropper's life, and, as Elijah Wald has rightly noted, the very high ratio of blacks to whites in the Delta, as high as nine to one in some counties, which meant that black folks, most of them migrants from the hill country to the east, dominated the Delta's vernacular musical culture in a way almost without parallel in other parts of the rural South.[17] And of course there's that deep, dark, primeval mud: the enduring trope of Delta authenticity.

Yet seductive as this Delta blues origin story has proven to be over the years, it rests on surprisingly shaky foundations. In "Blues in the Heartland" (1997), an article largely ignored by blues historians, anthropologist and blues scholar Harriet Ottenheimer makes the startling claim that blues music first emerged not in the Mississippi Delta but in the urban Midwest: "medium to large-sized . . . towns and cities such as St. Louis; Evansville, Indiana; and Henderson and Louisville, Kentucky." When you sort carefully through the available textual evidence, it turns out, the earliest account of somebody hearing something like blues in the Delta, Charles Peabody's "Notes on Negro Music" (1903) from Coahoma County near Clarksdale, dates from 1901–2. But there are half a dozen earlier accounts from midwestern towns, most of them strung out along the Ohio River, many of them in places where freed black southern migrants encountered German immigrants and their loud, heavily rhythmic "oom-pah" music. "In this scenario," Ottenheimer argues, "blues developed in the 1880s or 1890s, in multiethnic midwestern river towns, as a kind of urban party music. As the style gradually made its way down the Mississippi River it was adopted by rural musicians in Texas, Louisiana, Arkansas, and Mississippi, particularly in the region known as the Mississippi Delta. Itinerant rural blues singers and traveling minstrel troupes and tent shows also had a hand in spreading the music. By 1910 it was widespread throughout the South."[18]

Ottenheimer doesn't argue that the Delta plays no role in the development of the blues. Quite the reverse: she argues that African American singers there found ways of blending their "complex melismatic phrasing" with the new urban import and simplifying the AAB, three-chord underpinnings in a way that accounts for the power and immediacy of Delta blues. But she argues that blues scholars and aficionados alike have long been in thrall to a foundational error, one that began in the late 1920s when, after a decade dominated by urban blueswomen, "folklorists and recording engineers . . . encountered the rural Delta styles. [Because] these were simpler styles, it was generally assumed that they were also earlier styles." Not so, insists Ottenheimer.[19]

Some who hunger for Mississippi-based blues authenticity may be tempted to invoke melisma—long, undulating vocal lines that descend through the blues scale—and say, "*That* is the heart of the blues." Field hollers are in some ways the epitome of rough-hewn melismatic singing—a strong residual African element within the creole domain of American vernacular music. Melisma strongly flavors the congregational singing found in Delta churches. The slide guitar sounds made by Charley Patton, Son House, Robert Johnson, and other prewar Delta blues legends are an instrumental way of replicating vocal melisma, which is why that style of blues so often features guitar and voice doubling each other, or calling and responding to each other, or both. So, yes, melisma in a Mississippi context is bluesy. But there's a complication, as you may remember: the melisma that shows up in the blues, according to ethnomusicologist Gerhard Kubik, is more properly thought of as an Arab cultural inheritance, a "thoroughly processed and transformed Arabic-Islamic stylistic component" that worked its way into the musical fabric of those West African regions that were heavily Islamicized. The Muslim call to prayer—long, plaintive descending strains—ends up, centuries later, as the sound of the Mississippi cotton fields. Down-home Delta blues are layered with echoes from somewhere else.[20]

MR. HANDY'S FAMOUS BLUE NOTE

Which brings us to W. C. Handy and his 1941 autobiography, *Father of the Blues*. It was Handy, as much as anybody, who was responsible for gifting us with the mythology of Mississippi as ground zero for the blues. Virtually every blues history quotes or describes one or both of the key blues discovery moments in Handy's book, even as those histories frame the author himself as a less-than-bluesy figure: not a bluesman but a bandleader and songwriter who heard, adapted, published, *used* the blues, then wrote a life narrative featuring himself at the center of the blues origins-and-emergence story. This portrait of Handy isn't untrue, yet it lacks the sort of nuance that might enable us to distinguish Handy's real achievement from the hype and criticism.

To the extent that Handy is viewed as an illegitimate claimant, a misnamed "Father" rather than an important pioneer, he suffers for two reasons: his middle-class background, which is at odds with the conventional image of a down-and-out bluesman; and a remarkable lambasting that he

W. C. Handy and the "Birth" of the Blues

W. C. Handy
(courtesy of Special Collections, University of Memphis Libraries)

received at the hands of New Orleans jazzman Jelly Roll Morton. In March 1938, Handy had been introduced on a radio broadcast of Robert Ripley's *Believe It or Not* as "the originator of jazz, stomps, and blues." Morton heard the broadcast and immediately dashed off a long letter to Ripley, which was republished in *Down Beat* with the banner headline "'W. C. Handy Is a Liar!' Says Jelly Roll," insisting that he, not Handy, had invented jazz and that Handy was an incompetent pretender. "Mr. Handy," he insisted, "cannot prove anything is music that he has created. He has possibly taken advantage of some unprotected material that sometimes floats around. I would like to know how a person could be an originator of anything, without being able to do at least some of what they created."[21] *Father of the Blues*, dictated to an amanuensis in the year or two after the *Down Beat* letter, was Handy's shrewdly self-aggrandizing response to Morton, one that carefully frames and evidences his achievements.

As a black boy born in northwest Alabama in 1873, Handy was unusual in several ways. The first was his hometown of Florence, near Muscle Shoals, a relative oasis of racial harmony in a state and a region not known for such things. Florence and Lauderdale County had been borderlands during the Civil War; many white residents, small farmers and merchants, sympathized with the Union and distrusted the plantation elite of south Alabama. The Handy family, observed the local newspaper in Handy's birth year, "retained the good will of all persons, white and black."[22] This upbringing at a remove from the harshest elements of Jim Crow laid the groundwork for Handy's later ascent as an American icon, a songwriter, and music publisher with professional connections across the color line.

The second thing that set him apart was his parentage: both his father and his father's father were freed slaves and Christian ministers. This strong patriarchal line distinguishes him from the two most famous African American autobiographers who preceded him, Frederick Douglass and Booker T. Washington. Both of those men were the products — or so they heard tell — of liaisons between their mothers and white men: his mother's master in Douglass's case, a white man in a nearby town in Washington's. Neither man was certain who his father was. Neither knew his own date of birth. Handy knew both things: he proudly states his birth date in the opening paragraph of his book. He grew up in a log cabin built by his grandfather with a dirt floor refinished by his father. The trials of African American life — families scattered and men disappeared through imprisonment and death — have often rendered such firm familial bonds unavailable to black sons. Handy's future as blues father is anchored here, in the stability and identity conferred by a powerful paternal presence that is also, paradoxically, a source of oppression that must be struggled against.

Like many Christian ministers of the day, Handy's father believed that worldly music, any song or instrument not consecrated to the Lord's service, was of the devil. The famous childhood scene in *Father of the Blues* comes at the end of the first chapter, when young Will decides to buy a guitar. Most people think of Handy as a cornet player, but he also played piano and guitar, and it's the guitar — a "shiny store-bought instrument" — that he describes purchasing and carrying home after husbanding his pennies, then proudly displaying to his father. "Look at it shine," he says. But instead of being pleased, his father is outraged: "'A box!' he gasped, while my mother stood frozen. 'A guitar! One of the devil's playthings. Take it away. Take it away, I tell you. Get it out of your hands.'" "I was stunned," Handy writes. "The words dim and far away like words spoken in a dream." Handy's father forces him to exchange the guitar for a dictionary, a resonant action in the domain of African American autobiography since freedom and literacy — the ability to write your own freedom papers and slip past the patrollers — were a trope of slave narratives. Literacy in Handy's post-Emancipation black world meant uplift, education, moral elevation: the bourgeois virtues a minister's son was expected to hew to. Any sort of nonconsecrated music, in contrast — and especially the guitar and fiddle — bespoke not just the spendthrift dissipation of the Saturday night frolic but also the low-class world of professional black entertainment, a world that began to flower in the aftermath of slavery.[23]

The emergence of this world laid the groundwork for the black southern vaudeville and tent-show circuit on which performers like Ma Rainey, Bessie Smith, and Butler "String Beans" May paid their dues. Blackface minstrelsy — more precisely, the entrance of black actors and musicians into the previously all-white precincts of blackface minstrelsy, a trickle in the 1850s that became a flood in subsequent decades — was a key development, and a problematic one. Blackface minstrelsy, after all, traffics in racial burlesque: white actors blacken their faces with burnt cork, paint on huge red lips, and caper around onstage making tasteless jokes in exaggerated black dialect while strumming banjos and clacking bones. After the Civil War, the white men who owned blackface minstrel troupes paid free men of color to do what they had been paying white men to do — although those black actors and musicians pushed and prodded at the genre's aesthetic confines.[24]

Handy entered that world in the late 1890s as a cornetist and bandleader for Mahara's Minstrels, a touring company run by an Irishman named Frank Mahara. Even as the black middle class was aghast at such a career, Handy argues in *Father of the Blues* that minstrelsy was a crucial training ground for black entertainers. "It goes without saying," Handy writes, "that [black] minstrels were a disreputable lot in the eyes of a large section of upper-crust Negroes . . . but it was also true that all the best talent of that generation came down the same drain" (33). Handy's description of his time with Mahara's never makes clear whether he and his fellow minstrels blacked up, and he insists that he and his band "made few concessions to low-brow taste in our selection of music" (35). True to his bourgeois heritage, Handy recon structs a déclassé vernacular entertainment as an instrument of uplift within a brotherhood of ambitious young black men.

But Handy also makes clear that the Jim Crow world these young men traversed was a killing field in which the protocols of white supremacy had to be navigated on a daily basis. The genial, avuncular tone of his autobiography has lulled some readers into skating right by the moments of harshness, or underestimating Handy's own emotional engagement in them. He speaks, for example, about how "sudden, stark tragedy sometimes darkened our minstrel days," recounting the story of Louis Wright, a "slim, sensitive boy" who "resented insult" and who, defending himself and his girlfriend against some white harassers one night, cursed them out and fired his gun (43). In Handy's telling, a lynch mob accompanied by police officers shows up at the minstrel company's train in the railroad yard, brutally flogs many of them, then spies Wright. "He was lynched, his tongue cut out and his body shipped to his mother in Chicago in a pine box" (43). Handy's own hot temper gets him in trouble one night in Tennessee when he punches a misbehaving white man in the mouth; he escapes lynching only by hiding in a beneath-the-floorboards compartment in the minstrels' Pullman coach (46–47). A career move that begins with him buying "smart outfits" (33), including diamonds, and admiring his own reflection in the musical press when it "throws roses in [his] direction" (33) ends with him admitting that many of his minstrel peers had fled from America after "the nightmare of those minstrel days" (51).

This evocation of black minstrelsy in *Father of the Blues* shows us a violent and racist pre-blues world in which Handy and his peers *had* the blues, simultaneously mourning, bridling at, and laughing off their own subjugation, even as they sought to express themselves through an aging vernacular art form that was unfit for the task.[25] Handy, who wants more out of life, crafts an autobiographical self-portrait of a young songwriter with an ear preternaturally attuned to the sonic landscapes of his time and a hunger for pop musical success. One key transformation that he helped engender was a shift from the mocking laughter of minstrelsy to the bittersweet sadness of the blues. The blues aren't just sad, of course. They're infused with a spirit of resistance; harsh laughter, as Langston Hughes noted, is one means through which they generate that resistance.[26] (In "Crazy Blues," Mamie Smith sings, "I went to the railroad ... hang my head on the track / Thought about my baby ... I gladly snatched it back.")[27] Yet as a songwriter and autobiographer, Handy didn't just do his part to displace the minstrel grin. He also

W. C. Handy and the "Birth" of the Blues

helped install and celebrate two potent new archetypes of blackness: the blues "queen" and the rambling, guitar-toting "musicianer," both of whom he configures as powerful conveyors of race-wide grief. Handy emphasizes this point in *Father of the Blues*; it's a key element of the myth he weaves about his own place in the blues story. Nor is the myth without justification. His one indelible composition, "St. Louis Blues" (1914), may be the most famous blues song in the world, and it is surely one of the most widely recorded. The song, Hughes wrote in 1941, "is sung more than any other song on the air waves, is known in Shanghai and Buenos Aires, Paris and Berlin—in fact, is heard so often in Europe that a great many Europeans think it must be the American National Anthem."[28]

Handy dreamed up "St. Louis Blues," he tells us, during one long night in a Beale Street rooming house, a beachhead he established as a creative retreat from the distractions of domestic life. Narrating more than twenty-five years after the fact in such a way as to rebut Morton's charge that he had merely "taken advantage of unprotected material," Handy portrays the compositional process as a kind of epic reassembly of black musical resources intended both to glorify the race and result in the follow-up hit he yearned for after "Memphis Blues" (1912). "My first decision," he says, "was that my new song would be another blues, true to the soil and in the tradition of *Memphis Blues*. Ragtime, I had decided, was passing out" (118). The ragtime he has in mind isn't the orchestral art of Scott Joplin but the catchy, light-hearted backing for so-called coon songs, a heightened form of minstrelsy featuring boastful, razor-wielding, watermelon-eating black roughnecks. Handy knows all about such stuff and decides that his song "would have an important difference" from such retrograde material: "The emotions that it expressed were going to be real" (119).

The emotional core of "St. Louis Blues" is generated by a moment of profound empathy with a woman from that city who serves Handy as a folk exemplar, a native informant bearing the deepest of blues laments. A "flood of memories" places the Beale-Street–ensconced Handy back in St. Louis during his youthful wanderings—"broke, unshaven, wanting even a decent meal, and standing before the lighted saloon . . . without a shirt under my frayed coat"—and reminds him of "a woman whose pain seemed even greater than his own" as she muttered, "Ma man's got a heart like a rock cast in de sea" (119) and stumbled past him, drunk and grief-stricken. Handy's St. Louis sojourn, which he narrates earlier in the autobiography, is an elective encounter with vagrancy, an "excursion into the lower depths" (28) made by a privileged minister's son. "I wasn't compelled to sleep on cobblestones"

(29), he acknowledges, remembering a night he had done that with "a thousand men of both races" (27). But the experience opened his eyes and heart to a world of poverty and pain—and his ears, too. "Her language," he says, thinking back to the pained woman, "was the same down-home medium that conveyed the laughable woe of lamp-blacked lovers in hundreds of frothy songs, but her plight was much too real to provoke much laughter" (119).

Handy pointedly rejects the way blackface minstrelsy appropriated and misused black vernacular, trivializing black suffering in the process. The blues, *his* blues, he resolves, will honor, rather than mock, that emotional pain. Yet even as he makes that claim, he seems to contradict himself: "My plot," he decides, "centered around the wail of a lovesick woman for her lost man, but in the telling of it I resorted to the humorous spirit of the bygone coon songs" (120). That "humorous spirit" is muted in the well-known first verse but becomes more evident in the later choruses of Handy's original sheet music—in lines such as "Said a black-headed gal makes a freight train jump the track / But a long tall gal makes a preacher ball the Jack."[29]

If Handy's reminiscences and the song itself speak unevenly to the question of humor's appropriate place in black blues lyricism, then his overarching purpose—the creation of racially representative art with mainstream appeal—remains clear. Into the "St. Louis Blues" mash-up he throws a host of different elements from the African diaspora: ragtime syncopation; "a real melody in the spiritual tradition"; the tango ("derived from the African 'tangana'" and signifying a "tom-tom beat"); "Negro phraseology and dialect"; and "the folk blues' three-line stanza." "Altogether," he concludes, "I aimed to use all that is characteristic of the Negro from Africa to Alabama" (120–21). His creative process, in the telling, is almost comically overdetermined; he's a mad alchemist of the blues, trying to capture the protean magic of the folk form and transmute it into gold.

Of all the elements in Handy's synthesis, the most significant in the long run—and the key to the success of "St. Louis Blues"—is his brilliantly simple solution to the blues songwriter's quandary: how to render the microtonal subtleties of blues singing on the page, as sheet music. "The primitive Southern Negro," he begins,

> as he sang was sure to bear down on the third and seventh tones of the scale, slurring between major and minor. Whether in the cotton fields of the Delta or on the levee up St. Louis way, it was always the same. Till then, however, I had never heard this slur used by a more sophisticated Negro, or by any white man. I had tried to convey this

W. C. Handy and the "Birth" of the Blues

effect in Memphis Blues by introducing flat thirds and sevenths (now called "blue notes") into my song, although its prevailing key was the major; and I carried this device into my new melody as well. (120)

Handy knew where the melodic magic of the blues was buried — the "weird" sound that he and so many other early witnesses to the music remarked on. It inheres in the tension between major and minor: between the major "prevailing key" and specific minor-y pitches that good blues singers know how to hit as they move melismatically upward and downward through what we have learned in subsequent years to call the blues scale. Those minor-y pitches are *not*, in fact, flat thirds, fifths, and sevenths of the sort found on pianos and guitars. They don't exist in standard Western musical notation. They're in-between notes: quarter-tones, slides, slurs. More often than not, these pitches move subtly upward or downward in the brief interval after they're sounded. The best visual analogue for this is the way a blues guitar player squeezes the strings, pushing them incrementally across the fretboard — so that a flat third, for example, is raised five or ten cents in the direction of the major third.

Handy knew that it was impossible to accurately represent this sort of pitch-bending magic on the printed page, but he also knew how to approximate the magic, however roughly. It was possible to insert minor thirds and sevenths into a major key song. It was possible to use a minor third and major third *in sequence* in a song's melody. The opening "I" in the first published version of "St. Louis Blues" — "I hate to see the evenin' sun go down" — is sung to precisely that slurred sequence of notes. That's what Handy figured out: that the magic of the blues, to the extent that it was capable of being captured in sheet music and made available to the general public, was located there. Get some of that on paper and you could sell it and become famous around the world. (The minor-third-in-a-major-key trick was, in his own time, actually called Handy's "World Famous Blue Note.")[30] Handy didn't invent blues singing, but he did simplify and abstract one specific and crucial element of it. He salted this element into his sheet music as memorable melody behind feelingful lyrics that captured the public imagination. That, as much as any other achievement, is why he deserves our respect.

WEIRD MUSIC

Father of the Blues isn't just a songwriter's spirited self-defense; it's also the invaluable testimony of a witness to the earliest days of the Mississippi blues.

And here we come at last to the pair of passages for which Handy is justly famous. The prelude to both episodes was Handy's decision in 1903 to leave Mahara's Minstrels after seven years as musical director, move south to Memphis, and accept a new job leading a Knights of Pythias band in Clarksdale, Mississippi. He wasn't in search of the blues at that point. His ambition was to be the black John Philip Sousa—Sousa, "The March King," being the former musical director of the U.S. Marine Band and the most famous pop composer in turn-of-the-century America. But Handy had tasted the blues, especially the blues feelings bred by white supremacist violence, during his minstrel days, and his ears were open to new sounds. One night, while dozing at a train station in Tutwiler, a small Delta town, he is "wakened . . . with a start" (74) by a strange and captivating music.

Blues scholars invariably cite the date of the Tutwiler episode as 1903. Handy never offers that date. In fact, he sets up the episode by noting that it followed on an extensive work history that he'd accrued after accepting the band appointment in Clarksdale—such an extensive history that he'd come to know "by heart every foot of the Delta," so that travels through the region "became a familiar, monotonous round" (73). A much more likely date for the encounter is thus 1904. The 1903–4 variance matters only because it illustrates, once again, the way even established baseline facts about the blues can turn out to be spurious—more mythology than history. What is clear is how important Handy himself was to the process by which eyewitness accounts, history, and myth come to be mingled in the telling of the blues' emergence. The story begins, crucially, when Handy is jolted from sleep—a trope signifying the dawning of new consciousness. Then comes a passage familiar to any reader of blues histories:[31]

> A lean, loose-jointed Negro had commenced plunking a guitar beside me while I slept. His clothes were rags; his feet peeped out of his shoes. His face had on it some of the sadness of the ages. As he played, he pressed a knife on the strings of the guitar in a manner popularized by Hawaiian guitarists who used steel bars. The effect was unforgettable. His song, too, struck me instantly.
>
> *Goin' where the Southern cross' the Dog*
>
> The singer repeated the line three times, accompanying himself on the guitar with the weirdest music I had ever heard. (74)

That knife-sliding-on-the-guitar-strings technique is something that Handy rightly sources in a Hawaiian style—slack-key guitar—that had become

W. C. Handy and the "Birth" of the Blues

familiar to southern musicians thanks to the widespread touring of the Royal Hawaiian Band and other island ensembles in the decade before Handy encountered this guitarist.[32] But the guitarist's unusual slide style also, according to some scholars, has West African origins; it's a guitaristic elaboration of the diddley bow—a homemade one-string instrument, sometimes played by black southern children (especially in the Mississippi Delta) that derives from the monochord zither and mouth bow found in Malawi and elsewhere.[33]

The word "weirdest," applied to African American music, echoes down through American history and, before that, through the European colonial enterprise. In *The Souls of Black Folk* (1903), W. E. B. Du Bois called the spirituals "weird old songs"; Kentucky-born amateur musicologist Jeannette Robinson Murphy spoke, like Handy, of the "weird music" made by black southern men she'd known as a girl, African-born men for whom the "veneer of civilization" was "entirely superficial."[34] "Weird" gets at the unusual minor/major tonality, but it speaks more broadly to incomprehension: the Western listener's inability to make the encountered soundscape scan in accord with received ideas about musical meaning. The thrice-repeated line, with its obscure reference to a transit point, adds to Handy's confusion here. Hindsight allows us to recognize the song's verse form: it's an AAA blues, the precursor to the AAB verse that ultimately became the reference standard for both composed and performed blues.

But there's more to be learned from this passage. We might note, for example, the way that Handy, an educated middle-class bandleader, foregrounds the guitarist's ragged poverty—as though the real stuff, this "earthborn music," as Handy calls it a moment later, flows naturally out of a condition of low-down deprivation. As cultural historian Bryan Wagner has argued, the origin story Handy offers here "helped to sanctify the trainhopping threadbare drifter as a central character in the iconography of the black tradition." But by transforming the singer's imputed inner grief into an enduring racial legacy, "the sadness of the ages" revealed on his face, Handy turns away from the specifics of contemporary social history to create a legend. For, "the one thing we can know for sure about Handy's songster," Wagner argues, "is that he is legally vulnerable."[35] He was a vagrant, in the state's eyes—a social undesirable targeted by new laws that Mississippi and other Deep South jurisdictions were enacting to control the movement of black men no longer formally imprisoned by the institution of slavery.

What Handy mythifies as the sadness of the ages, in other words, may just be the weariness of a black drifter hoping to avoid arrest and banishment to the county farm. His one-line song makes perfect sense in this context: the Southern and the Dog, as he explains, were railroad lines that intersected in Moorhead, a small town forty miles to the south. He was singing about heading to the crossing-point—a good place to evade the law, although he doesn't say this in so many words.

The Tutwiler guitarist and blues singer becomes Handy's crossroad guide: he's a trickster in transit, a cipher with no name or identity, a guardian of the threshold across which the ambitious young composer must pass. Like his African antecedent, Esu-Elegbara, he's double-voiced, a skilled signifier who schools the educated but clueless Handy in local language use. What Handy needs to overcome, he admits a page or two later, is the prejudice engendered by his own musical training:

> I hasten to confess that I took up with low folk forms hesitantly. . . .
> I had picked up a fair training in the music of the modern world and
> had assumed that the correct manner to compose was to develop
> simples into grandissimos and not to repeat them monotonously.
> As a director of many respectable, conventional bands, it was not
> easy for me to concede that a simple slow-drag and repeat could be
> rhythm itself. Neither was I ready to believe that this was just what
> the public wanted. But we live to learn. (76)

The sticking point for Handy is repetition, something that characterized not just the Tutwiler musician's three-line lyric but also the rhythmic backing that propelled it and similar "low folk forms." We no longer use that sort of condescending language to talk about vernacular music, in part because we've had more than a hundred years to evolve listening skills adequate to the task. We've learned to appreciate the microtonal variants, intonational nuances (such as growls), and rhythmic emphases with which skilled blues musicians inflect AAA and AAB repetitions in order to give their songs emotional contours and a sense of narrative development. Handy, despite his formal musical education, or perhaps because of it, lacks those skills.

His enlightenment soon comes in another Mississippi town on a similarly memorable night. He is in Cleveland, twenty-five miles southwest of Tutwiler, leading his orchestra through a dance program, when someone sends up a note asking if he and the band would play some of their "native music." The implicit condescension of this request and the sociology of the Delta—where only whites, by and large, had enough money to hire Handy and his orchestra—strongly suggest that the crowd is white. Handy tries to meet this curious request, but the men in his orchestra sit at the high end of the black musical totem pole — they're full-time sight-readers who "bowed strictly to the authority of printed notes" — and the "sophisticated" melody they come up with leaves the crowd unmoved. So a second request is made: Would Handy's band take a break and give a "local colored band" a chance to play a few dance songs?

Handy is happy to relinquish the floor, but he eyes the competition with a sort of dismissive condescension that professional musicians reserve for those they consider to be less than legitimate:

> They were led by a long-legged chocolate boy and their band consisted of just three pieces, a battered guitar, a mandolin and a worn-out bass.
>
> The music they made was pretty well in keeping with their looks. They struck up one of those over-and-over strains that seem to have no very clear beginning and certainly no ending at all. The strumming attained a kind of disturbing monotony, but on and on it went, a kind of stuff that has long been associated with cane rows and levee camps. Thump-thump-thump went their feet on the floor. Their eyes rolled. Their shoulders swayed. And through it all that little agonizing strain persisted. It was not really annoying or unpleasant. Perhaps "haunting" is a better word, but I commenced to wonder if anybody besides small town rounders and their running mates would go for it. (76–77)

Again, as with the Tutwiler guitarist, Handy's attentions are first drawn to signs of poverty: "a battered guitar, . . . a worn-out bass." Again, as with the Tutwiler guitarist, Mississippi's musical soundscape offers a distinctive combination of weird (agonizing, haunting) tonality and seemingly excessive repetition. In a fascinating act of literary appropriation, Handy has represented the heavily accented timekeeping of this ragtag ensemble by borrowing and tweaking a line ("Thump, thump, thump, went his foot on the floor") from one of the most famous blues poems of all time, Langston Hughes's "The Weary Blues" (1925). Thanks to the detective work of a Handy scholar named Elliott Hurwitt, we know that the "long-legged chocolate boy" was twenty-one-year-old Prince McCoy: an up-and-coming Mississippi Delta bandleader whose regional popularity ultimately rivaled Handy's.[36] Handy is stretching the point when he configures McCoy and his trio as primitives. What they seem to have been is conversant with the blues — homegrown analogues and precursors to Handy and his band, ambitious young musicians who had figured out something that Handy was just about to figure out: blues was the new sound, and it sold:

> A rain of silver dollars began to fall around the outlandish, stomping feet. The dancers went wild. Dollars, quarters, halves—the shower grew heavier and continued so long I strained my neck to get a better look. There before the boys lay more money than my nine musicians were being paid for the entire engagement. Then I saw the beauty of primitive music. They had the stuff the people wanted. . . . My idea of what constitutes music was changed by the sight of that silver money cascading around the splay feet of a Mississippi string band. (77)

One dollar in the early 1900s is thirty dollars in our own time. Handy offers a tableau of transracial communion propelled by call-and-response aesthetics: a very early moment in the long history of the blues when black musicians are driving white dancers so wild with abandon that cash is literally being charmed from their hands.

Those who romanticize the early days of the Delta blues as an otherworldly tableau comprised of all-black jukes, deserted train stations, and midnight crossroads aren't entirely wrong—Handy did encounter that guitarist in Tutwiler, after all—but they're also missing significant elements of the story. The life stories of Charley Patton, Honeyboy Edwards, and other Delta blues players make clear that they, like Prince McCoy's trio here and the black vaudevillians at the "midnight rambles" of subsequent decades, made music that evoked powerful responses from white audiences, not just black audiences; they prized that response, along with the money it brought in, as a way of freeing themselves from the sharecropper's fate that swallowed up the mass of working-class black southerners.[37] Incorporating those new blues sounds into his orchestra's repertoire, scoring and publishing blues compositions, urging white singers like Marion Harris to record them, W. C. Handy greatly broadened the scope of this particular crossover move. He did so thanks to his willingness to forego the privileges of his black bourgeois background, at least briefly, and make a youthful excursion into the depths of working-class St. Louis, a transracial brotherhood on the cobblestoned levee of the Mississippi. But he also did so *because* of the privileges that his class position and education offered him: his skill as a sight-reader and composer as well as his self-confidence and sense of mission as the son and grandson of ministers who were viewed with respect by blacks and whites alike in their socially moderate corner of post-Reconstruction Alabama.

W. C. Handy and the "Birth" of the Blues

There is a long foreground, in other words, for the emergence of a mass white blues audience that began with the folk revival of the late 1950s and caught fire with the British blues invasion of the mid-1960s. Handy is a part of all this. He felt the power of the music, surging up from down below; he translated the complexities of blues singing into the profitable blue note; and he crafted a myth through which premodern Mississippi becomes the scene of transmission as threadbare black musicians open his eyes, schooling him in what he needs to know. As a witness to history, he's left us with an invaluable first-person account—as complicated, paradoxical, and suggestive, in its own way, as the music he sought to appropriate, champion, and memorialize.

part 7

Langston Hughes and the Scandal of Early Blues Poetry

SECULAR SONGS OF THE SOUTHERN NEGROES

The history of the blues is, among other things, a history of commentators who lament the appropriation, commercialization, dilution, sexing-up, stigmatization, or other misuse of the blues. White people are often the bad actors in this particular morality play, in part because they have long had a near monopoly on the cultural machinery that extracts profit from the music, but blacks sometimes take the heat as well. Langston Hughes, America's first great blues poet, contributes to this history with a pair of forceful statements, "The Negro Artist and the Racial Mountain" (1926) and "Note on Commercial Theatre" (1940), but he was himself castigated within the black community for daring to write frankly about blues people. People who engage deeply with the blues like to complain; sometimes their engagements precipitate complaints from others. This should not surprise us. The nature of the complaints, however, suggests something surprising: that the blues, for those cultural gatekeepers in whom it evokes powerful responses, functions simultaneously as something sacred and profane. It is a form of black folk expression whose racial and aesthetic purity must be safeguarded *and* a form of earthy, low-down, sex-charged communication, promiscuously easy to commodify and sell, that entrances a transracial public and creates various kinds of moral hazards and aesthetic problems. The history of the blues, in other words, encompasses a history of bluesy commentary *about* the blues —

as though a people's sacred trust were being defended, or degraded trash were being condemned, or both.

This pattern of critique is established at the very moment that the blues, although not yet a named idiom, first becomes audible to somebody with the power to represent the music to a broader audience. In "Notes on Negro Music" (1903), Harvard archaeologist Charles Peabody describes the range of vocal music, with and without guitar accompaniment, produced by the gang of black laborers hired to help him out on an excavation in Coahoma County, Mississippi, near Clarksdale, in 1901–2. The bulk of their material, much of it seemingly improvised and some of it offering sly commentary on his own position as white supervisor, pleases and holds his attention. But he's dismayed by the rapidity with which these men, asked to carry a tune for his wife, abandon their "autochthonous" music to sing what tradition-alists in our own time might call pop-cultural drivel: "very poor 'ragtime,' 'Goo-goo Eyes' with any number of encores, and 'Nigger Bully' and others quite as original probably with Miss May Irwin as with them."[1] A more per-ceptive commentator might have realized that these proto-bluesmen were merely trying to give Mrs. Peabody what they presumed she'd want: current and recent pop hits from the "coon song" songbook, including a swagger-ing comic number filled with violent and demeaning stereotypes of black roustabouts that had been a huge success for Irwin, a Canadian-born vaude-ville performer, after its publication in 1896. They were either debasing them-selves with "Nigger Bully" in an effort to please the boss's wife or taking a positive pleasure in the song's rough-edged portrait of black urban life, or both. Peabody misses all of this. What bothers him is the ease with which, in his estimation, these men sell out—abandoning the "real" stuff, their native Mississippi music, for the sake of degraded commercial fare, tawdry lyrics dreamed up by some Tin Pan Alley songwriter.

Peabody's complaint was repeated almost verbatim by pioneering southern folklorist Howard Odum in a 1911 article, "Folk-Song and Folk-Poetry as Found in the Secular Songs of the Southern Negroes." Attempting to separate the (authentic, traditional) wheat from the (degraded, modern) chaff in the songs performed by his African American subjects in Lafayette County, Mississippi, Odum sniffed dismissively at the latter. "All manner of 'rag-times,' 'coon-songs,' and the latest 'hits,' replace the simpler negro melodies. Young negroes pride themselves on the number of such songs they can sing, at the same time that they resent a request to sing the older melo-dies."[2] But Odum was far more scandalized by the songs his subjects generated themselves—an outpouring of Rabelaisian raunch, an "inexpressible wilderness of vulgarity and indecency," that blues scholar Paul Oliver would later call the "blue blues":

> Their songs tell of every phase of immorality and filth; they represent the superlative of the repulsive. . . . The prevailing theme of this class of songs is that of sexual relations, and there is no restraint in its expression. In comparison with similar songs of other peoples that have been preserved, those of the Negro stand out in a class of their own. They are sung by groups of boys and girls, of men and women, and they are sung by individuals who revel in their suggestiveness. Here the vivid imagination of the Negro makes his constant thought a putrid bed of rottenness and intensifies his already depraved nature. Openly descriptive of the grossest immorality and susceptible of unspeakable thoughts and actions, rotten with filth, they are yet sung to the time honored melodies.[3]

Both Odum and Peabody were passing judgment on the blues and the people who were in the process of inventing that music during what might be called the late pre-blues period, a moment just before W. C. Handy's "Memphis Blues" (1912) and "St. Louis Blues" (1914) gave the word "blues" cultural currency. They are bothered not by the blues' appropriation and commodification—the "blues scene" of those early days, as I noted in the previous chapter, was a muddle of sheet-music by black and white composers alike, including Antonio Maggio's "I Got the Blues" (1908)—but by the way *pre*-blues pop music seems to have claimed and aesthetically soiled black men whom these white men would have preferred to have encountered as pristine folk exemplars, innocents untouched by modernity. Odum, in addition, is bothered by the sex thing. Here his critique veers 180 degrees from folkloric purism, indicting his black subjects not for succumbing to the temptations of Tin Pan Alley but for being far too rambunctiously themselves: an entire folk community, in his view, sunk into extreme moral turpitude and entirely satisfied with that condition.

When African American commentators enter this stream of commentary, they do so as members of a Jazz Age intelligentsia who have watched the blues make the leap from an under-the-radar black southern folk music into nationwide crossover phenomenon. The issue of white appropriation has reared its head by this point, but so too has the issue of black capitulation to commercial pressures. In "The Blues as Folk Poetry" (1930), poet and professor Sterling Brown invokes the word "folk" as a marker of aesthetic purity and racial authenticity; although never mentioning white artists by name, he's unhappy with the way the music's popularity, abetted by modern technologies, threatens both domains:

> The Blues have deservedly come into their own, and, unfortunately for the lover of folk art, into something more than their own. They are sung on Broadway in nearly unrecognizable disguises, are produced on phonograph records by the thousands, are transmitted by radio. ... It is becoming more and more and more difficult to tell which songs are truly folk and which are clever approximations. ... The word ["blues"] has become part of the popular music vernacular, and has been widened to cover songs that by no stretch of the imagination could be considered Blues.[4]

"God only knows what the world has suffered from the white damsels who try to sing Blues," agrees Zora Neale Hurston in "Characteristics of Negro Expression" (1934), playing the race card more combatively than Brown and in a way that anticipates later Black Arts critiques of white appropriation during the Blues Revival of the 1960s.[5] But she mocks black crossover moves as well, the tidying-up and orchestrating of black religious music by the Fisk Jubilee Singers and others in an effort to cultivate a broader audience. "The Negroes themselves have also sinned in this respect. ... The spirituals that have been sung around the world are Negroid to be sure, but so full of musicians' tricks that Negro congregations are highly entertained when they hear their old songs so changed."[6]

Langston Hughes admired Brown's blues poetry, especially *Southern Road* (1932), and he was Hurston's friend and occasional collaborator. His "Note on Commercial Theatre" (1940), written in 1939 after a disillusioning stint as a Hollywood scriptwriter on *Way Down South*, a saccharine melodrama featuring cheerful slaves singing spirituals on their massa's plantation, neatly sums up the predicament of black blues in an age of grasping commercialization:

> You've taken my blues and gone —
> You sing 'em on Broadway
> And you sing 'em in Hollywood Bowl,
> And you mixed 'em up with symphonies
> And you fixed 'em
> So they don't sound like me.
> Yep, you done taken my blues and gone.

You also took my spirituals and gone.

You put me in *Macbeth* and *Carmen Jones*
And all kinds of *Swing Mikados*
And in everything but what's about me —[7]

The poem revolves around the tension between "you" and "me": the profit-centered world of "commercial theatre"—the profane white mainstream and its corrupting, diluting, appropriative machinations—on the one hand, and, on the other hand, the pristine, vulnerable, and exploited world of black folk artistry, a sacred trust in Hughes's eyes. The poem's presumptively black speaker signifies on a somewhat broader array of blues-tinged investments in the opening four lines than the titular word "commercial" might first suggest: not just Broadway's ersatz variants — about which more in a moment — but more substantial symphonic works by George Gershwin ("Rhapsody in Blue") and William Grant Still (the "Afro-American" symphony), both of whom Hughes admired. ("You sing 'em at Hollywood Bowl" may refer to Benny Goodman, whose band, featuring the jazz-and-blues singer Louise Tobin, famously played that venue in August 1939.)[8] The poem turns toward a prophetic assertion of a future reclamation of the blues (and spirituals), one enabling accurate and ennobling representations of black people (personalized as "me") rather than false and inauthentic ones:

But someday somebody'll
Stand up and talk about me,
And write about me —
Black and beautiful —
And sing about me,
And put on plays about me!
I reckon it'll be
Me myself!

Yes, it'll be me.

It's a powerful, memorable statement. The poem's opening line, "You've taken my blues and gone," resonates with contemporary African American complaints by Sugar Blue, Corey Harris, Roland L. Freeman, and others about the way white people have managed to achieve near hegemony in the mainstream blues scene—dominating awards shows and festival bookings, blithely profiteering and directing the conversation in a way that leaves some black blues performers feeling disenfranchised and some black communi-

Langston Hughes and Early Blues Poetry

ties feeling left behind. The poem's close, by contrast, imagines that what has been taken, spirited away, co-opted, will "someday" be put back into black hands.

As I suggested at the beginning of this chapter, forceful pronouncements about the blues have a habit of turning into morality plays: jeremiads about race, culture, power, and profit that take on an almost religious cast, demanding that we honor what is sacred and condemn what is profane. Here it might be good to remember Kalamu ya Salaam's insistence in his essay "the blues aesthetic" that "life is not about good vs. evil, but about good and evil eaten off the same plate."[9] Hughes is a key figure in the blues literary tradition not just because he voiced a prophetic complaint that remains relevant and unresolved to this day but also because he dared to be the black "me" that walked African American blues people and their music through the front door of American literature, incurring the condemnation of his genteel black elders even as he expanded the tradition in a way that empowered subsequent generations of black writers.

BLUES CRAZY

Since Hughes's poetic achievement was, in its own way, a vital part of the blues craze of the 1920s, it's worth briefly recapitulating that curious chapter in American cultural history. The craze began, as I noted in Bar 6, with the release of Mamie Smith's "Crazy Blues" (1920). The astonishing success of Smith's recording—75,000 records sold in Harlem alone in the first month, a million copies nationally in the first seven months—has been explained in several ways, including pent-up demand for a black blues recording artist among African American audiences. In *Seems Like Murder Here* (2002), I argued that songwriter Perry Bradford's lyrics, which veered from a lovelorn woman's complaint into a sensational mixture of drugs, guns, and cop-killing, might have something to do with those sales. "I'm gonna do like a Chinaman," Smith sang, ". . . get myself some hop / Get myself a gun, and shoot myself a cop." Harlem in 1920 was newly invigorated with black migrants from the South, people who had brought with them not only a taste for the blues but an immense relief at having escaped from a Jim Crowed region in which white southern lawmen routinely allowed lynchings to proceed and sometimes participated in them. The Ku Klux Klan, as it happened, was very much in the news when "Crazy Blues" was released; the organization was threatening to establish a beachhead in New York to assist (in the words of Imperial Wizard William Simmons) "the maintenance of white supremacy," and James Weldon Johnson was opining in the *New York Age* that if the Klan were foolish enough to set foot in Harlem, the organization "will have our sympathies, even our condolences, in advance." The song, I suggested, voiced a sort of black collective "Hell no!" not just to that specific threat but also to anything else, including local policing, that would undercut the promise held out by "the city of refuge," as author Rudolf Fisher termed Harlem in his 1925 story by the same name.

Whatever the reasons, Smith's recording was a huge hit and, as one narrative history put it, "the New York entertainment business went blues crazy."[10]

The so-called race records industry sprang up almost overnight, focused on providing commodified entertainment to an African American consuming public that hadn't previously been catered to. Record companies scrambled to find black female singers who could put across the new style, even as Tin Pan Alley songwriters, white and black, churned out recordable material. A fair number of them were natives of the South; a few, including Lucille Bogan, Birleanna Blanks, Cora Perkins, and Callie Vassar, were natives of Mississippi.[11] Many had come up in black vaudeville, the Theatre Owners Booking Association (TOBA) circuit. They weren't deep blues singers, as we might define that term now; their stylistics were more operatic, more indebted to Broadway than to tent shows and juke joints. Two singers who *were* indebted to Deep South tent shows and juke joints, Bessie Smith and Ma Rainey, came on the scene in 1923 and 1924, respectively, and their entrance decisively shifted the emergent genre's aesthetics. They were raw, deep, authentic, soulful, in a way that captivated black audiences and made believers out of music industry professionals who only a year or two earlier were dismissing them as too rough.

What often gets lost in the blues histories that narrate this period as a shift from "theatrical" black female blues singers to "down-home" black female blues singers is the degree to which both sorts of blues singers were working within an urban entertainment culture where white singers, songwriters, and playwrights had latched onto the blues craze and were dumping their own contributions onto the fire. Neglect this part of the story and Hughes's complaint, "You've taken my blues and gone," makes no sense. Jerome Kern, Noel Coward, Rogers and Hart, Irving Berlin — virtually every top Tin Pan Alley songwriter, according to historian Arnold Shaw, wrote songs with "blues" in the title.[12] Few of those songs were what we would today call blues; often they offered no more than a sprinkling of flatted thirds and fifths and the theme of romantic disappointment. "Blue Danube Blues," "Russian Blues," "Atlantic Blues," "Blue Ocean Blues," "The Yankee Doodle

Langston Hughes and Early Blues Poetry

Blues," "Half of It Dearie Blues," "When You and I Were Young Maggie Blues". . . the list goes on. The novelty song "Yes! We Have No Bananas," composed by Frank Silver and Irving Cohn for the Broadway revue "Make It Snappy" in 1922, was performed by comedian Eddie Cantor and became a hit for Billy Jones in 1923; both Cantor and Jones recorded the follow-up, "I've Got the Yes! We Have No Bananas Blues":

> Lately I've been off my nut
> I keep hearing nothing but
> "Yes, We Have No Bananas"
> I would like to find the guy
> Who composed that lullaby
> "Yes, We Have No Bananas"
> I wish that I could go
> To a cabaret or show
> Where someone wouldn't come along
> And sing that doggone song!
>
> I've got the "Yes, We Have No Bananas" Blues
>
> I've got the blues
> And when I hear it
> Oh how I fear it!
> It's just like hearing bad news.
> It hasn't got a bit of sense
> And I go wild when they commence
> "Bananas! Bananas!"
> I wish I could break up a million pianas! . . .[13]

Confronted with what surely feels to any student of African American blues like a razzmatazz-filled travesty of the form and a betrayal of the traumatic history encoded in the music, it's tempting indeed to shout, "You've taken my blues and gone!" But who is "you"? Even as white fascination with the blues led to the music's appropriation, dilution, and diffusion across the color line, black musicians were jumping onto the white-blues bandwagon, hoping for crossover sales. Pianist, composer, and music publisher Clarence Williams, a fixture on many of Bessie Smith's recordings, covered "I've Got the Yes! We Have No Bananas Blues" almost the moment it was released, backing up his wife, blues singer Eva Taylor, with his Blue Five ensemble. (The A-side of that recording featured "Oh Daddy Blues," a song that Williams also recorded with Smith.)[14] In 1926, Porter Grainger and Bob Ricketts, black entertainment professionals, published a booklet called *How to Play and Sing the Blues Like the Phonograph and Stage Artists*, offering advice to all comers — including white aspirants, one presumes. "To render a 'Blues' song effectively," they advised, "it is necessary to possess a fair knowledge of the spirit and circumstances under which this type of publication was created. If one can temporarily play the role of the oppressed or the depressed, injecting into his or her rendition a spirit of hopeful prayer, the effect will be more natural and successful."[15] Grainger and Ricketts were pianists, songwriters, arrangers, music publishers. The word "publication" makes clear that they presume their aspiring blues singer will be working from sheet music and suggests that they hoped, with the help of their instructional booklet, to sell more of that particular commodity. Their urging that the student "temporarily play the role of the oppressed" suggests that transracial sympathy — whites imagining themselves into low-down black subject positions — is being advocated by these black musical guides.

It won't do, in other words, to castigate a white-dominated entertainment industry in the 1920s as having taken the blues and gone and imagine that the final word has been said. The situation is more complicated than that. African American blues professionals also took the music and crossed over, parlaying their insider knowledge into increased profits and heightened mainstream visibility. And musically inclined whites, both amateur and professional, suddenly began to embrace blues music, in a variety of registers and however imperfectly, as something that spoke for and to them. The huge fees that Bessie Smith commanded as a recording artist and live performer during this period would not have been possible without such white responses and investments.

WITHOUT FEAR OR SHAME

Langston Hughes carved a singular path through the blues-besotted world of the Jazz Age. His signal contributions to the era are two volumes of poetry, *The Weary Blues* (1926) and *Fine Clothes to the Jew* (1927), plus an essay, "The Negro Artist and the Racial Mountain" (1926), in which, with a manifesto's polemical intensity, he defended his blues-based aesthetics. He was seeking, as one of Harlem's so-called New Negroes, to explode the strictures of the genteel tradition as that tradition was being maintained not by white literary gatekeepers — Vachel Lindsay, Carl Van Vechten, and other white writers strongly encouraged him — but by an anxious, snobbish black middle class. In our own age, shaped by the decades-long after-

Cover of sheet music for "I've Got the Yes! We Have No Banana[s] Blues"
(courtesy blogs.Harvard.edu, Creative Commons)

math of the Black Arts Movement with its revalorization of African origins and its sanctification of black popular music as the voice of the people, it may be hard for us to appreciate the strongly negative valence that an upwardly aspirant black bourgeoisie attached not just to blues and jazz during the first two decades of the twentieth century but also to the larger world of "popular entertainments." That negative valence has several sources. The most obvious is the long-standing scourge of blackface minstrelsy: the seemingly bottomless reservoir of denigrating, exaggerated, sometimes violent and/or sexual imagery through which white Americans had burlesqued and mocked black Americans for nearly a century before Hughes began writing his poems. A spate of coon songs beginning in the mid-1890s had reactivated the virus with the help of ragtime melodies; "ragtime," W. C. Handy notes in *Father of the Blues*, "was not [considered] respectable" by most black people, and that disreputability was grounded in a legitimate concern that blackface imagery, in profit-seeking white hands, had the power to undercut, even cripple, black attempts to forge and sustain images of dignified personhood. "Make the young negroes turn from coon songs and go to the songs of our mothers and fathers," pleaded Willie Councill, a leading black southern educator, before a capacity crowd in Memphis. "The coon songs . . . make sentiment against us."[16] The perils of popular entertainment, for those who shared Councill's perspective, were summed up in the title of a 1981 study by Sam Dennison: *Scandalize My Name: Black Imagery in American Popular Music*. Added to this broad, indisputable, and continuing burden of demeaning imagery was the fact that ragtime, blues, jazz, and other black vernacular musics were low-down and secular, rather than—like classical music and the spirituals—elevated and/or sanctified, a fact that cut directly against the black middle class's stated goal of "uplifting the race." They were musics associated with drinking, dancing, cursing, carousing, fornicating, and other forms of working-class and lower-class dissipation, rather than moral probity, aesthetic contemplation, and spiritual elevation of a sort that, if sustained over time, just might lead white Americans to accept their darker neighbors as fellow citizens. These musics were heathenish, in a word: hearkening back to the jungle. As such, their presence embarrassed, enervated, and sometimes outraged the black middle class.

Hughes stepped into the middle of this mess, and he did so with the principled determination of a poetic revolutionary. Like William Wordsworth in *Preface to Lyrical Ballads* (1800), who proposed to write about "incidents and situations from common life . . . in a selection of language really used by men," Hughes dared to write poems about the sort of people the

Langston Hughes and Early Blues Poetry

"dicty" (pretentious, uptight, classed-off) Negroes looked down on, and to do so in the pulsing, boisterous language of the blues, a language that had no compunctions about signifying with raunchy wit, as in "Ma Man," where the female speaker figures her lover's drunken lovemaking as a bravura musical performance: "He kin play a banjo. / Lordy, he kin plunk, plunk, plunk. / He kind play a banjo. / I mean plunk, plunk . . . plunk, plunk. / He plays good when he's sober / An' better, better, better when he's drunk."[17] To a black middle class heavily invested in respectability, determined not merely to guard black women against any imputation of unregulated sexuality but to reverse three centuries of slander driven by the Jezebel stereotype, such poetry was a deliberate insult, one that flaunted what needed to be rebutted. But to Hughes, there was no shame, *could* be no shame, in such poetry, as long as one was telling the truth: offering blues-based representations of black people that honored the complexity and vividness of their lives and the tragicomic sensibility that sustained them. Where Du Bois and other members of the Talented Tenth, the black elite, said, "The white world is so thoroughly against us that we need propaganda from our writers: uplifting representations that undercut demeaning stereotypes," Hughes said, in effect, "Stereotypes be damned. White people be damned! I'll tell the truth as I see it. The blues—and the African drum or 'tom-tom' that lies behind it—will be my muse." That was the argument advanced by "The Negro Artist and the Racial Mountain":

> Let the blare of Negro jazz bands and the bellowing voice of Bessie Smith singing Blues penetrate the closed ears of the colored near-intellectuals until they listen and perhaps understand. . . . We younger Negro artists who create now intend to express our individual dark-skinned selves without fear or shame. If white people are pleased we are glad. If they are not, it doesn't matter. We know we are beautiful. And ugly too. The tom-tom cries and the tom-tom laughs. If colored people are pleased we are glad. If they are not, their displeasure doesn't matter either. We build our temples for tomorrow, strong as we know how, and we stand on top of the mountain, free within ourselves.[18]

Hughes's manifesto was a youthful rebellion against the anxious strictures of an older generation, but it was also a bohemian embrace of lower-class black culture—a loud, edgy, disreputable culture that the black middle class viewed as a negative ideal, a spiritual contaminant to be avoided. Like Handy, Hughes was a blues translator: somebody who engaged in a self-

Langston Hughes, 1943
(photograph by Gordon Parks via Wikimedia)

conscious class descent, took deep joy and solace in what he found there, and returned from his hero's journey with what Joseph Campbell has termed boons, gifts from the depths bursting with vitality that offer the tradition — popular music in Handy's case, poetry in Hughes's — a needed renewal.[19]

"Class descent" is perhaps too strong a term for Hughes's engagement with the blues. Unlike Handy, who hailed from an intact middle-class household and an unusually secure paternal line, Hughes was an orphan of sorts, and a poor one. Born in Joplin, Missouri in 1902, he was raised by his grandmother in Lawrence, Kansas, until the age of twelve, then spent a couple of years with an aunt before being reclaimed briefly by his mother. Hughes's father had expatriated permanently to Mexico, where, according to Hughes, "he was interested only in making money" and speaking of his hatred for

Langston Hughes and Early Blues Poetry

Negroes. "I think he hated himself, too, for being a Negro," Hughes wrote in his autobiography, *The Big Sea* (1940). "He disliked all of his family because they were Negroes."[20] Hughes hated his distant, dismissive father and was profoundly aggrieved by his mother's abandonment—a fact which, according to his biographer Arnold Rampersad, led him to "install the black race in the place in his heart vacated by his absconding parents."[21]

Hughes's sympathies extended downward, not upward. He had no space in his heart for "upper class colored people," as he called those with whom he came into contact during a 1924 sojourn in Washington, D.C., "government workers, professors and teachers, doctors, lawyers, and resident politicians" who, he insisted, "were on the whole as unbearable and snobbish a group of people as I have ever come in contact with anywhere."[22] His sympathies lay instead with blues people; his conversion experience took place in Washington's Seventh Street district, where he connected the aesthetic and philosophical landscape offered by the blues with the folk-soul of a people, low-down people, his people:

> Seventh Street is the long, old, dirty street, where the ordinary
> Negroes hang out, folks with practically no family tree at all, folks
> who draw no color line between mulattoes and deep dark-browns,
> folks who work hard for a living with their hands. On Seventh Street
> in 1924 they played the blues, ate watermelon, barbecue, and fish
> sandwiches, shot pool, told tall tales, looked at the dome of the
> Capitol and laughed out loud. I listened to their blues:
> *Did you ever dream lucky—*
> *Wake up cold in hand?*
> ... I tried to write poems like the songs they sang on Seventh
> Street—gay songs, because you had to be gay or die; sad songs,
> because you couldn't help being sad sometimes. But gay or sad, you
> kept on living and you kept on going. Their songs—those of Seventh
> Street—had the pulse beat of the people who kept on going.[23]

This period of full immersion and conscious embrace had a long foreground. As Steven C. Tracy makes clear in *Langston Hughes and the Blues* (1988), the prelude to Hughes's incorporation of blues material into his poems was a surprisingly variegated set of encounters with the music, beginning with blind guitar players on Independence Avenue in Kansas City when he was a child, followed by similar street and nightclub experiences in Chicago and Harlem as a teenager. When he shipped out for Africa on the SS *Malone* in 1923, his shipmate George was "a Kentucky colored boy" and "real vagabond" who made up his own blues "about the gipsy who couldn't find words strong enough to tell about the troubles in his hard-luck soul." By the time Hughes published his second—and trouble-making—book of poetry, *Fine Clothes to the Jew* (1927), according to Tracy, he "had heard the blues in the country and in the city, in the South and in the North, in America and abroad, on the street, in house dives and theaters. He had heard folk blues, vaudeville blues, and recorded blues, and blues influenced by jazz, ragtime, and the Broadway stage."[24]

Hughes was not, himself, much of a blues singer, although he did try. As he recounts in *The Big Sea*, again remembering his time in the nation's capital:

> The blues poems I would often make up in my head and sing on the way to work. (Except that I could never carry a tune. But when I sing to myself, I think I am singing.) One evening, I was crossing Rock Creek Bridge, singing a blues I was trying to get right before I put it down on paper. A man passing on the opposite side of the bridge stopped, looked at me, then turned around and cut across the roadway.
>
> He said: "Son, what's the matter? Are you ill?"
>
> "No," I said. "Just singing."
>
> "I thought you were groaning," he commented. "Sorry!" And went his way.
>
> So after that I never sang my verses aloud in the street any more.[25]

Also meant to provoke a wincing chuckle in the reader is an anecdote he relates in "My Adventures as a Social Poet" (1947), in which he is invited to read some poems at a black church in Atlantic City, New Jersey, shortly after the publication of *The Weary Blues*, and encounters ministerial disapprobation for the devil's music that he has incorporated into his verse:

> During the course of my program I read several of my poems in the form of the Negro folk songs, including some blues poems about hard luck and hard work. As I read I noticed a deacon approach the pulpit with a note which he placed on the rostrum beside me, but I did not stop to open the note until I had finished and had acknowledged the applause of a cordial audience. The note read, "Do not read any more blues in my pulpit."[26]

Both negative responses pale, however, next to the widespread condemnation with which the black press greeted *Fine Clothes to the Jew* the following year. Hughes was convinced that he had upped his poet's game, purged his voice of voyeurship, hewed closer to "Negro folk-song forms," and been more faithful to the life struggles of the black people he wrote about. But black reviewers were scandalized. "LANGSTON HUGHES — THE SEWER DWELLER," blared the headline in Harlem's *Amsterdam News*; editor William M. Kelley called the book "100 pages of trash" that "[reek] of the gutter and sewer." In the *Pittsburgh Courier*, historian J. A. Rogers echoed Kelley: Hughes's "piffling trash" left him "positively sick." The *Chicago Whip*, according to biographer Rampersad, "sneered [at the] 'lecherous, lust-reeking characters that Hughes finds time to poeticize about. . . . These poems are unsanitary, insipid, and repulsing." Hughes, the paper announced, was the "poet low-rate" of Harlem. Not laureate, but low-rate. One week after the reviewer for the *Philadelphia Tribune* confessed that *Fine Clothes to the Jew* "disgusts me," the paper lamented Hughes's "obsession for the more degenerate elements of black life."[27]

All of this calumny rained down on the twenty-five-year-old author just as he was beginning a tour in honor of Negro History Week. He had been embraced by poet Vachel Lindsay several years earlier, promoted as the "bus-boy poet" when he'd passed three poems to Lindsay during an event at a Washington hotel. Now this. Yet Rampersad has called *Fine Clothes to the Jew* Hughes's "most brilliant book of poems, and one of the more astonishing books of verse ever published in the United States."[28] The Langston Hughes that I encountered in the course of my own high school and college education—and I suspect I'm not alone—was none of these things. He wasn't a blues poet. He certainly wasn't reviled by the black press. He was Hughes-as-Icon: America's "great black poet," a celebrated author of inspiring, easy-to-read verse that spoke to the trials of African American history and the ordinary people who suffered and survived it: "I, Too," "Mother to Son," "Montage of a Dream Deferred," "The Negro Speaks of Rivers." It was simple poetry—deceptively simple, but some (including me) might have wondered whether it wasn't a little simple-minded as well, at least in comparison with the work of Hughes's modernist peers Eliot, Stevens, and Crane.

THE WEARY BLUES

The best way of appreciating Hughes's achievement is to put yourself in his position as an ambitious young artist, someone thrilled by blues music, its makers, the world of experience it evokes. How best to capture the music's multidimensional dynamism and bittersweet stoicism and weave it into lines arranged on a page? (Handy does this when he incorporates a blues-moaning woman's overheard lament into the sheet music for "St. Louis Blues.") Understood this way, as the fulfilling of a self-generated assignment, Hughes's blues-poetic debut, "The Weary Blues" (1925), comes alive. It dramatizes the encounter of a supremely receptive audience member—a listener and witness—with a black pianist who sings and plays the blues in a Harlem dive.

The poem begins by establishing a distance between the spectator and the performer, evoking the performance through the spectator's responses:

> Droning a drowsy syncopated tune,
> Rocking back and forth to a mellow croon,
>   I heard a Negro play.
> Down on Lenox Avenue the other night
> By the pale dull pallor of an old gas light
>   He did a lazy sway. . . .
>   He did a lazy sway. . . .
> To the tune o' those Weary Blues.[29]

The race of the observing "I" is never specified, even as the race of the blues performer is highlighted. This immediately opens the poem to two possible readings: the witness is black and is responding to a culture hero of his own race; or the witness is white, a slumming tourist on a Harlem jaunt, and he is having his mind blown by one of uptown's exotic denizens. Harlem in the 1920s was a field of play on which both sorts of audience members roamed. We don't need to choose one reading or the other; the poem is more powerful if we allow both to coexist. This first verse, in any case, uses alliteration ("droning . . . drowsy") and assonance ("droning . . . syncopated," "lazy sway") to conjure a musical spell that instantaneously bewitches. The droning and rocking are things that the "Negro," not the "I," is doing—and yet the syntax of the first three lines confuses that issue, as though the witness, too, is droning and rocking: a one-person community drawn by the musician's call into a sympathetic response. The first eight-line stanza offers visual cues ("pale dull pallor") as well as musical ones; there's a tension between the poem's scenic aspect, in which the blues performer is a spectacle observed by the witness, and its participatory, soul-responsive aspect, through which the music and its accompanying dance (the "lazy sway") seem to fuse performer and witness into an intersubjective dyad, a party of two.

The poem's second eight-line stanza deepens the connection between the bluesman and the witnessing "I":

Langston Hughes and Early Blues Poetry

With his ebony hands on each ivory key
He made that poor piano moan with melody.
     O Blues!
Swaying to and fro on his rickety stool
He played that sad raggy tune like a musical fool.
     Sweet Blues!
Coming from a black man's soul.
     O Blues!

When I teach this poem, I offer my students three touchstones: three things that routinely show up in the texts we read and that we might provisionally stipulate as core elements of the blues literary tradition. All three manifest vividly in "The Weary Blues." The first, *blues form*, is the idea that blues literature often incorporates specific formal elements of blues music, including the AAB verse form and variations of that form, blues idiomatic language, and call-and-response dynamics. The second touchstone, *blues portraiture*, is the idea that many blues literary works offer compelling representations of blues performers, often within characteristic performance spaces (juke joints, house parties, theatrical stages), and often with a strong secondary focus on the audience. The third touchstone, *blues power*, asks us to attend not just to the mutual urgings of performer and audience but also to the more general way blues texts seek to evoke, conjure with, and contextualize the transformative energies that blues people and their music wield over the world—the power to arouse, seduce, curse, mourn, heal, and speak with prophetic foresight. Blues *does* something to people. Blues writers are fascinated by that.

I'll speak in a moment about blues form. As I've already made clear, the poem is a doubled blues portrait: an ideally receptive audience member wandering into a Harlem dive and observing, feeling, a blues-playing, blues-singing black pianist. The bluesman's age is never specified, but his environs are aged, worn-out, threadbare: the "pale dull pallor of an old gas light" and a "rickety stool" are what illuminate and support him. Yet out of such unpromising circumstances, the bluesman conjures an extraordinary spell. The poem evokes his blues power in several ways. The bluesman's "ebony hands on each ivory key" make the "poor piano moan with melody," an image-cluster that communicates not just an unexpected triumph of black (ebony) over white (ivory), as though a symbolic victory has been won over a world of race-based oppressions with the help of soulful black music, but also the way the pianist wrests expressive satisfaction—a melodic moan—from an inanimate object, a "poor piano." The poem interleaves these depictions of blues power in action with a series of apostrophes: "O Blues!," "Sweet Blues!," and "O Blues!" Confronting this trio of two-word exclamations in undergraduate and graduate classrooms, I always ask students the same questions. Where do they come from? Who is crying them out, or feeling them, or both? What is their ontological reality—their being-status? Is the first "O Blues!" the piano's moan, or the pianist's internal moan projected through the piano, or the poet-witness's ecstatic response to these moans? Hughes's genius lies in his ability to finesse these questions, to blur the boundaries between musician, instrument, and audience as a way of suggesting that extraordinary powers are being set in motion by this black musical shaman with the help of a magical potion called the blues.

Or at least that is how Hughes, aspiring young poet, wants us to envision the blues, in contradistinction to those who would demonize it as the devil's music, trivialize it as mere entertainment, or denigrate it as a low-down assault on uplift ideology and an affront to black female virtue. Hughes acknowledges the shoddy confines (Hurston's phrase) out of which the music emerges, but only as a way of highlighting its sublimity and power. And then, having evoked the music in this way, he does something new: he opens his poem wide, as no prior poet had thought to do, and incorporates actual blues lyrics, embracing and adapting blues form in a way that would have profound implications for the blues literary tradition:

> In a deep song voice with a melancholy tone
> I heard that Negro sing, that old piano moan—
>> "Ain't got nobody in all this world,
>> Ain't got nobody but ma self.
>> I's gwine to quit ma frownin'
>> And put ma troubles on the shelf."
> Thump, thump, thump, went his foot on the floor.
> He played a few chords then he sang some more—
>> "I got the Weary Blues
>> And I can't be satisfied.
>> Got the Weary Blues
>> And can't be satisfied—
>> I ain't happy no mo'
>> And I wish that I had died."

This passage contains two incorporated blues verses. Both verses evoke blues form not just by deploying black vernacular—"Ain't," "gwine," "ma," "mo" — but by the boldness with which they adapt several of blues music's distinctive stanzaic patterns. As Tracy has shrewdly noted, the first verse has an eight-bar song form as its substrate, not the more common twelve-bar form. "Trouble in Mind," an early blues, can be arranged in four similarly stacked lines:

> Trouble in mind, lord I'm blue
> But I won't be blue always.
> You know the sun's gonna shine
> In my back door someday.

Hughes's first blues verse, although it evokes loneliness, also summons a spirit of resistance, a core element of the blues ethos. The second stanza, surprisingly, gives up the ghost; the singer capitulates to weariness and sadness rather than fighting them off. The two stanzas in sequence, in other words, offer us one more example of the blues dialectic: a productive tension between two opposed orientations toward experience.

The second incorporated blues verse holds particular importance for Hughes, not just because it provides the title for both the poem and the volume that contains it, Hughes's first, but also because it was, Hughes wrote later, "the first blues verse I'd ever heard way back in Lawrence, Kansas when I was a kid."[30] It also represents an elegant innovation in the matter of how to represent blues singing on the page. Prior to this moment, such representations had been the product of professional songwriters and folklorists, not poets. Songwriters like Handy offered the lines sequentially, on a musical staff, with each subsequent verse stacked and numbered. These were blues lyrics for performing, not for reading and savoring. Folklorists like Odum, by contrast, offered each verse as stacked lines, so that the verses could easily be read in sequence, but each verse-stack was short: either three lines (AAB) or, more commonly, two lines with brief notation indicating that the A line was repeated. The "Weary Blues" verse, represented folklorically, would look like this:

> I got the Weary Blues and I can't be satisfied
> Got the Weary Blues and can't be satisfied
> I ain't happy no mo' and I wish that I had died.

or, more likely, like this:

> I got the Weary Blues and I can't be satisfied (2x)
> I ain't happy no mo' and I wish that I had died.

Hughes's innovation was to break each of the three lines at the point where the blues singer would ordinarily take a breath, thus preserving—or more properly, visually translating—that element of performance. Then he stacks those two half-lines on top of each other. He does this with each of the three lines, so that what was originally a three-line stanza has now become a six-line stanza. Why does he do this, and what does he achieve? Hughes himself joked that he'd divided, stacked, and thus doubled his blues lines because poetry editors at magazines paid by the line and he wanted to double his income.[31] But he gained two things apart from that. One gain, which he doesn't take advantage of in "The Weary Blues," is the ability to break individual lines not at the obvious breath point, but at some other point that increases tension, creates unexpected meaning, or both. He does this, for example, in the final stanza of "Bad Man," one of the poems that led critics to pan *Fine Clothes to the Jew*:

> I'm so bad I
> Don't even want to be good.
> So bad, bad, bad I
> Don't even want to be good.
> I'm goin' to de devil an'
> I wouldn't go to heaben if I could.

In performance, a blues singer would be more likely to sing the first two lines with a brief pause for breath after "bad": "I'm so bad . . . I don't even want to be good." By breaking the line where he does, so that the first line begins and ends with "I," Hughes reinforces the speaker's assertion of an indomitable spirit grounded in unrepentant bad behavior; he also creates a second half-line that begins with a negation, "Don't," that foregrounds its own opposition to the word "good." Hughes's stacked version of the blues line offers a brief but dramatic pause after that second "I," tumbling the reader into the second half-line. But there's another effect produced by these stacked lines, one designed, I believe, to compensate for what is not there in the visual rendering of the sung blues verse.

As any blues performer knows, each line of an AAB blues generally takes two bars to sing, a total of eight or nine beats, and is followed by two bars of empty space that are filled by an instrumental response or "fill"—piano tinklings, harmonica wails, bits of lead or slide guitar. One challenge of representing blues singing on the page is that these three two-bar fills—literally half of the twelve-bar sequence—simply evaporate. They're an intrinsic part of the performance, but they're purely musical, and thus nonverbal. Words

Langston Hughes and Early Blues Poetry

can't represent them. So how does a poet compensate for their absence? Hughes solves the problem, I suggest, by splitting and stacking his lines. He creates a plenitude of lines, an excess, and in so doing he masks, and makes up for, what has been lost — the fills — during the process of translating from performance to the page.

One element of blues form that Hughes brings vividly to life in the second incorporated verse within "The Weary Blues" is *worrying the line*, a way of subtly modifying the repeated A line so that the restatement emphasizes and adds nuance to the emotional dynamic set in motion by the initial statement. An important later blues poet, Sherley Anne Williams, defines worrying in her essay "The Blues Roots of Contemporary Afro-American Poetry" (1979) when discussing another of Hughes's poems from *Fine Clothes to the Jew*, "Young Gal's Blues": "Repetition in blues is seldom word for word and the definition of worrying the line includes changes in stress and pitch, the addition of exclamatory phrases, changes in word order, repetitions of phrases within the line itself, and the wordless blues cries which often punctuate the performance of the songs."[32] Williams is speaking here about what blues singers do, but she's also gesturing at the things that blues poets do, or might do, in order to translate blues singing into poetry. What Hughes does in "The Weary Blues" is precisely what she means by worrying the line:

> "I got the Weary Blues
> And I can't be satisfied.
> Got the Weary Blues
> And can't be satisfied
> I ain't happy no mo'
> And I wish that I had died."

Hughes omits the "I" when he repeats the A line. A seemingly minor change, it has important rhythmic effects and philosophical implications. The rhythmic effect is to emphasize "Weary" in line 3 and "can't" in line 4, subtly tilting the force of each half-line toward those words. The philosophical implication comes with the imputed erasure of the bluesman's selfhood as the "I" disappears: to have the Weary Blues is to be something less than fully alive, even while one perseveres in singing out that condition. It's almost as though Hughes had written, "I'm so weary, I can't even say I. So weary, so weary, can't even say my name." Casting this shadow across his own continuance even while continuing, yearning toward death in the final half-line, the bluesman conspicuously falls away from the blues ethos — or at least the version of it which demands that one anneal tragedy with comedy, hardening oneself to life's misfortunes and shrugging them off. There's no harsh laughter here. The poem ends on a curiously ambiguous note:

> The stars went out and so did the moon.
> The singer stopped playing and went to bed
> While the Weary Blues echoed through his head.
> He slept like a rock or a man that's dead.

All of the dynamism and musicality with which Hughes imbued the poem's opening stanzas through the sensorium of the witnessing "I"—the "I" who "heard a Negro play"—have vanished. The pianist, and the poem, have sung and played themselves out. These concluding lines are flat blunt statements of fact. The first, second, and fourth lines have almost exactly the same rhythm, a sing-song simplicity much more typical of children's verse. The quick, procedural, strike-the-sets momentum of these lines is brought up short by the poem's final word, "dead." Dead? Is that a good thing, to sleep that deeply? Perhaps it is, for one so weary who has worked so hard. Or perhaps it's a sign that he's been spiritually extinguished, which surely isn't a good thing.

The poem's ending raises many questions. One of the most intriguing, if we remember the witnessing "I" through whose eyes we first experienced the bluesman's pianistic spell, is, Where did that "I" go? The Harlem audience member seems to have disappeared in the course of the performance, so that the knowledge presented in these final lines—about the Weary Blues "echo[ing] through" the bluesman's "head," for example—is situated within the bluesman. Depicting that knowledge requires a kind of omniscience that the witnessing "I" doesn't possess at the beginning of the poem. The poem is engaging in a kind of perspectival sleight-of-hand, in other words. The poem dramatizes the process through which we, as readers, are introduced to the bluesman by way of exterior shots and with the help of a witness, then brought more deeply inside the bluesman's world, so that by the poem's end, after he's given us all he's got, we seem to be standing in his shoes—or, more properly lying with him in his bed, the tune he's just performed now echoing through our head as well as his.

Hughes does all that in his first published blues poem. He would write many others over the years. He paid a price for his boldness, at least in the short term, but he ultimately achieved his purpose. He made the blues—as lyrical statement, an act of witness-bearing, a conjuror's spell—an indelible part of American poetry.

par 8

Zora Neale Hurston in the Florida Jooks

SEX, VIOLENCE, AND THE CULTURAL INVESTIGATOR

Zora Neale Hurston, the third founding member of the blues literary tradition along with W. C. Handy and Langston Hughes, has arguably played a more complex and multilayered role than the other two. Like them, she was a translator, one who sought textual analogues — words on a page — that could do justice to the bittersweet lyricism, dynamism, and bold self-declarations found in blues music and the people who made and used that music, especially in the rural South during the early decades of the twentieth century. Like Handy, she was born in Alabama, although Florida raised and claimed her; like Hughes, who became a close friend and collaborator, she called Harlem her home during the Renaissance as a member of the so-called Niggerati, an upstart group of younger African American writers determined to think and live freely, reconfiguring the black image in white and black minds alike. Although Hurston has risen in stature since the mid-1970s to become a canonical figure in African American literature, American literature, and feminist studies on the basis of her novel *Their Eyes Were Watching God* (1937), her achievements as a blues-themed writer and folklorist have drawn less attention than they deserve.

The basic outlines of that achievement are easy to sketch. Hurston is the first cultural investigator, male or female, to write of black southern juke joints or "jooks" from the inside, both literally — she spent considerable time in one of them, the Pine Mill in Polk County, Florida — and figuratively, as a black female Floridian whose rural upbringing placed her in close imaginative proximity to the blues people whose songs and lives she was documenting. In both these respects she accomplished something that her widely traveled and intrepid white southern peers, Howard Odum and Dorothy Scarborough, were unable to do. Drawing on that experience, she wrote a major essay (a portion of "Characteristics of Negro Expression" subtitled "The Jook" [1933]), a pioneering folklore study (*Mules and Men* [1935]), a novel (*Their Eyes*), and an autobiography (*Dust Tracks on a Road* [1942]). Because she was a woman, and not an unattractive one, she found herself, as a cultural investigator who fraternized with male musicians and storytellers, drawn somewhat further into the fevered sexual economy of the jook than she had intended. It was a situation that aroused violent jealousies in several local women and equally fearsome threats on her behalf by one specific figure of power, Big Sweet, a swaggering, knife-wielding jook habituée. Both *Mules and Men* and *Dust Tracks* narrate versions of the same crisis: the night when her principal antagonist, Lucy, tries to knife her to death and Hurston is forced to flee the Pine Mill — concluding her participant-observation and saving her own life — as the jook erupts in spectacular fashion.

The understandings that Hurston evolved about blues people and their milieu, in other words, were both hard-won and problematic; they offer us a critical perspective not just on the limits of white privilege where certain kinds of cultural investigation are concerned but also on the understandable desire of some contemporary readers to view Hurston as an exuberant celebrant of black southern folk culture rather than a thoughtful and nuanced analyst and advocate who was vividly aware of the shadows that lurked within her broadly comic representations. Handy and Hughes, too, grapple with the violent vitality of southern blues people. Handy fears for his own safety as bandleader at a key moment in *Father of the Blues* when two of his men, a rougher class of Memphis musicians than he's employed in the past, start fighting on a parade float in Atlanta. "The band divided into factions," he remembers ruefully, "attempting to keep one from cutting or shooting the other."[1] Hughes drew the fire of black reviewers for poems like "Suicide" and "In a Troubled Key," from *Fine Clothes to the Jew*:

> I'm gonna buy me a knife with
> A blade ten inches long.
> Gonna buy a knife with
> A blade ten inches long.
> Shall I carve ma self or
> That man that done me wrong?
>
> . . .

Zora Neale Hurston in the Florida Jooks

Still I can't help lovin' you,
Even though you do me wrong.
Says I can't help lovin' you
Though you do me wrong—
But my love might turn into a knife
Instead of to a song.[2]

Hurston, like Handy and Hughes, played a vital role in the emergence of blues literature precisely because she truly *did* desire to celebrate, defend, and ennoble her working-class black subjects, even as she remained determined—as a cultural anthropologist and novelist—to honor their complexity, unconcerned with how some might judge the resulting portrait. She, like Hughes, was criticized harshly by some readers: not black newspaper columnists and other guardians of racial gentility, as in Hughes's case, but her black male peers, Sterling Brown and Richard Wright, both of whom insisted that she had egregiously underplayed the trauma that Jim Crow had inflicted on southern black folk.[3]

Where Hurston differs from both Handy and Hughes is the question of sexuality—a tricky question indeed, given the way black female sexuality had long been haunted by the lascivious Jezebel stereotype. Even as Handy and Hughes write frankly about the frustrated romantic passions out of which blues song emerges, both men expunge their own sexuality from their texts. The father of the blues, remarkably, is a kind of neuter, the opposite of a juke joint playboy. The only trace of sexual passion that he offers in his 1941 autobiography comes during an 1899 trip to Havana in the company of his wife, when he notices "Cuban senoritas" smiling at him from a balcony. "For a moment I was mesmerized by the hocus pocus of lovely dark eyes, red roses and fingers that threw kisses." Two pages later he reports that his wife, suddenly losing her appetite, has informed him that he "was destined to become a father." "I'd have excellent reason," he concludes, signifying on his own role in the pregnancy, "to remember the perfumed influence of sultry Havana."[4] In a blues tradition marked by sexual braggadocio of the crawling-kingsnake, little-red-rooster variety, Handy's sexual self-presentation is remarkably chaste, as though the blues' father figure was determined to steer clear of the messy, unruly passions he had taken as his chosen subject—and as befitted a good son of the Talented Tenth who was trying to win the blues broad cultural acceptance. Repressing his own desire in *Father of the Blues*, he enables white readers to identify with him as a benign elder statesman. Hughes, in *The Big Sea* and elsewhere, is equally discreet in the matter of his private erotic entanglements. "Only three times in his autobiographical writings would Hughes speak of being in love with women," notes his biographer, Arnold Rampersad. Although he did occasionally mention having visited prostitutes, his sexual persona was, according to Rampersad, marked by "a quality of ageless, sexless, inspired innocence, Peter-Pan like," something that led Hughes to be "regarded by many of his friends as asexual, without noticeable erotic feeling for either women or men."[5] Yet his blues poems were, or could be, hot, sexy, and violent. His blues people lived out what he apparently did not.

Hurston is a different story. Although she wasn't known for dressing in a revealing, hoochie-mama fashion, merely comporting herself with style and the occasional red scarf, she lived a far messier life, in erotic terms, than Handy or Hughes. She was married twice, both time to younger men, and had an extended, on-again, off-again relationship with a man more than twenty years her junior, the model for bluesman Tea Cake in *Their Eyes*. She put much more of herself into her works, in this respect, than did Handy or Hughes; indeed, she foregrounds her own inadvertent self-staging as an object of sexual interest and jealousy in the juke joint environment, and she confesses with playful astonishment in *Dust Tracks* that the men she encounters consistently, and mistakenly, see her as a sex object:

> They pant in my ear on short acquaintance, "You passionate thing! I can see you are just *burning* up! . . . Ahhh! I know that you will just wreck me! Your eyes and your lips tell me a lot. You are a walking furnace!" This amazes me sometimes. Often when this is whispered gustily into my ear, I am feeling no more amorous than a charter member of the Union League Club. I may be thinking of turnip greens with dumplings, or more royalty checks, and here is a man who visualizes me on a divan sending the world up in smoke. It has happened so often that I have come to expect it. There must be something about me that looks sort of couchy.[6]

Hurston is having fun with the Jezebel stereotype here, deflating it even as she coyly acknowledges her own Cleopatra-like attractions, but she's also aligning herself to some extent with Bessie Smith—whom she knew and admired—and other blues queens of her era: strong, independent, self-actualizing women who sang signifying songs full of sexual double-entendre and boldly pursued their passions. Writing of her extended affair with Percival McGuire Punter, the tall, dark, and dazzlingly handsome young graduate student at Columbia on whom she models Tea Cake, Hurston describes it as an "obsession," a love that wounds and must be escaped. "Everywhere I set my feet down," she admitted as she describes her flight to Jamaica, "there were tracks of blood. Blood from the very middle of my heart. . . . I tried to embalm all the tenderness of my passion for him in 'Their Eyes were Watching God.'"[7] Where African American clubwomen in the pre–Harlem Renaissance era had represented themselves as "supermoral" missionaries, deploying a politics of respectability in which, as religious scholar Evelyn Brooks Higginbotham has put it, "they represented their sexuality through its absence—through silence, secrecy, and invisibility," Hurston finds strength in a kind of shameless candor, a refusal either to carry the burden of respectability or to be shamed by those who do. She borrows this approach from the blues.[8]

To speak of Hurston's erotic life and to note the way she highlights that theme in her writings is in no way to discount her achievements as a cultural investigator and author. She was fearless, tireless, resourceful, and as resolutely independent of men as she was willing to engage deeply with them; she roamed the American South, including its northern migrant and Caribbean basin extensions, in pursuit of insight and material. But the sex in her texts, as African American literature scholar Henry Louis Gates Jr. notes in his essay "Why Richard Wright Hated Zora Neale Hurston" (2013), was something that got Hurston in trouble with her black male peers. "The politics of sexuality remained deeply problematic within black literary circles," writes Gates of the late 1930s, and he argues that the "heated, vitriolic exchange" between Wright and Hurston after the publication of *Their Eyes* was caused by "Hurston's creation of a black female protagonist who was comfortable with and celebrated her own sensuality, and who insisted on her right to choose her own lovers in spite of the strictures of the black community."[9] In a 1937 review in the Communist Party's *New Masses*, Wright had indicted Hurston's novel for "facile sensuality" and argued that she was trying to titillate white readers (i.e., men) "whose chauvinistic tastes she knows how to satisfy." Wright quotes, and Gates highlights, a by-now widely celebrated passage in which Hurston depicts the sexual awakening of her young black female protagonist, Janie Crawford, an awakening that is also a moment of spiritual enlargement:

> She was stretched on her back beneath the pear tree soaking in the altochant of the visiting bees, the gold of the sun and the panting breath of the breeze when the inaudible voice of it all came to her.

Zora Neale Hurston, 1937
(Library of Congress via Wikimedia)

She saw a dust-bearing bee sink into the sanctum of a bloom; the thousand sister-calyxes arch to meet the love embrace and the ecstatic shiver of the tree from root to tiniest branch creaming in every blossom and frothing with delight. So this was a marriage! She had been summoned to behold a revelation. Then Janie felt a pain remorseless sweet that left her limp and languid.[10]

"This is, I believe," Gates writes, "the first orgasm depicted in the entire history of African-American literature."[11] It is also, as I'll show later in this chapter, a textual moment that aligns Hurston with the blues tradition in several important ways. Neither of those things was apparent to Wright; he just knew that he was dealing with an author—a troublesome woman—who, in his view, substituted sex for social engagement, which is to say that she spent too much time exploring black pleasures and not enough time indicting the southern white man as an inflictor of black pain. This charge was a half-truth, but not the whole truth, and Hurston responded by trashing Wright's *Uncle Tom's Children* (1935) for the opposite sin, heartlessness and violence driven by a masculine hunger for racial revenge. It was, she wrote, "a book about hatreds," made up of "stories so grim that the Dismal Swamp of race hatred must be where they live. . . . There is lavish killing here, perhaps enough to satisfy all male black readers."[12]

In our own time, of course, Hurston has become canonical, a "voice of the folk," albeit one who complicates that project in ways that critics have begun to appreciate. Her erotic boldness now seems as tame as Bessie Smith singing, "Need a little sugar in my bowl." We are finally able to pause, neither scandalized nor inclined toward heroine-worship, and do our best to see Hurston clearly. Where did she come from, and how did those origins, that background, shape her approach to the blues?

LIES, SECRETS, AND SELF-MAKING

Zora Neale Hurston's entire life is founded on a lie—or, rather, a constructive bit of storytelling, a fantasy embraced and worked to her advantage. She was born in 1891 in Notasulga, Alabama, but in 1917, aged twenty-six and living on her own in Baltimore, she informed local school officials that she was sixteen years old, born in 1901, so that she could qualify for the free schooling that her unsettled and peripatetic life had prevented her from acquiring to that point. Her teachers and classmates bought the story. The scrubbed-off decade was a secret that she kept for the rest of her life: from friends, lovers, readers. Her first biographer, Robert Hemenway, gives her birth year as 1901 and her birthplace as Eatonville, Florida; Alice Walker, who tracked down Hurston's gravesite and erected a memorial in 1973, had that wrong year engraved on the stone. In *Dust Tracks*, Hurston cites Eatonville—again, wrongly—as her birthplace but never gives her birth year. Scholar Cheryl Wall finally discovered Hurston's true age with the help of census records.

Why did Hurston lie about her age and birthplace, and sustain the lie throughout her life? Valerie Boyd, author of a second biography, *Wrapped in Rainbows: The Life of Zora Neale Hurston* (2003), thinks that the mystery lies in an abortive, possibly abusive relationship with a man that Hurston may have endured in 1914 or 1915: the lowest point in a life in a life filled with many ups and downs. She never wrote explicitly of what happened. But she did describe in *Dust Tracks* a series of prophetic visions that she had had as a girl, and one of them, Boyd suggests, holds the key: a vision of a "shot-gun built house that needed a new coat of white paint, [and] held torture for me, but I must go. I saw deep love betrayed, but I must feel and know it."[13] At a key moment in *Dust Tracks*, just before changing her age and returning to school, Hurston refers to this vision—the house "that had threatened me with so much suffering that I used to sit up in bed sodden with agony"—as having "passed," which Boyd translates as the events themselves having actually come to pass. It's clear," writes Boyd, "that Zora suffered horribly during this buried time, so much so that she would never speak directly about her anguish or its causes."[14] Boyd takes this obscure and traumatic chapter of Hurston's life as a kind of skeleton key, one whose shaping power is revealed by the act of will required not merely to survive and escape it but also to live a remarkably full, empowered, and productive life in its aftermath.

What does not destroy me makes me stronger: that was Nietzsche's proclamation in *Twilight of the Gods*, but it is also the blues ethos in action. If we accept Boyd's claim about this black hole, so to speak, in Hurston's life story—a common-law relationship in her mid-twenties with a man who betrayed her love and physically abused her—then her decision to deny that part of her past after wrenching free from it, dialing back her age and reconfiguring her social identity in a way that enabled a fresh start and future triumphs, might strike us as an extraordinarily bluesy gesture. Yet her behavior stands notably at odds with the blues impulse, as Ralph Ellison describes it in his famous essay on Richard Wright's *Black Boy* (1945), "an impulse to keep the painful details and episodes of a brutal experience alive in one's aching consciousness, to finger its jagged grain, and to transcend it, not by the consolation of philosophy but by squeezing from it a near-tragic, near-comic

Zora Neale Hurston in the Florida Jooks

lyricism."[15] Hurston didn't finger the jagged grain of that particular disaster, at least not in her autobiographical writings. She squeezed it down to nothing, then buried it—the diamond, in a sense, that powered what followed. Appreciating this survival strategy helps us read the famous opening of her most famous novel with fresh eyes. "Women," she wrote in *Their Eyes*, "forget all those things they don't want to remember, and remember everything they don't want to forget. The dream is the truth. Then they act and do things accordingly" (*TE*, 1). Hurston's age—and her hometown, and her life—was hers to seize, reshape to her own needs, and work as she saw fit. Blues singers sing what could be true and what *feels* true, not the literal truth. Hurston embraces this concept with a vengeance, and gives it a gendered edge.

Hurston's determined resilience is sourced in her unusual upbringing. Notasulga, in eastern Alabama near the Tuskegee Institute, was her residence for scarcely a year, and she never referred to it, never cared about it, after being carried out of it as an infant. Home was the "pure Negro town" of Eatonville, today a small incorporated township (and still 90 percent black) within greater Orlando.[16] Her father, John Hurston, a preacher and carpenter, came upon the town by accident during one of his rambling journeys abroad, right around the time Zora was being delivered. A year later he sent for his wife, Lucy Potts Hurston, and the couple's five children. Hurston's parents were from somewhat different positions on the class spectrum of black southern life. John was an "across-the-creek Negro," as the saying went; he was from the wrong side of the tracks. His people worked on white plantations. Lucy's family was better off, more prideful. They were independent landowners, unhappy with their youngest daughter's choice of husband. But John Hurston was immensely ambitious, Lucy Potts was eager to support those ambitions, and Eatonville provided John, and soon Zora, with an unusually hospitable field of action. Within a couple of years, John had built an impressive homestead and become the minister of a church in Sanford, twenty miles away. He was a gifted, charismatic orator, sexually compelling to his female parishioners, and this eventually created problems within the marriage. Hurston was never particularly close to her father— she thought that he just didn't understand her—but her mother encouraged Zora to "jump at de sun," to pursue her own ambitions, and this encouragement stuck.

More important even than the family constellation was Eatonville itself. As a town founded, inhabited, and run by African Americans, it was a rarity in the early modern South: a place where segregation held no sway and first-class citizenship was each resident's birthright. In *The Souls of Black Folk*

(1903), published during Hurston's childhood, W. E. B. Du Bois wrote about what he called the "double-consciousness" that burdened black Americans, "this sense of always looking at one's self through the eyes of others," meaning whites.[17] Hurston's childhood in Eatonville, lived almost entirely out of sight of southern whites and their appraising, oppressive gazes, left her blissfully free from such double-consciousness. This is not to say that the specter of white violence was entirely absent. In the late 1930s, hired as a researcher by the Florida Writers Project, Hurston wrote "The Ocoee Riot," a stark historical essay about a 1920 lynching and racial purge that had taken place in Ocoee, a mostly white town thirteen miles from Eatonville, roughly a decade after she had moved away.[18] Zora personally confronted Jim Crow as a teenager when, after her mother's premature death, she was sent to boarding school in Jacksonville. "Jacksonville made me know that I was a little colored girl," she wrote, invoking the material and attitudinal signposts of southern segregation. "Things were all about the town to point this out to me. Streetcars and stores and then talk I heard around the school."[19] But this moral letdown came later, after Hurston's basic psychological orientation, her sense of racial wholeness in the safety of an all-black idyll, had been established.

Like Handy and Hughes, both of whom ended up in New York City in the 1920s, Hurston was a part of the Great Migration, an epic movement of black southerners up and out of their restricted southern "place" and into the uncertain freedom of a northern urban Promised Land. Like the other two, but even more so, Hurston's relatively privileged upbringing vis-à-vis the imprisoning, humiliating strictures of Jim Crow meant that, as a member of the black intelligentsia, she had little desire to shed her black southern cultural roots, including the blues, in an effort to rid herself of the stigma of having grown up down home. Quite the reverse: as a freshly minted member of the Harlem Renaissance, she played up her southern accent and locutions, remaking herself as a teller of tales and singer of folksongs at Harlem rentparties and soirees. She did this even as she was writing and publishing her first stories — "Spunk" took second place in a 1925 competition sponsored by *Opportunity*, a journal of Negro life — and enrolling at Columbia University to study anthropology with Franz Boas. Boas was her most significant intellectual influence, a German-born cultural relativist whose approach was an antiracist rebuke to a long-standing tradition of scientific racism by which "peoples" (i.e., races) and their cultures were organized in a hierarchy of biological, cultural, and moral advancement, with whites (Nordics, Caucasians) at the top, blacks (Hottentots, pygmies) at the bottom, and others (Malays) somewhere in the middle. Boas said to Hurston, in effect, "My European

Zora Neale Hurston in the Florida Jooks

academic culture isn't higher or lower than the folk culture that you imbibed as a girl in Eatonville, and that folk culture certainly isn't 'primitive.' Each culture is an equally valuable and evolved response to the social circumstances of the people who deploy it." By licensing Hurston to envision the intimate world of Eatonville — the porch of Joe Clarke's store where the men had told stories, played cards, bragged, swapped "lies" — as culture, Boas prompted an epiphany in Zora. Her lifelong campaign to explore, document, understand, explain, and body forth the power and brilliance of black southern folklore begins here.

THE NEGRO FURTHEST DOWN

Blues song was merely one cultural element, albeit an important one, in the archive that she sought to explore. With help from Boas, who rounded up several small research fellowships on her behalf, Hurston left New York early in 1927 on what turned out to be a six-month maiden voyage: the southern migrant returns home with the "spyglass of anthropology" as her guide, looking to collect material in Eatonville and beyond. Brimming with confidence but suspended awkwardly between the conflicting imperatives of a (former) native participant and university-trained investigator, Hurston failed to fill her trawling nets. "I knew where the material was all right," she confessed later, gently mocking her own cluelessness. "But, I went about asking, in carefully accented Barnardese, 'Pardon me, but do you know any folktales or folk-songs?' The men and women who had whole treasuries of material just seeping through their pores looked at me and shook their heads. No, they had never heard of anything like that around there. Maybe it was over in the next county. Why didn't I try over there? I did, and got the self-same answer" (DT, 175).

Although the trip was, in her view, a failure as a folklore collecting expedition, it paid unexpected dividends when Hurston ran into Langston Hughes in Mobile, Alabama. Hughes had been on his own tour of the South — Memphis, Baton Rouge, New Orleans — after being invited to read his blues poetry at Fisk University's graduation in Nashville the previous month. The two friends ate fried fish and watermelon, then headed north in Hurston's beat-up car, according to biographer Boyd, pausing frequently "to pick up folk songs and tall tales, to meet guitar players and conjure doctors, to visit small-town jooks and country churches."[20] They ended up in Macon, where they attended a concert by Bessie Smith, overnighted at a local hotel, and woke in the morning to hear her voice: she was staying down the hall, it turned out, and "practice[ing] . . . with gusto." The blues writers lingered to chat with the Empress of the Blues, who delivered a memorable chestnut: "The trouble with white folks singing the blues is that they can't get low down enough."[21]

In December 1927, Hurston headed south out of New York on a second and much more consequential expedition. This time she was subsidized by Charlotte Osgood Mason, a wealthy white patron—"Godmother," as she insisted her beneficiaries call her—who was also assisting Hughes, poet Claude McKay, painter Aaron Douglas, and other of Harlem's young black creatives. Mason would provide substantial cash subsidies; Hurston would do the fieldwork, bring her news of "the negro furthest down," and, importantly, hand over her findings at the end, for publication in Mason's name. It was a devil's bargain of sorts, one that Hurston struggled to navigate for the next half-dozen years. Ever the survivor, Hurston bought a new car, packed a pistol, and hit the road. The voyage, which she dramatized in *Mules and Men* and reprised in *Dust Tracks on a Road*, led once again to Eatonville, where blues guitarist Bubber Mimms and his fellow front-porch layabouts urged Hurston on toward Polk County, forty miles southwest. Familiar with "Polk County Blues," incited by their tales of the strong, salty women who haunted the region's backwoods jooks, Hurston headed south for "corn (likker) and song."[22] And it was there, in the town of Loughman, that Hurston moved into the living quarters of the Everglades Cypress Lumber Company and spent the next four-and-a-half months immersing herself in the rough, boisterous, blues-filled culture of Florida's inland frontier.

Rough means *rough*. Hurston's autobiographical writings make much of the fact that she was a tomboy, unafraid to use her fists; she writes of savagely beating her stepmother when tensions between them reached a boiling point and confesses that she and Punter slapped each other around at a similar moment of aggrieved high feeling. But Hurston, for all her feistiness, was a minister's daughter and child of privilege compared with the men and women of the lumber camp. Much of the drama in her encounter with the camp's denizens emerges from the class difference that frames their interactions. She registers this difference in a range of ways: in their colorful vernacular language ("yo' entrimmins" for "your name" [*MAM*, 63]), in their suspicion of her new car (they think she's a revenue agent; she convinces them that she's a bootlegger), and in the way the men are intimidated by her "$12.74 dress from Macy's" (*MAM*, 63) that she had on "among all the $1.98 mail-order dresses" (*MAM*, 63) worn by the camp's women. "I did look different," she admits, "and resolved to fix all that no later than the next morning" (*MAM*, 63). She is, she realizes very quickly, a high-class woman—or somebody being seen as one—trying to connect with a low-down crowd. She connects through music: convincing Jim Presley, one of the camp's leading musicians, to back her up on guitar as she sings "John Henry." It's a ballad, not a blues, but this moment of musical teamwork has precisely the effect she yearns for, dissolving class differences and embedding her within the folk community:

> So he played and I started to sing the verses I knew. They put me on the table and everybody urged me to spread my jenk [Have a good time], so I did the best I could. Joe Willard knew two verses and sang them. Eugene Oliver knew one; Big Sweet knew one. And how James Presley can make his box cry out the accompaniment!
>
> By the time that the song was over, before Joe Willard lifted me down from the table I knew that I was in the inner circle. I had first to convince the "job" that I was not an enemy in the person of the law; and, second, I had to prove that I was their kind. "John Henry" got me over my second hurdle.
>
> After that my car was everybody's car. James Presley, Slim and I teamed up and we had to do "John Henry" wherever we appeared. We soon had a reputation that way. We went to Mulberry, Pierce and Lakeland. (*MAM*, 65)

This passage offers us a vivid illustration not just of the way Hurston leverages her own modest musical talents—she was an enthusiastic but mediocre singer—to connect with a folk community and enable her folklore-collection mission, but also of the blithe cluelessness with which she cozies up to the local men, never thinking about how this might make other women in the camp feel. To say that her car became everybody's car is to say that she had suddenly become Queen Bee, a focus of masculine attentions. The women, it turns out, are furious at the interloper who is making music with, traveling with, and presumably sleeping with, their boyfriends. They have knives in hand that they are itching to use on Hurston—a powerful way of making their feelings known to her and the community.

What a bluesy situation! And what an extraordinary opportunity for a cultural investigator, to be drawn this deeply into the seething passions of the people you're trying to understand. Hurston's guide in all this, her native informant *par excellence*, is Big Sweet: a big, strong, fierce, trash-talking mama bear who vividly clarifies the dangers that await her naive guardian as the two women play cards in the Pine Mill jook, the rollicking, blues-music-filled social center of the logging camp. The most pressing problem is a rival of Big Sweet's named Lucy and her side-girl, Ella Wall:

> "Dat li'l narrer contracted piece uh meatskin gointer make me stomp her right now!" Big Sweet exploded. "De two-face heifer! Been hanging' 'round me so she kin tote news to Ella. If she don't look out she'll have on her last clean dress befo' de crack of day."
>
> "Ah'm surprised at Lucy," I agreed. "Ah thought you all were de *best* of friends."
>
> "She mad 'cause Ah dared her to jump *you*. She don't lak Slim always playing JOHN HENRY for you. She would have done cut you to death if Ah hadn't of took and told her."
>
> "Ah can see she doesn't like it, but—"
>
> "Neb' mind 'bout ole Lucy. She know Ah backs yo' fallin'. She know if she scratch yo' skin Ah'll kill her so dead till she can't fall. They'll have to push her over." (*MAM*, 149)

In *Seems Like Murder Here,* I wrote at length about Hurston's unsettling encounter with the violent folkways of the Pine Mill jook. I framed it both biographically—a tough girl herself, Hurston wasn't *this* tough, and knew it—and with reference to the blues tradition as a whole, where "cutting and shooting" and the braggadocio associated with those two forms of interpersonal violence were routinely confronted by Deep South blues performers who worked the juke joints.[23] Indeed, countless blues recordings make lyric capital out of the sort of mayhem Big Sweet and Lucy are threatening here. "Don't you bother my baby," Muddy Waters sings of his female lover in "Gone to Main Street" (1952), "no tellin' what she'll do / She might cut you, she might shoot you too." In this respect, the violence that Hurston confronts at the Pine Mill testifies to the fact that she has encountered the Real, in sociocultural terms: seriously low-down blues people, this at the very moment when Broadway and Tin Pan Alley, as both she and Hughes knew well, were being flooded with emotive white damsels and various sorts of pop-lyrical confections to which the word "blues" had been dubiously appended.

Yet when we take into account Valerie Boyd's claim about the anguish that a twenty-something Hurston had suffered a dozen years earlier during her "buried" time in the shotgun house, at the mercy (or so Boyd believes) of a lover who physically abused her until she managed to break free, then another perspective on this juke joint immersion experience suggests itself. I believe that Hurston found Big Sweet, Lucy, and their hyperviolent threats so compelling because they offer her living models of feminine indomita-

Zora Neale Hurston in the Florida Jooks

Willie King playing for dancers at Betty's Place in Prairie Point, Alabama
(courtesy of the photographer, Bill Steber)

bility: women who could not possibly have allowed themselves to be man-handled and forced into the sort of soul-killing subordination that Hurston herself apparently was, if only briefly. They may be fighting over men, but they don't depend on men to do their fighting for them. They are figures of power: black southern badwomen who take shit from nobody, and certainly not from men, including white men. (When the white quarters-boss, trying to keep order on a particularly raucous evening, demands that Big Sweet give him her knife, she shouts, "Naw suh! Nobody gets mah knife," and "Don't you touch me, white folks!," an act of resistance that thrills the juke joint crowd. "You wuz a whole women and half uh man," pronounces Joe Willard after he leaves. "You made dat cracker stand off a *you*." (*MAM*, 152). Hurston saw in Big Sweet a version of the woman she might have been—or might have been saved by—at that vulnerable earlier moment in her life.

Hurston's vivid rendering of the Pine Mill is animated not just by this sort of threatened mayhem, deadly serious one moment and playful the next, but also by her attention to the way blues music provides the soundtrack to after-hours carousing once these lumber workers get off work. "The jook was in full play when we walked in," she writes, evoking the scene of communal performance. "The piano was throbbing like a stringed drum and the couples slow-dragging about the floor were urging the player on to new lows. 'Jook, Johnnie, Ah know you kin spank dat ole pe-anner.' 'Jook it Johnnie!' 'Throw it in de alley!'" (*MAM*, 143). Even this brief passage is chock-full of cultural insight, from the way a percussive approach shapes the pianist's barrelhouse dance aesthetic—keeping the African drum alive in America's portion of the Global South—to the call-and-response urgings from multiple audience members and the way those urgings reinforce both the drum-song element and "get down" aesthetics, another African cultural bequest. Lowering or dipping the body is, in West Africa, a way of connecting with the earth and deepening spiritual intent; to "throw it in de alley" and explore "new lows," in musical terms, is to dig down into the nitty-gritty, play for real, testify from the soul, but also, in this New World context, to get nasty, incite sexual heat, facilitate the mating dance of the slow-dragging couples.[24] Hurston gets all this into her thick description. Like Handy and Hughes, she also finds a place for the familiar AAB blues stanza, rendering melismatic sung vernacular as written text in a way that foreshadows the violence that is about to explode through the jook:

> Heard the new singing man climbing up on
> > Tell me, tell me where de blood red river ru-u-un
> > Oh tell me where de blood red river run
> > From mah back door, straight to de risin' sun.
> > Heard Slim's bass strings under the singing throbbing all
> Africa and Jim Presley's melody crying like repentance as four or
> five couples took the floor. Doing the slow drag, doing the scronch.
> Joe Willard doing a traveling buck and wing towards where I stood
> against the wall facing the open door. (*MAM*, 178)

This passage comes just before Lucy heads toward Hurston with an open switchblade in hand, precipitating a free-for-all brawl. Before discussing that moment, it's worth pausing to note a fascinating element of her participant-observer fieldwork that Hurston leaves out of *Mules and Men*: the fact that she introduced these lumber camp laborers to the poetry of Langston Hughes.

"I read from 'Fine Clothes' to the group at Loughman," she wrote to Hughes in March 1928, "and *they got the point* and enjoyed it *immensely*."[25] They understood and enjoyed Hughes's blues poems, surely, because the formal, attitudinal, and imagistic elements that he employed—AAB repetitions, a preoccupation with troubled male-female relationships, and a brooding focus on sex and violence, especially knives—were everyday currency in the Pine Mill, as was the vernacular voice in which he wrote. Hurston left *Fine Clothes to the Jew* out of her narrative because including it would have undercut her portrait of a preliterate backwoods folk community, but she was so astonished by the response that, according to biographer Boyd, she started reading Hughes's poetry everywhere she went—railroad camps, phosphate mines, turpentine stills—during the remainder of her trip. "They call it 'De Party Book,'" she wrote to Hughes in July in during an extended stay in Magazine, Alabama. "They adore 'Saturday Night' and 'Evil Woman,' 'Bad Man,' 'Gypsy Man.' They sing the poems right off, and [on] July 1, two men came over with guitars and sang the whole book. Everybody joined in. It was the strangest and most thrilling thing. They played it well too. You'd be surprised. One man was giving the words out—lining them out as the preacher does a hymn and the others would take it up and sing. It was glorious!"[26]

This remarkable passage shows us that the process through which she and Hughes used blues song as raw material, transforming oral performance into literary text, could be reversed by the black folk community, so that blues literature itself became the raw material for a collective vernacular performance. This picture of a warm and convivial celebration is complicated, however, by the contents of the four "adore[d]" poems mentioned by Hurston, which together sketch the sort of violent and profane good-timing world that led black southern church people to condemn the blues as the devil's music. "I ain't gonna mistreat ma / Good gal any more," begins "Evil Woman, "I'm just gonna kill her / Next time she makes me sore." "Bad Man" is narrated in the voice of a similarly ill-tempered lover, one filled with "meanness" and "likker" who beats his wife and his "side gal too."[27]

Black southern blues culture was a thrilling scene of discovery for Hurston, one that offered her a wealth of folkloric material and encounters with memorable individuals, but it was also a culture pervaded by interpersonal violence: brags, threats, and hands-on retribution. Women were men's equals in this last regard; Hurston found this gender equity compelling—and humorous, at least at first. "Negro women *are* punished in these parts for killing men," she joked shortly after arriving in Loughman, "but only if they exceed the quota" (*MAM*, 60). But she also found the violence chilling when she realized that she, too, had been drawn into the charmed circle: a woman marked for death by a vengeful, knife-wielding rival. When Big Sweet advises Hurston that she should be prepared to run for her life if Lucy or Ella comes after her, the participant-observer suddenly bears witness to her own fear: "I thought of all I had to live for and turned cold at the thought of dying in a violent manner in a sordid sawmill camp" (*MAM*, 151). A week later, Lucy makes a play for her that Big Sweet disables, upping the ante. "I shivered," writes Hurston, "at the thought of dying with a knife in my back, or having my face mutilated" (*MAM*, 154).

All of this leads inexorably, as Hurston tells it, to a final showdown at the Pine Mill jook. Hurston's panicked response, as she sees Lucy heading toward her with knife in hand, is a stunning reversal of the generally comic tone with which she has narrated her immersive experience in the lumber camp's social world. "I didn't move but I was running in my skin. I could hear the blade already crying in my flesh. I was sick and weak" (*MAM*, 179). Then Big Sweet leaps once again to her defense and Jim Presley punches Hurston violently, protectively, hurling her toward the door and shouting, "Run you chile! Run and ride!":

> Slim stuck out the guitar to keep two struggling men from blocking my way. Lucy was screaming. Crip had hold of Big Sweet's clothes in the back and Joe was slugging him loose. Curses, oaths, cries and the whole place was in motion. Blood was on the floor. I fell out of the door over a man lying on the steps, who either fell himself trying to run or got knocked down. I don't know. I was in the car in a second and in high just too quick. Jim and Slim helped me throw my bags into the car and I saw the sun rising as I approached Crescent City. (*MAM*, 179)

The guitar, which has been instrumental in opening this blues community to Hurston and her cultural investigations, has been transformed into a weapon that opens a path to escape. Hurston's tone is flat and affectless, her narrative kinetic and open-eyed; she offers us a stunned epiphany, it would seem, as four-and-a-half months of participant-observation end in an adrenalized rush. When Hurston narrates this same episode in *Dust Tracks*, seeking perhaps to entertain a white audience, she plays up the weaponry angle in a way that veers toward coon-song cliché: "Switch-blades, ice-picks and old-fashioned razors were out. One or two razors had already been bent back and thrown across the room, but our fight was the main attraction" (*DT*, 190–91). But the gist of the story, in both cases, is the same: forcibly exiled by the blues-filled black folk community that she has sought to understand, inadvertently inciting a murderous rage in a local woman, Hurston flees the jook to save her own life.

Why is this, of all things, the story that Hurston chooses to tell about her encounter with the blues and blues people? I've already suggested several possible answers, including her desire as a cultural anthropologist to find and honor the Real—a self-contained backwoods locale, intense passions, authentic blues—at a moment when Broadway and Tin Pan Alley were diluting, trivializing, and profiting from the music. Hurston also shapes her representations, as I've noted, in a way that highlights the fearsome power of women: a feminist point, surely, and one that perhaps addresses a deep psychological need evoked by Boyd, but a point that is also undercut by the way she represents herself as foolishly naive and ultimately disempowered within the world of the Pine Mill jook. The best answer to the question, it turns out, is *Their Eyes Were Watching God*, a novel written not long after the publication of *Mules and Men*.

A PAIN REMORSELESS SWEET

One of the most important prewar blues novels, along with Claude McKay's *Home to Harlem* (1928) and Gilmore Millen's *Sweet Man* (1930), *Their Eyes* is Hurston's attempt to rewrite her Florida backwoods blues immersion experience in a way that wins her a victory in the juke joint rather than allowing her be driven into exile. She accomplishes this through a surrogate, Janie Crawford, and specifically through Janie's midlife romance with Tea Cake, a younger bluesman who embodies the paradoxes of blues culture as Hurston had come to know them. Tea Cake has many virtues as a lover; he ministers to Janie in ways that deepen and intensify her emotions, heal her from wounds engendered by previous husbands, connect her with a black folk community, and help her claim her fullness as a self-possessed subject. But he, like the blues culture he emblematizes, has a violence problem. He is a juke joint fighter, adept with razor and gun, and he brags about his willingness to use violence on others—an aspect of his character that Janie initially disavows but is ultimately forced to confront. Tea Cake doesn't merely resemble Big Sweet in this regard: Hurston literally puts Big Sweet's words in Tea Cake's mouth, a verbatim transfer of threatened mayhem from the folklore study to the novel. She also has Tea Cake do for Janie precisely the thing that Big Sweet won't do for Hurston: instruct her in the arts of violence. Big Sweet pooh-poohs the idea of teaching Hurston how to handle a knife; "You can't do dis kind uh fightin'," she insists (*MAM*, 175). But Tea Cake—Hurston's creation—is delighted to teach Janie how to handle a gun. "Oh," he said, "you needs tuh learn how" (124). As it turns out, Janie will use the skills Tea Cake has taught her to kill him in self-defense late in the novel, thereby preserving her own life and symbolically purging the novel of the violence he embodies. Yet even as she kills off Tea Cake, she keeps his memory alive in the final scene, a moment of "singing and sobbing" (183) that evokes a kinder, gentler blues. Here, I argue, Hurston works a complicated spell and achieves a retroactive triumph over the spirited but volatile blues community at Loughman that had driven her from its doors.

Their Eyes is an exemplary blues novel, and not just because it features a Florida bluesman—he plays piano and guitar—as a key protagonist. As several critics have noted, Janie's three marriages together constitute an AAB blues verse: the first two are similarly unfulfilling (both men care more for material things than for her), the second is worse than the first (the reiteration + intensification of the A-prime line), and the third is a triumphant answer to the problem posed by the doubled romantic disaster (the B line as a response to the call of the repeated A line).[28] The novel also illustrates Angela Y. Davis's influential claim in *Blues Legacies and Black Feminism* (1997) that the themes of travel and sexuality were so prevalent in early blues because the freedom to travel and the freedom to choose one's lover(s) were two crucial things that distinguished African Americans in the postslavery years from their slave-born parents and grandparents, who'd been chained to the plantation and, in the matter of intimate relations, subject to the whims of the master.[29] Janie Crawford's life is marked not just by multiple husbands of her own choosing and, with the third husband, a large helping of sexual satisfaction, but by several consequential journeys in pursuit of love, including a trip with Tea Cake down onto "de muck"—rich farmland adjacent to Lake Okeechobee—that enables her to forge an immersive connection with a blues-playing, blues-using community. Finally, both the plot and imagistic patterning of *Their Eyes* can be glossed with uncanny precision by one specific blues recording, "Bumble Bee," a hit for Memphis Minnie in 1929:

> Bumble bee, bumble bee, where you been so long
> Bumble bee, bumble bee, where you been so long.
> You stung me this morning, I been restless all day long.

Zora Neale Hurston in the Florida Jooks

I met my bumble bee this morning as he flying in the door.
I met my bumble bee this morning as he flying in the door
And the way he stung me, he made me cry for more

Hmmmmm, don't stay so long from me
Hmmmmm, don't stay so long from me
You is my bumble bee, you got something that I really need.

I'm gonna build me a bungalow, just for me and my bumble bee.
I'm gonna build me a bungalow, just for me and my bumble bee.
Then I won't worry, I will have all the honey I need.

It's likely, although not provable, that Hurston knew of "Bumble Bee" or one of the four follow-up versions released between 1929 and 1931, including this recording, "Bumble Bee #2"; she had a lot to say about race records—not always kind things, to be sure—and she had a particular interest in raunchy vernacular song, the culture of "the man in the gutter," as she termed it.[30] This song is relatively tame by those standards but still provocative in the way it configures sexual intercourse as a mixture of sex and violence, a "sting" administered by a lover who is imaged as a bumble bee. In the first three stanzas, it evokes the singer's desire as something that is intensified by her lover's absence, and this element turns out to be a crucial part of the interpretive framework that the song extends toward the novel. (The wayward, stinger-bearing bumble bee is a perfect symbolic rendering of Davis's travel-and-sexuality thesis.)

If we think back to the scene of Janie's sexual awakening under a pear tree, we might remember that it is precipitated by a "dust-bearing bee sink[ing] into the sanctum of a bloom"—which is to say, by a generative symbolic sting, a sexual union of bee and blossom—and that the orgasm it precipitates in Janie fills her with "a pain remorseless sweet." The relevance of Memphis Minnie's song should be obvious here. Pain and pleasure, apparent opposites, are yoked to create yet another example of the blues dialectic: in this case, a sexual sting that awakens Janie into desire and, in Minnie's words, makes her cry for more. The novel images that cry as her response to a newly sensed lack that begs to be filled by an as-yet unidentified lover. "Where were the singing bees for her?" wonders Janie, gazing longingly at the world after her orgasmic reverie. "Nothing on the place nor in her grandma's house answered her" (*TE*, 11).

Unfolding according to the logic encoded in this bluesy scene, *Their Eyes Were Watching God* takes the form of a quest-romance designed to win Janie a man who will sting her thrillingly — ravish her, fill her with sweet remorseless pain, bring her to sexual completion surcharged with romantic passion — in a way that fulfills the promise made by the bees under the pear tree. The novel gains power from the way Hurston frames Janie's erotic journey with reference to the markedly different experience of Nanny, the slave-born grandmother who has raised her. Both Nanny and her daughter Leafy, Hurston's absent mother, were raped — by a white slave owner in Nanny's case, a black schoolteacher in Leafy's — and gave birth out of wedlock. Nanny sees sexuality, especially among the unwed, as a dangerous thing, a source of heartbreak and unfreedom, and doesn't want to Janie to become a "spit cup" used by men (19). Janie, freeborn, sees sexual fulfillment as her birthright, a component of the ideal marriage into which the pear tree and buzzing bees have initiated her. Grandmother and granddaughter come into conflict; Nanny slaps Janie across the face, then hugs her; Janie bursts into tears. (We notice, if we're paying attention, that the novel has, with that back-and-forth exchange, engaged the pain-and-pleasure dialectic of the blues.) Nanny dies shortly after convincing Janie to marry Logan Killicks, a property-owning but sexually unattractive black farmer.

In the novel's blues schema, Killicks is the establishing complaint of the initial A-line. During a postslavery era when black southern folk are trying to figure out what it means to live a free and self-possessed life, Killicks, with his sixty acres and a mule, looks like a great catch to Nanny — but of course Nanny isn't Janie, and to Janie, who doesn't love him, doesn't enjoy looking at him, and feels exploited by him like a kind of mule-woman for her labor power, he's "desecrating" the pear-tree vision that serves as her soul's North Star. So she abandons him within a year. In so doing, she rejects Nanny's slavery-era vision of what freedom should look and feel like for a young black woman in the early years of the new century. It just doesn't fit her.

Janie leaves Killicks for Joe "Jody" Starks, who will soon become her second husband.[31] He wanders into view as her first marriage is on its final legs: a "cityfied, stylish dressed man" (26) whistling as he strolls along the road that fronts the farm. Smooth-talking and self-confident, he chats her up and confesses his desire to be a "big voice" (27) in a community that will allow him to realize his ambition. He engages her deep hunger to journey the world — the travel imperative Davis identifies as a key blues theme — even as she assesses him skeptically in line with her pear-tree hunger to be sexually stung in a thrilling way. "Janie pulled back a long time because he did not represent sun-up and pollen and blooming trees, but he spoke for the far horizon" (28). After wooing her for a week while Killicks is off in the fields, he wins her hand and carries her away toward a future that will, she is now convinced, fulfill her vision of romantic completion. "From now on until death," she tells herself as she leaves her old life behind, "she was going to have flower dust, and springtime sprinkled over everything. A bee for her bloom" (31).

In the novel's blues schema, Starks is the A-prime line: the problem repeated, with emphasis. The disaster he represents takes a while to become apparent. Driven by overweening ambition, Joe transports Janie to a brand-new all-black town of Eatonville—Hurston models him on her own father—and becomes the mayor and proprietor of the general store, where he installs Janie as checkout clerk and figurehead. He's entrepreneurial; he takes the town over, helps build it. But he also begins to play out a second vision of post-Emancipation black freedom: not Killicks's forty-acres-and-a-mule vision of independent yeoman farmers, but a recapitulation of slavery, of white mastery. Joe builds a "gloaty, sparkly white" house (44). He has spittoons, and spits in them. He bosses his fellow black townspeople around in such a way that they complain about the "bow-down" sound of his voice (44). Hurston is attentive to the supreme irony: here, at a postslavery moment in an all-black town, Joe's vision of freedom is a recapitulation of the slavemaster's prerogatives. With the help of his "big voice," he wants to be boss over every living thing, including Janie. He wants his wife to sit in the "high chair" like a queen, separated from the townspeople the way he is, but he also wants her to submit to his every command and accept his periodic belittling silently, without protest. When his belittling becomes violent—he slaps Janie around one night until her ears ring when she accidentally scorches the dinner she's cooked for him—she watches her dream of a bee for her bloom disintegrate. "She wasn't petal-open anymore with him," Hurston tells us. "She had no more blossomy openings dusting pollen over her man" (67–68).

If Boyd's claim about Hurston's painful lost time under a lover's violent thumb in the shotgun house is correct, then Hurston's portrait of Joe Starks as a suffocating oppressor revisits that primal scene: the novelist digs down into her own crushing disillusionment to find a buried strength within Janie that will be the grounds for future action. "She had an inside and an outside now," Hurston tells us after Janie recovers from the beating, "and suddenly she knew how not to mix them" (68). Keeping her own counsel, Janie holds return fire until the day when Joe and a handful of locals are standing around the store; prompted by one man's comment about the way she has cut a plug of tobacco, Joe mocks her incompetence with a knife and then insults her middle-aged woman's body. That knife is important: Hurston has put into Joe's mouth essentially the same critique that Big Sweet made of Hurston: "You don't know how tuh handle it" (*MAM*, 176). But the public humiliation superadded by Joe distinguishes his comment utterly from the big-sisterly protectiveness of Hurston's juke-house friend, and in that moment, Janie suddenly finds her own voice—a voice that echoes Big Sweet's aggressive woofing. "You big-bellies round here and put out a lot of brag," she tells Joe, "but 'tain't nothin' to it but yo' big voice. Humph! Talkin' 'bout *me* lookin' old! When you pull down yo' britches, you look lak de change uh life" (75).

In one stunning moment, signifying mercilessly on Joe's shriveled penis, Janie executes a death blow to her husband's vanity. Furiously resentful, he dies within a few pages, at the end of the following chapter. And then, after a brief but important interregnum in which Janie dwells in the lonesomeness of an empty house, sounds her own soul, finds it fit, and takes joy in the "freedom feeling" (86) that has come over her, Tea Cake enters the picture.

BLUES MADE AND USED

In the novel's blues schema, Tea Cake is the answering B-line: the response to the doubled disaster that has been Janie's marital life to this point. In almost every respect he is the antithesis of Logan and Joe. They were older than Janie; Tea Cake is younger. They demanded that she work; he invites her to play (checkers, late-night fishing, back-and-forth banter). They were men of means, focused on the future and determined to accumulate property; he's a man of no means, a musician and lover focused on the here and now. They seemed incapable of taking pleasure in her beauty and telling her so (or at least Joe devolved to this condition as the marriage proceeded); Tea Cake takes pleasure in her beauty, tells her so, and holds up a mirror, insisting that she do the same. Tea Cake stimulates, challenges, liberates, and heals Janie, and the blues that he lives and plays are an intrinsic part of this, although they also introduce complications. One way he steals her heart, for example, is by playing out the logic of "Bumble Bee #2": summoning up sexual passion and then absenting himself from the scene in a way that leaves her restless all day long. Where Joe, with his big voice, was omnipresent in a way that Janie found suffocating, Tea Cake stays away for a full week after their initial encounter, giving her a chance to miss him. He brings his guitar—"mah box" (96)—when he returns; the following night he sits down at her piano and begins to play and sing the blues. An adjunct to his playful flirtations, the music becomes the soundtrack to their blossoming romance. He leaves suddenly that second night, after the subject of the twelve-year age difference has come up, and his masterly deployment of call-and-response aesthetics—insisting that he has to "struggle aginst" (101) his feelings for her, then parrying her skepticism—awakens her passion. Her feelings, echoing the restless sexual hunger evoked in "Bumble Bee," promise the fulfillment of her youthful initiation under the pear tree:

> All next day in the house and store she thought resisting thoughts about Tea Cake. She even ridiculed him in her mind and was a little ashamed of the association. But every hour or two the battle had to be fought all over again. She couldn't make him look just like any other man to her. He looked like the love thoughts of women. He could be a bee to a blossom—a pear tree blossom in the spring. (101)

Even as Tea Cake plays Janie in every sense of the word, Hurston makes clear that his skills, such as they are, derive from the low-down, blues-filled world in which he spends his time. "Bet he's hanging 'round some jook or 'nother," Janie sneers the first time he absents himself. "Glad Ah treated him cold. Whut do Ah want wid some trashy nigger out de streets? Bet he's livin' wid some woman or 'nother and takin' me for uh fool" (102). The morning after they make love for the first time, Janie wakes to feel Tea Cake "almost kissing her breath away" (103), and that line is a near-verbatim quote from Bessie Smith's "Empty Bed Blues" (1928), where a "new man" thrills the singer "night and day," leading her to proclaim, "He's got a new way of lovin' almost takes my breath away."

As the romance between Tea Cake and Janie develops, it becomes clear that she is deepening as a subject under his been-here-and-gone ministrations: becoming at once more feelingful and more edgy, filled with strong and contradictory passions yoked together in a familiar blues dialectic:

> In the cool of the afternoon [after they first made love] the fiend from hell specially sent to lovers arrived at Janie's ear. Doubt. All the fears that circumstance could provide and the heart feel attacked her on every side. This was a new sensation for her, but no less excruciating. If only Tea Cake would make her certain! He did not return that night nor the next and so she plunged into the abyss and descended to the ninth darkness where light has never been.
>
> But the fourth day after he came in the afternoon driving a battered car. Jumped out like a deer and made the gesture of tying it

to a post on the store porch. Ready with his grin! She adored him and hated him at the same time. How could he make her suffer so and then come grinning like that with that darling way he had? (103)

Certainty and doubt, love and hate, pain and pleasure: rarely has a work of American literature offered a more pointed object lesson in the emotional lineaments of blues romance. Hurston *wants* Janie to get thoroughly bluesed up: pulled out of the "classed-off" high chair in which Nanny and Joe wanted to keep her and down onto the rich, fragrant muck of open-hearted, fully embodied life. But Hurston also wants us to attend to a related educational process through which Janie's eyes are opened to the violence of Tea Cake's world, a violence that is an intrinsic part of who he is.

Tea Cake, like Big Sweet, is a skilled knife-fighter. He takes as much pleasure in those abilities as he takes in his facility as a gambler, lover, and blues musician. An attentive reader will notice Hurston hinting slyly at this element of his makeup in one of the earliest descriptions she offers of him — as seen through Janie's eyes, significantly, although Janie doesn't recognize the import of what she sees: "She looked him over and got little thrills from every one of his good points. Those full, lazy eyes with the lashes curling sharply away like drawn scimitars" (92). The question of Tea Cake's violence is first raised overtly when Hezekiah, who helps Janie in the store, warns her against dating such a low-class man. "Is he bad 'bout toting pistols and knives tuh hurt people wid?" she asks, pushing back. "Dey don't say he ever cut nobody or shot nobody neither" (98), Hezekiah concedes. But Hezekiah is wrong. And Janie, who watches her lover buy a new switch-blade knife and two decks of playing cards before he heads out alone on a juke joint expedition, is wrong when she insists to herself, anxiously, "Tea Cake wouldn't harm a fly" (120). When he falls back through the front door at daylight, he has been cut in several places and lost some blood; $300 richer, he regales her with a story about how he beat up the man who accused him of cheating at dice. "Baby," he brags, "Ah run mah other arm in mah coat-sleeve and grabbed dat nigger by his necktie befo' he could bat his eye and then Ah wuz all over 'im jus' lak gravy over rice. He lost his razor tryin' tuh git loose from me. He wuz hollerin' for me tuh turn him loose, but baby, Ah turnt him every way *but* loose" (121).

Big Sweet's phrase, bragging about her readiness for a knife fight with Ella Wall, was "Ah'll be all over her jus' lak gravy over rice." Hurston changes the tense and gender, then puts those words in Tea Cake's mouth. Her boisterous working-class hero isn't just a playful bluesman-lover but also a skilled and enthusiastic brawler. As she paints iodine on his wounds and cries, Janie is burdened by this new knowledge; he has, in fact, been "hanging 'round some juke or 'nother," but she's in too deep for sneering now. And the "self-crushing love" she feels for him, a love that leads her soul to "[crawl] out from its hiding place" (122), suggests that she is spiritually enlarged by the relationship, regardless of its problematics.

Blues culture, as Hurston had experienced in at the Pine Mill and as she dramatizes it in the person of Tea Cake, was animated by a powerful expressive need that sometimes spoke through violence. In black working-class social spaces like the jook, brags and boasts were backed by deadly force, as were romantic claims. Hurston "shivered" in the lumber camp when she began to understand the risk to her own person. But she also found herself intoxicated by the energy, joy, and creative spirit that surged within the camp's juke house. *Their Eyes* conjures with this paradox in pointed ways as the love affair between Janie and Tea Cake plays out. Tea Cake liberates Janie, for example, by teaching her how to shoot "pistol and shot gun and rifle" (125). She thrives under his tutelage, becoming a better shot than he is. This subplot, in symbolic terms, shows the violence of the jook being put to constructive use. Tea Cake disciples Janie more deeply into the blues by taking her down on "de muck," an agricultural district in the Everglades bordering Lake Okeechobee where migrants and fieldwork are plentiful and where the music thrives as well. "All night now the jooks clanged and clamored. Pianos living three lifetimes in one. Blues made and used right on the spot. Dancing, fighting, singing, crying, laughing, winning and losing love every hour. Work all day for money, fight all night for love. The rich black earth clinging to bodies and biting the skin like ants" (125).

Janie's spiritual liberation requires that the imprisoning dream of class ascent that Nanny inculcated in her and Joe Starks did his best to impose on her be extinguished. Allowing herself to be romanced by Tea Cake began the process; accompanying him onto the muck and choosing to work in the fields with the migrant community's other women continues it. The room she and Tea Cake share in the "quarters" is transformed into a veritable juke joint, filled every night with trash-talking gamblers, storytellers, and an audience for Tea Cake's box-picking. Janie has left the big white house and its high chair far behind; blues culture, the all-black space and sociality of the jook, has wholly supplanted the spiritually retrograde vision shared by Nanny and Joe, a white inheritance at odds with the truth of black being.

As an egalitarian space in which labor and play fuse under the sign of blues, the muck is also an Id-space in which the "lower" human passions flower fully and can thus be experienced and explored. Here, too, Tea Cake disciples Janie by misbehaving in the way that bluesmen do—letting his erotic attentions wander toward a "little chunky girl" (130) named Nunkie. Nunkie attracts his interest in the fields, importantly, by hitting him "playfully," mingling sexual enticements and low-level violence. "Janie learned what it felt like to be jealous," Hurston writes. "She never thought at all. She just acted on feelings" (131). Seized by a "cold rage" (131) when she discovers them together, Janie angrily confronts Tea Cake; later, back at the quarters, she hits him, chasing him from room to room and hurling accusations. She's seething, fully activated, wildly alive—and sexually receptive, even voracious:

> They wrestled on until they were doped with their own fumes and emanations; till their clothes had been torn away; till he hurled her to the floor and held her there melting her resistance with the heat of his body, doing things with their bodies to express the inexpressible; kissed her until she arched her body to meet him and they fell asleep in sweet exhaustion. (132)

Here is the sexual completion that Janie has been seeking ever since the pear-tree revelation, when she saw a "dust-bearing bee sink into the sanctum of a bloom; the thousand sister-calyxes arch to meet the love embrace." This passage is the fulfillment of that prophecy. The "sweet exhaustion" she shares with Tea Cake echoes the "pain remorseless sweet that left her limp and languid" in that earlier moment. So this *is* a marriage. Hurston wants us to know that. A deep, primal, and fulfilling connection has been established.

And yet, and yet. The endgame of *Their Eyes* is a complicated exercise in which the violence that Tea Cake carries—a violence associated with the jook, an enlivening, passion-deepening, and even life-sustaining violence in certain contexts—is also revealed for what Hurston herself knew it to be: a mortal danger to be evaded. The word "also" is crucial here. Hurston's vision is capacious, multivariate; Tea Cake's descent into violent jealousy and madness is governed by a both/and logic, not an either/or logic. At bottom, however, is a wound inflicted on one black bluesman's soul by an ideology of whiteness that seems to have infected the world in which he lives. When a thin-lipped, light-skinned woman named Mrs. Turner praises Janie for her "coffee-and-cream complexion" (134) and badmouths Tea Cake for being dark, Tea Cake later whips Janie to relieve "that awful fear inside him" and to "[reassure] himself in possession" (140). Racism, rendering him insecure about his masculine prerogatives, accentuates a preexisting condi-

tion—a jealous possessiveness and willingness to use violence as its guaran-
tor that the jook has bred in him. Later, after Tea Cake and Janie have barely
survived a hurricane and Tea Cake, struggling to protect Janie, has been bit-
ten by a mad dog that is "nothin' all over but pure hate" (158), the bluesman
is forcibly impressed into service by a pair of white men with guns seeking
black laborers to bury the dead. Tea Cake bridles and later escapes to the
Everglades with Janie, complaining broodingly about how the town he just
left was "full uh trouble and compellment" (163). The novel, which has effectively banished white people for most of its length, succumbs to whiteness,
or at least acknowledges whiteness's dispiriting presence, in these late pages.
Tea Cake's own violence has always subsisted in uneasy relation with the
"compellments," the disciplinary prerogatives, of Jim Crow. Now the bluesman becomes the novel's version of a Jesus figure: not a blameless innocent
but still a good man and husband who is forced to suffer for the sins of this
particular southern world. In a final paroxysm of violent, rabies-induced jealousy, Tea Cake pulls a pistol out from under his bed and shoots—or shoots
at—Janie. She kills him with a shotgun blast, knowing even as she does that
"Tea Cake was gone. Something else was looking out of his face" (172). He
has, we are to understand, finally been driven mad by the virus of white supremacy that has corroded his being. But that virus has acted in a way that
simultaneously licenses, and exaggerates, his knife-fighter's predilection for
hands-on violence.

It is easy to miss the subtlety with which Hurston interleaves the forces
that ultimately destabilize Tea Cake and require Janie to kill him. The brilliance of *Their Eyes Were Watching God* is that it finds a way of encoding this
complexity even while offering us a moving love story, a blues story with a
tragic ending that is also redemptive and even liberating. In killing Tea Cake,
the novel kills off the violent mayhem spawned by his juke joint world, even
while conferring on Janie the ability to defend herself with righteous violence. In the glorious love affair between the bluesman and Janie, of course,
the novel insists that the passions conveyed by the blues are a great and noble
thing. They deepen and transform lives. They save a good woman, helping
her escape from containment and despair.

bar 9

Ralph Ellison, Richard Wright, and the Southern Blues Violences

BRUTAL EXPERIENCE AND LYRIC FLIGHT

If Handy, Hughes, and Hurston help usher the blues literary tradition into being, then one thing that unites them is a shared concern with two issues that have proven to be central to that tradition: the dialectical energy—pain and pleasure, tragedy and comedy—marshaled by the music and its congregants, and the representational strategies through which blues lyricism can be displaced onto the written page. Ralph Ellison, too, is a canonical blues literary figure, and his description of the blues in a 1945 review-essay, "Richard Wright's Blues," has been extraordinarily influential over the years, in part because it addresses both issues, embracing the blues' bittersweet tonality and enlarging their scope to encompass prose literature. "The blues," Ellison proposed,

> is an impulse to keep the painful details and episodes of a brutal experience alive in one's aching consciousness, to finger its jagged grain, and to transcend it, not by the consolation of philosophy but by squeezing from it a near-tragic, near-comic lyricism. As a form, the blues is an autobiographical chronicle of personal catastrophe expressed lyrically.[1]

In Bar 8, I invoked Memphis Minnie's "Bumble Bee" and Bessie Smith's "Empty Bed Blues" as plausible sources for the pleasure-and-pain dialectic evidenced by *Their Eyes Were Watching God*; Ellison opens that interpretive door in another famous passage from the same essay. "Like a blues sung by such an artist as Bessie Smith," he wrote of Wright's autobiography, "its lyrical prose evokes the paradoxical, almost surreal image of a black boy singing lustily as he probes his own grievous wound. . . . *Black Boy* represent[s] the flowering — cross-fertilized by pollen blown by the winds of strange cultures — of the humble blues lyric" (91).

Many decades later, we're still exploring the implications of those words "flowering" and "cross-fertilized." In what way, precisely, do the "humble blues lyric" — more specifically, tens of thousands of blues recordings — and the African American literary tradition speak to each other? Is the fusion of blues lyrics with more traditional Western literary forms, such as the autobiography, the only way, or the most important way, or merely one important way, in which blues literature flowers into being? Or does the blues impulse, as Ellison conceives of it, animate the tradition: a desire not merely to narrate (or sing) an experience characterized by the words "painful," "brutal," and "aching," but to beat it back with an admixture of humor so that the blues ethos is embodied? And where, in all this, are the blues musicians themselves — performers who sing the songs, exemplify the impulse, and live out the ethos? Janie's autobiographical chronicle in *Their Eyes*, after all, was shaped by the active intervention of Tea Cake, a guitar-picker and piano-tickler; he was the bumble bee who cross-fertilized her world with the blues and contributed directly to her flowering. When we're seeking to assess the blues content of particular literary texts, how critical is the presence of such blues-musical figures?

One way of exploring such issues, I suggest, is to make *Black Boy* a test case. Does Wright's autobiography truly deserve to be called a work of blues literature? Wright makes no attempt, after all, to depict the blues culture that was thriving in the Mississippi and Arkansas of his youth, a culture of street-corner busking and all-night-long house parties presided over by a loosely organized brotherhood of skilled, promiscuous, highly mobile songsters — a world rendered in rich autobiographical detail by Honeyboy Edwards in *The World Don't Owe Me Nothing*. Young Richard does, at one point, stand outside a saloon in Memphis; somebody gives him a drink and teaches him some filthy language — language he repeats for the amusement of the bar's patrons until, later, he is beaten badly for repeating it at home. This could be an urban juke joint, except that no music is audible, here or elsewhere in *Black Boy*. Nor does Wright offer us blues lyrics rendered on the page, as three-line stanzas or briefer lyric echoes, in the manner pioneered by Handy, Hughes, and Hurston. Wright doesn't actually sing the blues per se; Ellison is being purely metaphorical when he characterizes young Richard as "singing lustily." Where, then, is the presumed bluesiness of *Black Boy* sourced? Did Wright just somehow *absorb* the blues, thanks to his blackness and his Deep South upbringing?

In the summer of 1921, when Wright was fourteen, he made a brief, disillusioning tour of the Mississippi Delta as an assistant to W. Mance, an illiterate black insurance agent. "I saw a bare, bleak pool of black life and I hated it," he wrote in *Black Boy*. "The people were alike, their homes were alike, and their farms were alike."[2] Where young Wright saw a bleak and uninspiring tableau of subsistence-level peasantry, devoid of the individuating expressiveness enabled by the blues, Edwards speaks of a Delta childhood animated and enriched by the music — but also marked by the violence that pervaded southern blues culture:

> Mama . . . could play guitar and harp. She'd put a guitar across her lap with a pocket knife and play "Par-a-lee" on it. We was all kind of musical people. Didn't none of her family but her play music, but on my father's side was musicians. He played violin and guitar but he got rid of them after I got up to be a little size; he quit playing.
>
> Papa used to hold country dances on a Saturday night, sell whiskey and play guitar at the house. Sometimes he'd go off to play at jukes. He got in a fight one time at one of them Saturday night dances. My daddy got to fighting and hollering with a guy and they run out of the dance and into the field. My daddy had a plaid shirt on and this guy Jack shot at him with a Winchester rifle. The bullet just missed Papa, but it shot a hole through his shirt! Then he quit playing.[3]

Although Wright was not, according to biographer Hazel Rowley, "tempted by saloons, shooting craps, or houses of ill repute" after moving to Memphis with his mother in 1925, he did occasionally visit the Palace Theatre on Beale Street during his two-and-a-half-year residence and listen to Gertrude Saunders, a touring vaudevillian, sing the blues.[4] That's not much cultural exposure, at least when compared with the much deeper well from which Hughes and Hurston were drawing. Ellison later backpedaled, as it happens, on his early claims about Wright's literary bluesiness. "For all of his having come from Mississippi," Ellison told interviewer Robert O'Mealley in 1976,

Ralph Ellison and Richard Wright

"he didn't know a lot of the folklore. And although he tried to write a blues, he knew nothing about that or jazz."[5]

The written blues Ellison disparages here is almost surely "King Joe (Joe Louis Blues)," a thirteen-stanza blues song that Wright composed in 1941 at the suggestion of producer John Hammond in honor of boxer Joe Louis's recent triumphs. A shortened version of "King Joe" was set to music by Count Basie and performed on record by actor Paul Robeson in his deep, powerful, operatic basso. "The man certainly can't sing the blues," Basie later mused of Robeson, but Wright's labored lyrics were no help to the swing-challenged singer—although the producers were shrewd enough to leave a half-dozen of the clunkiest stanzas off the recording, including the following:

> Big black bearcat couldn't turn nothing loose he caught (2x)
> Squeezed it 'til the count of nine, and just couldn't be bought
>
> Now molasses is black and they say buttermilk is white (2x)
> If you eat a bellyful of both, it's like a Joe Louis fight
>
> Wonder what Joe Louis thinks when he's fighting a white man
> Say wonder what Joe Louis thinks when he's fighting a white man
> Bet he thinks what I'm thinking . . . 'cause he wears a deadpan[6]

Although Wright would, in later years, occasionally revisit the blues in poems such as "Blue Snow Blues" and "The FB Eye Blues," liner notes for albums by Josh White and Big Bill Broonzy, and an influential foreword to Paul Oliver's *Blues Fell This Morning: The Meaning of the Blues* (1960), his commitment to blues vernacular culture pales beside that of Hughes, Hurston, Brown, Sherley Anne Williams, August Wilson, Albert Murray, and Ellison himself.[7] Yet a crucial distinction needs to be made here between blues *expressiveness* and blues *feeling*. Wright may not, as Ellison claimed, have known how to write a convincing blues song, and there is no record of him singing the blues. But it might be argued—and I am about to argue—that he *had* the blues as a Mississippi black boy, lived a life structured by blues feelings that he shared with his peers and elders—including the sorts of blues performers whom he chose later, as a writer, not to represent. The source of these feelings, as Ellison suggests, is a brutal experience composed of painful details and episodes that the blues subject, a subject half-created by this experience, chooses to keep alive in aching consciousness.

As a way of making that argument and teasing out the implications of Ellison's statement, I'll begin with a claim that I've already evidenced: blues expressiveness is grounded in and shaped by the encounter of working-class black folk with violence in the Jim Crow South. There's more to blues expressiveness than that, of course, as other critics have argued. The aesthetic and attitudinal contours of the music are also shaped by the spatial mobility made possible by a post-Reconstruction southern railway system and the sonic textures engendered by that system's horizon-bound trains; by the consolidation of a mass audience with the emergence of a race records market and its technologies of reproduction; and by the way the new sexual freedom of post-Emancipation life was explored by the music's black producers and consumers.[8] Yet southern violence is, I would argue, a more thoroughgoing influence on blues lives, blues feelings, and blues song than these other three domains, in part because it hovers behind them—prompting dreams of escape and fears of pursuit, for example, and infecting intimate relationships. This violence consists of three distinct but interlocking forms of interpersonal violence: *disciplinary* violence, *retributive* violence, and *intimate* violence.

Disciplinary violence, to reiterate, is white-on-black violence that aims, in white southern parlance, to keep "the Negro in his place"; it consists primarily of lynching, police brutality, and related forms of white vigilantism. When Ellison speaks in "Richard Wright's Blues" about young Richard having come of age in a world ruled by "an elaborate scheme of taboos supported by ruthless physical violence" (95), he is offering a succinct definition of disciplinary violence as it functioned in Mississippi between 1890 and 1965. Little Brother Montgomery's 1936 recording, "The First Time I Met You," with the singer's cry of having been "run from tree to tree" by the blues and his plea, "Mr. Blues, don't murder me," exemplifies the blues response to disciplinary violence.[9] Robert Johnson's preternaturally restless "Hell Hound on My Trail" ("I got to keep movin' / I've got to keep movin' / blues fallin' down like hail") is similarly haunted by the presence of white violence in the landscape it evokes, in the mobility it both enacts and laments.

Retributive violence, somewhat less common in both southern history and blues song, is black-on-white violence that strikes back, or threatens to strike back, at disciplinary violence and other forms of racist oppression, sometimes with a kind of badman swagger. "Stackolee," which features a St. Louis lawman who is leery of confronting that "bad son-of-a-gun they call Stackolee," is a badman blues ballad that flirts with retributive violence.[10] Luzanna Cholly, the nattily attired Alabama bluesman in Albert Murray's novel *Train Whistle Guitar* (1974), is a hero to the young black narrator precisely because, with inimitable cool, he threatens retributive violence. "The idea of going to jail didn't scare him at all," Murray tells us,

Ralph Ellison and Richard Wright

and the idea of getting lynch-mobbed didn't faze him either. All I can remember him ever saying about that was: If they shoot at me they sure better not miss me they sure better get me that first time. Whitefolks used to say he was a crazy nigger, but what they really meant or should have meant was that he was confusing to them. . . . They certainly respected the fact that he wasn't going to take any foolishness off of them.[11]

Intimate violence, the third kind of blues violence, is black-on-black violence driven by jealousy, hatred, and other strong passions, particularly the cutting and shooting that cut a wide swath through blues song and blues literature. Ma Rainey's "See See Rider Blues," which climaxes with a verse in which the singer swears she's going to kill her abandoning lover with "a pistol just as long as I am tall," exemplifies this sort of intraracial vengeance. Intimate violence is a particularly fruitful axis around which to align blues lyrics and blues literature; knives, for example, surface not just in songs such as "Got Cut All to Pieces," "Good Chib Blues," and "Two-By-Four Blues," but novels such as Walter Mosley's *RL's Dream*, Murray's *Train Whistle Guitar*, Gayl Jones's *Eva's Man*, and Hurston's *Their Eyes Were Watching God*, poems such as Hughes's "In a Troubled Key" and "Suicide," plays such as August Wilson's *Ma Rainey's Black Bottom* and *Seven Guitars*, and autobiographies by David Honeyboy Edwards, Henry Townsend, and others.

FINGERING THE JAGGED GRAIN

Richard Wright may not have known how to write a blues, as Ellison later insisted, but he did know how to evoke these three Jim Crow violences, which together constitute much of the brutal experience he suffered and survived, and which likewise reveal his underlying affinity with the blues textual tradition I've just sketched. In this respect, Ellison's characterization of *Black Boy* as a kind of literary flowering of the humble blues lyric is apt. Not only were Wright (b. 1908) and Little Brother Montgomery (b. 1910) contemporaries who came of age in the Delta, for example, but Montgomery's signifying protest against lynching in "The First Time I Met You" is uncannily echoed in *Black Boy*'s evocation of the terror produced in his youthful imagination by the phantasmic lynch mob. "I had already grown to feel that there existed men against whom I was powerless," Wright insisted of his Deep South boyhood, "men who could violate my life at will. . . . I had already become as conditioned to their existence as though I had been the victim of a thousand lynchings" (87). Here is one audible blues-note in Wright, a note born out of the black southern subject's confrontation with the threat of disciplinary violence. Another blues-note can be heard when Wright reports a story he's been told about one woman's response to such violence. "One evening," Wright tells us,

> I heard a tale that rendered me sleepless for nights. It was of a
> Negro woman whose husband had been seized and killed by a
> mob. It was claimed that the woman vowed she would avenge her
> husband's death and she took a shotgun, wrapped it in a sheet, and
> went humbly to the whites, pleading that she be allowed to take her
> husband's body for burial. It seemed that she was granted permission
> to come to the side of her dead husband while the whites, silent and
> armed, looked on. The woman, so went the story, knelt and prayed,
> then proceeded to unwrap the sheet; and, before the white men
> realized what was happening, she had taken the gun from the sheet
> and had slain four of them, shooting at them from her knees. (86)

Wright's tale resonates with blues singer Josie Miles's 1924 recording, "Mad Mama's Blues," which threatens shotgun-wreaked vengeance against a blues-inducing world:

> Wanna set the world on fire, that is my one mad desire
> I'm a devil in disguise, got murder in my eyes
>
> Now I could see blood runnin' through the streets
> Now I could see blood runnin' through the streets
> Could be everybody layin' dead right at my feet
>
> . . . .
>
> I took my big Winchester, down off the shelf
> I took my big Winchester, down off the shelf
> When I get through shootin', there won't be nobody left.

In his review of *Black Boy*, Ellison evokes this sort of blues-bearing retributive violence when he speaks of "three general ways" in which black folk confronted their destiny "in the South of Wright's childhood," the third way being to "adopt a criminal attitude, and carry on an unceasing psychological scrimmage with the whites, which often flared forth into physical violence" (94).

What interests Ellison far more than black badman (or badwoman) vengeance against whites, however, is the linkage he glimpses in Wright's

Ralph Ellison and Richard Wright

Mississippi boyhood between white disciplinary violence, especially lynching, and black intimate violence, an intimate violence that took the form not of mayhem in the jooks but of beatings Wright suffered at the hands of his mother and grandmother. "Wright saw his destiny," Ellison writes, ". . . in terms of a quick and casual violence inflicted upon him by both family and community" (94). This family violence, the violence of black southern elders against their children, is viewed by Ellison as a problematic but understandable attempt to suppress a rebellious individuality that, were it expressed by these children, would be met with white reprisal against the entire black community. Later he elaborates: "One of the Southern Negro family's methods of protecting the child is the severe beating—a homeopathic dose of the violence generated by black and white relationships. . . . Even parental love is given a qualitative balance akin to 'sadism'" (101). Many would dispute Ellison's depiction of black family life under Jim Crow—a sympathetic paraphrase, clearly, of Wright's unremittingly bleak rendering. Yet Wright's vision of intimate violence as the passion-driven inflicting of beatings on the people one is closest to is a blues vision of sorts, one that links his autobiography with blues song and the blues literary tradition.

In blues song, this sort of intimate violence issues more frequently against a lover than a child—as when Robert Johnson in "Me and the Devil Blues" (1938) sings, "I'm goin' to beat my woman / until I get satisfied," or Muddy Waters in "Oh Yeah" (1954) cries, "Oh yeaaah, someday I'm goin' to catch you soon / cut you in the morning, whup you in the afternoon." The beatings that slowly infect the relationship between Janie and Tea Cake in *Their Eyes* offer similar testimony. It might be argued that what I am calling intimate violence in Wright's case—black southern elders whipping a child to keep him in line—is actually a kind of second-order disciplinary violence, the internalization, transformation, and anticipatory staging of a far more deadly and indiscriminate white disciplinary violence that those elders hope to ward off. This is precisely Ellison's claim, in fact. In *Black Boy*, however, boundaries between the two sorts of violence begin to break down; the black disciplining gesture is resisted and thereby forced into the open, revealed to be a form of naked aggression not much different from a knife-slashing. The starkest example of this is the moment where young Richard watches his Uncle Tom tear "a long, young, green switch from the elm tree" (186) and determines not to be beaten by the older man. Richard goes to his dresser drawer, gets out a pack of razor blades, and arms himself with "a thin blade of blue steel in each hand" (186–87). This gesture aligns him with the blues lyric and literary tradition—with Waters (in "Walking thru the Park" [1959]) singing, "Don't you bother my baby, no telling what she'll do / She might cut you, she might shoot you too," and with Tea Cake arming himself with blades and cards before leaving Janie and heading off to a local juke. "I've got a razor in each hand!" young Richard warns his uncle in "a low, charged voice." "If you touch me, I'll cut you! Maybe I'll get cut too, but I'll cut you, so help me God!" (187). If intimate violence is a way southern blues people and their migrant peers express some of their fiercest feelings, then young Richard's gesture of revolt transforms the scene of parent-child discipline into a kind of juke joint brawl—albeit a brawl lacking both the rich musical context and elaborate social context (frontier brags, half-mocking threats at the gambling table, sexual possessiveness) that Hurston encountered in the Pine Mill jook.

Richard Wright's rebellion against his uncle's threatened beating closely parallels an encounter described by St. Louis bluesman Henry Townsend in his autobiography, *A Blues Life*. Townsend, born in Shelby, Mississippi, the year after Wright was born in Natchez, is catapulted into his future career the day he learns, as a nine-year-old, that his father is going to beat him for blowing snuff in his cousin's eyes. "My daddy was gonna get me for that," he claims,

> and that's when I first left home. You don't know how bad it hurts my feelings for me to think that somebody is gonna physically interfere with me, like hitting on me. You don't know how bad it hurts me. My heart jumps and tears in two like busting a string. I can't stand that. I don't dish it out and I can't stand it. I've been whipped but it wasn't a pleasant thing for the man that whipped me—or me—I'll tell you that.
>
> ...I didn't give [my daddy] no chance [to whip me]. I caught the train. I didn't know where I was going—I didn't care. I knew I wasn't gonna stay there and get a whooping.[12]

Wright is the Mississippi black boy who silently suffers the blues of disciplinary and intimate violence, finally rebelling when pressed to the breaking point but escaping only later to exorcise his blues up north in the form of a literary autobiographical chronicle. He has, in Trudier Harris's memorable phrase, "no outlet for the blues," or at least no musical outlet for those feelings.[13] Townsend, by contrast, is the Mississippi black boy who refuses to stay put and allow those particular blues to be inflicted on him; his escape to East St. Louis is a creative liberation, the first step into eventual self-ownership marked by a mastery of blues song's expressive vocabulary.

Henry Townsend (guitar) and Henry Brown (piano)
(courtesy of the photographer, Hans Andreásson)

Townsend is a blues lyricist as well as performer; when I spoke with him backstage at B. B. King's Blues Club in New York in the summer of 2001, he mentioned pridefully that he was the composer of the blues standard, "Every Day I Have the Blues"—the original 1935 version by pianist Pinetop Sparks, on which he played guitar. Although he can't take credit for the well-known lines added to the song by Memphis Slim in his influential 1949 version— "Nobody loves me, nobody seems to care / Worries and troubles, you know I've had my share"—it's tempting to see the song as the declaration of a bitterly rebellious but euphoric nine-year-old runaway riding the rails north, away from his father's blows. It's also tempting to see those lines as the crystallization of young Richard Wright's predicament: "Every Day I Have the Blues" is the humble blues lyric from which *Black Boy* seems to have sprung, even if Wright himself was incapable of singing that song in so many words.

Southern violence, considered in its entirety, doesn't just hurt feelings. It produces a range of abject black bodies: beaten, battered, dismembered, dead. The bodies produced by white violence show up at several points in *Black Boy*—most notably, as the corpses of Uncle Hoskins and an acquain-

tance of Wright's named Bob, both of whose lynchings-by-shooting are related to Wright by others — but these bodies are represented in a sketchy,
fleeting way. The traumatic effect they have on young Wright is out of proportion with the unspectacular representations themselves, as though his
own imagination were doing most of the terrorizing. In one of the few moments in *Black Boy* where retributive violence is imaged, the tale about the
black woman who wraps a shotgun in a sheet to avenge the death of her
mobbed husband, Wright is similarly circumspect; this story compels his
attention by the sheer audacity of the woman's act rather than the morbid
details of the revenge-murders themselves. The most graphic spectacles imaged by Wright in *Black Boy*, it turns out, are the beatings he suffers at the
hands of his mother and grandmother. The novel opens with such a scene
after he has accidentally set the family's house on fire:

> "You almost scared us to death," my mother muttered as she stripped
> the leaves from a tree limb to prepare it for my back.
> I was lashed so hard and long that I lost consciousness. I was
> beaten out of my senses and later found myself in bed, screaming,
> determined to run away, tussling with my mother and father who
> were trying to keep me still. I was lost in a fog of fear. A doctor was
> called — I was afterwards told — and he ordered that I be kept abed,
> that I be kept quiet, that my very life depended on it. My body
> seemed on fire and I could not sleep. Packs of ice were put on my
> forehead to keep down the fever. (7)

If intimate violence produces shocking images of Wright's battered body in
Black Boy, where disciplinary and retributive violence only sketchily represent the bodily violations wrought on, and by, others, then all three violences
intermingle in Wright's imagination to evoke a portrait of southern black
blues life as a desperate and humorless struggle, a living nightmare.

When we pay attention to the way this linked set of southern violences
circulates within blues song and blues literature, it becomes clear that *Black
Boy* stands simultaneously at the margins and the center of the blues textual
tradition. The fact that it erases all traces of Mississippi's thriving blues culture from the world it describes, with the ideological intent of depicting the
unrelieved bleakness of black southern life, makes it marginal. Where are the
belted-out blues songs described by James Cone as "an expression of fortitude in the face of a broken existence"?[14] Where is the temporary but vital
liberation claimed by black Mississippians — including Honeyboy Edwards's
father — at house parties and juke joints every Saturday night? Yet to the ex-

tent that Wright's own life is an expression of fortitude in the face of a broken existence, one shaped by disciplinary, retributive, and intimate violence, *Black Boy* is indeed an exemplary blues text, one animated by the deepest of southern blues feelings.

ELLISON'S VIOLENT BLUES HUMORS

In his own writings, Ralph Ellison represents the blues violences somewhat differently from Wright. Most important, perhaps, Ellison steers clear of the horror provoked by white racial terrorism, refusing to hold those experiences in aching consciousness as Wright does; he redeems desperation with humor rather than seconding it with unrelieved grimness. One explanation for this difference in approach is the social milieu in which each author grew up: relations between blacks and whites were considerably more benign in Oklahoma City during Ellison's boyhood than in Mississippi and Arkansas during Wright's, granting Ellison a more detached perspective.[15] Ellison knows that lynching is a source of agony for black folk, as his short story "A Party Down at the Square" makes clear. But his decision to make the narrator of that story a white boy who admires the lynchers, rather than a black witness who shudders at them, reveals an inclination to reject helpless subjection in favor of very dark satire.[16] The same impulse to heighten the comedic side of the blues' tragicomic dialectic is at work in *Invisible Man*, where Ellison has Dr. Bledsoe, a Booker T. Washington stand-in who rules his Tuskegee-like empire with a ruthless hand, echo a pronouncement made by Mississippi's most infamous white demagogue, James Vardaman. "I'll have every Negro in the country hanging on tree limbs by morning," thunders Bledsoe, "if it means staying where I am."[17] One can hardly imagine Richard Wright making this sort of joke. In his essay "An Extravagance of Laughter," Ellison evokes a related form of disciplinary violence, aggressive southern policing, in a way that rejects Wright's bitter pronouncements about "days lived under the threat of violence" for a more benign stoicism. "I gave Jeeter Lester types a wide berth," Ellison acknowledges of his college days in Alabama, "but found it impossible to avoid them entirely—because many were law-enforcement officers who served on the highway patrols with a violent zeal like that which Negro slave narratives ascribed to the 'paterollers' who had guarded the roads during slavery.... (Southern buses were haunted, and so, in a sense, were Southern roads and highways).... Even the roads that led *away* from the South were also haunted; a circumstance which I should have learned, but did not, from numerous lyrics that were sung to the blues."[18]

Ralph Ellison
(courtesy of Rockefeller Archive Center, Sleepy Hollow, N.Y.)

Ellison knows that white death haunts the southern roads traveled by black folk, but he refuses to be rendered psychologically brittle by this fact. The prospect, enactment, or aftermath of a lynching doesn't function in Ellison's work as the sort of destabilizing phantasm it becomes in Wright's story "Big Boy Leaves Home" and his poem "Between the World and Me." It functions instead as an existential challenge to be mastered and moved beyond. The metaphorical outlines of spectacle lynching, for example, surface in the celebrated Battle Royal scene of *Invisible Man*, where the narrator, wrestling blindfolded with a group of black boys while white onlookers take bets, is kicked by one white man onto an electrified carpet. "It was," he tells us, "as though I had rolled through a bed of hot coals. It seemed a whole century would pass before I would roll free, a century in which I was seared through the deepest levels of my body to the fearful breath within me and the breath seared and heated to the point of explosion."[19] When lynching victims were burned, as the black victim in "A Party Down at the Square" is burned, the ritual was often referred to by whites as a "Negro barbecue." Ellison is signifying on that ritual here: not, as Wright does, to image black abjection as a form of protest, but to dramatize the capacity of the black blues subject to resist tragedy with the help of improvisational dexterity — figuring out how to roll off the carpet without being hurt too badly. What Ellison's Invisible Man is always seeking, often without knowing it, is the half-comic insight that wrings transcendence out of misery and frustration.

Retributive violence bursts forth on the second page of *Invisible Man*, and the instrument of retribution is a blues knife, a knife deployed against oppressive whiteness with a raging sense of grievance. "Oh yes, I kicked him!" exclaims the narrator, speaking of a "tall blond man" who has called him "an insulting name" and repeatedly cursed him after the two men have accidentally bumped into each other one night on the street and begun to struggle:

> And in my outrage I got out my knife and prepared to slit his throat,
> right there beneath the lamplight in the deserted street, holding him
> in the collar with one hand, and opening the knife with my teeth —
> when it occurred to me that the man had not *seen* me, actually; that
> he, as far as he knew, was in the midst of a walking nightmare! And
> I stopped the blade, slicing the air as I pushed him away, letting
> him fall back to the street. I stared at him hard as the lights of a car
> stabbed through the darkness. He lay there, moaning on the asphalt;
> a man almost killed by a phantom. It unnerved me. I was both
> disgusted and ashamed. I was like a drunken man myself, wavering

about on weakened legs. Then I was amused: Something in this man's thick head had sprung out and beaten him within an inch of his life. I began to laugh at this crazy discovery. Would he have awakened at the point of death? Would Death himself have freed him for wakeful living? But I didn't linger. I ran away into the dark, laughing so hard I feared I might rupture myself.[20]

Knives that show up in blues literature almost always do damage, from the razor with which a "little woman" in a Mississippi juke joint slits her abusive husband's throat in Edwards's autobiography, to the knife that Levee plunges into Toledo's back at the end of *Ma Rainey's Black Bottom*, to the knife that leads Bea Ella Thornhill to get rechristened "Red Ella" after she eviscerates her faithless lover Beau Beau Weaver in *Train Whistle Guitar*. These blues-blades are instruments of a fierce passion that rarely subsides without bloodshed. The Invisible Man's knife is an exception. The hysterical laughter that wells up in Ellison's protagonist at the absurdity of his situation and causes him to run away without using his knife — a violence-dissolving hilarity — is a calculated divergence from the harsh truth of blues culture. Ellison has taken what might be called the "hardening" laughter of the blues tradition and deployed it in a way that defuses his protagonist's explosive feelings. This is a creative but fertile misreading of the tragicomic thrust of the blues.

Blues people may have told violent stories and sung violent songs that were annealed with humor, but that humor was a way of dealing with the fact that blues culture was, or could be, fearsomely violent, rippling with interpersonal grievances that mere laughter could *not* defuse. "They tell me she shot one old man's arms off, down in Mississippi," bluesman Johnny Shines recalled of blues singer Memphis Minnie, chuckling at the memory. "Shot his arm off, or cut it off with a hatchet, something. Some say shot, some say cut. Minnie was a hellraiser, I know that!"[21] This sort of blues laughter is a way of maintaining psychological equilibrium in the face of a Jim Crowed social environment rendered deadly by the double-barreled threat of white disciplinary and black intimate violence. Ellison transforms this blues laughter, in his book's opening scene, into something quite different: a psychological tool for defusing one's *own* violence. There is little evidence to suggest that this is the way blues people in the Deep South actually dealt with the rage, terror, and sadness that white disciplinary violence provoked in them. They may have sometimes grinned in the white man's face, as Levee's father grins in the face of the white men who have raped his wife, but these grins dissolved neither their aggrieved feelings nor their fantasies of violent retri-

Ralph Ellison and Richard Wright

bution. For the most part, blues people expressed their fury either by murdering the white men who had wronged them, as Levee's father does, or, more typically, by redirecting those feelings at an acceptable target—which is to say, by using guns and knives against each other in juke joints and Chicago recording studios.

Ellison's divergence from the harsh realities of blues violence in his novel's opening scene can help us see more clearly what he's trying to do in the novel's portrait of Jim Trueblood, a blues-singing sharecropper who accidentally rapes his own daughter while dreaming restlessly in the family bed one night. Ellison elides from that portrait the feelings of bitterness that Trueblood might be expected to harbor after his wife Kate has furiously attacked and wounded him, and he transforms the disciplinary violence that haunted the South in the form of "Jeeter Lester types" into an instrument of comic vengeance. The sharecropper tells the narrator and Mr. Norton how "biggity school folks up on the hill" (52)—higher-class black folk—have tried to shut him up so that he won't embarrass them in white eyes with his tale of low-down degradation. "They sent a fellow out here, a big fellow too, and he said if I didn't leave they was going to turn the white folks loose on me. It made me mad and it made me scared" (52). But Trueblood's fear of white reprisal fades in the face of profitable white fascination with his tale of dream-provoked incest. The rest of Trueblood's portrait is free from the sort of looming redneck threat that marks "A Party Down at the Square" and "Flying Home." Ellison's satiric purpose leads him to make the white folks Trueblood's "friends" and the "biggity [black] school folks" Trueblood's ineffectual antagonists, stewards of a white lynch mob that never forms.

Ellison similarly soft-pedals the harsh realities of black southern blues culture when he depicts Trueblood as a man willing to sit still and allow his own wife to beat him down. Blues musicians do not generally let blows directed at them go unanswered; the life stories of Skip James, Henry Townsend, and Leadbelly offer us hardened survivors who don't hesitate to strike back at anyone who manhandles them. But sometimes, as Honeyboy Edwards acknowledges, one's wife is delivering justified payback for one's transgressions. "Most of the time when we did fight," Honeyboy admitted, speaking to this point, "I would be the cause of it. Because I would come in drunk, jump on her sometimes. Which I had no business doing. She'd cut on me! I'd be wanting to fight and she'd cut me up! She'd be right on me with that pocketknife. I got cuts all over me. Bessie was tough; she was bad with a razor blade."[22]

Trueblood's Kate, although not Bessie's sort of natural-born brawler, levels a comically exaggerated attack on her sinful husband. Her determination to use every available object as a weapon — including, in sequence, "little things and big things," "somethin' cold and strong-stinkin'," something that sounds "like a cannonball," a double-barrel shotgun, some unnamed thing that digs into Trueblood's side "like a sharp spade," an iron, and finally an ax (61–63) — places her squarely in the blues tradition of intimate violence as expressive violence, violence that vividly communicates feelings. Ellison, in turn, forces us to look at the wounds suffered by Trueblood, including the "scar on his right cheek" (50) and the "wound" (53) around which "flies and fine white gnats" (53) swarm, in a way that connects him with August Wilson's Levee, who lifts his shirt to show his bandmates his scarred chest. Flesh wounds, in both cases, bespeak deeper emotional wounds. What Ellison doesn't offer us with Trueblood, however, is Levee's sort of violent response. Trueblood suffers his wife's blows, passively resigned. Yet he also transmutes his fate into self-acceptance with the help of the blues. One night, rejected by his family and his preacher, he gazes up at the stars and starts singing. "I sing me some blues that night ain't never been sung before," he remembers later, "and while I'm singin' them blues I make up my mind that I ain't nobody but myself and ain't nothing I can do but let whatever is gonna happen, happen." Months after the episode, living an uneasy truce with Kate and his daughter, he is also profiting richly from white folks who come by his shack to gaze at his wounds, listen to his story, and give him money. (They, Ellison wants us to understand, are the "flies and fine white gnats," ethically diminished by their voyeuristic fascination with black misery.) Trueblood hasn't just survived but prospered.

The blues are grounded in paradox — above all, the paradox that was African American life in the segregated South during slavery's long aftermath. How can one be both free and imprisoned? And how can one get by in such a world? That was the situation confronted by blues people: free in name, significantly freer than they had been as slaves, but also hemmed in by white violence, part of the brutal experience Ellison invokes in his celebrated definition. Hemmed in by family, too, as Wright and Ellison tell it. The mother and grandmother that protect you also beat you; the daughter you love is also the daughter you have somehow ended up raping in your sleep. How can the blues do justice to these painful paradoxes? It can chronicle personal catastrophe, squeeze from that tale a near-tragic, near-comic lyricism, and hope for the best, as Jim Trueblood does — beaten down, regretful, but determined to persist, whistling a bittersweet melody as he rises to confront the uncertain life that awaits him.

Ralph Ellison and Richard Wright

bar 10

The Blues Revival and the Black Arts Movement

"Look like ah, what the Klan couldn't kill, look like we gonna
let die for lack of love. Look like now we don't, we don't much
listen to ourselves, you know what I mean. We don't really
listen to ourselves any more, Mister Can't Sing Blues Black
Man, be telling me the blues is 'bout submission, shuffling,
and stuff too ugly to hang on yonder wall. But submission is
silence, submission is *silence*, and silence is NOT my song!"

Kalamu ya Salaam, "My Story, My Song" (1990)

OUR STORY, OUR SONG

A central theme of this book is that we, as a variegated contemporary global
community of people with musical and literary investments in the blues, are
dwelling, whether we're conscious of it or not, in the aftermath of significant historical and cultural developments. We're the survivors, and inheritors, of things that happened decades, and centuries, ago. The long shadow
of New World slavery hovers darkly, indisputably, over our project. In her
influential theoretical-autobiographical meditation, *In the Wake: On Blackness and Being* (2016), African American literature scholar Christina Sharpe
insists that "transatlantic slavery was and is the disaster. The disaster of Black
subjection was and *is* planned; terror is disaster and 'terror has a history' . . .
and it is deeply atemporal." Her intention, she says, is to do "wake work":
to explore "the afterlives of slavery" as they manifest in literary texts and
in the daily lives of black people. "Living in the wake," she explains, "means
living the history and present of terror, from slavery to the present, as the

ground of our everyday Black existence."[1] Sharpe's haunted vision of our contemporary moment, a Faulknerian vision in which what is supposedly past refuses to remain there but instead suffuses and suffocates the present, is part of a so-called Afro-pessimist movement within black diasporic circles. It is a blues vision shorn of comedy—much closer to Wright's than Ellison's—and it resonates with the ghastly fall from grace marked by President Obama's eight years in office: from the dream of beloved community evoked by the black First Family's triumphant election-night appearance on Chicago's Grant Park stage before a huge multiracial crowd in November 2008 through a now-familiar litany of dead young black men whose killings, beginning with Trayvon Martin in February 2012, sparked the emergence of Black Lives Matter and mass public protest.

It is no coincidence that the reemergence of black bluesism, a conscious, principled, and angry reclamation of the blues as black culture, takes place during that period. The phrase "a new black consciousness" may feel slightly dated today, evoking as it does a specific moment in the mid-1960s, but that sort of awakening, evoked by the word "woke," is what we are witnessing—not just in American society at large and in academic circles, but anywhere the blues is/are at issue. The keynote panel at the 2019 International Blues Challenge was titled "The Blues and Race"; moderated by Dr. Noelle Trent of the National Civil Rights Museum, its participants included performers Bobby Rush, Teeny Tucker, and Marquise Knox, representing three generations of prideful black blues claimants.[2] Younger black writers, including Derrick Harriell, Tyehimba Jess, Kiese Laymon, Zandria Robinson, and Kevin Young, are laying claim to the blues with directness and urgency as well. In her essay "Listening for the Country" (2016), sociologist Robinson, a Memphis native, listens deeply into the curated collection of blues CDs in her father's old truck a decade after his death, tantalized by the traces of personal and familial grief interleaved with racism and black precarity that she hears there:

> Daddy had a blues all his life that I couldn't begin to know, though I had so desperately tried to understand it as his first-born and accomplice. . . . I put on my ethnographer hat and went back to the CDs [I had burned for him] that I had found in the truck. . . .
>
> Daddy had given me a list of requests for Bobby "Blue" Bland. . . . When I first saw the list, I thought it was mighty narcissistic of Daddy to be having the blues with all he had done to Mama. But listening to that music in the wake of Daddy's death some ten years

later, I was compelled to consider for the first time the shape of Daddy's hurt—and his right to it. He had hurt Mama and the rest of us, but I had not given him space to hurt, not about anything, really, beyond a stubbed toe. His upbringing in Jim Crow Mississippi with disappearances and violences and the concomitant beatings from Big Mama Rosie. A missed scholarship opportunity because a racist counselor hadn't turned in a form. His visit to Memphis that was only supposed to be a stop on the way to St. Louis that turned out to be an entire life and abrupt death. His guilt about what he had done to Mama, or to us. His mama's death, the only time I saw him cry, and all the other people he loved who had died or gone missing. Having to tell his daughter about the hole in her child's father's head. And those women who weren't Mama. I wondered if Daddy was thinking of them when he listened to Bland sing. . . . Had they broken my daddy's heart while he was breaking Mama's? Did he hear Mama's city pain in Bland's declaration that he had a "hole where [his] heart used to be"? Or was he thinking of his own heart, and how he had turned Mama mean?[3]

This is wake work, in Sharpe's terms, work that registers the disappearances and violences that were the ground of everyday black southern existence during that period, even as it evokes a complex of blues feelings accessed through a daughter's intersubjective encounter with her father through the medium of blues recordings. "When you're talking about the blues," Jess recently told an interviewer, making a broader pitch for blues' continuing utility to black writers, "you're talking about the roots of African American literature, really the core of American literature. . . . That was the literature we had before we could read and write. And once we were allowed to read and write without the force of death being put upon us, all that imaging went right into the literature. And that's the connection between African American literature and the blues. So there's no separation between the two."[4] "When I think about blues," Harriell agrees in words that align the music with Black Lives Matter, "I think about marginalized lives. I think about black lives. . . . I don't need to go to a blues bar in the Delta to hear blues. I think that pain, that anguish, that legacy is in music right now."[5]

Today's new black consciousness, especially when it takes blues as its purview, has two important historical precedents. The first is the Harlem Renaissance, especially Hughes's manifesto "The Negro Artist and the Racial Mountain," with its invocation of "the bellowing voice of Bessie

Smith singing Blues" as a "prod" with which to "penetrate the closed ears [of] colored near-intellectuals." The second, which bears directly on our own moment and is a principal focus of this chapter, is the Black Arts Movement, a decade-long (1965–76) creative eruption that tends to be remembered not for its investments in blues but for a soundtrack anchored in jazz. Archie Shepp, Sun Ra, and Albert Ayler—jazz-revolutionist proponents of the "New Thing"—played downtown fundraisers and uptown marches for Amiri Baraka's Black Arts Repertory Theatre School in the heady spring of 1965, joining the faculty as founding members. Black Arts poets embraced saxophonist John Coltrane as a secular saint after his death in 1967, modeling their spoken-word performances on his shrieking, onrushing, freedom-yearning style to create what literary critic Kimberly Benston has termed "the Coltrane poem." Poet-shamans as diverse as David Henderson, Haki Madhubuti, Sonia Sanchez, Jayne Cortez, A. B. Spellman, and Michael Harper, made this sort of elegiac spoken-word praise-song into one of the movement's signal innovations and enduring achievements.[6]

Yet blues, a politically problematic but equally vital expressive legacy, was also a crucial instrument of racial and cultural self-definition for a wide array of Black Arts writers and their academic fellow travelers, including Sanchez, Cortez, and Madhubuti, Amiri Baraka, Larry Neal, Ron Karenga, Stephen Henderson, Ben Caldwell, Eugene Redmond, Henry Dumas, Quincy Troupe, Al Young, Stanley Crouch, Nikki Giovanni, James Cone, Kalamu ya Salaam, Tom Dent, and a host of lesser-known writers published in *Negro Digest* and *Black World* and anthologies such as *Black Fire* (1968), *The New Black Poetry* (1969), and *The Black Aesthetic* (1971). To this list might be added writers and critics such as Toni Morrison, August Wilson, Sherley Anne Williams, Ishmael Reed, Sterling Plumpp, Alice Walker, Gayl Jones, Arthur Flowers, Angela Davis, Yusuf Komunyakaa, John Sinclair, Jon Michael Spencer, Harryette Mullen, Allison Joseph, Sharon Bridgforth, and the younger black writers I've just discussed: contemporaries and inheritors of the Black Arts Movement whose work significantly engages with blues forms, blues themes, and the black ancestral "Blues God" invoked by Larry Neal. Far from being the shortest and least successful movement in African American cultural history, as Henry Louis Gates Jr. has provocatively claimed, the decade-long Black Arts Movement has had a broad and enduring impact on African American literature.[7] It has remade that literature as a blues-toned legacy—proudly invested in, and supremely conscious of, its own southern-born vernacular taproot, a survivor's ethos of self-willed mobility, self-determined sexual personhood, and bittersweetly lyric self-inscription elaborated in the face of continuing legacies of black precarity and the spiritual and epistemological failures of whiteness.

To the extent, however, that the Black Arts Movement envisioned a splitting-off of black art from white America and a purification of that separate sphere, it has indeed proved to be a failure—at least with respect to contemporary blues culture. Although the so-called chitlin' circuit of juke joints, clubs, and concert venues lingers on in the modern South, supplying a small but loyal black audience, the mainstream universe of festivals, nightclubs, bands, record labels, DJs, blues societies, websites, and internet discussion groups has grown in the past sixty years from a coterie audience of folk blues fans into a multimillion dollar, worldwide enterprise: predominantly white-administered and white-attended and, except for a modest admixture of black blues musicians on the bandstands, a palpably non–African American thing. Blues are *white* culture these days: a way a certain kind of earthy, hip, antiracist whiteness (and a certain kind of geeky, volunteerist, middle American whiteness) knows itself, and shares that knowledge with like-minded others.

The irreversible onslaught of white blues fandom and musicianship is a fact, one that some African American blues performers, indebted to such audiences for their livelihoods, have noted with a dismay that shadows the contemporary scene.[8] In one branch of blues literature, too, the rising white tide is unmistakable. The 1990s witnessed a remarkable flowering of black blues autobiographies by Sammy Price, Mance Lipscomb, Willie Dixon, B. B. King, David Honeyboy Edwards, Ruth Brown, Yank Rachell, and Henry Townsend; the next decade and a half added the life stories of Etta James and Buddy Guy. In every case, black vernacular voices were shaped into print by white ghostwriters. The very existence of such autobiographies is partly a result of the folk-and-electric Blues Revival of the 1960s, which gave performers such as Lipscomb and King access to large new white audiences, and partly a result of the traditionalist tenor of the contemporary scene, which venerated Edwards (d. 2011) and King (d. 2015) and today venerates Guy and Bobby Rush as sources of badly needed Deep South authenticity within a strange new blues world made uneasy by its own whiteness.

This world, grounded in the drama of cross-racial connoisseurship, had already become visible to black intellectuals as a cultural crisis in the early 1960s, when Amiri Baraka, then LeRoi Jones, did his best to dynamite the rails. "Old bald-headed four-eyed ofays popping their fingers," rages Clay, the wildly antagonized young black protagonist of *Dutchman* (1964), accusing white blues lovers—and by extension his slinky white seductress/antagonist Lula—of being utterly clueless about the inner life of black folk,

> and don't know yet what they're doing. They say, "I love Bessie
> Smith." And don't even understand that Bessie Smith is saying,
> "Kiss my ass, kiss my black unruly ass." Before love, suffering, desire,
> anything you can explain, she's saying, and very plainly, "Kiss my
> black ass." And if you don't know that, it's you that's doing the
> kissing. . . . If Bessie Smith had killed some white people she wouldn't
> have needed that music. She could have talked very straight and plain
> about the world. No metaphors.[9]

Lula, offended by Clay's truth-telling, stabs him in the heart shortly after this outburst and, with the help of other white passengers, hustles his warm corpse off the subway car.

Where do things stand, decades later? "Pack your bags & head to Memphis! for the Blues Foundation's BluesFirst," proclaims the website for the nation's premier blues advocacy organization:

> The ONLY International Convention and Expo for Blues Societies,
> Fans, Musicians and Industry . . . Learn Important Strategies for
> Successful
> > Blues Retail
> > Publicity
> > Studio Recording
> > Budget Preparation
> > Newsletter Production
> > Blues Radio
> > Internet Marketing
> > Grant Writing
> > Blues in the Schools Programs
> > Plus a Special Information Panel by The BMA
>
> *Includes:*
> > 3 Days of Strategy-Packed Learning Opportunities
> > > to Make Your Blues Organization Succeed
> > 3 Days of Fun, Friends and Blues Networking
> > A VIP Pass to All the Clubs on Beale Street for the
> > > International Blues Challenge Competition

The Blues Revival and the Black Arts Movement

Plus admission to:
>   Shake and Howdy Reception
>   The Keeping the Blues Alive Awards Brunch
>   Blues, Brews & BBQ Party
>   The International Blues Challenge Competition[10]

Bessie Smith would have to kill a whole lot of white people to make a dent in this particular blues world, and whether or not she "need[s] that music" has become a moot point: Marcia Ball, an older white Texas pianist and mainstay of the contemporary scene, is more than ready to cover the gig. Baraka's Lula has become a blues diva, and Baraka's Clay still doesn't stand a chance against her.

BLACK POWER AND BLUES POWER

Ironies abound on the postmodern blues scene; one of the most poignant was evoked by Kalamu ya Salaam, Black Arts poet and historian, at the end of his pithy and provocative treatise "the blues aesthetic" (1994). "Why and when," he laments, "did blues people stop liking the blues?"[11] Salaam's plaint about waning black interest in the quintessential black art form, one he had voiced four years earlier in a spoken word performance, "My Story, My Song," from which this chapter's epigraph is drawn, is not new. Although there are signs these days of a modest renaissance among younger black musicians and writers, the loss of the black blues audience remains the changing same of all blues commentary, white and black, during the past sixty years.[12] In its white incarnation it led to the founding of *Living Blues* magazine ("A Journal of the Black American Blues Tradition") by a group of white aficionados in 1970 and still animates white-run blues societies intent on "keeping the blues alive" by teaching "blues in the schools" to compliant black children. In its black version the complaint echoed through the pages of *Ebony* in the late 1950s and early '60s in articles with titles such as "Are Negroes Ashamed of the Blues?"[13] As the 1960s progressed and James Brown and Aretha Franklin became the rage, the complaint was picked up by black DJs and blues musicians such as B. B. King, who watched helplessly as the black youth audience for blues melted away. "On this particular night in this particular city," King remembered later of a soul show he'd played during the period, "the audience booed me bad. I cried. Never had been booed before. Didn't know what it felt like until the boos hit me in the face. Coming from my own people— especially coming from young people—made it worse."[14]

If by "liking the blues" one means believing in the cultural value and political efficacy of the blues, then a significant number of Black Arts poets and
theorists—the self-appointed intellectual vanguard of the blues people—
stopped liking the blues around 1965, when LeRoi Jones broke faith with
bohemian interracialism and took the A Train from Greenwich Village up
to Harlem. The integrationist tenor of Mississippi's Freedom Summer experiment the previous year, along with its Delta blues groundnote, were
swept out as Black Power angrily swept in. Fanon's dismissal of the blues in
Towards the African Revolution (1967)—a "black slave lament . . . offered up
for the admiration of the oppressors"—undergirded the Black Arts revaluation; the song-form was guilty by association with the now intolerable social conditions that had produced it.[15] "The blues are invalid," Maulana Ron
Karenga declaimed in an influential essay in *Negro Digest* (1968), "for they
teach resignation, in a word acceptance of reality—and we have come to
change reality."[16] For Karenga, Madhubuti (*Don't Cry, Scream* [1969]), Sanchez ("liberation / poem" [1970]), and others, blues were the embarrass-
ing residue of an older generation's helpless passivity, no longer useful in a
time of revolutionary transformation and expressive license. "We ain't blue,
we are black," insisted Madhubuti, deploying blues repetitions only to reject the stance of black dejection he construed them as signifying. "We ain't
blue, we are black. / (all the blues did was / make me cry)."[17] "no mo / blue /
trains running on this track," agreed Sanchez. "They all be de / railed."[18] Soul
and jazz were the sounds of the urban North: hip, inspiring freedom-songs.
"Soul music is an expression of how we feel today," black DJ Reggie Lavong
at New York's WWRL told Michael Haralambos in 1968, "blues was how we
felt yesterday."[19] Blues *could* be the sounds of the urban North, and hip in
their own fashion—white scholar Charles Keil helped clarify this in *Urban
Blues* (1966)—but for an influential segment of Black Arts proponents, blues
signified the benighted rural South: they were the cry of the slavery/share-
cropping continuum, the sorrow-songs associated with what Baraka, in *Blues
People*, had termed "the scene of the crime."[20]

Yet for another, considerably larger cohort of Black Arts writers led by
Larry Neal, the blues were something quite different: a cherished ancestral rootstock, an inalienably black cultural inheritance that could be put to
political as well as aesthetic good use. "The blues," countered Neal in "The
Ethos of the Blues" (1972),

> with all of their contradictions, represent, for better or worse, the
> essential vector of the Afro-American sensibility and identity.

Album cover for *Don't Cry, Scream* by Don L. Lee (Haki Madhubuti)
(courtesy of Archives & Special Collections,
J. D. Williams Library, University of Mississippi)

Birthing themselves sometime between the end of formal slavery and the turn of the century, the blues represent the ex-slave's confrontation with a more secular evaluation of the world. They were shaped in the context of social and political oppression, but they do *not*, as Maulana Karenga said, *collectively* "teach resignation." To hear the blues in this manner is to totally misunderstand the essential function of the blues, because the blues are basically defiant in their attitude toward life. They are about survival on the meanest, most gut level of human existence. They are, therefore, lyric responses to the facts of life.[21]

These blues are not sorrow songs but survivor songs: the soundtrack of a spiritual warriorship that refuses to say die. These blues wrest far more than their share of swaggering lyric joy out of an evil world, inscribing person-hood and sustaining the tribe in the process. "To write a blues song," wrote Etheridge Knight in "Haiku" (1968), "is to regiment riots / and pluck gems from graves."[22] Such are the blues defended and celebrated by Neal ("For Our Women," "Can You Dig It?"), Salaam ("The Blues (in two parts)"), Stanley Crouch ("The Big Feeling," "Howlin' Wolf: A Blues Lesson Book"), Jayne Cortez ("Lead," "Dinah's Back in Town," "You Know"), James Cone (*The Spirituals and the Blues*), Al Young ("A Dance for Ma Rainey"), Stephen Henderson ("Blues, Soul, and Black Identity: The Forms of Things Un-known"), Quincy Troupe ("Impressions / of Chicago; for Howlin Wolf"), Eugene Redmond ("Double Clutch Lover"), Nikki Giovanni ("Poem for Aretha," "Master Charge Blues"), Tom Dent ("For Walter Washington"), and Henry Dumas ("Keep the Faith Blues"), among others.[23]

"Blk people have done it to the english language," insisted the southern-born Salaam in "The Blues (in two parts)" (1972), making his case for the aesthetic revolution wrought by those blue-toned survivor songs. "They have niggerized it. . . . We are finding that blk poetry has to do mostly with rhythm, images, & sound. . . . Most good images come from blues, blues singers were our 1st heavy poets."[24] "The blues," proclaimed Crouch in "The Big Feeling" (1969),

> is the most important art form ever produced in America, ever, possibly in the West. Because it has the "big feeling," as John Lee Hooker says: It broke past the lie, became rudely vulgar in its exposition of truth, spit in the face of Venus de Milo (the armless bitch incapable of embrace), stumbled through the flung lye of loneliness, so often scalded walking barefoot in the glass-strewn

alleys of anguish, maimed by memories, suffering the treason against the self which is called sentimentality, but, at the end with its tongue hanging out, in love: "Dun't you want to rock?" Or, "Got a good rocking mama and the way she rock is all right!" That, is the final specificity of feeling and, of life: The woman reached, or wished for—"And say, babe, don't you remember me?" That is, the Blues to me means: No one is crushed if he, or she, can summon the strength to understand what has happened, which is identity. Therefore, B. B. King need not be threatened by white musicians, he knows who he is and knows, as we all must: "As long as you've got Black People, you'll have the blues."[25]

Theomusicologist Cone, like Neal and Crouch, defended the blues in the name of black identity-formation; in *The Spirituals and the Blues* (1972) he had one eye on those white folklorists who claimed that the blues had no real protest content and another eye on Karenga, who argued the same point from a Marxist perspective. "The political significance of the blues," wrote Cone, "is not very impressive to those who have not experienced black servitude. Neither is it impressive to persons who are fascinated by modern theories of political revolution. But for black people who live the blues, who experience and share that history with their black fathers and mothers, the blues are examples of Black Power and the courage to affirm black being."[26]

Blues Power is Black Power! Both the white folklorists and the black revolutionists, Cone argues by implication, miss the liberationist moment in blues: the way, as he puts it elsewhere in his study, the "ritual and drama" of blues performance "preserve the worth of black humanity" and "affirm the somebodiness of black people" in the face of oppression. At once functional, collective, and committed, the blues foster a continuing revolution of black spirit, excavating and purging despair—rather than surrendering to it—on a daily basis.[27]

Some Black Arts writers, most notably Baraka, articulated a multivalent vision of the blues' cultural and ideological function. *Blues People* (1963), *Dutchman* (1964), and "The Changing Same (R&B and New Black Music)" (1966) together sketch a capsule history of the evolving Black Arts attitude toward the blues: from a relatively benign index of "the Negro's" changing attitudes toward America, to a register of political impotence and aestheticized black rage ("If Bessie Smith had killed some white people, she wouldn't have needed that music"), to a rich, enduring, and endlessly inspiring black ancestral wellspring ("Blues (Lyric) its song quality is, it seems, the deepest expression of memory.... It is the racial memory").[28] Even Don L. Lee (Haki Madhubuti), who rejected the blues in *Don't Cry, Scream* (1969) as an art that "exhibits illusions of manhood" and is "destroyed" by John Coltrane's freedom-yearning ascension into "scream-eeeeeeeeeeeeee-ing," could seemingly reverse his revaluation, celebrating Delta bluesman Son House in an untitled but closely observed praise poem published in 1970:

> to himself he knew the answers
> & the answers were amplified
> by the sharpness of the broken bottle
> that gave accent to the muddy music as it screamed
> & scratched the unpure lines
> of our many faces,
> while our bodies jumped to the sounds of
> mississippi.[29]

House, a Delta blues recording star in the 1930s and early '40s, had been tracked down in the summer of 1964 by young white blues enthusiasts Nick Perls, Dick Waterman, Phil Spiro, and Nick Perls, who found House in Rochester, New York, after searching to no avail down in Mississippi. The trio put a guitar in House's hands, coaxed him out of retirement, and worked the levers of white power to get him onto the bill at the Newport Folk Festival by summer's end. With Waterman acting as his manager and booking agent, House played Carnegie Hall the following year, was featured in several documentaries, and enjoyed an entirely unexpected second act as a performer and recording artist.[30] Without those efforts, paradoxically, House would have died in obscurity and Lee would never have had the occasion to observe him in action, or write the poem that resulted.

If white blues aficionados and black poets could, on occasion, be secret sharers of the music they loved and admired, then the polarized racial climate of the period tended to preclude overt acknowledgment of that common bond. Virtually all Black Arts writers, in fact, saw white enactments of and claims on the blues as an insult and a threat, one more invidious example of cultural theft rife with minstrelsy and false consciousness. "It should come as a surprise to no one," critic Stephen Henderson told a black college audience in 1970,

> that white people have tried to usurp the concept of "Soul" and to
> dilute its meaning. That is a function of their historical relationship
> to us, and that relationship has been parasitic, cannibalistic....

The Blues Revival and the Black Arts Movement

The history of our national music, i.e., so-called serious music, the history of popular music, the history of the American popular theatre, would be pallid indeed without the black energy and forms which were appropriated from us, and which we have foolishly called "contributions" to American culture. This is only now becoming clear, only now being publicly admitted. . . . The Janis Joplins of this world, and the Mike Bloomfields, and the Laura Nyros, and the Tom Jones' are merely carrying on a time-honored tradition of swallowing the nigger whole. They are cultural cannibals. But how do you deal with the sickness?[31]

The sickness to which Henderson's polemic refers is the Blues Revival, which by 1970 had shifted into high gear and by 1971 had been officially certified in Bob Groom's slim monograph by that name.[32] Henderson's jeremiad, which was seconded in the writings of Don L. Lee, Ron Welburn, Calvin C. Hernton, and others, makes clear the degree to which the Black Arts Movement's desire to reclaim and define the blues as a black cultural inheritance rather than a Negro "contribution" to American culture was being pressured by the truly daunting emergence of a mass white blues audience—an audience no less galvanized, it must be added, by established black performers such as B. B. King and Muddy Waters than by white insurgents such as Joplin and Bloomfield. The white culture industry seemed determined to overwhelm any Black Arts separation-and-purification scheme by capitalizing on white omnivorousness for the music, recasting black ancestral lines of descent in a way that seemed anathema to black aesthetic radicals. "Paul Butterfield worships Muddy Waters," inveighed Ron Welburn in his essay on black music in *The Black Aesthetic* (1971),

> who has never had so much money in his life. In fact, a black fathers/ white sons syndrome is developing. A Chess label album cover pictures a black god giving the life-touch, a la Michelangelo, to a white neo-Greek hippie in shades. This is part of the Euro-American scheme. The black music impetus is only to be recognized as sire to the white world; a kind of wooden-Indian or buffalo-nickel wish. A vampirish situation indeed!
>
> . . . African-Americans should continue to move as far away from this madness as humanly possible, spiritually, psychologically, and in the immediate physical sense at least. . . . Black music should not be allowed to become popular outside the black community, which means that the black community must support the music.[33]

Fathers and Sons (1969) was the title of a highly successful double LP that paired Muddy and Otis Spann with Butterfield, Bloomfield, Sam Lay, Donald "Duck" Dunn, and Buddy Miles: four black guys and three white guys, but also three fathers (Muddy, Spann, and Lay) and four sons, which is to say a thread of black ancestral connection in the person of Miles, a point obscured by the album's iconographic cover art.

The "shoulds" and "musts" that mark Welburn's jeremiad are a holding action in the face of a troubling and indisputable social fact: the young white audience for blues had swelled to fill a vacuum created by a vanishing young black audience. Even younger black intellectuals such as Henderson, enamored of the blues and angered at white borrowings, were forced to admit this. "About three years ago," he chided a black college audience in 1970, "I wrote a short article in which I lamented the seeming indifference of young black people to what I call the most characteristic feature of black cultural life—the blues."[34] Like Welburn's jeremiad, Henderson's address at Southern University in New Orleans was an attempt to drum up black community support for an art form that suffered as many negative connotations within the race as it enjoyed positive (and profitable) ones out in the wider world. The black blues musicians themselves, as Welburn is too honest not to note, followed the money trail. "Until the mid-1950s," observed *Time* magazine in 1971, "the music of Muddy [Waters] and his fellow bluesmen was marketed as 'race music' aimed almost exclusively at black communities. Today his new audience is largely young whites; Muddy now makes 20 to 30 college appearances a year, and he plays mostly in white clubs and theaters. For one thing, says Muddy, young whites are more responsive. 'The blacks are more interested in the jumpy stuff. The whites want to hear me for what I am.'"[35] "Yes, the blues is alive and well, all you people," Hamilton Bims informed his *Ebony* readers in 1972, before cataloging the ways African American performers were oppressed by crime, class snobbishness, and shifting cultural politics within their own communities:

> Indeed it is the subject of a worldwide craze. Blues performers are toasted in Europe and at open-air festivals from Monterey to Newport....
>
> Chicago bluesmen have had their crosses to bear. Many are respected, even idolized in Europe—yet the places that await them when they venture back home are often dungeons of violence and the paychecks are absurd. They have also been the victims of an intraracial snobbery—a legacy of the times when the blues was

The Blues Revival and the Black Arts Movement

the property of contemptible old men hawking dimes on a street corner. Urbanized blacks have tended to deprecate the blues in favor, initially, of contemporary jazz and more recently that ethnic amalgam described as "soul." The blues is often seen as an Uncle Tom expression, a cowardly admission of impotence and despair; while the "positive" projections of the James Brown school are viewed as infinitely more consistent with the current black mood.[36]

Even as Black Arts poetry readings and theatrical troupes were flowering in urban centers and on college campuses across the country during the late sixties, even as Crouch, Al Young, Tom Dent, and other young poets were crafting praise songs to blues performers such as Howling Wolf, Ma Rainey, and Walter "Wolfman" Washington, there remained a fundamental disconnect between the younger black generation and their blues-playing elders. Was this merely a black variation on the period theme, "Never trust anybody over thirty"? Yet the burgeoning white youth audience for blues not only trusted those elders, it venerated them in a way that most black kids — except that segment of the Black Arts vanguard — didn't begin to. As late as 1969, after his remarkable success at the Fillmore West had certified his star status in the eyes of young whites, B. B. King could tell an interviewer, "I've never been asked to appear at a black college."[37] Junior Parker, according to cultural historian Michael Haralambos, hungered for but never achieved the sort of crossover success King, Waters, and Albert King had enjoyed; "the title of his last LP, 'You Don't Have To Be Black To Love The Blues,' shows he was still trying to break through to that audience."[38] If the title of Parker's 1974 album says little about Parker's real designs on the mainstream market and much about his record label's marketing strategy, then it makes painfully clear just what sort of pressures the Blues Revival was exerting on a black folk/popular form that Black Arts poets and theoreticians were intent on defining *away* from grasping whiteness and mainstream Americanness, away from capital-driven exoticism of the sort that Hernton lambasted in *Black Fire*: "Ray Charles, Mahalia Jackson, Lightning Hopkins, Little Richard — sex, soul, honkytonk! — it all represents something that will turn white folks on, something that will gratify their perversities."[39]

To further complicate the cultural politics of the moment, 1969 marked the birth of the Ann Arbor Blues Festival: the first major blues festival held in North America, featuring Muddy Waters, B. B. King, Lightnin' Hopkins, Junior Wells, Howlin' Wolf, James Cotton, Otis Rush, T-Bone Walker, Luther Allison, Magic Sam and Son House. It also marked the emergence,

Album cover for *You Don't Have to Be Black to Love the Blues* by Junior Parker
(image courtesy of Archives & Special Collections,
J. D. Williams Library University of Mississippi)

in the festival's program notes, of an ideology of self-conscious white blues universalism. The specter of "black rage," evident on both college campuses and in the urban riots inventoried by the Kerner Commission Report (1968), had clearly roused the anxieties of white blues aficionados about the possible bad faith attendant on so thoroughgoing a white embrace of a black art so closely identified with the oppression of blacks by whites. White anxiety compensated by insisting on the black social provenance of the blues (no white folks at *these* origins!), even while elaborating a narrative of popular music's "roots" in the blues and naturalizing the ascendance of contemporary white blues performers to a position alongside their black elders and peers. "Somewhere in this headlong rush of publicity and profit," a certain Habel Husock informed Ann Arbor festivalgoers,

The Blues Revival and the Black Arts Movement

contemporary music has stumbled on its roots in a joyous reunion. What that means is a full-fledged revival of the blues, the unique music of the American black man that has infused popular music with its echoes of Africa, slavery, and rural and urban poverty. . . .

The blues evolved in the secret culture of black America; a pure, ethnic form of self-expression. (Blues was neither invented by a Columbia recording engineer nor by the Cream). . . .

. . . The blues is alive and very well — it cannot be relegated to history for it continues to answer needs for man and has come to reach an audience much larger than a ghetto bar, a new audience which has recognized in itself the same passions and emotions that found their form in blues. The blues grows continually in the artistry of such men as James Cotton, Junior Wells and Buddy Guy. Many faithful white musicians refine the blues and mold the blues to suit the emotions of their backgrounds further, blues has been a launching pad for jazz riffs and improvisations.[40]

Husock is happy to grant Black Arts theoreticians their racial-ancestral claims — blues as "a pure ethnic form of self-expression" that evolved as "the secret culture of black America" — but only in order to clear a space for his universalist claims about "new audience[s]" outside the ghetto and "faithful white musicians" who "refine" and "mold" the blues. It was these latter sorts of sentiments, not merely antithetical to the ethnic-consolidationist project of the Black Arts Movement but an insult to black intelligence — was Janis Joplin really *refining* Big Mama Thornton's blues? — that justifiably infuriated Henderson, Welburn, Hernton, and Lee. "Our music," wrote Lee in 1970,

is being stolen each and every day and passed off as another's creation — take Tom Jones and Janis Joplin, two white performers who try to sing black. They've not only become rich, while black musicians starve in their own creation, but those two whites, plus others — who are at best poor copies of what they consider black — will, after a short period of time become the *standard*. It will get to the point where when you speak of soul and black music, you will find people automatically thinking of white imitators.[41]

Whether or not Lee's prophecy about white imitators has, in fact, come true in our own day is debatable. The white blues audience's hunger for what the Europeans are fond of calling "real black blues" has, if anything, grown stronger in recent decades; Buddy Guy, Taj Mahal, and other headliners on the mainstream blues circuit command premium prices, and the European festivals (Burnley, Notodden, Blues Estafette) are notorious for preferring lesser-known black blues artists to rising white stars such as Kenny Wayne Shepard and Samantha Fish. At the same time, it is possible to find blues festivals advertised in the pages of major American blues publications such as *Blues Blast* and *Blues Festival Guide* in which six of the eight acts are all-white or contain a single black member, making white blues the acceptable de facto norm, if not exactly the standard.[42] Often that token black member is a drummer or bassist, but not infrequently he is the Old School legend, the aging or elderly master—W. C. Clark, Henry Gray—backed up by willing white apprentices. Black fathers and white sons all over again, staging rituals of fellowship and reconciliation.

BLUES AIN'T NOTHING LIKE IT USE TO BE

Or are they symbolic transfers of cultural power in the service of profiteering white universalism? Once the fathers die, after all, the anointed sons take over; guitarist Bob Margolin makes a living these days on the basis of having played behind Muddy Waters in the early 1970s. The white blues audience today seems only too happy to embrace the actual children of deceased black blues legends—Shemekia Copeland, Bernard Allison, Big Bill Morganfield—as performers in their own right, and the last few years has seen the emergence of a new cohort of younger black male artists, both electric and acoustic, including Gary Clark Jr., Jerron "Blind Boy" Paxton, Marquise Knox, and Mr. Sipp, among others. But there was no way that Black Arts spokesmen could have anticipated these particular plot twists in the late 1960s. It was the white blues-kids, cultural interlopers and harbingers of the future, who bedeviled them. "For the 1970s and beyond," insisted Welburn in "The Black Aesthetic Imperative," "the success of political, economic, and educational thrusts by the black community will depend on both an aesthetic that black artists formulate and the extent to which we are able to control our culture, and specifically our music, from theft and exploitation by aliens."[43]

At the height of the Blues Revival, black anxiety and annoyance at the displacement of black people from blues performance was an understandable response to a combination of factors: not just the swelling white audience and shrinking black audience for the music, not just the emergence of white blues stars such as Joplin and Butterfield but also the historical parallel offered by the rock 'n' roll "cover" phenomenon of the 1950s (Pat Boone and Bill Haley profiting off the songs of Fats Domino and Big Joe Turner), and the rapidly evolving ideology driving the revival—a putatively antiracist, universalist ideology based on "feeling the blues," an ideology that cleared space for white participation by either rejecting privileged black claims on the music or asserting them with a fervency that hoped to fend off black nationalist objections. In the former case the ideology might be summarized, "Now that we play the blues, we have made them our own"; in the latter case, "Now that we listen to your blues, we feel them as intensely as you do."

Exhibit A in the former case was journalist Albert Goldman, author of a *New York Times* article headlined "Why Do Whites Sing Black?" that Henderson vigorously deconstructed before his college audience in 1970:

> When he [Goldman] waxes ecstatic about Stevie Winwood, whom he calls "Super-Whitey No. 1," who pretended that he was "Ray Charles crying in an illiterate voice out of the heart of darkness," we see finally what it is all about. White people really understand black people and black culture better than black people, so why shouldn't they get the credit. Thus Stevie Winwood, "Attaining a deeper shade of black than any dyed by Negro hands . . . became the Pied Piper of Soul." And Paul Butterfield has created "a new idiom," which is "half black and half white," and has "done for the blues what no black lad could do—he has breathed into the ancient form a powerful whiff of contemporary life." So there you have it. If that isn't plain enough, Goldman ends his article with the following statement, which really shows the extent of his perversion.
>
>> Next Friday night at Madison Square Garden, Janis Joplin and Paul Butterfield will lock horns in what should be the greatest blues battle of recent years. The audience will be white, the musicians will be black and white, and the music will be black, white and blue, the colors of a new nation—the Woodstock Nation—that no longer carries its soul in its genes.
>
> That is as plain as it has to be, for Goldman is sanctioning the use, the exploitation of black music for white nationalist purposes, without really owning that the music still belongs to us at all. And the technique of expropriation is plain—detach the music from its cultural context under the guise of liberalism and integration, then ZAP them niggers again.[44]

One may feel, as I do, that Paul Butterfield was a true innovator — one of the few white blues instrumentalists who extended the tradition rather than merely ventriloquizing his black influences — and at the same time share Henderson's assessment of Goldman's invidious fatuity here. That fatuity is a byproduct of Goldman's hyperbolic style: he burlesques Winwood in the original article even as he celebrates him ("a fey pixie, who looks as if he was reared under a mushroom"), and he characterizes Joplin as "this genera-tion's campy little Mae West."[45] Yet Goldman, precisely by virtue of his tact-lessness, asks all the right questions about the musical miscegenation that marked the heated late sixties moment at which the Black Arts Movement and the Blues Revival came to loggerheads:

> Driven apart in every other area of national life by goads of hate and
> fear, black and white are attaining within the hot embrace of Soul
> music a harmony never dreamed of in earlier days. Yet one wonders
> if this identification is more than skin deep. What are the kids doing?
> Are they trying to pass? Are they color blind? Do they expect to
> attain a state of black grace? Let's put it bluntly: how can a pampered,
> milk-faced, middle-class kid who has never had a hole in his shoe
> sing the blues that belong to some beat-up old black who lived his life
> in poverty and misery?[46]

Goldman shrewdly frames the Blues Revival in the context of racial polariza-tion — a polarization abetted by (if not reducible to) the Black Arts Move-ment's dedication to, as Larry Neal put it, "the destruction of the white thing, the destruction of white ideas, and white ways of looking at the world."[47] It seems entirely plausible, in fact, that the passion which drove white blues fans into the "hot embrace" of musical blackness as the sixties progressed was in fact an anxious response to the hot, angry *rejection* of white patronage, white solicitude, and interracial fraternity by a politicized blackness mani-festing variously as Black Power, the Black Panthers, the Black Aesthetic, the Black Arts Movement, and *Black Rage* (1968). In the black blues recordings with which they established private rituals of communion, in the black blues artists who were delighted by (if sometimes also puzzled and unnerved by) their adulatory attentions at clubs and festivals, white blues fans during the Black Power years made a separate peace with blackness of a sort that ideo-logically driven public tensions (not to mention the Kerner Commission's celebrated warning about the emergence of "two societies, one black, one white — separate and unequal") made almost impossible in any other civic setting. *Blues Power,* the title of albums by Albert King (1968) and Eric Clapton (1970), was, by this reading, a kind of anxiety formation against Black Power. *The World of Blues Power!* and *Blues Power, Vol. 2*, bestselling Decca compilations in 1969 and 1970, were anthologizing integrationist responses to the anthologizing separatist calls made by *Black Fire* (1968) and *The Black Power Revolt* (1968).

For all his trash-talk about "the white thing," it was *Black Fire*'s coeditor Larry Neal, alone among his Black Arts peers, who was willing to entertain the idea that the Blues Revival's white audiences might testify to the power and universal reach of black music. "Even though the blues were not addressed to white people and were not created by white artists," he told Charles Rowell in 1974, "when white people heard the blues they knew it was a formidable music."[48] But of course the blues were being *played*, if not precisely created, by a sizeable cohort of white performers by the time the sixties drew to a close: what had begun at the Newport Folk Festival in 1963 as a charmed encounter between superannuated, somewhat exoticized black country bluesmen and an audience of white folkies had metastasized by 1968 into Eric Clapton and Cream transforming Robert Johnson's "Cross Road Blues" into sheets of sound at the Winter Garden in San Francisco with the help of banked Marshall amps and hallucinogens. It had also morphed into Jimi Hendrix's "Voodoo Child" version of the same New Thing. Musical miscegenation was a two-way street in the late sixties; Black Arts sensibilities betrayed considerable unease about what seemed like treacherously shifting blues ground, a postmodern hall of mirrors in which blue-eyed blues people were determining the idiom's prevailing feeling-tone and those few younger blacks who had embraced the blues seemed to be losing contact with their essential blackness. James Thompson's poem "Media Means," published in *Negro Digest* in 1969, clearly signifies on the media-driven "scene" that embraced both Clapton and Hendrix:

> . . . speaking
> to Young Blacks
> whom MEDIA has made
>   BELIEVE
> that a Black Blues Chord
> played by BLACKS
> is an
> ACID ROCK TUNE
> that White imitation
> of a very black feeling/

I was forced to scream:
INTEGRATION IS DREADFUL
when you don't control
the media which makes
ZOMBIE/ISM a constant
condition.) IT SELLS IMAGES —
imitations of REAL
and REALITY imitates
       IT:
Black folks imitating
        white folks
        who
        imitate
        THEM![49]

"Blues done gone and got / Americanize," complained poet Mae Jackson in a similar vein, also in *Negro Digest* (1969):

tellin' me that I should
stay in school
get off the streets
and keep the summer cool
i says
blues ain't nothing like it use to be
... and the folks singing it
ain't singing for me
no more.[50]

Both of these poems sing the Blues Revival blues, voicing in the first-person "I" a collective black sense of outrage, enervation, and loss: loss of a familiar low-down blues-home safe from the encroachment of whiteness. Jackson's vernacular voice reconstructs that home as a complaint against blues-singing white interlopers and their co-optive liberal platitudes — or, more precisely, against a comprehensive whiteness that manifests as *both* blues singing and platitude-mongering. "The Black Arts Movement," Neal had famously declared a year earlier, "is radically opposed to any concept of the artist that alienates him from his community."[51] Means and Jackson embody this creed — their own black community orientation is evident — but the song they sing is a lament about their alienation from a brave new blues world that no longer speaks to or for them. Does their complaint sound familiar?

For both the Blues Revival and the Black Arts Movement's engagement with blues, 1970 was a watershed year, a transitional moment in which two very different social formations suddenly came into uneasy alignment. One index of this shift was *Living Blues*, a mimeographed newsletter featuring lengthy interviews with black blues musicians founded that year in Chicago by a group of seven young white journalists, oral historians, and proponents of French surrealism. What made the magazine unusual and controversial was an editorial policy that hewed to a black aesthetic critique of white blues later summarized by Paul Garon, one of the founders: "For those interested in the support and study of African-American culture, blues as purveyed by whites appears unauthentic and deeply impoverished; further, it too often represents an appropriation of black culture of a type sadly familiar. Finally, it can be economically crippling to black artists through loss of jobs and critical attention."[52] Each of these statements was a half-truth. The flailing, gravel-voiced, minstrelsy-tinged excesses of Janis Joplin could and did coexist with the preternaturally wise—and black-mentored—blues stylings of Bonnie Raitt, who took pains to acknowledge and share stages with her mentors; although middling rock-blues boogiemen such as Canned Heat and Alvin Lee may indeed have made more money than they deserved off of black-authored blues songs, black bluesmen such as B. B. King and Muddy Waters found the loss of the black youth market far more economically crippling than any such white appropriations, and were gratified by their sudden ascension into the mainstream. What was significant, in any case, was the emergence of black aesthetic radicalism among young white blues fans. Larry Neal's call for the destruction of the white thing had drawn an unexpected response from his self-declared white allies.

Neal himself was hard at work on his black bluesist reclamation project: in the January 1970 issue of *Negro Digest*, he used his review of Phyl Garland's *The Sound of Soul* to celebrate B. B. King's achievement in terms that constituted an implicit rebuttal of Ron Karenga's dismissal of the blues in the magazine's pages two years earlier. "We are the continuation of Black memory," Neal insisted,

> our songs are the emanations of that memory; our rhythms the force
> that drives that memory.
>   Bessie Smith sang: that the meanest folks in the whole wide
> world lives on Black Mountain. She was singin' 'bout niggers, evil and

bad but surviving in spite of everything. Nigger/Black. Black music/
niggers/the "nigger" in the music being its dominant force. . . .

But it is nigger energy that will rule. B. B. King has more to tell
me about the world that I can use than most poets and intellectuals.
Here he is talking to Phyl Garland:

> "*Blues* is B. B. King. Yes, and I've been a crusader for it for 21
> years. Without this, I don't think I could *live* very long — not that
> I think I'm goin' to live a long time anyway, but I don't think I
> could live even *that* long if I had to stop playin' or if I couldn't
> be with the people I love so, the people that have *helped* me so
> much. . . . I couldn't live! I try to give them a message. I try hard."

How many of us are so dedicated to whatever it is that we do?
How many of us commit ourselves so thoroughly to our work? How
many of us link our work to the survival of both ourselves and our
people?

> . . . *We will write our own scriptures.* We will seek validation of the
> truths that we sense must exist in the holiest work of each one of us.
> From spirits like B. B. King, Jimmy Reed, Son House, James Brown,
> Smokey Robinson, Moms Mabley . . . an ethnic [*sic*] will be fashioned
> whose fundamental truths can be denied by no one. . . .
>
> . . . New scriptures are in order. New mythologies. New
> constructs: Black Music as the Model for the Black Nation. . . .
>
> We are a new species of Man, child. Liberation will come out of
> honky-tonk bars, gut-bucket blues, and the meanest niggers that have
> ever walked the planet. (Saw Bobby Blue Bland singing Uptown.
> He had on silver dashiki *and* his process.) The current Soul Music
> explosion illustrates the mass culture of Black America is still strong;
> and still dominated by the eternal spirit of the Blues God.[53]

According to Neal, not only don't King's blues teach resignation, as Karenga
had insisted, but they powerfully respond to Karenga's call for revolutionary black art: they are functional, collective, and committed — as committed as soul music, which the blues underpin spiritually and aesthetically as "the eternal spirit of the Blues God." In the figure of soul-crooner
Bobby Blue Bland, sporting Afrocentric clothes and a blues-identified hair-
style, Neal finds a way of dissolving the seeming contradiction between
the ancestral African origins, the gut-bucket New World transformations,
the freedom-demanding soul extensions, and the pan-African revolution-

ary consciousness that together constitute the black aesthetic in his eyes. "He was compelled by the evolving/changing critical discourse of his era to go through changes," Houston A. Baker Jr. notes of Neal, "but in the synapses of all those connections made with Western thought were sounds of an African/Caribbean/New World/Afro-American/Funky-But-Downhome/ Journeyed-Back/Gut-Bucket/Honky Tonk changing same called the blues. . . . He was a pivotal figure in the evolution of a vernacular, blues theory of Afro-American expression in the United States."[54] Neal's Blues God was an emblem of black cultural survival— "the god that survived the middle passage," as he put it in a 1978 interview—but also a god of native lyricism, one inflected by the race's American oppressions. "We are *an* African people, but we are not Africans," Neal insisted in "New Space: The Growth of Black Consciousness in the Sixties" (1970): "We are slave ships, crammed together in putrid holds, the Mali dream, Dahomey magic transformed by the hougans of New Orleans. We are field hollering Buddy Bolden; the night's secret sermon; the memory of your own God and the transmutation of that God. You know cotton and lynching. You know cities of tenement cells."[55]

It is striking to compare Neal's 1970 statements with the program copy for the 1970 Ann Arbor Blues Festival and realize that the Blues Revival, too, was struggling to articulate a version of the Blues God: an ancestral source, indisputably black, yet one in which whites as well as blacks could be baptized. The 1970 program, Exhibit B in the evolving ideology of blues universalism, relinquished Habel Husock's claims of the previous year that faithful white musicians could refine the blues. This year the ideological core wasn't "Now that we play the blues, we have made them our own," but "Now that we listen to your blues, we feel them as intensely as you do." What the festival organizers felt more than anything was a sense of mourning for the pantheon of black blues performers who had died since the previous year's festival and whose photographs and capsule biographies were featured in the program: Kokomo Arnold, Slim Harpo, Earl Hooker, Skip James, Magic Sam, and Otis Spann. "Their deaths," wrote the organizers, "have left a vacancy in our hearts that will never be filled."[56] One might, if one wanted to be irritable, dismiss such effusions as an updated version of the plantation sentimentalism that accompanied the death of a faithful black slave: sadness for the passing of the Old Negroes imbued with nostalgia for an integrationist/ paternalist idyll that had been exploded by black social assertiveness in the Black Power era. Or one might decide that real family feeling across racial lines is being evidenced: a beloved black-and-white blues community. Or both. (In this book, as I've made clear, I'm trying to hold down the space between black bluesist skepticism and blues universalist idealism.) The roots of the modern "keeping the blues alive" movement, in any case, are visible in the 1970 Ann Arbor Blues Festival program, along with a surprisingly forceful articulation of the black aesthetic:

> The Blues will never die. We of the Blues Festival Committee whole heartedly believe this, but we also accept that time changes everything, even the blues. The Ann Arbor Blues Festival is set up as a tribute to an American musical genre that has been part of black culture in this nation since slave days. It is from and of the black experience. Those who bemoan the passing of the so-called rural blues fail to realize that the same intensity and feeling is apparent in the blues that pour from the black urban community today. The blues are the same — only the problems are different. . . .
>
> We of the festival hope to achieve, as last year, a true rapport between the audience and the performing artist. This shouldn't be too difficult as this year's show contains some of the greatest blues acts around.[57]

"The black experience," a linguistic marker deployed in the Black Power era for the anti-assimilationist assertion of black singularity, is bent to different ideological purposes here. A critique is implicitly being leveled, for one thing, at folk blues purists such as Alan Lomax and Samuel Charters who had famously denigrated urban blues artists such as B. B. King as too commercial — and whom Charles Keil had skewered so effectively in *Urban Blues*. Hip white blues aficionados, these program notes suggest, fall into Larry Neal's camp: they groove to the Blues God's unities rather than engaging in silly cultism. But Neal's claim about the Black Arts Movement's being "radically opposed to any concept of the artist that alienates him from his community" has also been stealthily reworked here: what had been a description of the black performer's organic relationship with his *black* public has been transformed into a prophecy about the black performer's relationship with what would turn out to be an almost entirely *white* festival audience. What guarantees the "true rapport" between black performer and white audience is a seemingly effortless marriage between black artistry and the emotional response such artistry compels. The social solvent here is white blues feeling, understood as the evoked and adequate correlate to black blues power. Such feeling celebrates a pantheon of black blues gods only to explode the idea of a black nation: an integrationist rather than ethnic-consolidationist ethos. It is counterrevolutionary to the core — if by revolutionary you mean intent

James Cotton and fans at the Ann Arbor Blues Festival, 1969
(© Tom Copi / San Francisco)

on forging a close bond between black performer and black community of a sort that discourages or precludes white participation.

It was perhaps inevitable, amid so much ideological struggle, that black blues promoters with sensibilities shaped by the Black Arts Movement would stage their own Blues Revival event. "The Washington [D.C.] Blues Festival held in November 1970," according to Michael Haralambos, "was the first blues festival produced by blacks for blacks. According to the press handout it was "an attempt to return blues to the black community given that many white interests have exploited the music at the expense of many of the black musicians who will be performing.'"[58] The lineup was a treasure-trove of black cultural riches: Luther Allison, Libba Cotton, Sleepy John Estes, Buddy Guy & Junior Wells, Richie Havens, J. B. Hutto, John Jackson, B. B. King, Furry Lewis, Mance Lipscomb, Fred McDowell, Muddy Waters, Rev. Robert Wilkins, and Howlin' Wolf. The multiday event announced its departure from mainstream festival practice by kicking off, on Thursday evening, with what *Jazz Journal*'s correspondent characterized as "the volatile and exciting African Heritage Dancers and Drummers[, who] began by taking us back to the African motherland in the highly skilled and rigorous performance of ceremonial dances of West Africa."[59] This prideful framing of the blues as a New World extension of African musical practice was new—a logical extension, perhaps, of the Pan African Cultural Festival in Algiers the previous summer, which had been attended by at least one blues-loving Black Panther, Stokely Carmichael.[60] New, too, was the venue: Howard University, which made the festival, according to *Jazz Journal*, the first such event to be held on a black college campus. What was also new, and at the same time uncannily familiar for black blues advocates during the Blues Revival, was the spectacle of Black Art overrun by white blues fans. "Topper Carew," reported the *Jazz Journal*,

> (Director of The New Thing Art and Architecture Center which sponsored the event) had hoped to instill pride and interest in the cultural heritage of a 76% black communtiy [*sic*] of Washington by presenting the blues—the raw-boned music which so essentially encompasses the experience of the black man in America.
>
> Sadly, only a small percentage of blacks were in attendance, sprinkled amongst a predominantly white, hippy crowd who came to listen to the blues and dig the overall scene. The blues are created by blacks but are apparently supported by whites! The magnetic grip of the soul genre, tawdry in comparison with the rugged purity instrinsic [*sic*] to the blues idiom perhaps has its slick hooks in the young generation of blacks. Or maybe with the growing black pride, the blues are all too unpleasant reminders of a wishfully forgotten past; and understandably so.[61]

What to make of such a flagrant sociological paradox? If such an event, carefully framed to enable the unembarrassed participation of a politicized young black audience, had failed to draw such an audience, or much of any black audience, it would seem hard to continue to rail, as Stephen Henderson had railed a few months earlier on a different black college campus, against white "cultural cannibalism." In this case, the culture cannibals shored up *somebody*'s profit margins, and not a white man's.

THE BLUES IS ALRIGHT

What is the shared legacy, finally, of the vexed and unacknowledged partnership between the Blues Revival and the Black Arts Movement? One might argue that the disco craze of the mid-1970s helped undo both social formations, dissolving the dirty realism of the former and the ethnocentric advocacy of the latter in a multiracial bath of depoliticized beats-per-minute. The truth, somewhat more complex, allows for a pair of striking generalizations about the past fifty years:

The Blues Revival and the Black Arts Movement

1. White blues fans and musicians have taken blues music—including an ever-shrinking cohort of black blues elders—and run with it, letting (blackened) white blues feeling blossom into blues societies, blues festivals, blues magazines, blues instructional videos, and the like.

2. Black blues writers and cultural custodians, unable to prevent these proliferating appropriations, have taken their stand on the printed page; black literature has become the locus of a fresh, wide-ranging, and profound re-engagement with black ancestral and post-soul blues, a cultural legacy that is effectively off-limits to white writers.

White folks came away from the sixties with the music, in short; black folks came away with the talking books. (White folks also came away with the ghostwriting credits for a series of black blues autobiographies—a genre that requires them selflessly to suppress their own voices so that the voices of their black subjects may emerge.) The result in our own day is a curiously bifurcated blues culture in which hardcore white blues aficionados who can easily list Robert Johnson's recorded sides (including unreleased alternate takes) and various rumored burial sites draw a blank when literary works such as "The Weary Blues" and *Their Eyes Were Watching God* are mentioned; a culture in which younger black poets who can name a dozen poems by Langston Hughes, know enough about Albert Murray to reject his cultural politics, and are hip to Jess, Kevin Young, and Harryette Mullen, will draw a similar blank when two of blues music's brightest young black stars, Jarekus Singleton and Marquise Knox, are mentioned.

Such sweeping generalizations, true as they may be, obscure significant local exceptions. One of these is poet and former White Panther John Sinclair, whose volume, *Fattening Frogs for Snakes: Delta Sound Suite* (2002), takes a series of interviews with black blues musicians gathered by white journalists over the years and transforms them into a kind of documentary free verse, so that Sinclair's own poetic voice disappears for long stretches into the voices of Howlin' Wolf, Sonny Boy Williamson, Robert Junior Lockwood, Bukka White. "The book," insists Amiri Baraka in his foreword, a helpful authenticating document in this post–Black Arts era, "is not a Homage to the Blues, it is a long long long blues full of other blues and blues inside of them. John all the way inside, and he got the blues."[62] A white man has written a literary blues beyond color, it would seem, but also a blues securely anchored in a griotic ambition to sing the black ancestors—Sinclair's, Baraka's, ours.

Another exception — in this case, to the hoary truism that blues is no longer a black popular music — can be found in the soul blues scene in Mississippi. In the fall of 2002, shortly after moving down from New York, I attended a heavily advertised show in Canton, a northern suburb of the state capitol. By my count, I was one of four whites in a crowd of perhaps 3,000 blacks, all of whom had come to spread lawn chairs on the dirt infield of an indoor rodeo facility and groove to heavy-rotation soul blues stars Sir Charles Jones ("Love Machine"), Marvin Sease ("A Woman Would Rather Be Licked"), Peggy Scott-Adams ("Hot and Sassy"), and Willie Clayton ("Call Me Mr. C"). The endless round of Chicago shuffles and revivalist acoustic fingerpicking that mark the post–Blues Revival mainstream were conspicuously absent, but blues — as a timbral and microtonal vocabulary, a harmonic home, a familiar place that an otherwise conventional soul composition could suddenly go — was very much in evidence. "Do you mind if I sing you some *blues*?" Clayton demanded of the crowd midway through his exhilarating set. "Do you mind if I throw a *hurtin'* on you?" The deafening roar, the hands raised in willing testimony, the brisk CD and T-shirt sales I noticed later at Clayton's merchandizing table, all suggest — as *Living Blues*, to its credit, has been insisting for some time — that blues music for certain sectors of the black community is alive and well, albeit in a form that the mainstream can't quite bring itself to acknowledge *as* blues.

A final paradox begs to be considered. The revitalized black market for blues that I've just described, roughly thirty-five years in duration, can be traced to two releases, Z. Z. Hill's "Down Home Blues" (1982) and Little Milton's "The Blues Is Alright" (1984). Both songs, twelve-bar shuffles of the sort that white blues audiences and musicians had been keeping alive through several decades of black popular neglect, were also, with their roots-and-pride ethos, the answer to a prayer sung by Black Arts spokesmen Neal, Henderson, Welburn, and Karenga: black art for the black community. Both songs were functional, collective, committed to self-respect and spiritual uplift. They were and are popular with whites, too: once they'd broken through, Little Milton worked the mainstream as well as the soul blues circuit, and made a good living doing it; Bobby Rush currently does the same thing. The title of Milton's song, in fact, was the official motto in the congressionally certified "Year of the Blues" (2003). *The blues is alright*: not quite the revolution many thought they were having, way back when, but still an achievement worth noting. The Blues Revival and the Black Arts Movement, unacknowledged coconspirators, did indeed transform our world.

par II

Giving It All Away: Blues Harmonica Education in the Digital Age

My primary means of employment for the past two decades—my day gig, in musician-speak—is teaching English and Southern Studies at the University of Mississippi. I've written a handful of blues-focused books over the years, including a couple of academic monographs, a memoir, and a novel. But I've also been a blues harmonica player for more than forty years, and my life in and around blues music has taken many forms. I've been a busker in Europe and America, including four years on the streets of Harlem, and I still play the occasional street fair. Like every journeyman, I've played countless concerts, club dates, and restaurant gigs, plus dozens of festivals from New Orleans to Neuchâtel. I've taught blues harmonica in a range of settings, from private lessons and small group classes to lecture-style workshops and jam camps, and I've organized and produced a Mississippi-based event, Hill Country Harmonica. I've recorded ten albums, both duo and solo projects, and produced half of them, along with the debut by a young African American harmonica player from Memphis whom I'll be talking about later.

Yet in terms of global impact, my various investments in the blues are dwarfed by what happened when, more than decade ago and quite by accident, I decided to take my blues harmonica teaching ministry into the world of digital media. Back in February 2007, when YouTube was still a wild and commercial-free frontier, I decided to upload a video with the title "Blues

Harmonica Secrets Revealed (Gussow.ooo)," in which I proclaimed my intention to "give it all away"—every last bit of carefully guarded esoteric knowledge and spiritual guidance I could muster. On the digital end I was an utter novice. I had no idea how wireless networks worked; my wife and I didn't even have internet access, much less a router. But when I stood outside my rental house in Oxford, Mississippi, with my new MacBook, I was able to find something named Belkin hovering obscurely over the power lines, and when I pressed YouTube's upload button and waited for ten or fifteen minutes, I suddenly had a video on YouTube. One video led to more—forty videos in forty days, a deluge that seemed to delight the rapidly accumulating subscribers to my Dirty-South Blues Harp Channel as much as it surprised me—and the videos kept on coming. That was the beginning of my long and implausible voyage as a digital-age blues harmonica educator and web entrepreneur.

More than 500 videos later, my YouTube channel has 20 million views and 70,000 subscribers. But YouTube and the roughly 100,000 monthly hits it delivers to my videos is only half the story: the free half, so to speak, since none of those views makes me a cent. I used too many copyrighted blues recordings early on, showing my subscribers how to copy cool licks, and have, in YouTube administrative parlance, been "disabled from monetization."[1] If you search the phrase "blues harmonica" on Google, you'll find a website that I created back in April 2007, ModernBluesHarmonica.com, hovering somewhere on the first several pages. According to Google Analytics, Modern Blues Harmonica, in calendar year 2018, had 137,000 discrete users (i.e., individual visitors) and more than 750,000 page views from 192 different countries and territories around the world, including 35 of the 54 countries in Africa. The website makes a little money, although not as much as a competent full-timer would surely extract. I sell blues harmonica video lessons for $5 and my own hand-drawn tablature sheets—simplified musical notation—for $2. My prices have remained unchanged since 2007. Giving it all away on YouTube exists side by side with extracting a modest profit: the creed of the journeyman musician and small-scale entrepreneur. Composing hand-drawn tab sheets is time-consuming work. Often my tabs consist of twelve or twenty-four bars' worth of a harmonica solo by one of the black or white greats—Big Walter Horton, Junior Wells, Paul Butterfield, Kim Wilson—that I've painstakingly pulled off a recording and notated. Sometimes my tabs consist of beginners' songs of my own invention, with introductory melodies designed to usher raw beginners through the door. As web-based businesses go, Modern Blues Harmonica is a quirky, creaky, one-off little operation with information-stuffed pages that look ten years out of date and are drastically in need of redesign.

I haven't written about my life as a digital-age blues harmonica teacher before now, perhaps because the spirit of market-focused entrepreneurship that undergirds the profit-accruing half of it seems jarringly at odds with the reflective, service-oriented creed that drives my work as a university-based intellectual. But there is a way, I think, of bringing those two worlds together: by investigating blues harmonica education as both a practice and an ideological investment; as something that teachers and students "do," in a range of ways, but also as a business enterprise that might be interrogated on racial grounds.

Who am I, as a white man, to profit from the blues with the help of digital technologies? As Gil Scott-Heron might say, *that* particular scenario ain't no new thing—and yet it *is* a new thing, this teaching of blues harmonica on a global scale through the medium of free YouTube videos and low-cost downloadable videos and tabs. I have students in every corner of the world, men (and a few women) I've never met who claim me as their teacher and copy my video improvisations with a skill that astonishes me: KomsonBlues in Hainan, China, or Predrag Antic from Bosnia-Herzegovina.[2] Yet it's worth noting, again, that what I'm dispersing and profiting from isn't "black music" in any straightforward sense but a polyglot jumble of melodies drawn from the past sixty years' worth of blues harmonica history, a black-and-white pantheon that I've transcribed, adapted, and supplemented with my own inventions. The experiment I'm conducting is radical and open-ended, one in which I've been joined by a gaggle of other internet blues harp teachers from around the world, and none of us has any idea what its long-term effects will be. This seems like a good moment to take stock of the near-term effects. In particular, I'd like to think critically about how people used to learn blues harmonica and how that process has been changed by digital technologies.

The broader sociological context for this change is of course the widely noted whitening of the mainstream blues world over the past sixty years. Interviewed by *Newsweek* in 1969 about his recent performance at the Fillmore West in San Francisco, B. B. King expressed astonishment at the rapidity of the change. "The last time we played there it was 95% black in 1963," he said. "This time it was 95% white. I was shocked."[3] But King was also delighted—moved to tears, in fact—by the embrace of this new audience.[4] Even as black youth abandoned the blues for soul music during the 1960s, younger white blues musicians, including harmonica players Paul Butterfield and Charlie Musselwhite, were suddenly making their presence felt, and white audiences, for the most part, were happy to embrace that whiter shade of blues with the same ardor they brought to the black originals. At this point, in the second decade of the new millennium, one can find local blues scenes, complete with musicians, audiences, and jam sessions, in almost every corner of the world. (Google "Vietnam blues club" and you'll find the Facebook page for an affinity group called the NOLA Blues Club Saigon, with news of an upcoming live show featuring the BBQ Blues Band at Snap Cafe in Ho Chi Minh City.) Blues has been transformed in the last half century from what had for many decades been primarily a black folk and popular music into a global subculture. In purely numerical terms, African American blues audiences and musicians have been swamped by a mongrel sea of blues-playing, blues-loving, non–African American others.

By uploading free lessons to YouTube and selling videos and tabs off my website for the past decade, I've helped further this development. Like their Black Arts brethren of another era, some contemporary African American blues musicians are alarmed by the continuing expansion of blues music's audiences, the increasing heterogeneity of its performing cohort, and the loss of black cultural stewardship that this process represents. Such change is a threat, as they see it, to the core values of the blues, a threat grounded in the erasure of the very history—painful, suffered-for black history—that helped bring the music into being. Sugar Blue's statement at the 2012 conference on "Race, Gender, and the Blues" at Dominican University, a Chicago-area hotbed of black intellectual resistance to the music's appropriation, remains a touchstone for this point of view. "This is a part of my heritage in which I have great pride," he proclaimed, invoking the blood-debt he owed to enslaved ancestors who had suffered the scourge of whips, guns, knives, chains, and branding irons. "You cannot and will not take this music, this tradition, this bequest, this cry of freedom and dignity from bloodied, unbowed heads without a struggle."[5] In a subsequent statement to journalist Howard Reich, Blue slightly softened his pushback, making a space for passionate white investments in much the same way Larry Neal had, even as he reiterated his warning against those who would decontextualize and/or claim ownership of the music:

> There are a lot of people that love the blues but know little about its origins and have no concept as to how closely it is tied to the black experience. . . . The fact that it has become universal is a wonderful thing, because it says how important and influential and powerful this music is. But it must be remembered that though you are

Blues Harmonica Education in the Digital Age

welcome to the house, do not try and take the home. Come on in, visit, enjoy, do your thing. But remember whose house you're in.[6]

Blue's statement encapsulates the paradox of our contemporary moment: a moment when a sense of black community ownership of the blues, blues as a vital ancestral inheritance, is in tension with the music's global spread, its use-extension into countless non–African American communities that are in the process of mastering the music as best they can and making it a part of their own developing cultural inheritance. Should we celebrate this change, or condemn it? Should we embrace the postmodern globalization of the blues as a kind of progress, a victory for blues music as a cultural form, or critique that global spread as a crisis of cultural expropriation and dilution, a tragic erasure of the burdens and meanings of black history as lived by the music's originators and encoded into the very fabric of the music?[7]

MASTERS AND APPRENTICES

One way of beginning to answer that question, I suggest, is to pay close attention to the way blues harmonica education has changed over the years. Here I hope to sidestep ideological disagreements by swerving toward lived experience and the specifics of knowledge transmission. Both my scholarship in blues autobiography and my own musician's life convince me that there is what might be called an old-school process of blues education, one best expressed by analogy with the skilled trades. There are apprentices, journeymen, and masters. The young blues wannabe, of whatever age, seeks out a master and says "Teach me." Or, alternately, the master identifies the promising apprentice and says, "I can teach you." Ideally, both things happen in a dance of mutual convenience and the apprentice's education commences. This old-school model, which held sway for many years in the predigital world and still carries significant force in our own day, was both grounded and local: learning depended on face-to-face, fully embodied encounters between master and apprentice, and such partnerships were generally struck up in specific locations on the blues highway where talent, old and young, tended to gather, especially towns and cities with active blues scenes like New Orleans, Memphis, Chicago, and Clarksdale, Mississippi. In some cases the master and apprentice set off together on the road, the older musician guiding the younger musician, showing him the ropes and profiting from his presence as a sideman. The word "protégé'" means "protected." The protégé is the protected one who flies under the master's wing. Eventually, at some critical moment of arrival, the apprentice becomes a journeyman and is certified by his master and the public as such. Not yet a master but no longer an apprentice, the journeyman blues performer realizes, *knows*, that he is capable of lighting out on his own.

I'm using a masculinist vocabulary here because the world of blues-playing men is the world I know, but the educational process I'm describing can be applied to female performers as well; Bessie Smith's approach to the blues, for example, was profoundly shaped by the time she spent touring in a tent show with the older Ma Rainey. If we move back beyond 1960 into a black southern blues world before the dawn of "white blues" and its attendant dilemmas, we find a mentoring process that proceeded unevenly, sometimes harshly. Guitarist Big Joe Williams took on Honeyboy Edwards as his apprentice in 1929 — "Joe was the first man that learned me how to hustle on the road," Honeyboy told an interviewer — and the two men spent a profitable nine months traveling down through Mississippi to New Orleans. But "Joe started drinking heavy in New Orleans," Honeyboy remembered. "I was young, I didn't weigh but 110 pounds, and Joe started wanting to fight me. So I slipped off and left there walking."[8] Later, standing on a bridge in Bay St. Louis, Mississippi, and entertaining passersby, Honeyboy discovers that he can make money playing solo guitar, without Joe, and becomes a journeyman in that moment. Although Honeyboy's blues apprenticeship involves a certain amount of formal musical instruction — the partnership begins, in fact, when Big Joe first watches young Honeyboy play guitar and says, "I can learn you" — the education process is as much about how to *work* the music, how to travel with it and make money with it, as it is about how to play it.

This is old-school, hands-on blues education. Honeyboy's bumpy but fruitful apprenticeship is a gentleman's handshake, however, compared with that of harmonica player Junior Wells, who described to an interviewer the brutal way Sonny Boy Williamson taught him about the blues when he was an ambitious tween in the mid-1940s:

> I had asked him about teachin' me somethin' and he say, "Where's your harp at?" I took it out and showed it to him. He took it and throwed it on the ground and stomped it. He said, "That's not a harmonica." He said, "You gotta go get one. And you gotta buy me a drink." I say, "Okay." So I went up there to the drugstore and I got me a Marine Band and I come back and I brought him back a half pint of whiskey. 100 proof Granddaddy. He said, "No. What do I look like to you? Some little boy or something' another?" And I said, "No."

He say, "I need a fifth." I went and got that fifth and brought it back to him. And he took the drink of it, big drink of it. Drink him some more and he sat down and went to blowin' the harp. He said, "Now, I want you to listen to this." So he blowed it and I tried to play it. He said, "You know what?" I say, "What?" He said, "Now, I'm gonna show you one more time." And he did. And I did the same thing. He said, "You know what? You ain't never gonna learn how to be nothin' or do nothing' with your dumb ass. And you know what else? You see that bottle of whiskey you bought?" He say, "You bought it, right?" I said, "Yeah." And he say, "And it's mine." And he took his knife out and licked it and laid it down there by his bottle of whiskey, said, "And if you touch it, you little bastard, you, I'll cut your damn throat. Now get up and get the hell away from me."

Man, nothin' ever hurt me before like that before in my life. I told him, "You just doin' this to me 'cause I'm a kid, but if I was a grown man you wouldn't do that to me." He said, "Well, I did it. Now get out of my face." I cried, that hurt me to my SOUL. I said, Lord Jesus. And, ah-oooh, man, I was more determined then I was gonna do it.

Wells headed north to Chicago and pursued his education with a vengeance on the streets and in the clubs. One evening a few years later, Sonny Boy showed up at a Blue Monday jam at Theresa's Lounge and offered to buy Wells a drink. Wells was furious:

I said, "Let me tell you one thing. Don't mess with me. Just leave me ALONE." He said, "I know what's wrong with you. You mad with me about what I said to you and the way I treated you a long time ago, right?" And I said, "Yeah." He said, "Well, listen at you now. You learned how to play. And you're doin' it right. I'm proud of you." Said, "Now just think. If I had a' babied you around you still wouldn't be blowin' the harmonica. Do that make sense to you?"

And I'll be damned, it just run through my head just like that, said boom! He's right. I said, "You're right." He said, "Well, come on and have a drink then. Now treat the next son of a bitch that come up and tell you to show him something, treat 'em like I treated you. [Laughs] The dumb son of a bitch'll learn somethin' then." I was proud of him then, you know. 'Cause he was right about it. I probably wouldn'ta.[9]

There's no love lost early on between the young blues wannabe and the older bluesman, and yet blues education does take place—inspired mentoring, one might even say, although others might call it the cruelest sort of hazing. Regardless, a musical and spiritual lineage is created. At the appropriate moment, face-to-face, Sonny Boy anoints Junior not just as a journeyman but also as his successor, someone who, in some appropriate future moment, will rough up, bluesify, his own young and naive apprentice.

What happens to this old-school model of blues education in the 1960s and '70s? One thing that happens is that young white blues players begin to show up in black blues scenes that are themselves in the process of adapting to an influx of white blues fans, and black blues elders, for a range of reasons, begin taking on these young white men as apprentices. Many of today's white blues elders, players like Rick Estrin, Steve Guyger, and James Harman, Charlie Musselwhite, Paul Oscher, Rod Piazza, and Kim Wilson, had transracial mentoring relationships of this sort with blues harmonica players like George "Harmonica" Smith and guitarist/bandleaders like Muddy Waters and Jimmy Rogers. As with the previous generation of black harmonica players, locale critically inflects the mentoring process: blues-rich cities like Chicago and Memphis remain vital centers of blues harp activity, but Los Angeles becomes a staging area because Smith relocates there—Piazza and the late William Clarke, his protégé, gigged frequently with him—and Austin enters the picture thanks to one particular blues club, Antone's, founded in 1975, which gives Wilson, harpist in the house band, the chance to back up his mentors Muddy and Jimmy in the course of extended residencies. "To have all those guys that you listened to on records all those years while you were playing, for them to treat you like an equal," Wilson has said, "that's success. I really think I'm one of them. In fact, I *know* I'm one of them. . . . They made me one of them. I can never pay them back for what they did for me."[10]

What we hear in Wilson's words isn't just a sense of earned pride in his accomplishment and gratitude for the lessons he's been taught by his African American heroes and mentors but also something like a heritage claim: a white bluesman's insistence that his transracial mentorship has culturally blackened him in a way that secures him a spot in the grand lineage of blues harmonica. Black history isn't something Wilson is making a claim on; in that respect, his heritage claim is quite different from that of his black peer, Sugar Blue. He's making a claim based on lived and earned *proximity* to blackness, rather than on lived blackness, and on a wealth of shared experience on and off the bandstand: a history of interracial fraternity among blues musicians made possible by the transformations wrought by the civil rights struggle.

Kim Wilson and Muddy Waters
(courtesy of the photographer, Kathy Murray)

Wilson's blues harmonica education, as he understands it, is anchored in the ethos put forward by the Reverend Martin Luther King Jr.: a "solidarity of the human family" which recognizes that "we are tied together in the single garment of destiny, caught in an inescapable network of mutuality."[11] Wilson's transracial apprenticeship carries the integrationist spirit of the 1960s forward into the '70s and beyond. In this respect it is markedly different from the fierce, in-group hazing that Junior Wells received at the hands of Sonny Boy. Cultural knowledge is still being transmitted face to face in this brave new blues world, older men are still mentoring younger men into the blues life, blackness is still pressingly relevant, but it's a kinder and gentler educational process all around. (A black bluesist might respond, of course, that an older black man like Muddy Waters would have been reflexively disinclined to slap around a younger white man, in Chicago or elsewhere, thanks to the prohibitive penalties that accrued to such behavior in the segregated South, where he'd been born and raised.)

BLUES HARP AND THE NEW OLD SCHOOL

I'm seven years younger than Kim Wilson. In blues harmonica generational and educational terms, we're a world apart. When I bought my first harmonica in 1974 at the age of sixteen, a white kid from the suburbs of New York City, I knew nobody else who played—nobody except Magic Dick of the J. Geils Band, a Jewish guy with an Afro whose recorded harmonica stylings on an up-tempo instrumental called "Whammer Jammer" I was determined to decode and master. I had never been to a blues club, never heard or seen an actual blues musician. So I did what culturally challenged white guys across America did back then when they had a hankering to learn blues harmonica: I bought a copy of the coolest available instruction manual at the local mall, a book called *Blues Harp* (1965) by a tough-looking white guy named Tony "Little Sun" Glover. The shadowy, oddly framed cover photo showed the long dark fingers of a black man in a suit holding a harmonica to his lips. Glover's voice on the page was gruff, knowing, a little edgy—the voice of a hipster, a disreputable Kerouackian uncle—and incredibly comforting because of that. On my very first day as a blues harmonica player, I had a mentor and guide. All the players Glover profiled were older black men, a pantheon of greats that would quickly become my own. All the songs he broke down into tablature were drawn from them.

Here, it now seems apparent, was the next stage in the evolution of blues harmonica education: blue-blackness at second hand, rendered as written text rather than living song, and in the voice of what we might now call a white Negro: a white guy who'd lived the life and earned his way deep inside the music, or seemed to have done so. The master/apprentice relationship I established with Glover's book, although vividly real to my sixteen-year-old self, was disembodied and abstract: a second-order simulacrum of the on-stage partnership Kim Wilson had enjoyed with Muddy Waters, and a third-order declension from the vicious hazing that Sonny Boy had given Junior Wells when Junior was my age. Glover couldn't reach out of his book's pages and slap me around—but his voice *could* reach out and make demands on me, hip me the finer points, and confuse me in a way that led me deeper into the mystery of the blues. "At first," he advised me,

> you'll probably model your style after your favorite harpman, and try to sound as much like him as you can—and that's cool, because you need a sound and technique to aim for. But you should look beyond that. Say that Sonny Terry is your man, and you've worked and practiced and sweated until you've come close to his sound—now you can sit back, take a deep breath and grin at yourself. You sound like Sonny. Now why not go the next step and sound like yourself?
>
> After all, Sonny already sounds like Sonny—and he *is* Sonny.

Blues Harmonica Education in the Digital Age

And you ain't. But you're something he's not—and that's *you*. You've got your own ideas, scenes and perceptions. Why not play your own sound? That's one thing that nobody else can or will do for you.[12]

What I did with what Glover had given me was strictly up to me, as it was up to each of his book's many readers. *Blues Harp* couldn't take me all the way. But it was a start. Among other things, it pointed me toward the records I began to buy at my local mall, jam along with, and copy licks from: black players like Sonny Terry, James Cotton, and Little Walter but also other players—white guys—I found in the blues section, like Paul Butterfield and Charlie Musselwhite. My disembodied blues masters.

Still in print today, Glover's *Blues Harp* established the paradigm for blues harmonica education as distance education as it currently manifests in digital media: a massive open online jumble of teaching videos offered primarily by white journeymen of various degrees of competence willing to share what they know with whomever cares to watch, often for free but sometimes for a modest fee. In terms of blues lineage, Glover is my white hipster daddy. When I inaugurated my YouTube ministry in 2007, declaring my intention to "give it all away," I was working within the Gloverian tradition—except, of course, I was now the heir apparent to Tony Glover, not his youthful apprentice. And I wasn't charging a cent.

How I went from apprentice to journeyman is its own unlikely story. Suffice it to say that ten years after I first picked up a harmonica and long after I'd given up my ambition of becoming a serious blues player, a personal crisis led me to plunge back into music, determined to master my instrument, unburden my heart, and make my mark as a performer. At that point, quite unexpectedly, I was given a chance to live out the old-school model of blues education thanks to the intervention of two older black men: Nat Riddles and Sterling "Mr. Satan" Magee.

I met Nat, six years my elder, on the streets of New York one night in the spring of 1985.[13] He heard me wailing as I paced uptown on Amsterdam Avenue, then swung his cab into a U-turn and yelled at me out the passenger window, grinning as though we already knew each other. A generous, thoughtful, and singularly charismatic man, Bronx-born, who told tales of Sugar Blue's epic one-man street performances and Kim Wilson's dazzling stagecraft, Nat was, from my star-struck perspective, the embodiment of blues harmonica tradition. The sounds he produced were strident, swinging, complexly layered; they were like nothing I'd heard up close, filled with nuances I'd never encountered on the records I owned. Nat pointed me toward John Lee Williamson — the first Sonny Boy, not the second — and demanded that I learn Big Walter Horton; I'd somehow managed to bypass both players, even though they appeared in Glover's book. I took several sit-down lessons with Nat, then chased him down outside an East Village blues bar called Dan Lynch one afternoon and played him what I'd learned as he drank from a brown-bagged forty-ounce malt liquor. Lynch's was his home base, the place where he gigged and hung out. That locale, with its endless Sunday jam sessions and glad-handing interracial fraternity, now became my second home as well. Nat worked the sidewalks of the Village that summer with his guitarman, Charlie Hilbert, as a duo he called "El Café Street"; he made me sit in, applauded my efforts, and certified my modest achievements with a bottle or two of Heineken. Then, at summer's end, he disappeared. He'd been shot in the chest outside Lynch's, people told me, after a lover's spat or a drug deal gone bad.

Over the next six years, until he died of leukemia at age thirty-nine in 1991, Nat and I evolved from master and apprentice into friends. He not only transformed my blues harmonica playing, so that some of his distinctive sound worked its way into my own, but he made the blues real to me, offering me a living, breathing exemplar that no thumbed-through book or copied record possibly could. In part because his own friends, lovers, guitarmen, and harmonica heroes were white as well as black, Nat lived his blues ministry like a prophet of blues universalism, refusing the temptation to reify "black blues" and "white blues" in a hierarchy of authenticity or legitimacy; he just wasn't interested in making those sorts of heritage claims. As he was fond of pointing out, several of his own teachers, Bob Shatkin and Lenny Rabenovets, were Jewish guys from Brooklyn. He stole licks and techniques from everybody, without apology; he made the music into his own thing and demanded that I do the same. His willingness to share freely of his knowledge made him an ideal mentor; he laid the groundwork not just for my later decision to share my knowledge on YouTube but also for a specific mentoring role I would play in a young black harmonica player's life. His periodic crises and disappearances, painful as they were, schooled me in the sense of loss that it is the job of the blues musician to confront and overcome.

Since I've written at length about my second blues master in a memoir called *Mister Satan's Apprentice* and spoken earlier about how he schooled me in the blues ethos, the briefest of summaries will have to suffice. Sterling Magee, when I first encountered him on a Harlem sidewalk in 1986, was a gray-bearded fifty-year-old who played guitar, stomped on a hi-hat cymbal, and shouted the blues with intimidating ferocity. His name, bystanders told

Blues Harmonica Education in the Digital Age

me, was Mister Satan. He called himself that; everybody called him that. Awed by his power and brilliance, determined to connect with him, I returned the next day with my harmonicas, microphone, and battery-powered amp. I sat in with him on a long jam and we drew a larger crowd as a duo than he'd drawn as a one-man band. From that moment on, as though fated, we were partners. Sterling was Mississippi-born and Florida-bred. Buoyant with Harlem spirit, he'd already lived a long and peripatetic life when I met him, one that involved several deceased wives and a nervous breakdown half a dozen years earlier that led him to renounce his birth name for his current name. He was on the upswing these days, as was I—I'd finished my first year of study with Nat—and we were, we both sensed, exactly what each of us had been looking for: a powerful and charismatic blues master in my case, an energetic and willing accomplice in his.

For the next four years we worked that same outdoor spot in Harlem, giving me a priceless opportunity, as Mister Satan's protégé, to deepen my blues education with the help of a demonstrative black audience, including a circle of older men who brought fold-up chairs to our daily concerts and became the amen corner we could count on. In 1991, the year Robert Johnson's reissue CD went platinum, Mister Satan and I suddenly got picked up by major management—the devil-at-the-crossroads thing made us an easy sell, apparently—and for the next seven years we were a national touring act and a *Living Blues* cover story, until Sterling had another breakdown and, like Nat, disappeared down South for a while.

What lessons can be drawn from this brief narrative of my own blues apprenticeship and the larger story of the evolution of blues education? I'll offer three. First, the apprentice/journeyman/master model has managed to survive the marked whitening of the blues scene over the past fifty or sixty years, although the specific contours and texture of that culture transmission process have modulated as white apprentices have entered the picture. Second, as the relative number of African American blues elders diminishes, the apprenticeship model, if it is to survive in America and around the world, will find ways of expanding to encompass *non*black blues elders: men of a certain age who've lived the life and know the music, not just white guys but Japanese guys, Chicano guys, whomever the local subculture considers worthy—and women, too, like my friends Roxy Perry and the late Big Nancy Swarbrick, tough but nurturing harmonica-playing bandleaders who have been important mentors in the New York metro scene.

Third, precisely because blues music is an African American inheritance, and a vital one, the blues educational process will always value a teaching lineage that connects present-day students, white as well as black, with African American masters. My Jersey-born friend Deak Harp served his apprenticeship with James Cotton back in the 1990s—following him on the road for five years, hanging out backstage, living in his Chicago basement, then driving his van for another six years. Cotton's huge tone is audible in everything Deak plays, but he's got his own distinctive sound as well, a repetitive, groove-centered growl in which he doubles his harp lines on a homemade diddley-bow guitar. Now, as a contemporary (white) master relocated to Clarksdale, Mississippi, Deak has accumulated his own protégé, a young Indiana relocatee named Carson Diersing. Cotton finally passed away in 2017, but his lineage will continue in part thanks to people like Deak and Carson. Even as Corey Harris angrily denigrates white interlopers in his *Blues Is Black Music!* blog, even as he journeys to Mali in search of Ali Farka Touré and other African roots-music masters in whom to anchor his own ancestry, he is teaching blues guitar to all comers, white as well as black, on the video-centered distance-learning platform Sonic Junction, creating a new generation of blues players who will someday invoke him as a mentor. In racial and aesthetic terms, lines of descent within the contemporary blues educational world are more tangled than they've ever been. Whether or not that's a good thing—and I sincerely believe that it is—it's certainly a new thing: a distinctive feature of our postmodern musical moment.

Before discussing my own endeavors in web-based blues harmonica education, I should say a few words about three of my professional peers, a cohort that might be termed the "new old school." All of them have websites through which they solicit gigs and sell CDs and other merchandise, but all of them also rely on the traditional model of fully embodied, face-to-face mentorship, often in group contexts. Billy Branch (b. 1951), a three-time Grammy nominee based in Chicago and a contemporary of Nat Riddles (b. 1952), is the best known and the only African American of the three. He, too, is in the lineage of James Cotton—and Big Walter and Junior Wells and Carey Bell; he learned firsthand from Chicago's best—and he is eloquent testimony to the fact that the white guys, plentiful as they've been in recent decades, haven't yet displaced their black peers from center stage in the cultural transmission process. Billy has been teaching blues in Chicago's largely black public schools for almost forty years, passing along the tradition in that way, but his teaching ministry is ecumenical and international, extending to Europe, South America, Asia, and Mexico. "Branch has delivered his empowering curriculum to students all over the world," proclaims his website, noting with an accompanying photo that "the Ford Foundation funded a

2 week [Blues in the Schools] program in Xalapa, Veracruz, Mexico to demonstrate the common legacy of African-American and African-Mexican cultural roots." He has no equal as a player and teacher.

Yet Branch is, for all that, an exception to the general trend, which is that white men dominate the blues harmonica instructional market in our postmillennial era. David Barrett (b. 1973), a teacher, performer, and author based in San Jose, California, describes himself as "the world's leading expert in blues harmonica education" and "the world's most published author of blues harmonica lesson material," and it's hard to dispute those characterizations.[14] Mentored by Gary Smith, a white Bay Area harmonica legend who was himself mentored by Charlie Musselwhite, Barrett can in turn take credit for mentoring one of today's best young players of color, Mumbai native Aki Kumar (b. 1980). (I discuss Kumar's unusual career arc in the final pages of Bar 12.) A longtime columnist for *Blues Revue* magazine and the e-zine harmonicasessions.com, Barrett founded Harmonica Masterclass in 1994, organizing a series of multi-pro-celebrity-player weekend workshops that drew up to 250 registrants at a time. By 2002 he had organized his teaching ministry into a full-blown School of the Blues, offering individual and group classes, and BluesHarmonica.com, a website launched in 1999 that aggregated and promoted his various activities, merchandise, and publications, including book/CD packages and videos such as *Basic Blues Harmonica Method* and *Building Harmonica Technique*.

Jon Gindick (b. 1948), ten years older than me, first achieved notoriety for a self-published book, *Country & Blues Harmonica for the Musically Hopeless* (1984). A California native with a shambling, bear-hugging Big Lebowski persona, Gindick has published half a dozen other harmonica books since then and bills himself as "the best-selling music instruction author in the world."[15] In 2003 he pioneered the concept of harmonica jam camps, four- and five-day retreats costing roughly a thousand dollars in which coaches interact with campers in a range of individual, small-group, big-lecture, and performance settings. Between 2006 and 2009, I taught at ten of Gindick's camps—St. Louis, Jacksonville, Virginia Beach, Dallas, then half a dozen in Clarksdale, Mississippi, where he has purchased a refurbished sharecropper's shack as a second home.

Jon has a gift for making anybody, of whatever age, sex, race, or talent level, feel brave enough to stand up at a jam session and wail their head off. Essentially he views the harmonica as a tool through which he can conduct workshops in personal empowerment. He hasn't, to my knowledge, been mentored in the old-school way that Deak Harp, David Barrett, and, in an earlier generation, Kim Wilson and Rod Piazza were mentored—although Gindick did convince B. B. King to back him up on several songs in his 1987 instructional video, *Country & Blues Harmonica for the Absolute Beginner*. From my perspective and for all his virtues, he lacks grounding in the stylistic and attitudinal orientation of the African American blues tradition, at least as I came to know those things during my doubled apprenticeship.

But who am I to talk? Relative to Wilson, Piazza, and Barrett, I'm strictly a part-time lightweight. I never had the cool, stylish, greased-back, vaguely dangerous look that real blues harmonica pros were supposed to have, nor did I have the serious music-school training, including the ability to sight read, that enabled Barrett to write all his books. By temperament, I'm a modernist, not a traditionalist—the fruit of my years with Sterling, who took great pride in his originality and demanded that I do the same. Like Sterling, I wanted to kick the blues forward into a new place, not keep the music anchored in a white hipster's dream of 1950s Chicago. It was for this reason, among others, that I made my move on YouTube. In some perverse, not-fully-thought-through way, I hoped that my promise to "give it all away" would break the clubhouse wide open, flood the inner sanctum with light, and rout the white traditionalists once and for all. But I also felt, more altruistically, that somebody had to serve the players of the future in an online context, sharing the fruits of their professional experience in the virtual world, and that just wasn't happening.

BLUES HARMONICA SECRETS REVEALED

In February 2007, YouTube was a very different place than it is now. It was strictly noncommercial; the website's terms of service insisted on that.[16] Monetization—the incorporation or overlay of ads into videos—hadn't yet been introduced. Where blues harmonica was concerned, it was more like a picked-over steam table than the world's largest big-block video library. There were several dozen grainy videos of the African American greats— James Cotton, Sonny Boy Williamson, Carey Bell—and some vintage amp bench tests by a German player named Harpsucker. Gindick was there with his "Jamcamp06" channel, strumming guitar and tooting. Ronnie Shellist, an Austin-based journeyman, had uploaded a half-dozen jam-along-in-your-bedroom videos, including one called "Funky Blues Harmonica" that had 20,000 views then and has more than 2 million now. That was pretty much it.

So, stumbling blindly forward, powder-kegged with energy, I set up my

Sony videocam, made a video, and uploaded it. By labeling it "Blues Harmonica Secrets Revealed (Gussow.000)," I announced my disruptive intentions and committed myself to a course of action. I had no thought of financial gain and I was explicit about my guiding ethos, which I'd taken from Lewis Hyde's 1983 classic, *The Gift: Imagination and the Erotic Life of Property*. "A gift only lives if you give it away," I announced in my thirty-eighth video, six weeks in.[17] I had 792 subscribers by that point, and the comments and emails I'd received told me that I had indeed found my public. "The reason I'm giving you guys these lessons on YouTube," I said, mentioning my maiden voyage as a sixteen-year-old with Tony Glover's book, "is because I wish that *I* had had somebody who knew how to play, who knew how to teach, who had thought through and lived with this stuff for a long time, to come along to *me* when I was desperately searching for information, to give me his personality, to give me his knowledge, to give me whatever wisdom he'd learned in the course of his blues and life's journey." I mentioned how important Nat Riddles had been to my own development. I finished up by directing my subscribers toward a trio of good teaching websites: gindick .com, harmonicalessons.com, and bluesharmonica.com. Maybe Gindick and the others would make a few dollars from the mention. I was happy to help out.

Then, just as I'd reached equilibrium, everything broke open again. It started when my subscribers said, "We want to give you money. A tip, as thanks." It hadn't occurred to me to ask for donations, but the busker in me was intrigued. I searched the terms "build website" and found Macwebsite builder.com, which offered an idiot-proof template and a ten-day free trial. I picked the first domain name that came to mind and managed to create a cheesy-looking homepage. I rented a P.O. Box and—because several overseas subscribers insisted on PayPal, something I'd never used—I signed up for the service and figured out how to put a "donate" icon on the homepage. Then, because YouTube's terms of use forbade any sort of advertising or commercial use, I put on my ratty old busker's hat and a bright red Hawaiian shirt and made a video in which I informed my subscribers, tongue in cheek, that I had just founded a new church, the Joyous Disciples of Blues Harmonica Anarchism, and would be happy to accept donations. I held up large-font signs on which I'd typed the relevant real and virtual addresses. I figured I'd take whatever trickled in, then kill the website before I got charged.

Over the next seven days, $700 worth of donations flooded in. My PayPal account suddenly resembled an international depository. Tens and twenties fluttered out of hand-addressed envelopes cluttering my new P.O. box, but most people preferred instant electronic largesse. I was floored. Giving it all away had led to *this*?

Then I had what felt like a staggering insight, although it seems trivially obvious now, more than a decade later, when ideas about the disruptive power of digital technologies and the dematerialization of books, movies, and recorded music have played themselves out on a grand scale. The old model of retail blues harmonica education back in 2007, if you didn't have a local pro, was books, CDs, and DVDs. You put a $15 or $20 check in the mail, and somebody—a top pro like Jerry Portnoy, who played for Muddy— sends you back what you've ordered. The process takes a couple of weeks from the moment you act on your impulse. Suppose I took the hand-drawn tab sheets I'd developed over the two decades I'd been giving private lessons and created video tutorials that revolved around them, then found a way of uploading those videos and tabs to a file-hosting website, with links from my new website, so that people, for a modest PayPal charge, could instantly download them? Little Walter's "Juke," for example, or "Born in Chicago," or Big Walter's "Easy"? Plus "Same Old Blues," "Bittersweet Boogie," and all the beginners' exercises I'd worked up for my students over the years. Virtual presence and low-priced digital files, one song at a time, cafeteria-style. No muss, no fuss.

If my insight was correct, if I was able to configure the various moving parts into something that actually worked, time and distance would be scrubbed for the first time from the blues harmonica educational delivery system and the book-and-instructional-CD model would be consigned to the dustbin of history.[18] I was sure that somebody more tech-savvy than I had already figured this out—David Barrett at bluesharmonica.com, for example—but a half hour's research revealed that nobody had. They'd barely figured out that YouTube was there. Any would-be blues harmonica student with internet access would be able to purchase and download my lessons instantly at any hour of the day or night, anywhere in the world. The old-school, face-to-face, long-form apprenticeship that I had served with Nat Riddles and Mister Satan was a great thing if you could find it, but most people couldn't find it. They, too, deserved a chance to learn how to play blues harmonica.

That was the birth of modernbluesharmonica.com. I'm aware, even as I narrate this history, that what I've described could easily be caricatured as a baroque example of the "white thing" that Black Arts spokesperson Larry Neal wanted to destroy: white ideas and white ways of looking at the world that suck all the humanity, all the funk, out of a music that deserves better. Some may object that the dream of global domination that I've confessed to above, albeit in a playful, mock-epic voice, puts me into perilously close alignment with the bad actor Sugar Blue was referring to when he warned against those interlopers who would not only enter the "house" that is the African American blues tradition but also try to claim ownership. "Do not try and take the home," he warns us. "Come on in, visit, enjoy, do your thing. But remember whose house you're in." It's a nontrivial advisory, one that distills the core dilemma explored by this book. The house that is blues harmonica was indisputably built by African American men, and this is truer the further one goes back in time. But white men, too, have built additions to that house over the past half century—and quite a few of them were mentored by older black men. At what point does the white apprentice become a master in his own right, bringing honor to his black master by doing so? At what point does he truly enter the tradition, contribute something original to it, earn the right to speak on behalf of it? And where does this leave player/teachers like me—determined to share the gifts that have been bestowed on us, determined to keep the tradition alive and vital, pushing students around the world to embrace it and perhaps even leave their mark on it? Digital technologies exist; blues harmonica is a sound that people across the globe clearly hunger for. In spreading the gospel far and wide, as I have sought to do, have I taken something away from Sugar Blue, his living black blues brethren, the departed black masters we all revere? Or, in talking them up to my subscribers and customers, have I helped ensure that there's a continuing audience for their work?

Or, despite my mentoring by two black elders and my academic training in African American literature and culture, am I perhaps distorting the meaning of the music—subtly, crucially, inevitably—by virtue of the fact that I do, after all, walk through the world as a white man? Yet even as I frame that question, my critical reflexes lead me to look askance at that phrase "the meaning of the blues." Surely we all realize, in this late postmodern moment, that there is no one unitary "the" when speaking of the blues, unless you're preaching fundamentalism. Meanings are contingent, if significantly inflected by social history. Shaped by dialogue and critique, sustained by community endorsement, they emerge from, and help guide, social practices. Lots of people other than African Americans have attached meanings to the blues over the past half century. Although some of them—sponsored by the Blues Brothers' costumed burlesque, for example—are trivial, even demeaning, others are not so easily dismissed. In a review of *Weeds Like Us* (2019), an autobiography by (white) blues singer Janiva Magness, Mary Katherine Aldin writes,

> Her childhood was one of nearly Gothic tragedy, including the suicides, separately, of both her parents, a succession of foster homes during her early adolescence, and her encounters with abuse, drugs, alcoholism, rape, and serious depression. A runaway at 14, a teenaged pregnancy ended with her surrendering her daughter for adoption; many of her siblings died too young (the body count in this story is unusually high) and she herself attempted suicide several times. ... She writes "Blues is a lot more than my vocation. It's been my salvation."[19]

None of us, not even Willie Dixon, author of an autobiography titled *I Am the Blues* (1989), has the final word on what the blues mean, have meant, and can mean. Still, Dixon's bold claim — "I am the blues" — is not one that I, or any white player I can imagine, would or could ever make. And *that* differential surely means something.

And what about money? How does profit-accrual factor into the social justice equation? I've invested not just time but brains and heart in learning how to play blues on my instrument and figuring out the most effective ways of teaching others how to do the same thing. Nobody has yet suggested that I was wrong or unethical to give my teaching away for free, although I suppose that argument could be made. Am I wrong, then, for seeking to profit from my teaching? Am I somehow misusing the blues when I, as a white man, do that? Or am I doing what people who play this music have always done: trying to scrounge some portion of a living with the help of whatever talent, industry, and originality they could muster? Honeyboy Edwards viewed the blues that way; so did Robert Johnson.

Even as I ask these questions, I'm aware that several younger generations of white players (and non–African American players more broadly) are coming up behind me who do *not*, in fact, see blackness as an essential constituent of the blues, either because they haven't had black mentors and bandmates, or because they aren't particularly conversant with the sociohistorical origins of the music and the feelings that underlie it, or both. I find this every bit as concerning as Sugar Blue does; here he and I suddenly find common ground. But what is to be done?

The realm of digital commerce, it turns out, offers several ways of addressing these problematics.

One of the best things about the sort of widely dispersed virtual communities enabled by the internet is that they give us a chance to create real embodied communities, if only briefly. This is why, in 2010, a partner and I cobbled together an event called Hill Country Harmonica, a long-weekend homecoming in north Mississippi for my YouTube and Modern Blues Harmonica students—I invited them via video uploads and posts on the MBH forum—that over the next three years featured contemporary masters like Billy Branch, Sugar Blue, Phil Wiggins, Charlie Sayles, Terry "Harmonica" Bean, and Robert "Feelgood" Potts, along with young guns like Aki Kumar, Andrew Alli, and Damion Pearson. As a promoter, I've sought to hire African American players, something that a fair number of contemporary blues festivals no longer seem to consider a priority. I do this out of admiration and respect: for the inspiring music they make, the values they carry, the vernacular traditions they embody. I invite them not just to come and headline the evening concerts but also to sit with us under the big gazebo on long lazy afternoons and allow me to interview them, sharing the lessons they were taught by their own teachers, reinventing the face-to-face mentorship for a new era.[20] Not surprisingly, videos taken by registrants are freely shared on YouTube in the event's annual aftermath, so that the embodied community has a long afterlife in cyberspace.

My own curatorial efforts as YouTube uploader and majordomo of modernbluesharmonica.com are part of this flowering of contemporary blues harmonica culture. Here, paradoxically, I use my position as (white) blues harmonica spokesperson to blend an all-comers ethos with a continuing emphasis on the blues as an African American cultural inheritance. As a way of quickly orienting students toward the tradition's vital center, for example, my website offers a top-ten list of greatest all-time players; nine are African American, and Sugar Blue is on the list. (A cranky black bluesist might argue, of course, that nothing is whiter and *less* in the spirit of a cussed old soul like Sonny Boy Williamson than a top-ten list.) Several years ago, moved by Blue's statement about how many fans and players "love the blues but know little about its origins and have no concept as to how closely it is tied to the black experience," I created a sequence of twelve one-hour YouTube lectures under the heading "Blues Talk" in which I tried to address that lack, using my training as an African American literature scholar to talk about works by W. C. Handy, Langston Hughes, Zora Neale Hurston, August Wilson, and the black southern blues worlds they sought to evoke. This book, growing out of those lectures, is my considered response to Sugar Blue's call.

The final chapter of this story is the tale of how I met and mentored a young African American player from Memphis, and how we changed each other's lives.

In February 2008, to celebrate my one-year anniversary on YouTube, I uploaded a performance video in which I showed myself playfully struggling to execute "Whammer Jammer," the song that first led me to pick up a harmonica as a sixteen-year-old. Apart from my high school graduation, I'd never actually performed it live, but I'd been working on it for thirty-odd years and had it 99 percent right. The great majority of viewers offered praise in the comments section, but somebody with the handle "superchucker777" wrote something like "Actually, you're playing that lick wrong." Who the hell are *you*? I thought, intrigued.

I was more intrigued when, after a back-channel exchange, I discovered that he was a sixteen-year-old high school kid named Brandon Bailey who lived up in Memphis and was about to perform "Whammer Jammer" in the semifinals of the Orpheum Star Search competition. We spoke on the phone; he was extremely polite, almost nerdy, and refreshingly direct. His long-term career goal, he said, was pediatric oncology. He asked me to drive up from Oxford and watch him compete. Remembering how generous Nat had been to me, remembering my own hunger for guidance at Brandon's age, I drove eighty miles up to Memphis on the appointed evening, found the concert hall at the foot of Beale Street, and slipped into a seat. He was well-dressed in a pinstriped suit and hat, one of twenty-five contestants. He was the only harmonica player. Most of the other contestants were singers of the professionally groomed, stage-mothered variety. His solo performance through a small amp was dynamic—he played the song properly, Nat would have said—but he didn't move around much. Still, the solo harp thing was unique enough and his playing was strong enough that he made the cut and was passed along to the finals, one of eight who would perform six months later on the same stage.

I realized almost immediately that I had something to offer him: a lesson in stagecraft that an older man—an actor friend of my family's—had given me when Satan and Adam were about to tour internationally for the first time back in 1991, opening for Bo Diddley on big stages in the United Kingdom. So a couple of months later I booked a rehearsal room in a Memphis studio and drove up again from Oxford. Brandon lived with his mother and grandmother in a garden apartment complex in South Memphis. "It's nice to see you again, Mr. Gussow," he said in his slow, formal way as we shook hands. His mother got into the back seat and we drove over to the studio and walked into the carpeted room, harmonica cases in hand. Then Brandon and I got to work. I asked him to sit with his mother in a pair of chairs along the wall while I stepped up onto the low stage and turned to face him. "In the semifinals," I said, holding my arms wide, "you moved between here and here." I walked the length of the small imaginary box I'd just outlined. "If you want to beat everybody in the finals, you need to use the whole space, including the corners. You need to *own* the stage." He came up and stood where I'd stood and I walked out and sat where he'd been sitting, next to his mother. "Lift your head," I called out. "Look out at us." As he started to play, I remembered Nat's words to me—his very first bit of guidance in our very first lesson, in fact. "Open your hands," I urged. "Let it out."

Half an hour later we were done. It was a warm June afternoon. We drove over to Beale Street, strolling and basking, eventually connecting with Vince Jackson, an African American bluesman who was working the outdoor stage in Handy Park with his band. Intrigued by Brandon's youth, pleased to meet a pair of fellow harp players, Vince invited us to sit in. It was the first time Brandon had ever played with a blues band, or any band. Two weeks later, on the Fourth of July, Brandon and his mother drove down to Oxford and I had him sit in with Sterling Magee at a house party I'd organized to celebrate Satan and Adam's official comeback tour after a decade's absence. He fit right in. (The YouTube video is titled "Introducing Brandon Bailey (with Mister Satan).")

Three months later my wife and I drove up to Memphis for the Orpheum Star Search finals. First prize was $5,000 and a recording contract. We sat in the front row. Brandon, now seventeen, would be competing against seven other seventeen-to-twenty-year-olds. All were white; at least half of them, according to the program, had won or placed highly in other talent competitions. They'd appeared at county fairs, starred in semipro productions of Broadway classics. One girl, a trained opera singer, had unbelievable power and vocal range. They'd had all the advantages. Several of them could easily have made the cut at *American Idol* and been sent to Hollywood.

Brandon was the last contestant of the night and the only one who didn't sing. What chance did he have? He was backed up by the house band. He cued them with a finger the way Nat used to do—not a move I'd shown him—and hit the opening chord, then nailed the bent high note and started jamming. He strode into the floodlights as he worked the groove, pivoting side to side, keeping his head high. By the time the band fell in behind him,

Brandon Bailey
(photograph by Tucker Walsh, courtesy of National Public Radio)

the crowd was clapping in time. And then, rocketing along through a half-dozen stop-time choruses, he came into his full power. He'd gone far beyond the couple of moves I'd shown him back in June. The stuff he'd figured out isn't stuff you can teach. He owned the stage, the song. I stared up at him as he ended with a screaming bent high note — Magic Dick's signature, and my own — followed by a thundering crash that dissolved into the roar of the crowd. He pulled his hands away from his face, allowed himself a small grin, and took a bow. I trotted up the aisle to the rest room, excited, as we waited for the judges' tally. The event photographer, who'd been to the previous five finals, was shaking his head. "I'd pay to see that," he said. "Me too," I said. Nat would be proud, I thought. The announcement of the winner, when it came, was icing on the cake.

Brandon and I have remained friends; our real and virtual lives have continued to intersect in unexpected ways. The year after his Star Search triumph, as he was exploring a cutting-edge synthesis of harmonica playing and beat-boxing, he surprised me with a gift: the most basic of stomp-boxes, not much more than a small block of wood with a quarter-inch phone jack. That sent me off on a voyage of discovery as a one-man band, leading me within a year to record a solo harp-and-foot-drums debut, *Kick and Stomp* (2010). (The remake of "Crossroads Blues" has a shout-out to Sterling Magee; the

Blues Harmonica Education in the Digital Age

music video, enlivened by an awkward dance move or two, has managed to accumulate 3 million views.) The following year, donating my services in exchange for the experience, I produced Brandon's debut CD at Royal Sound, the same Memphis studio that turned out Al Green's hits and Bruno Mars's "Uptown Funk." That album, *Memphis Grooves* (2011), landed Brandon on NPR's *All Things Considered* ("Harmonica Blues with a 'Brand' New Beat") and briefly rose to #1 on the iTunes blues chart.[21] One track, an instrumental arrangement of Stevie Wonder's "Superstition," featured the two of us blasting out a long intertwined series of blues harp improvisations, all of them driven along by the foot drums that I'd never have ended up playing if a certain cocky sixteen-year-old hadn't commented on my YouTube video three years earlier.[22] Brandon was already light-years ahead of his Orpheum performance. Hard as he made me work to keep up, I was thrilled to hear echoes of my sound and approach in his, along with lots of stuff I couldn't take credit for and had no desire to. The truth was, I'd never actually given him a formal, face-to-face harmonica lesson. We'd just hung out, jammed, and talked harp. He'd done the rest.

bar 12

Turnaround

It's necessary for Black people in America to understand how
powerful and far reaching the Blues influence is. It's necessary
for us to understand that this music, and in many ways, lifestyle,
has helped many people around the world discover themselves
and feel freedom previously not experienced. The Blues is
giving, altruistic. The Blues is a healer. . . . There are many
Blues music aficionados around who are often completely
out of touch with Black life, and further out of touch with
Living Creatively. Yet they have categorized Black music like
laboratory specimens; and the sad thing is that some artists
believe what someone else has told them about who they are.

Lincoln T. "Chicago Beau" Beauchamp

Amis de la musique du "blues" et de l'harmonica, Bonny B. le
bluesman suisse, bonjour. Aujourd'hui nous allons apprendre
une deuxième riff du blues avec les chiffres que vous pourriez
voir au-dessous de la tablature. Donc, je vais jouer la premier
tournée seul et la deuxième tournée vous jouerez tout seul.

[Friends of the blues and the harmonica, good morning from
Bonny B. the Swiss bluesman. Today we're going to learn a second
blues riff, using the numbers that you can see at the bottom of
the tab sheet. Okay, I'm going to play the first chorus by myself,
and then you're going to play the second chorus by yourself.]

*Bonny B., Cambodian-born player, teacher, and proprietor
of "Blues TV" in Fribourg, Switzerland, in a video titled
"Bonny B Harmonica Lesson 'Riff 2' avec tablature" (2011)*

IN THE WORLD OF BLUES PERFORMANCE, the twelfth bar of a twelve-bar blues is called the turnaround.[1] In harmonic terms, it represents a momentary drop from the resolution or return-to-home feeling conveyed by the tonic ("I") chord in bar 11 down into the solidly anchored basement represented by the dominant ("V") chord. It's a pause that refreshes, even as it carries the music, in the space of four beats, from the end of the line back to the beginning, preparing us to cycle through another twelve-bar chorus.

When religions, political philosophies, and arguments about culture claim that truth can only be found by returning to the beginnings, the presumptively simpler "early days"—the early church, the intentions of the authors of the U.S. Constitution, the first day an enslaved African set foot on American soil back in 1619, the real blues from the dusty old Mississippi Delta—they are endorsing fundamentalism. Fundamentalism, especially in our postmodern moment, is an anxious response to contemporary uncertainties. It bespeaks a hunger for firm moral anchoring, a desire to condemn and purge what it judges to be impure and intermixed, even as it lays down the law that sanctifies true believers. The pronouncement "Blues is the devil's music," so widespread and potent in black southern communities during the first half of the twentieth century, was the motto of black Christian fundamentalists: ministers and church-going parents confronting a freeborn younger black generation's desire to live life to the fullest in a modernizing America with the help of blues music and its sensual incitements. The slogan "Blues is black music," insurgent (if not precisely widespread) in our own time, reflects an admirable desire to celebrate black cultural achievement, a justifiable concern with who profits from that achievement, and an understandable hunger to claim the music as a site of memory for the trauma wrought by slavery and Jim Crow, accompanied by a problematic desire to evade the complexities of American (and world) musical history and to trivialize and disparage a broad range of non–African American investments in, and claims on, the music. The slogan "No black. No white. Just the blues," meanwhile, seeks fundamentalist certainty, along with freshly minted white innocence, by deploying what it imagines to be a morally unassailable call to transracial brotherhood under the sign of the blues ("I don't see color, I just hear talent"), even while insisting, in its first two words, on erasing black history, black culture, and the indisputable blackness of 92 percent of the blues performers celebrated in Memphis's "Blues Hall of Fame."[2] (A slightly less tone-deaf slogan creator would have reversed the order of the slogan's first two sentences, disinvesting in whiteness before banishing blackness.)

The truth offered by blues music in performance, unlike the truth offered by these three fundamentalist slogans, arises from a repeated return to the beginning: a repeated ritual pause-and-plunge from the turnaround into one more twelve-bar chorus, not for the purpose of consolidating and hardening an ideological position but for the purpose of extending the creative journey, testing out alternate positions, refining and extending key statements, and giving the song a chance to sing itself out. In that spirit, here are five choruses of contemporary blues life from the second decade of the third millennium. Make of them what you will.

ASIA, TOO (1): SHOJI NAITO, TARO SENGA, AND KEN "SUGAR BROWN" KAWASHIMA

Why should we presume that the blues-and-race debate can or should be confined to black and white? A more honest discussion would acknowledge that blues music has long had not just a significant Asian audience, one tracing back at least as far as the mass popularity of "St. Louis Blues" in Japan during and after World War II, but also an expanding cohort of Asian musicians who have coalesced into bona fide local and national scenes in India, Indonesia, the Philippines, Thailand, Singapore, Japan, and Hong Kong. Some of these musicians, having proven themselves in their native lands, often by backing up touring and expatriate African American blues performers, make their way to Chicago, Memphis, and other American blues meccas, where they pay additional dues—again, often in bands led by African American elders—and contribute to the ongoing vitality of local blues culture. But that is merely one sort of contemporary Asian blues journey, and there are others.

Well-known in Chicago blues circles, Japanese guitarist/bassist/harmonicist Shoji Naito moved to the Windy City in 1996 and learned his trade playing behind John Primer, Carey Bell, Jimmy Burns, Willie "Big Eyes" Smith, and Lurrie Bell: a classic old-school apprenticeship.[3] A longtime member of the Eddy Clearwater Band, Naito also occasionally plays bass and guitar with Billy Branch and his Sons of Blues, and he helps anchor a regular Monday evening class at the Old Town School of Music taught by Joe Filisko, a (white) mainstay of Chicago's blues harmonica scene, subbing for Filisko when the latter musician is out on tour. Naito has recorded several collections of jam-along "Shoblues Harp Tracks"—traditional Chicago grooves for developing blues players, with fanciful titles like "Joke" and "Mad Hours" (instead of "Juke" and "Sad Hours") designed to skirt copyright troubles while faithfully evoking the sound of Little Walter's guitarists.

He's also recorded an album of his own, *New Cool Old School* (2016), which features veteran African American singers Willie Buck, Katherine Wilson, and Milwaukee Slim, and has produced a handful of albums for other local artists, black and white.[4]

Naito is a traditionalist, one whose career reflects a desire to study, recuperate, body forth, and honor a classic Chicago blues style from an earlier era. Harmonica player Taro Senga, also a native of Japan, has a somewhat different aesthetic approach and career arc. A child prodigy in that country back in the 1990s, Senga was a protégé of Danish harmonicist Lee Oskar, a funk-and-jazz-based stylist best known for his time with War, a multiethnic funk-rock band. Senga and his father, Akimitsu, a blues guitar player with a traditionalist bent, appeared in *Tokyo Blues* (1999), a documentary about the history of blues in Japan; Akimitsu beamed as he described a recent American trip in which the father-son blues duo, billing themselves as the Blind Lemon Brothers, played a black nightclub in Los Angeles and were warmly received there.[5] (The earned approval of a black audience remains an authenticating touchstone for many non–African American blues players, a phenomenon that blues critic Paul Garon invoked in an influential 1995 essay, "White Blues," to insist that such music and performances were innately inauthentic. "If white blues is autonomous and self-authenticating, why is black approval needed? If it is not autonomous and self-authenticating, and the craving for black approval seems to suggest this, why is it not the weak and imitative form its detractors claim?")[6] As a series of YouTube clips from 2007, shot in a Japanese bar, make clear, Taro's playing has evolved over the years, driven by his father's proficiency in jazz as well as blues guitar. Like many non–American musicians, especially those who attend the annual International Blues Challenge in Memphis, the Blind Lemon Brothers eventually made a full-scale American blues pilgrimage, one that took them from Memphis (Taro, like Brandon Bailey, sat in with Vince Jackson and his Juke Joint All-Stars in Handy Park), to the Mississippi Delta (they met veteran blues educator Johnny Billington and jammed at Ground Zero in Clarksdale), to Chicago (they visited the House of Blues, sat in with Mississippi native and longtime Chicagoan Jimmy Burns), with a side trip to New York City (a jazz jam at Cleopatra's Needle).[7]

Some, including Garon, might denigrate this sort of blues touristic itinerary as a spiritually vapid exercise in (white-ish) blues romanticism, a craven attempt at self-authentication through an imagined absorption of African American blues energies. Others might view it as a legitimate pilgrimage, one made with sincere spiritual intent: to listen, to learn, to be inspired, to connect more deeply with the sources of one's art, and to pay homage to specific individuals—in this case, almost all of them older African American men—who are living masters and carriers of that art. One always has the option, of course, of playing the blues without making such a pilgrimage or paying such homage. Would that be a better course of action? If so, for whom, and in what way?

Regardless of how one adjudges such contemporary Asian investments in the blues, one is left with Taro Senga himself in his current incarnation as the frontman of Monster, a hard-swinging all-Japanese rock-blues quartet. Their up-tempo harmonica instrumental, "The Call," has audible echoes of several African American masters, including Little Walter (it samples the opening riff from "Juke") and James Cotton, but it also, at the same time, does what good modern blues has always done, which is update, reconfigure, and make an indelible personal statement. A dynamic contemporary blues harmonica boogie, it holds its own with the best on the world stage, including Billy Branch's "Son of Juke" and Jason Ricci's "Goenopheny."[8]

Finally, there is the case of Ken "Sugar Brown" Kawashima, a blues performer and political theorist who came to my attention late in the process of assembling this book and whose words provide the fourth and final epigraph to Bar 1. Kawashima's aggressive pushback against black bluesist heritage claims is grounded not just in his lived experience within the Chicago blues scene but in his Marxist orientation toward the marketing of this thing called "blues," a skepticism about racial labeling that he grounds in his reading of Karl Hagstrom Miller. "Segregating Sound," he explains in a short documentary titled Sugar Brown: The Shade of Blues (2016), "is about how certain genres of popular music come into being, mostly through marketing of the record companies, and how they racialize genres of music, how musicians themselves internalize that representation of the genre through race and embody race . . . and embody the racialized representation of the music."[9]

A University of Chicago graduate with a PhD in history from NYU, currently an associate professor of East Asian studies at the University of Toronto, Kawashima has spent decades navigating his singular path through the blues' available array of identitarian and transracialist stances. Product of a Korean mother and Japanese father who emigrated to America in the 1960s, he grew up in Bowling Green, Ohio, headed north to Chicago for college, and, as a harmonica player and guitarist, quickly became part of that city's still-vibrant blues scene in the late 1980's, almost a decade before Naito arrived. After sitting in with John "Ice Cream Man" Brim and his Ice Cream Men, an African American elder accompanied by four younger white tra-

Dr. Ken "Sugar Brown" Kawashima
(courtesy of Mark Maryanovich Photography)

ditionalists, Kawashima was picked up by Tail Dragger Jones, an Arkansas-born local, and soon found himself working three or four gigs a week while still in his early twenties, often at all-black venues like the Delta Fish Market. It was Tail Dragger who gave him his stage name, no trivial thing in Chicago's blues subculture. "He said no one can remember or pronounce my last name," Kawashima remembered. After trying out "Japanese boy" and "Korean kid," the grizzled black front man settled on Sugar Brown — a handle shrewdly indexed to his racial in-betweenness, according to Kawashima. "That's the way he wanted somehow to give meaning to me. Not as white, but as brown."

But Kawashima's presence in Tail Dragger's band created tensions in the black blues community. "There were musicians that wanted gigs that I was on." One of those musicians, Boston Blackie, angrily confronted Tail Dragger while the young Asian American blues player stood by. "How come you're hiring a white boy and a Chinaman when there's fifteen other black guys in the neighborhood who need the job?" Angered at being reduced to an ethnic stereotype ("I'm not even Chinese," he told an interviewer), disillusioned with the scene after Tail Dragger shot Boston Blackie to death in an unrelated episode at the fish market, Kawashima left Chicago for Japan.

There, incongruously, he was embraced as a locus of authenticity: a bearer of Chicago street cred who could sing blues with an American accent and blow some down-home harp. "I felt good singing with other Japanese people. I didn't have this big stark racial difference standing in the way. I didn't feel this alienation of race. And maybe that allowed me to feel comfortable enough to start really singing."

Since returning to America, earning a PhD in East Asian History, and taking a teaching job at the University of Toronto, Kawashima has seemingly managed to embrace all sides of his singular identity as a Korean-Japanese-American-Canadian bluesman-intellectual with a Chicago pedigree, winning the Toronto Blues Society talent search (2013) and making it to the finals of the International Blues Challenge (2017). He is Dr. Ken Kawashima, author of *The Proletarian Gamble: Korean Workers in Interwar Japan* (Duke UP, 2009) *and* he is Sugar Brown, bandleader and recording artist with three solo albums to his name: *Sugar Brown's Sad Day* (2014), *Poor Lazarus* (2015), and *It's a Blues World (Calling All Blues)* (2018). His ethos of the blues, as befits his singular journey, is edged with a fierce individualism earned during his immersion in three radically different blues communities. "I would lose all confidence in myself," he insists, "if I let racist people get me down. 'Cause I know myself. I know what I can do. I love myself for doing what I can do."

THE BLUES COALITION

One significant concern expressed by participants in the "State of the Blues Today" panel at the 2012 "Blues and the Spirit" symposium at Dominican University was the degree to which contemporary blues festivals tended to slight African American–led acts and African American performers more generally; a similar indictment was leveled at the Blues Music Awards bestowed annually by the Blues Foundation in Memphis. In his comments, Branch referenced recent research by the Blues Coalition, an anonymous working group. Its preliminary findings were posted in the comments section of the 2011 *Chicago Reader* article in which Alligator Records head Bruce Iglauer made what many felt were disparaging comments about black Chicago blues artists. (On its Facebook page, the group describes itself as "an independent group of blues artists, industry professionals, activists, writers and educators committed to preserving and promoting the Blues, an american [sic] art form.") The two research summaries were "Food for Thought:

Some Preliminary Data on Blues Festival Bookings" and "Let the Numbers Roll," which focused on the BMAs.[10]

All of the festivals analyzed in "Food for Thought" were located on the mainstream festival continuum: a broad, geographically diverse range of North American events with predominantly white audiences. (I have played many such festivals over the years.) Some of those festivals have large corporate sponsors; some charge admission while others are free city-fest type events. At least one, the Legendary Blues Cruise, is a well-funded private endeavor that charges the same multithousand-dollar fees to stateroom-ensconced attendees that one might pay for any seven-day cruise to the Caribbean. The Chicago Blues Festival, intriguingly, was not mentioned by the Blues Coalition. As one of the largest and best-known free blues festivals and one that highlights Chicago's own African American blues stars and stalwarts, it draws a significant local black audience, albeit one that skews, like all contemporary blues audiences, older rather than younger. Nor were any of the festivals analyzed by the Blues Coalition the sort of all-black events, billing themselves unabashedly as blues festivals, that regularly take place in contemporary Mississippi — events featuring soul-blues performers like O. B. Buchana, Willie Clayton, Rev. Theodis Ealey, Ms. Jody, and one or two younger hip-hop themed newcomers in dark shades, styling and profiling on the gaudy website poster.[11] Those events, staged by black promoters for black audiences, are not a subject of interest, much less concern, for the Blues Coalition. Its concern arises only when the festivals, promoters, and audiences are predominantly or entirely white, and when the structural effect of that white-majority rule is what it adjudges to be a self-evident deficit in black blues representation on stage.

So what did the Blues Coalition find when it looked at a limited but reasonably representative sample of major North American blues festivals for calendar year 2011, ten in total, assessing them, in raw numerical and percentage terms, for "bands that are predominantly African American and are led by African American bandleaders"? The results fall into three categories: one bad outlier, two good outliers, and seven festivals in the middle range — a middle range that the researchers, who use the word "only" to characterize African American representation in four out of those seven cases, view as problematic and unjust.

The bad outlier, presented first in the report, is the Edmonton Labatt Blues Festival, the one Canadian festival assessed by the study. Only 2 out of 13 bands (15 percent), according to the Coalition, had African American bandleaders and were predominantly African American in composition, and neither of those bands were headliners, although one white band, the report noted, had a black performer as a featured guest. If one tracks down the program for the three-day festival, which is not provided by the study, the situation becomes somewhat more complicated than the Blues Coalition findings suggest, although there are certainly problematics worth attending to.[12]

Here are the daily lineups for the festival:

FRIDAY

5:30 p.m. — David Gogo

6:55 p.m. — Reba Russell

8:30 p.m. — Kim Wilson's Blues All Stars

SATURDAY

2:30 p.m. — Duffy Bishop Band

4:00 p.m. — Dave Riley and Bob Corritore

5:30 p.m. — Chubby Carrier and the Bayou Swamp Band

7:00 p.m. — John Nemeth Soul Revue

8:30 p.m. — Nick Moss and the Flip-Tops
      with special guest Guitar Shorty

SUNDAY

2:30 p.m. — David Vest

4:00 p.m. — Sean Carney Band

5:30 p.m. — RJ Mischo with Mike Morgan and the Crawl

7:00 p.m. — Diunna Greenleaf and Blue Mercy

8:30 p.m. — Delta Groove Harp Blast with Bob Corritore,
      Randy Chortkoff, Mitch Kashmar and "Big Pete" Van der
      Pluijm on harps, Kirk Fletcher and Paris Slim on guitar,
      Willie Campbell bass, Bob Rio keys, and Jimi Bott drums

The only native Canadian, (white) guitarist David Gogo, opened the festival on Friday; the only other Canadian resident, (white) Alabama native David Vest, was the Sunday opener. So although this was a Canadian blues festival, the promoters, who have a long track record and a major Canadian sponsor, went to the effort and expense of importing and foregrounding American blues acts. (The expense includes not just airfares but also taxes and border fees.)

Where, in this mix, do African American blues performers show up? The one all-black band, as it happens, is Louisiana zydeco rather than straight-up blues: Chubby Carrier, positioned in the middle of Saturday's lineup. Diunna Greenleaf, slotted into a desirable showcase position on Sunday evening, is an award-winning Houston-based black blues belter—real blues, by anybody's standards—but her band is white. The Blues Coalition's reference standard, bands that are "predominantly African American," is, it would seem, a standard that many black bandleaders in Greenleaf's position either can't meet (because black sidemen aren't available) or aren't particularly trying to meet. Dave Riley and Bob Corritore, preceding Chubby Carrier on Saturday, are a well-known interracial duo hailing from Mississippi and Chicago respectively; guitarist Riley is seven years older than his harmonica-playing white partner, but Corritore, who runs a blues club in Phoenix and is extremely active as a blues producer and DJ, has performed and recorded with a legion of African American blues stars. Black Houston native Guitar Shorty was originally scheduled to headline with his own band on Saturday night, but the promoters apparently decided, late in the game, to punch things up publicity-wise by pairing him with Nick Moss, a well-known younger white Chicago-born guitarist, and his Flip Tops—an all-white ensemble, like Shorty's.

It's unclear which of the three acts I've described is, after Chubby Carrier, the second of two acceptably African American acts from the Blues Coalition's perspective, since none of the three is "predominantly African American in composition." In terms of stage image and the bodying forth of African American blues prowess, all three acts feature strong and distinctive black frontmen and frontwomen, southern-born exemplars of the blues. But each act also images the interracial character of contemporary blues performance, reinforcing the idea not just of blues as transracial American culture but also of black and white musicians sharing power and space, actively supporting and taking pleasure in each other's playing. This latter element undercuts the Blues Coalition's black bluesist viewpoint, which sees African Americans, individually and collectively, as the only legitimate carriers of blues music's legacy.

One all-black act; three salt-and-pepper acts with black leaders. The other nine acts are, with a couple of passing exceptions, all white from top to bottom. And here a real, regrettable, nontrivial racial disparity becomes visible in a category I know well: harmonica players. Thanks in part to the Delta Groove Harp Blast that headlines on Sunday night, the festival is loaded with blues harmonica talent, a total of seven players: Randy Chortkoff, Bob Corritore, Mitch Kashmar, R. J. Mischo, John Nemeth, and "Big Pete" Van der Pluijm, and Kim Wilson. Two of the seven, Kashmar and Wilson, are on anybody's top-ten list of living players; three others (Corritore,

Mischo, and Nemeth) are leading pros only half a notch down from that; and Chortkoff and Van der Pluijm are solid but unexceptional journeymen. All seven are white. If I were Billy Boy Arnold, Sugar Blue, or Billy Branch, or Omar Coleman or James Cotton (who was still alive and gigging in 2011), I would find it hard not to feel that I, and my black Chicago peers had been ignored, shut out, shunted aside. As a player and occasional promoter, somebody who has hired Kashmar and Nemeth for my own events, knows Corritore and Mischo, and thinks the world of Wilson, I'm nevertheless troubled by the *de facto* exclusion of black players — not an intended outcome, surely, but still the end result of a complex process involving a range of priorities (or lack of certain priorities) in the creation of a festival program, mediated by preexisting blues industry friendships and the price and availability of performers for specific dates.

At the other extreme from the Edmonton Labatt's Blues Festival — headlined "a few exceptions to the pattern" in the Blues Coalition report — were the North Atlantic Blues Festival in Rockland, Maine, and the Pennsylvania Blues Festival (formerly the Poconos Blues Festival), which featured 76 percent and 90 percent African American acts, respectively. (Michael Cloeren, the majordomo of the latter festival, has been a longtime white advocate for African American blues performers.) The other seven festivals inventoried by the Coalition ranged from 28 percent to 41 percent African American bands led by African Americans. The higher percentages were often in metro locations (Tampa; Wilmington, Delaware) with substantial black populations — places where a desire to please black as well as white audiences might have guided promoters in their choices about bands. The lower percentages were in locations (Telluride, Colorado; Portland, Oregon; Bedford, Texas) with notably smaller black populations. (Portland is the "whitest city in America," according to the *Atlantic*.)[13]

There's an honest debate to be had about whether the 28-to-41 percent norm unearthed by the Blues Coalition evidences a lamentable failure of racial representation on the part of mainstream blues festival organizers or, alternately, is an unsurprising and not entirely unreasonable outcome. To somebody who considers "white blues" fundamentally invalid, a category error sustained through false consciousness and thoroughgoing white dominance in the ideological and commercial marketplace, *any* significant proportion of white acts on a blues festival program is a bad thing. By the same token, the contemporary blues scene does sometimes present us with self-evident absurdities: the all-white blues festival decried by Billy Branch is no imagined unicorn but a real American phenomenon. (For the record, the 2018 Mahindra Blues Festival in Mumbai, India, consisted of five acts: a white Brit (John Mayall), a Mexican American (Coco Montoya), an African American (Walter "Wolfman" Washington), a white Canadian (Layla Zoe), and an Indian (Blackstratblues featuring Warren Mendonza).[14] Is that admirable diversity or a regrettable lack of African American representation?)

In "Let the Numbers Roll," their second report, the Blues Coalition subjected the Blues Music Awards in Memphis to the same process of racial parsing it had applied to blues festivals. In the categories inventoried by researchers, 30 to 50 percent of the awards over the previous ten years (2002–11) had gone to African American performers—with one stunning exception. In the category "Blues Instrumentalist of the Year—Harmonica," no African American player had ever won an award, not just during the decade in question, but since the creation of the separate harmonica category back in 1993. James Cotton, Carey Bell, Sugar Blue, Billy Branch, and Billy Boy Arnold had all been nominated during that nineteen-year period. But none had ever won. Even more dismayingly, this shutout has continued to the present day.[15]

Twenty-six years! But no one person is to blame. Certainly the white blues harmonica players who have monopolized the award during the past quarter-century—with Charlie Musselwhite, perennial winner, at the top of the list—aren't to blame. They just play their gigs, make their albums, and let the chips fall where they may. So who, or what, is to blame? We don't really have a name for it. Structural racism? A popularity contest skewed by the accrued judgments of white blues aficionados (including reviewers, journalists, and bloggers) functioning within a white-dominated organizational infrastructure—blues societies, DJs, record labels, booking agencies? White folks consciously, or unconsciously, rewarding their own?

Something is wrong here.

JUS' BLUES MUSIC AWARDS

It should come as no surprise that some African American blues people, fed up with the current state of affairs, have gravitated toward their own advocacy organization and their own set of annual blues awards. The nonprofit Jus' Blues Music Foundation was established in Atlanta in 1995 by African American impresario Charles Mitchell out of a desire to honor that city's, and the South's, long and storied blues heritage. In a 1997 article previewing Mitchell's Atlanta Blues Heritage Festival and the second Jus' Blues Awards (he skipped 1996 because of the Olympics), Mitchell offered no overtly ideological justification—although all ten of the blues performers he mentioned were African American, ranging from classic 1920s blueswomen Bessie Smith and Ida Cox through contemporary soul-blues and mainstream stars like Trudy Lynn and Lucky Peterson.[16]

Twenty years later, in August 2017, I attended the foundation's Jus' Blues Music Awards weekend at the Horseshoe Casino in Tunica, Mississippi. The word "music," which apparently became a part of the awards' title at some point, allows the Jus' Blues Music Awards to signify on the Blues Music Awards: the Jus' Blues Music Foundation, as it were, shadowing the big bad Blues Music Foundation. Apart from a journalist who showed up briefly to interview Millie Jackson, I was one of only two whites attending the event. The other was David Whiteis: a contributing editor of *Living Blues*, a member of the "State of the Blues Today" plenary panel, and the author of culturally informed books on southern soul-blues and Chicago blues.[17] No white women were present. As a professor who regularly teaches blues courses at Ole Miss, I came to broaden my knowledge base, hear good music, and have some candid conversations. I was not disappointed. Mitchell himself was friendly, ebullient, happy to chat; the same could be said of pretty much everybody I met. The event itself consisted of several different performance-based events in the evening—an awards ceremony, a "juke joint fish fry"—plus a mid-morning "tech conference" in a smaller seminar room that represented a gathering of the tribe to discuss issues of felt relevance to contemporary African American blues performers and those who consider themselves stewards of the music and its legacy. Ms. Jackson and Bobby Rush were present, sitting side by side at one of the rowed tables, elbowing each other like show-business survivors. Singer Teeny Tucker, daughter of Tommy "Put on Your Red Dress" Tucker, sat at a table just behind me. Ronnie Baker Brooks talked about how important it was to control your own music—retaining your own publishing, owning your own masters, trusting no one except yourself to take care of business. Many expressed concern about the way digital technologies had changed the game, rendering CDs, a key blues industry profit center, increasingly obsolete. There was just as much concern about how to guarantee the preservation of the blues' African American legacy in an age when young black people didn't seem very interested in the blues.

Hovering behind the entire conversation, but never expressed in so many words, was the feeling of being an aging and besieged community—besieged above all by the seemingly inexorable tide of whiteness, although the word "white" was rarely spoken, perhaps because it didn't need to be. ("They" was the working substitute.) Information was exchanged; tips and

Turnaround

hacks were shared. Rush, that rare performer whose stock is equally high on the soul-blues and mainstream scenes, presided like a genial elder, the mischievous great-uncle who knew just the right moment to drop a cackling piece of mother wit and break up the room. Later that night, at the fish fry in a low-ceilinged ballroom at the Roadhouse Casino, Rush came down off the stage to sing and blow solo harp. I'd seen Rush in performance a handful of times, but never in this sort of all-black setting. He has always cultivated a trickster persona—a sex-crazed old playa who asks his apple-bottomed pair of dancers to turn toward the crowd so that he, and the crowd, can ogle their curves and be taken in once again by the Goddess, she who holds all the power over poor Bobby. He did none of that here. He just sang a song, an old Mississippi blues, a blues so old that the line he sang— "They got me arrested for murder . . . and I ain't even harmed a man" —was sung by the black Delta laborers who worked for Charles Peabody back in 1901. "They got me arrested for forgery," he sang a moment later, "and people, you know I can't even write my own damn name." He blew some harp, and then he sang some more—drawing a laugh or two, indicting the criminal justice system, insisting that black lives matter. He did something that blues and only blues can do. It's not a thing that white people can do with the blues.

I'd had a different version of that same feeling at the awards ceremony the previous night, when a singer named Sheryl Youngblood took the stage and sang Etta James's "At Last." Those of us who have been in and around the music for a long time sometimes make the mistake of thinking that we've heard everything worth hearing; we assume, half-consciously, that we're incapable of being blindsided by somebody we've never heard of. Dr. Johnny Jones, an administrator at Mississippi Valley State University and the head of educational development for the Jus' Blues Music Foundation, insisted on pulling me through the crowd and seating me at a table near the front—right next to Denise LaSalle, as it happens, someone whose *Love Talkin'* (1984) album had instantly made her one of my heroes as a twenty-something blues wannabe. Grateful and slightly abashed to realize how generously I'd been seated, I looked up to see Youngblood, powerfully built, resplendent in a sleeveless white pantsuit. She was, I found out later, a drummer and bandleader, not to mention a 2015 Chicago Blues Hall of Fame inductee, but she's not somebody they play on "Bluesville" (perhaps because her one CD, which I purchased later, doesn't do her justice), not somebody whose name shows up on BluesFestivalGuide.com the way that Samantha Fish and Ana Popovic do. She's not that sort of mainstream draw. She's not the flavor of the month. So I'd never heard of her. But that's just me—and the rest of the

Sheryl Youngblood
(courtesy of the photographer, Aaron Porter)

mainstream blues world outside Chicago, I daresay. As she began to work her magic on the song, mixing the power of a gospel singer with the finesse of a jazz diva, I had only one thought: This is the big leagues. All the rest — and specifically, 95 percent of the white female blues singers I know — are playing Triple A ball at best. I'd had precisely the same intuitive response back in 1985 when I first ventured into Showman's, a Harlem jazz bar, and heard organist and singer Jimmy "Preacher" Robins work his magic on that crowd: This is the stuff. The other stuff — the blues we play downtown — is what it is, but it ain't this.

The crowd — that in-group vibe — is key. When we talk about race and blues, we need to keep in mind the way call-and-response functions in the intimacy of all-black settings. The crowd's urgings, their needs and knowledge, their connoisseurship and felt approval, make a difference. They enable superior performance. The sort of hand-in-glove connection that fused Youngblood with her audience was the ballast out of which she powered herself into the heart of the song. Once you've heard that, *felt* that, you can't forget it. It becomes a touchstone for what great blues is. And the fake stuff, the let's-get-dressed-up-and-pretend stuff, or the merely less-than-great stuff, stands starkly revealed for what it is. If you haven't heard Sheryl Youngblood—or a performer of comparable majesty—do what she does in that sort of all-black setting, of course, what I'm saying won't make sense and may even annoy you.

We all love Bonnie Raitt. She's the exception that proves the rule. I know a handful of white female blues singers who can break your heart—Danielle Nicole just might do that in "Cry No More" (2018)—and a fair number who can throw down on guitar, although few with the earned swagger of Chicago veteran Joanna Connor. But let's not pretend. Blues has a range of use-values as it spreads outward from African American culture, wending its way across America and around the globe. That's a good thing. It's a great thing, in fact. But let's stop pretending that Double A and Triple A ball are the major leagues, or that the gatekeepers of the mainstream scene know everything that's going on out there.[18] If there was any justice in the world, Sheryl Youngblood would be playing at a blues festival near you.

TOO SWEET TO DIE

For the past few years, Delta State University in Cleveland, Mississippi, has been hosting an annual International Conference on the Blues. I've presented there several times; it's a good place to network and share ideas. Evening blues performances are always a part of the proceedings. My Blues Doctors duo played there in 2016, in fact.

Cleveland is an important town in blues history, which may explain why it has four Mississippi Blues Trail markers, including one titled "The Enlightenment of W. C. Handy" that recounts the story of Handy's dance band stepping aside to let Prince McCoy and his "local colored band" play a song or two during a concert. The money showered on McCoy's blues trio by the white dancers convinced Handy that the blues, a "primitive music," had crossover potential.[19] In 2017, capitalizing on Cleveland's civic history, the conference organizers put together a free evening concert at the downtown courthouse—a tribute to John Lee Hooker, right on the front steps. Among other things, the concert demolished the claim that young black people don't play the blues anymore.

The concert featured a trio of young men who are arguably the best blues players and singers of their generation: Marquise Knox (age twenty-six), Jontavious Willis (age twenty), and Christone "Kingfish" Ingram (age eighteen). They had never previously performed together. Ingram, a Clarksdale native, is somebody I'd seen a handful of times, most recently at Double

Decker, our annual festival in Oxford, where he'd done the high-speed Buddy Guy–style shredding he's famous for. The others, especially Knox, came bearing considerable advance notice of the "You gotta see this guy live" sort. Since I am professionally inclined to view white blues hunger for the Next Big Thing with skepticism, I wasn't expecting much. It was just three young black men with guitars, dimly lit on a lukewarm October night, sitting on chairs in front of mics.

As the purveyor of a blues harmonica website with the word "modern" in it, my own taste inclines away from traditionalism, away from older sounds, in part because a significant number of white blues harmonica players make a fetish of those sounds and the African American greats who summoned them into being many years ago. Although I teach the tradition, I'm always looking for players willing to take a risk for the sake of discovering the sound that speaks to *right now*—which is, after all, what Little Walter did back in 1952 when he copied sax players like Jimmy Liggins and Sonny Stitt in order to come up with "Juke." Sugar Blue has been pursuing that brash, bebop-inspired, in-your-face sound throughout his career, which is why he'll be remembered long after the traditionalists are dead and gone.

By that standard, there was nothing modern about what Knox, Willis, and Ingram did—except for the fact that they'd chosen to play and sing deep, old Mississippi blues when most of their young black peers were into rap and R&B.[20] (Afrodiasporic music scholar Ali Colleen Neff argues, in this context, that the blues live on in Clarksdale's African American community not just *as* blues—as an audible distillate, for example, of John Lee Hooker and Muddy Waters that white blues fans would find palatable—but as the hip-hop stylings of Jerome "Top Notch the Villain" Williams and other young rappers, the sort of music against which white blues aficionados often define their own musical tastes.)[21] Staking their claim on traditional blues repertoire was, in fact, a cutting-edge move for the trio, part of a small but growing blues and roots revival among younger African American musicians, including Jerron "Blind Boy" Paxton, Valerie June, Andrew Alli, Damion Pearson, and the Carolina Chocolate Drops. What immediately became apparent was that these three young men were doing something that no comparable trio of young white blues guys was remotely capable of doing. They weren't doing a traditionalist turn; they weren't just replicating a certain kind of sound and feel. They were reoccupying the music, reclaiming it in the deepest, most deliberate, and yet most natural way one can imagine. They had accessed the source, wherever it was, and created the sound freshly out of that. What sort of wake work was this? Knox, his face half-shadowed in the angled spotlight, sang Hooker's "I'm in the Mood," and his rough, tired, hungry, menacing voice *was* Hooker's — and his own voice, too, supported by his own version of Hooker's spattery, finger-picked guitar. To call it a brilliant homage is true enough, but the word "homage" doesn't capture the uncanny power of Knox's vocal performance, a performance that erased the distance between reanimator and honoree without once seeming like mere imitation. Willis and Ingram, meanwhile, were adding spontaneity and rhythmic counterpoint to the song by trading off chording and fills on second and third guitar, then, when the song was over, taking turns at the mic, their voices preternaturally wise, giving Hooker his due without ever subsuming their own personalities. Rarely have such young musicians paid such a dynamic tribute to the spirit and work of a deceased blues great.

All this was merely a prelude to what happened later, across the street. Knox and Willis, facing each other across a bottle of bourbon, had taken up residence at a darkened picnic table adjacent to the café where a post-concert jam session and party were taking place. Several fans, including blues poet and conference organizer Don Mitchell, were shoulder to shoulder with them; another half dozen or so were gathered in a loose circle. A few cell phones were out, capturing the proceedings. Kingfish, standing at one end of the table with guitar in hand, was playing a familiar old Mississippi standard, "Catfish Blues," as Knox and Willis passed the bottle back and forth and traded verses, most of which seemed to be improvised and all of which were interrupted by roars of laughter and shouts of "Uh huh" and "God dog!" from around the circle:

Knox
I thought I had four kids . . . but I only got three
My daddy said I'll feed the last one . . . he'll look like me
Ever since then . . . my life has changed
Two can play your game
Honey, two can play your game

Willis
If you got . . . got one woman
You better get . . . hey hey . . . four of mine
Cause two might quit you and the . . . other two might die
Other two might die
Mm mm mm

Knox
Ever since I . . . was a young man
I've had the guitar . . . in my hand
But when you see me . . . you know you can't deny
I'm too sweet to die
Oh lordy
Oh well is I
Oh well is I
All right, she's all right . . .
She's all right, she's all right
She's all right, she's all right

Knox
Now the woman you had . . . used to have tender feet
And then she come to St. Louis . . . trying to get some of this
I said now now . . . you pretty heifer . . . go on back to the devil

Willis
Well that woman . . . that I had
I said You-oooou . . . got her now
Tell you the truth now pardner, I got seven others . . . and I
Didn't want her no more . . .
Didn't want her no more . . .
Didn't want her no more . . .

Knox had a harp his hand and was blowing fills at this point. Another young black man whom I'd seen earlier at the party, a student at Delta State, joined in and sang a verse:

Student
And my baby . . . she came back home
Smelling just like a . . . lowdown rag
And she got . . . in my bed
I can't take it like that
I can't take it like that
Just like a dirty rag.

Knox answered with a fierce, playful harp solo: love moans and cries. "Whip it to a jello!" Willis chuckled. "That's why she like it so much!

Knox
Well Kingfish . . . look what you done started
She used to be nice . . . but the girl's downhearted
Whatever you done . . . come change it for me.[22]

"I'm like John Lee Hooker," Knox said, interrupting himself. "It don't got to rhyme." More explosive laughter from all sides. On and on they went, trading choruses at the picnic table as cell phones blinked, capturing everything but the feeling of being right where we were, in that circle, with those young men in that Mississippi night. Too sweet to die.

ASIA, TOO (2): KOMSON BLUES AND AKI KUMAR

One day a few years ago I was surfing YouTube and came across a video "blues harmonica : Adam Gussow solo cover," uploaded to a channel called "komson blues."[23] It featured a young man, apparently of Asian descent, with glasses and a white T-shirt, sitting in what appears to be a bedroom — a large stuffed animal is splayed on a dresser just behind him — and playing solo harmonica along with a metronome. During the ninety-second video, he replicates a harmonica part that I had improvised for a Swatch watch commercial featuring guitarist Sterling Magee and myself, shot on a Greenwich Village stoop back in the late 1980s, several years before we became known as Satan and Adam.[24] I'd uploaded the commercial to YouTube some years earlier; he had apparently found it and made it a study tape: something to break down, copy, and put back out there as a way of demonstrating his prowess to the world. He played the part so well, with such exemplary tone and attention to detail, that I signed in and left a comment.

He quickly tracked down my email address, which isn't hard to do, and emailed me:

dear adam
    i am the guy who imitate your solo from the Swatch watch ad, and thank you for your comments, and i got some questions, can you explain for me or give some tips. thank you so much~~
    Q: i heard the song named "good morning little school girl" its sonny boy williamson version, but seems its not 12 bar blues, cause i lost the beat every time, and i am not clear about the 8bar blues, its this the 8bar blues song?
    Q: i really love playing blues harmonica, but i know its not sound

good if I play all the time, but i am not good at singing, could you
give some advices how to singing blues songs?

    Q: do you got plan to come China to play? nowadays, blues
harmonica fans all know adam, hahaha, you are my teacher~~

    thank you so much

    Best wishes

    komson[25]

I gave him what help I could, and we began an occasional correspondence.
I still don't know Komson's real name. But he tells me that he lives in Guang-
zhou, in Guangdong province, just across the strait from Hong Kong. To date,
Komson has uploaded sixty-five videos to his channel. A few of them are his
own improvisations, but the great majority, taken together, constitute a remarkable student portfolio: a curated series of self-designated masterworks
faithfully replicated on camera, offering a Who's Who of the blues harmonica
world as he sees it. Departed greats James Cotton, Sonny Terry, Big Walter,
Little Walter, and Sonny Boy Williamson are there, along with Magic Dick,
Rick Estrin, Jerry Portnoy, and Kim Wilson, but Komson has also covered
younger American teacher/performers like David Barrett, Joe Filisko, and
Jason Ricci, and he's thrown a handful of the best-known players from other
parts of the world: Bonny B (Cambodia/Switzerland), Steve Baker (United
Kingdom/Germany), Flavio Guimarães (Brazil), Paul Lamb (United King-
dom), Jean-Jacques Milteau (France), Victor Puertas (Spain), Lee Sankey
(United Kingdom), and Frédéric Yonnet (France/United States). Living
African American players—Billy Boy Arnold, Sugar Blue, Billy Branch—are
curiously absent from this otherwise inclusive pantheon, as are well-known
contemporary women players such as Annie Raines and Cheryl Arena.[26]

    One of Komson's masterworks is "Bombay Stroll" by Akarsha "Aki"
Kumar, a superb young West Coast player. If there's one contemporary blues
musician who best exemplifies the possibilities inherent in the idea of blues
as simultaneously a black music, an American music, and a global music, a
music staking its claim to our attention in this late postmodern moment, it
is Aki. A longtime student of David Barrett, majordomo of BluesHarmonica
.com and founder of San Jose's School of the Blues who was himself a student of Bay Area legend Gary Smith, Aki had the sort of pedigreed face-to-
face mentorship—from a white teacher, as it happens, not a black one—that
merits the word "lineage." His own website tells the rest of the story:

> Indian-born, San Jose–based Aki Kumar, aka "The Only Bombay
> Blues Man," left his home in Mumbai with the intention of working

as a software engineer in Silicon Valley. Then he discovered the blues, and his life dramatically changed. Singing and playing harmonica, he steeped himself in the music and became a fixture in blues clubs throughout Northern California. . . .

When he began performing, Kumar initially attempted to downplay his ethnicity. . . . "I wanted to make a statement that I was a traditional blues man, so I wanted to be playing blues and have nobody even wonder where I came from." His attitude soon changed, and with his Little Village Foundation debut, *Aki Goes to Bollywood* [2016], he began integrating elements of Indian music into his musical and visual presentation, making for a multi-cultural mash-up that sounds like no one else, yet never loses touch with its blues foundation. That unique blend of East and West reaches a new creative plateau on Aki's second Little Village Foundation album, *Hindi Man Blues* [2018], which boasts Aki's most ambitious cross-cultural fusion to date, and features liner notes by veteran blues great Charlie Musselwhite.[27]

It was losing his job as a software engineer at Adobe in 2013 that convinced Aki to pursue the blues as a full-time occupation, a decision endorsed by the notice he drew in a 2014 article in *Living Blues* featuring rising stars of blues harmonica, virtually all of them men of color. What his website biography doesn't make clear is the degree to which Aki's transformation from slickly styled blues revivalist into a deliberately "ethnic" crossover provocateur dressed in a turban and kurta has been a response to shifting political currents in the United States, specifically the demonization of "Islamic terrorists," "Mexican rapists," fearsome dark-skinned others. "It was really a personal transformation for me," he told a journalist in 2018, "because of changes in the U.S. political climate and the rise of this maniac Trump and the poison he's spewing. I thought it was time to stop trying to gain authenticity as a Chicago style blues harmonica player and be more about who I really am, which is part Indian and part American, and to put that out in the blues community in a very visible way."[28]

Hindi Man Blues, a title that signifies on *Hoodoo Man Blues*, the celebrated 1964 album by Junior Wells and Buddy Guy, shows Aki continuing to develop both his Indian-blues fusion and his political critique. "Dilruba," the lead music video from the album, frames Aki's performance within a Red State tableau: an older white man in a cowboy hat and dark sunglasses approaches a big chrome microphone, cringes at a squeal of high-pitched feed-

Aki Kumar
(photograph by Marilyn Stringer, courtesy of Akarsha Kumar)

back, glances down at a piece of paper, and then haltingly introduces the next act as "Ah-KAI Cummer" as the camera pans across the audience — half a dozen bored Heartland Americans, one in farmer's overalls, sitting in half-empty bleachers. How ya gonna play to *that* crowd? Cut to a floodlit stage where Aki stands, chromatic harp and mic in hand, clothed in light cream-colored Indian formal wear buttoned to the neck. His jump blues quartet, arrayed behind him, launches into a familiar up-tempo retro-jump beat. The fourth member of his quartet, sitting on the floor, is playing not a piano but a small Indian harmonium. Aki blows a harp intro, then begins to sing — in Hindi, with subtitles. A beautiful dark-haired Indian woman in a sari slowly works her way down to a seat in front as he sings and then blows a solo; Aki, stunned by her beauty, takes the harp out of his mouth as the solo continues on without him. The frame dissolves into a dream reverie: Aki and the woman, now clothed in magenta, circle each other in a rural setting that appears to be Sonoma wine country as Kid Andersen, a Norwegian-born guitarist and mainstay of the West Coast blues scene, plays a spirited solo on the sitar. Later, after the seduction reverie and its accompanying dance has played itself out—Aki voices both his own pleas and the spiky demurrals of his intended beloved, all in rapid-fire Hindi—we're back on stage, where Aki, like Mumbai's version of Louis Prima or Desi Arnaz, urges his band members onward with exaggerated "hot" cries and gestures, a seemingly deliberate self-burlesque. If the earlier dance sequence is an homage to Bollywood, this routine suggests, mischievously, that Red State America will love *this* sort of "wild" Ethnic Guy, even if they can't understand a word he's saying.[29]

If the social commentary is visible but muted here, clothed in a playful exoticism and a catchy fusion sound, then it's front and center in "All Bark No Bite," an angry, funny, English-language blues, powered by old-school acoustic harp and a familiar slow-rolling stop-time format; a signifying blues that boldly calls out the forty-fifth president of the United States. It's "Big Boss Man" for the tweet-storm era:

> Now looky here man . . .
> Don't you kid yourself
> You say we need fixin' . . .
> But you're the one who needs help
> You're acting high and mighty . . .
> An entitled fool
> You got a big-name degree . . .
> But we'll take you to school
>
> *Chorus:*
>
> You're just a barking dog . . .but you ain't got no bite
> Now that you've taken us on . . . you gonna gonna lose this fight
>
> A fast-food connoisseur . . .
> More ketchup than steak
> Like that rug on your head boy . . .
> You're just a flimsy fake
> Now all your talk is cheap . . .
> Your best words are just lies
> Your bluster don't scare us, boy . . .
> We'll cut you down to size

You're just a barking dog . . . etc.

You talk a big game . . .
Waving tiny little hands
Still a low-class billionaire . . .
With a two-dollar tan
All your huffin' and a puffin' . . .
Ain't nothin' but a whole lotta jive
You're just a big old zero, boy . . .
Acting like 45

You're just a barking dog . . . etc.

Now you're stumbling and s-s-s-stuttering . . .
As you fall on your face
Now the only thing you're winning, man . . .
Is a shot at last place
You're a historic blunder . . .
A blemish and a stain
Soon you'll be forgotten . . .
And we'll be great again.[30]

The song ends abruptly on "again." No familiar walk-it-down cadence, no
last lingering chord followed by a collective final cutoff. The song just . . .
stops. It's a drop-the-mic moment — Trump's own slogan, "Make America
Great Again," turned against him in an unanswerable way — but it's also a
modern touch, a structural innovation that defamiliarizes the blues, for a
moment, and makes them new.

ACKNOWLEDGMENTS

The debt of gratitude I owe to those who helped bring *Whose Blues?* into being begins with the nameless scribes of Rev.com, who transcribed eight hours' worth of "Blues Talk" YouTube videos quickly and accurately. Thanks for sparing me that thankless task! Thanks, too, to Ted Ownby and Ivo Kamps, my supervisors at the Center for the Study of Southern Culture and the English Department, both at the University of Mississippi, who offered to pay the cost of transcription at a very early moment when more prudent administrators might have wondered whether the book I envisioned would actually emerge from such an unlikely source.

Three chapters of *Whose Blues?* have previously been published in slightly different form as an outgrowth of that transcription-and-development process. Heartfelt thanks to Marcus Tribett at *Arkansas Review,* Jimmy Thomas at *Study the South,* and Emma Calabrese (and Ayse Erginer) at *Southern Cultures* for their conscientious editorial guidance, including many suggestions for revision that strengthened the resulting articles and book. I am grateful to all three journals for extending me the right to reprint.

Bar 9 began life as a paper delivered at the 2001 "Ralph Ellison: The Next Fifty Years" conference at the University of Pittsburgh. I was invited to Pitt at the suggestion of two early mentors, Jonathan Arac and Marcus Rediker, who encouraged my fledgling attempts at scholarly writing and dreams of an academic career and whom it gives me great pleasure to thank here. Shepherded by editor and conference cochair Ronald Judy, the revised paper later appeared in *boundary 2* and has been substantially rewritten for this volume. Bar 10 was originally published in slightly different form in *New Thoughts on the Black Arts Movement,* edited by Margo Natalie Crawford and Lisa Gail Collins, my esteemed colleagues in the Africana Studies Program at Vassar College between 2000 and 2002. I first delivered Bar 11 as a keynote lecture for the Twenty-Fourth annual Midwestern Conference on Literature, Language, and Media at Northern Illinois University in DeKalb in 2016 at the invitation of Tim Ryan, one of my favorite blues literature scholars. A revised version was published in the *Journal of Popular Music Education* and has been further revised for its somewhat different audience here. I extend my grateful thanks to all parties for permission to reprint, and for encouragement tendered along the way.

I'm fortunate to have blues poet Derrick Harriell as a colleague at Ole Miss; a joint interview that E. M. Tran recently conducted with him and Tyehimba Jess helped deepen my understandings of contemporary African American literary investments in the blues. I've also benefited greatly from supervising the doctoral work of Josh-Wade Ferguson; his focus on Africadian blues writer George Elliott Clarke as well as Sherman Alexie, Joy Harjo, Kiese Laymon, and Jesmyn Ward has given me a keener sense of blues' range of use-values in the modern world. (Josh-Wade's interview with Laymon, titled "Perpetual Reckoning," provides the epigraph for Bar 4.)

The way I think about the blues has been critically shaped at every turn by the musicians I have been lucky enough to work, talk, and share time with over the years. Sterling "Mr. Satan" Magee has been a source of continuing inspiration since the day we first met on 125th Street in Harlem back in 1986; I'm delighted that the documentary *Satan & Adam*, twenty-three years in the making, finally saw widespread release in 2018, when both Sterling and I were still alive and kicking and ready to do our thing one last time at the Tribeca Film Festival. My thanks to filmmaker V. Scott Balcerek for having faith in our story. Since my relocation from New York City to Oxford, Mississippi in 2002, I've gotten to know a whole new crew of local players, most of whom I've jammed or gigged with, some of whom I've hired to teach and perform at Hill Country Harmonica and/or visit with my graduate and undergraduate blues literature classes at the university. These include Bill Abel, Terry "Harmonica" Bean, Sam Carr, Jimmy "Duck" Holmes, Bill "Watermelon Slim" Homans, Mark "Muleman" Massey, Bill "Howl-N-Madd" Perry, Anthony "Big A" Sherrod, Josh "Razorblade" Stewart, Sharde Thomas, Andrew "Shine" Turner, and Leo "Bud" Welch. Sam, Josh, and Leo have passed on; the rest are still here—making superior music, bearing witness, teaching us things we need to know. Thanks, friends. Additional thanks to Aki Kumar for permission to reprint his lyrics and to Brandon Bailey for getting me started on that foot drum adventure and trusting me to produce his first album. My current blues partner, Alan Gross, appears nowhere in *Whose Blues?*, but he and our Blues Doctors duo have greatly enriched the last half-dozen years of my life. Sterling Magee's nephew Rod Patterson, a singer, dancer, and motivational speaker, recently contacted me after seeing *Satan & Adam*, asking to join Alan and me in a trio featuring his uncle's songs—one more example of the unlikely story lines that percolate through contemporary blues culture. (We call ourselves Sir Rod and the Blues Doctors.) My harmonica mentor Nat Riddles, who passed in 1991, has missed the last thirty years of our collective history, but I know he'd be chuckling at where we've ended up. This book is dedicated to his memory.

From time to time I had a research question that needed better answers than I could come up with on my own. I was lucky to have, both in-state and within easy email reach, Greg Johnson, blues curator at the department of Archives & Special Collections here on campus, and Scott Barretta, former editor of *Living Blues* and coauthor with Jim O'Neal of all the Mississippi Blues Trail markers. They have my warmest thanks for their help — including Greg's late-stage help in locating, sourcing, and scanning several photos. Clay Motley, a scholar and fan of the Mississippi blues, helped solve the mystery of an untraceable Ma Rainey quote when I put the question to my Facebook friends, for which I'm grateful. I owe special thanks the two peer reviewers retained by UNC Press for their many excellent suggestions; this book benefited greatly from their shrewd appraisal. Thanks, too, to all the photographers whose images appear herein, a richly evocative cache testifying to the beauty, majesty, and dynamism of the performers who make this music.

Finally, I'd like to thank my son, Shaun, on the cusp of fourteen as I write these words, for the continuing provocation of his expanding musical instrumentarium, which has featured, in turn, trumpet, cello, electric bass, keyboard, tuba, bass clarinet, trombone, alto sax, flute, and hi-tension marching snare drum. For the moment he has settled on trumpet, bass, and snare, and is our resident master of Guitar Hero 3. I'm proud to have taught him his first blues scale and delighted finally to be out of hock from Amro Music in Memphis, where the salesmen look at Dad with bemusement every time we walk through the door. I have no idea what sort of music will be blasting or thumping or tinkling or tooting out of Shaun's room next, and that is a great thing.

As for Sherrie: the adventure continues. Thanks for encouraging me to hit the road when you see that gleam in my eye, and for welcoming me home with a hug and a kiss when I return.

NOTES

BAR 1

1. Harris, "Can White People Play the Blues?"

2. "Businessman Tries to End Mississippi's Bad Rap."

3. Upholt, "Up All Night on Farish Street."

4. "Opening Plenary: Blues Summit on the State of the Music Today."

5. Outrage at Iglauer within Chicago's blues community was focused primarily on the following statement: "If I'm criticized, and I assume I am, for not signing more African-American artists, the answer is: show me an African-American artist who has got a vision for where to carry some blues into the future, who is an efficient bandleader, who has their act together businesswise enough so that I can work with them, who doesn't have a significant drug or alcohol issue, and who has live charisma, and I will take that artist real seriously." Qtd. in Whiteis, "At 40 Years Old, Alligator Records Continues to Evolve."

6. For a quick overview of this scene, see "Top 30 Southern Soul, Rhythm & Blues Albums." An equally enlightening overview recently showed up in my mailbox at the Center for the Study of Southern Culture: a distribution copy of a CD called *Blues Mix 28: Dance Party Soul* (2019) issued by Ecko Records of Memphis, featuring O. B. Buchana ("You're Welcome to the Party"), KT ("Kitty Kayt Tamer"), Gerod Rayborn ("I Love My Blues"), Sweet Angel ("Don't Let the Clean Up Woman Pick Up Your Man"), Jaye Hammer ("I Ain't Leaving Mississippi" remix), and others.

7. One significant exception to my claim is Nellie "Tiger" Travis; a participant on at least one other panel in the "Blues and the Spirit" symposium, Travis does indeed have experience, and an audience, in both the southern soul blues scene and Chicago's mainstream club scene.

8. "Blues Talk."

9. For more on the possible Native American origins of the blues, see Gioia, *The Guitar and the New World*, esp. 83–126; and Briggs, "Exploring Native American Influence on the Blues." Also see "ITTA BENA."

10. In a brief but still-useful survey, Barlow divides blues scholarship circa 1989 into three broad approaches: "blues as folklore, blues as oral literature, and blues as cultural history." Barlow, *"Looking Up at Down,"* 344–45.

11. Neal, "Any Day Now," esp. 424–25, 432–33.

12. Leitch, "Blues Southwestern Style"; Grazian, *Blue Chicago*.

BAR 2

1. Freeman, "Don't Forget the Blues."

2. Wilson, "Preface to Three Plays."

3. According to Google Analytics, my two YouTube channels, Modern Blues Harmonica and Gussow's Classic Blues Harmonica Videos, had a total of 3,289,742 video views in

calendar year 2018. A total of 137,247 users from 192 countries and territories visited ModernBluesHarmonica.com during that same period.

4. "Award Winners and Nominees."

5. Kubik, *Africa and the Blues*, 93–95.

6. Gussow, "Blues Heard 'Round the World," 9–12. For a photo of the Guam Blues Scholars, see Gussow, *Journeyman's Road*, xv.

7. I am using scare quotes around the word "white" to acknowledge both the occulted African and African American contribution to bluegrass—the banjo and black fiddling traditions in old-time string bands—and the occasional presence of African American players (such as mandolinist Richie Brown) in otherwise all-white settings. See Durman, "African American Old-Time String Band Music."

8. Wilson, "Preface to Three Plays," 564–65.

9. Wilson, *Ma Rainey's Black Bottom*, 57–58.

10. For a discussion of this historical dynamic, see Lemann, *The Promised Land*; and Dittmer, *Local People*, esp. 384–88.

11. Edwards, *The World Don't Owe Me Nothing*, 49.

12. Qtd. in Levine, *Black Culture and Black Consciousness*, 237. LeRoi Jones argues both sides of the equation in the space of three paragraphs in *Blues People*. "It is impossible to say simply, 'Slavery created blues,' and be done with it," he writes, "or at least it seems almost impossible to make such a statement and sound intelligent saying it" (50). But he also writes, "Blues did begin in slavery, and it is from that 'peculiar institution,' as it was known euphemistically, that blues did find its particular form" (50).

13. Salaam, *What Is Life?*, 7.

14. Edwards, *The World Don't Owe Me Nothing*, 47.

15. Edwards, 49.

16. This figure is drawn from the U.S. Census of 1860. See "Selected Statistics on Slavery in the United States."

17. Johnson, *Soul by Soul*, esp. 78–116.

18. Ferris, *Blues from the Delta*, 19.

19. Haralambos, *Soul Music*, 72.

20. Harris, Untitled referee's report.

21. Murray, *Stomping the Blues*, 6, 10, 45, 68–69.

BAR 3

1. Gussow, "Teaching the Blues."

2. Rowe, *Chicago Blues*, 165–68; Goins, *Blues All Day Long*, 112–15.

3. Berlin's song, made famous by Ruth Etting in the 1927 Ziegfeld Follies, was recorded by Etting and many other artists. "Ruth Etting."

4. Rogin, *Blackface, White Noise*, 111.

5. Keil sketches the "moldy fig" syndrome among blues commentators in *Urban Blues*, 34–39.

6. King, *Blues All around Me*, 242.

7. Gussow, "'If Bessie Smith Had Killed Some White People,'" 239–40.

8. Jahn, *Muntu*, xxi.

9. Edwards, *The World Don't Owe Me Nothing*, 45, 47.

10. Edwards, 47.

11. Baker, *Turning South Again*, 93.

12. Edwards, *The World Don't Owe Me Nothing*, 121.

13. Ferris, *Blues from the Delta*, 19. The saying appears in many versions; Ferris collected his from Shelby "Poppa Jazz" Brown, a resident of Leland, Mississippi, he interviewed in the late 1960s who had run a juke joint for more than thirty years.

14. Foster, *'Til Death or Distance Do Us Part*, 22, 36.

15. Salaam, "the blues aesthetic," 14.

16. Handy, *Father of the Blues*, 145–47.

17. Dollard, *Caste and Class in a Southern Town*, 359.

18. Wilson, *Ma Rainey's Black Bottom*, 68. All subsequent citations of this work in this chapter are included parenthetically in the text.

BAR 4

1. For an extended discussion of enactments of beloved community in contemporary blues culture, see Gussow, "Where Is the Love?" Also see Barlow, *"Looking Up at Down,"* 346. "An unusual cross-section of people are currently engaged in blues culture. Their race, class, and generational differences have made it one of those rare, eclectic, and in many ways utopian social experiments that can take place only on the fringes of the dominant culture. . . . This proclivity to break down cultural barriers and to refashion race and social relations along more egalitarian lines gives the blues culture its utopian potential."

2. Edwards, *The World Don't Owe Me Nothing*, 142.

3. For a critique of "colorblind" thinking in a blues context, see Herrick, "Performing Blues and Navigating Race in Transcultural Contexts," 6.

4. The world of rock offers an important parallel for recent black bluesist critiques of the mainstream blues scene. The BRC (Black Rock Coalition) Manifesto (1985), a statement around which that insurgent cohort of African American rock musicians organized, insisted that "rock and roll is Black music and we are its heirs. . . . BRC members assert cultural ownership, stressing that African American innovators made central contributions to the development of rock." The BRC was particularly angered by two issues: the way in which rock music (as opposed to 1950s rock and roll) had been defined as white by rock journalists and historians, and the way in which white radio programmers and record labels had effectively conspired to exclude black rockers from radio playlists and deny them recording contracts. See Mahon, *Right to Rock*, esp. 86–103.

5. Cone, *The Spirituals and the Blues*, 100.

6. The two entries read as follows: "(1930) N.Y. Times 5 Jan. VIII. 2 x/4 Riverside— Ted Lewis, the moaning blues man, is the week's big item in this house; (1953) Zanesville (Ohio) Signal 3 July 4/3 Mez Mezzrow, the Big Blues Man, was arrested in Paris for peddling merrywanna." "bluesman," *Oxford English Dictionary*.

7. Clar, "Sammelreferat," 225; Wilgus, "From the Record Review Editor," 284.

8. Wilgus, "The Blues," 185.

9. See, for example, Love, "Down and Dirty with G. Love": "When I think about Mississippi John Hurt, I think of adjectives like gentle, soft-spoken, soothing, sly, charming and personable."

10. Davis, "Charley Patton."

11. Wald, *Escaping the Delta*, 58.

12. Wald, 60.

13. Wald, 118.

14. Wald, 118.

15. Wald, 7.

16. Recent scholarship has eroded the claim made by both Wald and McGinley that the classic blueswomen were the first stars of the blues. In Bar 5, I discuss Butler "String Beans" May, a black male vaudevillian who never recorded but who rose to prominence in the decade before the blues craze, working in a duo with his wife, Sweetie. Abbott and Seroff make a convincing case that he, not the blueswomen, was the first widely known blues star. See Abbott and Seroff, *The Original Blues*, 67–123.

17. Wald, *Escaping the Delta*, xv, xxiv.

18. *"Publishers Weekly* List of Bestselling Novels."

19. Abbott and Seroff, *Ragged but Right*, 217.

20. Edwards, *The World Don't Owe Me Nothing*, esp. 119–27.

21. Wald, *Escaping the Delta*, 3.

22. Reich, "Sugar Blue a Soaring Voice for the Blues."

23. Tran, "Obsession, Desperation, and Curiosity," n.p.

24. Tran, n.p.

25. Lomax, *Blues in the Mississippi Night*, n.p.

26. Gussow, *Seems Like Murder Here*, 11–12, 45–59.

27. King, *Blues All around Me*, 56–57.

28. King, 55–56.

29. Gussow, *Seems Like Murder Here*, 22, 45, 57–59.

30. Edwards, *The World Don't Owe Me Nothing*, 47.

31. Ferris, *Give My Poor Heart Ease*, 114.

32. "Five Stages of Grief."

33. Edwards, *The World Don't Owe Me Nothing*, 121.

34. O'Neal and van Singel, *The Voice of the Blues*, 235.

35. Gussow, *Journeyman's Road*, 113–14.

36. Tate writes, for example, of how his mother "once wrote a poem of the same name [i.e., "Everything but the Burden"] to decry the long-standing, ongoing, and unarrested theft of African-American cultural properties by thieving, flavorless whitefolk. A jeremiad against the ways Our music, Our fashion, Our hairstyles, Our dances, Our anatomical traits, Our bodies, Our Soul continue to be considered ever ripe for the plucking and the biting by the same crafty devils who brought you the African slave trade and the Middle Passage." Tate, *Everything but the Burden*, 2.

37. zur Heide, *Deep South Piano*, 36–37.

BAR 5

1. "Examined Life—Cornell West."

2. Hughes, "Bad Luck Card."

3. Ellison, "Richard Wright's Blues," 90.

4. Calt, *I'd Rather Be the Devil*, 34–38.

5. Kubik, *Africa and the Blues*, 42–46; Ottenheimer, "Comoro Crossroads," 34.

6. Handy, *Father of the Blues*, 79.

7. Hazzard-Gordon, *Jookin'*.

8. Cone, *The Spirituals and the Blues*.

9. Hurston, *Mules and Men*, 143.

10. DeSalvo, *The Language of the Blues*, xiv.

11. See Steptoe, "Big Mama Thornton, Little Richard, and the Queer Roots of Rock 'n' Roll," 61.

12. Qtd. in Oliver, *Screening the Blues*, 166.

13. Qtd. in Gates, *The Signifying Monkey*, 85.

14. Berlin, "If You Don't Want My Peaches." Also see Cartwright, "Guess These People Wonder What I'm Singing," 288–91; Oliver, *Songsters and Saints*, 72; and McGinley, *Staging the Blues*, 31–79, esp. 36–37.

15. McGinley, *Staging the Blues*, 31–79, esp. 36–37.

16. Davis, *Blues Legacies and Black Feminism*, 4.

17. Murray, *Stomping the Blues*, 10.

18. Salaam, "the blues aesthetic," 13–14.

19. Langston Hughes to Carl Van Vechten, qtd. in Rampersad, *The Life of Langston Hughes*, 111.

BAR 6

1. Jones, *Dutchman*, 30.

2. "Bridging the Blues"; "Clarksdale, Mississippi."

3. "The Blues Were Born."

4. Albertson, *Bessie*, 12.

5. Work, *American Negro Songs and Spirituals*, 32–33.

6. Abbott and Seroff, *The Original Blues*, 170.

7. Abbott and Seroff, 287.

8. Reich, "Sugar Blue a Soaring Voice for the Blues."

9. Brackett, *Categorizing Sound*, 84.

10. Handy, *Father of the Blues*, 199–200.

11. Muir, *Long Lost Blues*, 83–85, 182.

12. Abbott and Seroff, *The Original Blues*, 67–123, esp. 70, 74–76, 104, 106, 115, 116–20; 125, 127, 136, 144.

13. Keil, *Urban Blues*, 233.

14. Abbott and Seroff, *The Original Blues*, 262–63, 275–76. "When [Houston-based blues pianist] Sammy Price traveled with the Theatre Owners Booking Association (TOBA) in the 1920s, he performed for a 'white only' audience during 'Midnight Rambles' on the weekend and for African Americans on other nights." Steptoe, *Houston Bound*, 173.

15. The phrase appears in Neal's essay "The Black Arts Movement" (1968): "The motive behind the black aesthetic is *the destruction of the white thing*, the destruction of white ideas and white ways of looking at the world."

16. For histories of the blues that example this paragraph's claims, see Palmer, *Deep Blues*, 23–25, 43–46, 48–57; Barlow, "Looking Up at Down," 25–40; and Davis, *The History of the Blues*, 23–29.

17. Cobb, *The Most Southern Place on Earth*; Wald, *Escaping the Delta*, 85.

18. Ottenheimer, "Blues in the Heartland," 16, 36.

19. Ottenheimer, 36.

20. Kubik, *Africa and the Blues*, 94.

21. Morton, "I Created Jazz in 1902, Not W. C. Handy."

22. Robertson, *W. C. Handy*, 30.

23. Handy, *Father of the Blues*, 10. All subsequent citations of this work in this chapter are included parenthetically in the text.

24. For more on this development, see Toll, *Blacking Up*, 195–233.

25. I write at length about this idea in Gussow, *Seems Like Murder Here*, 81–93.

26. Tracy, *Langston Hughes and the Blues*, 115.

27. Qtd. in Gussow, *Seems Like Murder Here*, 194.

28. Hughes, "Songs Called the Blues."

29. Handy, *Blues: An Anthology*, 85.

30. Robertson, *W. C. Handy*, 97.

31. Blues histories that quote this passage include Oakley, *The Devil's Music*, 9; Barlow, *"Looking Up at Down,"* 31; and Davis, *The History of the Blues*, 25.

32. Troutman, *Kika Kila*, 156–59.

33. Kubik, *Africa and the Blues*, 16–20; Powell, "The Diddley Bow."

34. Du Bois, "Of the Sorrow Songs," 264; Murphy, "The Survival of African Music in America."

35. Wagner, *Disturbing the Peace*, 27, 37.

36. "Prince McCoy."

37. See, for example, Evans, "Charley Patton," 152, 158–59; and Edwards, *The World Don't Owe Me Nothing*, 60, 62.

BAR 7

1. Peabody, "Notes on Negro Music," 148–49.

2. Odum, "Folk-Song and Folk-Poetry," 137.

3. Odum, *Social and Mental Traits of the Negro*, 470.

4. Brown, "The Blues as Folk Poetry," 540–41.

5. Hurston, "Characteristics of Negro Expression," 66.

6. Hurston, 66.

7. Hughes, "Note on Commercial Theatre," 190.

8. Thanks to Elijah Wald and David Hall for clarifying this point.

9. Salaam, "the blues aesthetic," 14.

10. Charters and Kunstadt, *Jazz*, 96.

11. Thanks to Greg Johnson for answering my question about Mississippi-born blues singers other than Bogan who recorded during this period.

12. Shaw, *The Jazz Age*, 76–77.

13. "I've Got the Yes, We Have No Bananas Blues!"

14. Laird, *Moanin' Low*, 533.

15. Qtd. in Melnick, *A Right to Sing the Blues*, 169–70.

16. Qtd. in Dickerson, *Goin' Back to Memphis*, 24.

17. Hughes, "Ma Man," 66–67.

18. Hughes, "The Negro Artist and the Racial Mountain," 694.

19. Campbell, *The Hero with a Thousand Faces*, 30.

20. Hughes, *The Big Sea*, 40.

21. Rampersad, introduction, xxii.

22. Hughes, *The Big Sea*, 206–7.

23. Hughes, 208–9.

24. Tracy, *Langston Hughes and the Blues*, 113.

25. Hughes, *The Big Sea*, 217.

26. Hughes, "My Adventures as a Social Poet," 206.

27. Rampersad, *The Life of Langston Hughes*, 140.

28. Rampersad, 141.

29. Hughes, "The Weary Blues."

30. Hughes, *The Big Sea*, 215.

31. Qtd. in Tracy, *Langston Hughes and the Blues*, 155.

32. Williams, "The Blues Roots," 448.

BAR 8

1. Handy, *Father of the Blues*, 176.

2. Hughes, *The Collected Poems*, 82, 249.

3. See Hemenway, *Zora Neale Hurston*, 219, 241.

4. Handy, *Father of the Blues*, 54.

5. Rampersad, *The Life of Langston Hughes*, 20, 46.

6. Hurston, *Dust Tracks on a Road*, 262.

7. Hurston, 260.

8. Higginbotham, "African-American Women's History," 266.

9. Gates, "Why Richard Wright Hated Zora Neale Hurston."

10. Hurston, *Their Eyes Were Watching God*, 10–11. All subsequent citations of this work (*TE*) in this chapter are included parenthetically in the text.

11. Gates, "Why Richard Wright Hated Zora Neale Hurston."

12. Qtd. in Gates.

13. Hurston, *Dust Tracks on a Road*, 58.

14. Boyd, *Wrapped in Rainbows*, 69.

15. Ellison, "Richard Wright's Blues," 90.

16. Hurston, *Dust Tracks on a Road*, 4. All subsequent citations of this work (*DT*) in this chapter are included parenthetically in the text.

17. Du Bois, *The Souls of Black Folk*, 45.

18. Hurston, "The Ocoee Riot."

19. Hurston, "How It Feels to Be Colored Me."

20. Boyd, *Wrapped in Rainbows*, 151.

21. Boyd, 151.

22. Hurston, *Mules and Men*, 57. All subsequent citations of this work (*MAM*) in this chapter are included parenthetically in the text.

23. Gussow, *Seems Like Murder Here*, 235–52.

24. See "The 'Get-Down' Quality: Descending Direction in Melody, Sculpture, Dance," in Thompson, *African Art in Motion*, 13–14.

25. Hurston, *Zora Neale Hurston*, 113.

26. Hurston, 122.

27. Hughes, *The Collected Poems*, 112.

28. See Johnson, "'The World in a Jug,'" 401–15.

29. Davis, *Blues Legacies and Black Feminism*, 4, 8–9.

30. Hurston, *Zora Neale Hurston*, 131–32.

31. For a reading of young Joe Starks as the embodiment of the "Jody" figure in black

folk culture, a well-dressed, seductive "back-door man" who steals Janie away from hardworking but unglamorous Logan Killicks, see Steptoe, "'Jody's Got Your Girl and Gone,'" esp. 253, 258–59.

BAR 9

1. Ellison, "Richard Wright's Blues," 90. All subsequent citations of this work in this chapter are included parenthetically in the text.

2. Wright, *Black Boy*, 161. All subsequent citations of this work in this chapter are included parenthetically in the text.

3. Edwards, *The World Don't Owe Me Nothing*, 4–5.

4. Rowley, *Richard Wright*, 43.

5. Ellison, "'My Strength Comes from Louis Armstrong,'" 283.

6. See Fabre, *The Unfinished Quest of Richard Wright*, 237; and Rowley, *Richard Wright*, 256–57.

7. For brief mentions of Wright's blues poetry and liner notes, see Fabre, *The Unfinished Quest of Richard Wright*, 516; Rowley, *Richard Wright*, 227; and Werner, "Bigger's Blues," 143. Folklorist William Ferris, invoking commonalities between Wright and his black Mississippi contemporary, blues bassist and lyricist Willie Dixon (1915–92), offers a notably more generous assessment of Wright as a blues writer, someone who "saw a clear parallel between his work and the lyrics of the blues performer." Ferris, "Richard Wright and the Blues."

8. For "spatial mobility," see Baker, *Blues, Ideology, and Afro-American Literature*; and Murray, *Train Whistle Guitar*. For "mass blues audience" and "technologies of reproduction," see Titon, *Early Downhome Blues*; and Harrison, *Black Pearls*. For "new sexual freedom," see Davis, *Blues Legacies and Black Feminism*.

9. Qtd. in Sackheim, *The Blues Line*, 391.

10. "Stackolee."

11. Murray, *Train Whistle Guitar*, 13.

12. Townsend, *A Blues Life*, 6–7.

13. Harris, "No Outlet for the Blues," 58.

14. Cone, "The Blues," 236.

15. Ellison, "Remembering Richard Wright," 199.

16. Ellison, "A Party Down at the Square," 3–11.

17. Ellison, *Invisible Man*, 141.

18. Ellison, "An Extravagance of Laughter," 167, 180.

19. Ellison, *Invisible Man*, 28.

20. Ellison, 4–5.

21. Garon, *Woman with Guitar*, 69–70.

22. Edwards, *The World Don't Owe Me Nothing*, 199.

BAR 10

1. Sharpe, *In the Wake*, 5.

2. Blues Foundation, "2019 Blues and Race Panel, Part 1."

3. Robinson, "Listening for the Country."

4. Tran, "Obsession, Desperation, and Curiosity."

5. Tran.

6. See Benston, "Renovating Blackness."

7. Gates, "Black Creativity," 74–75.

8. This list includes panelists Sugar Blue and Billy Branch at the "State of the Blues Today" at the Dominican University symposium discussed in Bar 1, along with Guy Davis and Corey Harris. For Davis, see Matheis, "Favored Son." For Harris, see Frede, "Words Sound Power," 31. "You know," Harris told *Living Blues*, "one time this guy took my picture after I told him not to. I was on the street. He had one of those little disposable cameras. I said, 'Why'd you take my picture?' He said, 'Well, my son said, 'I just want a picture of this big fucking black guy playing a guitar.' He was talking about me. I said, 'You're a real idiot, you know that. You sit here and say that to me, how do you think I'm going to react.' I said, 'Give me your camera.' I took his camera and I threw it in the sewer.'"

9. Jones, *Dutchman*, 34–35.

10. "BluesFirst." This source shows the Blues Foundation's web-based pitch for the previous year's event in February 2001. Much of the language is identical or similar to that used to promote the 2002 event, but the latter event was expanded to three days.

11. Salaam, *What Is Life?*, 19.

12. The phrase is from Jones, "The Changing Same."

13. Wood, "Are Negroes Ashamed of the Blues?" See also "Why I'll Always Sing the Blues, 95" "Although B. B. considers the type of songs he plays and sings America's greatest contribution to the music world, he realizes 'a lot of people don't like to be associated with the blues because the songs embarrass them. . . . It's a drag. You know why? Because it is Negro music and they are afraid of anything Negro while we're going through this integration business.'. . . B. B. realizes that the blues are still going through their period of disgrace as did ragtime, jazz and swing."

14. King, *Blues All around Me*, 213.

15. Fanon, *Toward the African Revolution*, 37.

16. Karenga, "Black Art," 9.

17. Madhubuti, *Don't Cry, Scream*.

18. Sanchez, "liberation / poem."

19. Haralambos, *Soul Music*, 118.

20. Jones, *Blues People*, 95.

21. Neal, "The Ethos of the Blues," 42.

22. Knight, "Haiku."

23. Neal, "For Our Women" and "Can You Dig It?," 55, 71–72; Ferdinand (Kalamu ya Salaam), "The Blues (in two parts)," 375–77; Cone, *The Spirituals and the Blues*; Cortez, "Lead," "Dinah's Back in Town," and "You Know"; Crouch, "The Big Feeling" and "Howlin' Wolf"; Dent, "For Walter Washington," 372–73; Dumas, "Keep the Faith Blues," 370; Giovanni, "Poem For Aretha," "Master Charge Blues"; Henderson, "Blues, Soul, and Black Identity"; 348; Redmond, "Double Clutch Lover"; Troupe, "Impressions / of Chicago; for Howlin Wolf"; Young, "A Dance for Ma Rainey," 366.

24. Ferdinand (Kalamu ya Salaam), "The Blues (in two parts)," 378–79.

25. Crouch, "The Big Feeling," 45.

26. Cone, *The Spirituals and the Blues*, 122.

27. Cone, 105.

28. Jones, "The Changing Same," 180.

29. Madhubuti, *We Walk the Way of the New World*, 5.

30. See Beaumont, *Preachin' the Blues*, esp. 9–25.

31. Henderson, "Blues, Soul, and Black Identity," 36.

32. Groom, *The Blues Revival*.

33. Welburn, "The Black Aesthetic Imperative," 147.

34. Henderson, "Blues, Soul, and Black Identity," 14.

35. "Down Home and Dirty."

36. Bims, "Blues City."

37. Qtd. in Haralambos, *Soul Music*, 91.

38. Haralambos, 91.

39. Hernton, "Dynamite Growing Out of Their Skulls."

40. Husock, untitled essay, n.p.

41. Madhubuti, *We Walk the Way of the New World*, 19.

42. An advertisement for the 1999 Santa Cruz (Calif.) Blues Festival featured headliners Jimmie Vaughan (Saturday) and Gregg Allman (Sunday), with John Mayall and the Bluesbreakers, Rod Piazza and the Mighty Flyers, the BoneShakers, Nina Storey, Ronnie Earl, and W. C. Clark. The BoneShakers are a "mixed" band; W. C. Clark is African American. *Blues Revue* 47 (May 1999): 61.

43. Welburn, "The Black Aesthetic Imperative," 132.

44. Henderson, "Blues, Soul, and Black Identity," 38.

45. Goldman, "Why Do Whites Sing Black?"

46. Goldman.

47. Neal, "The Black Arts Movement."

48. Rowell, "An Interview with Larry Neal," 29.

49. Thompson, "Media Means."

50. Qtd. in Amini, "Books Noted," 51.

51. Neal, "The Black Arts Movement."

52. Garon, "White Blues."

53. Neal, "The Sound of Soul," 43–47.

54. Baker, "Critical Change and Blues Continuity," 82.

55. Qtd. in Harrison, "Larry Neal," 173.

56. Ann Arbor Blues Festival program, 1969, n.p.

57. Ann Arbor Blues Festival program, 1970, n.p.

58. Haralambos, *Soul Music*, 169.

59. Gilmore, "Washington Blues Festival '70."

60. "Don L. Lee Interviews Stokely Carmichael," 72.

61. Gilmore, "Washington Blues Festival '70."

62. Baraka, foreword, 9.

BAR 11

1. In September 2015, responding to the fact that my Dirty-South Blues Harp channel (currently the Modern Blues Harmonica channel) had been permanently disabled from monetization, I created a new channel, Gussow's Classic Blues Harmonica Videos, monetized it from the outset, and obeyed YouTube's guidelines. It now has 6.6 million lifetime views and 100,000 subscribers.

2. Komson Blues, "Blues Harmonica"; Antic, "Predrag Antic Testimonial for Modern Blues Harmonica."

3. Haralambos, *Soul Music*, 90.

4. King, *Blues All around Me*, 242.

5. Reich, "Sugar Blue a Soaring Voice for the Blues."

6. Reich.

7. "Postmodern globalization for the blues," according to Vincent Leitch in his study of the contemporary Oklahoma City blues scene, "has meant becoming multiracial, decentralized, international, and heterogeneous." Leitch, "Blues Southwestern Style," 140.

8. Edwards, *The World Don't Owe Me Nothing*, 42, 44.

9. O'Neal, "Junior Wells," 11.

10. Field, *Harps, Harmonicas, and Heavy Breathers*, 229. When he was a teenager in Memphis, Charlie Musselwhite, seven years older than Wilson, spent time at the homes of Noah Lewis and Will Shade. "Musicians regularly gathered [there] and often 'were very willing to show me things on the guitar,'" Musselwhite remembered, "at a time when 'black kids my age weren't interested in their music.'" Herrick, "Performing Blues and Navigating Race in Transcultural Contexts," 14.

11. King, "The American Dream," 22.

12. Glover, *Blues Harp*.

13. I write at length about my apprenticeship with Nat Riddles in Gussow, *Mister Satan's Apprentice*.

14. Barrett, "About David Barrett."

15. Gindick, "Jon's Mail Order Store."

16. Advertising first appeared on YouTube on August 22, 2007, six months after I uploaded my first video. Sweney, "First Ads Appear on YouTube Clips."

17. Gussow, "Modern Blues Harmonica"; Hyde, *The Gift*.

18. I am exaggerating slightly. Of course blues harmonica instructional books and the occasional instructional CDs and DVDs continue to be released, sold, and shipped; you can find most of them on Amazon. But in the past decade, a number of blues harmonica teachers have begun to offer downloadable and/or paywall-protected video instructionals, including Ronnie Shellist, David Barrett, Jason Ricci, Sandy Weltman, and, in the United Kingdom, Tomlin Leckie and Ben Hewlett.

19. Aldin, review of *Weeds Like Us*, 78–79.

20. Hill Country Harmonica is merely one of several contemporary workshop environments in which African American blues elders teach groups of students in face-to-face settings. Other significant examples include the Port Townsend (Wash.) Acoustic Blues Workshop; Blues & Swing Week at the Augusta Heritage Center at Davis & Elkins College in Elkins, W.Va.; Traditions Weeks at Common Ground on the Hill in Westminster, Md.; Fernando Jones's Blues Camp in Chicago; and, in the United Kingdom Blues Week at the University of Northampton.

21. "Harmonica Blues with a 'Brand' New Beat."

22. Bailey and Gussow, "Superstition."

BAR 12

1. Sometimes the eleventh and twelfth bar together are called the turnaround; a few people even refer to bars nine through twelve as the turnaround.

2. As of 2018, only 13 out of more than 170 performers in the BHOF were white (7.5 percent). This calculation is derived from the list of inductees (1980–2018) provided in the Wikipedia entry "Blues Hall of Fame."

3. For other examples of Japanese / African American collaboration in the contemporary Chicago blues scene, see Herrick, "Performing Blues and Navigating Race in Transcultural Contexts," 4 (on the partnership of Shunsuke "Shun" Kikuta and J. W. Williams); and Lee, *Sugar Brown: The Shade of Blues* (the blues journey of Dr. Ken Kawashima, PhD, including his time with Tail Dragger Jones).

4. This biographical portrait draws on information found on the bio page and elsewhere on Naito's personal website, www.shojinaito.com, along with my personal knowledge, based on several visits to Filisko's Monday-night class at the Old Town School of Folk Music and a longtime subscription to *You Missed Monday*, Filisko's weekly newsletter.

5. McTurk, *Tokyo Blues*.

6. Garon, "White Blues."

7. "Blind Lemon Brothers."

8. "M1 The Call Performed by Monster."

9. Lee, "Sugar Brown." This portrait of Kawashima was assembled from Lee's documentary and the following online sources: "About Sugar Brown," "Samm Bennett Interviews Sugar Brown," and "Sugar Brown, blues singer_songwriter."

10. Whiteis, "At 40 Years Old, Alligator Records Continues to Evolve."

11. See, for example, "The Mississippi Blues Fest."

12. The festival's programming over three days was assembled from the following sources: "Edmonton's Labatt Blues Festival"; "Edmonton's Labatt Blues Festival 2011"; Levesque, "Blues Festival Cooks Up Tasty Combos"; Levesque, "Guitar Shorty Stands Tall at Blues Fest."

13. Semuels, "The Racist History of Portland."

14. "Mahindra Blues Festival 2018."

15. "Award Winners and Nominees."

16. Rollins, "Festival to Celebrate Blues Roots."

17. In his important new study, *Blues Legacy: Tradition and Innovation in Chicago* (2019), Whiteis perfectly illustrates the tensions and paradoxes of our contemporary blues moment. He argues that his book's "multigenerational, multisubgenre perspective" emphasizes Chicago's "living [blues] tradition as a dynamic and flexible one, capable of maintaining both its cultural specificity and its universal humanistic appeal as it continues to widen its scope and its range among musicians and audiences, both locally and on the national and international levels" (257). Although the contemporary Chicago blues scene has produced a number of significant non–African American performers in recent years, including Sumito "Ariyo" Ariyoshi, Barrelhouse Chuck, Rockin' Johnny Burgin, Joanna Connor, Bob Corritore, Joe Filisko, Billy Flynn, Steve Freund, Pierre Lacocque, Tad Robinson, Matthew Skoller, and Dave Specter, and although some of those musicians are mentioned and even praised by the performers profiled in *Blues Legacy*—as peers, bandmates, fellow recording artists—all forty-nine of the blues performers listed in the table of contents are African American. There's a disjunction, in other words, between the actual transracial texture of contemporary Chicago blues culture, a texture evoked by Whiteis's informants, and the all-black cast of that city's "living tradition" as configured by Whiteis's larger structural decision about who deserves profiling.

18. A page on guitarist Joe Bonamassa's website proclaiming "The Best Modern Female

Blues Musicians" lists seven white women, most of whom play electric guitar (in the order he ranks them: Ana Popovic, Samantha Fish, Joane Shaw Taylor, the Larkin Poe duo, Heather Gillis, Susan Tedeschi, Danielle Nicole) followed by three African American women (Ruthie Foster, Shemekia Copeland, Southern Avenue fronted by Tierinii Jackson). Macaluso, "The Best Modern Female Blues Musicians."

19. "The Enlightenment of W. C. Handy."

20. Here it is worth noting two different ways blues music lives on in contemporary hip hop: sampling and father/son duos. In "They Just Don't Know" (2009), to cite a representative example, the Memphis-based rapper Gyft samples the opening bars of "Come On (Let the Good Times Roll)" (1960), a widely covered hit for New Orleans blues singer Earl King. Recordings by Albert King, B. B. King, and Howlin' Wolf have all been sampled in this way. In a pair of father/son duos, "Bridging the Gap" (2004) by Olu Dara and Nas and "Uncle Tom Is Dead" (2004) by Guy and Martial Davis, the sonic and attitudinal difference between blues and hip hop, along with underlying continuities, is dramatized as a call-and-response dialogue between a blues-voiced father and a rap-voiced son—a dialogue that, in the case of the Davises, becomes a dozens-style exchange of insults.

21. "The blues community," Neff argues, "preserves culture on its own terms . . . ; instead of fading away, the blues defies the strains of time by updating and strengthening itself, remaining relevant to the community's contemporary needs. . . . The dynamic nature of Black Atlantic music defies genre labels and historical definitions, which in turn frustrates a dominant market that relies on the branding of an 'authentic' product. . . . Cultural practice in the Mississippi Delta resists, at its deepest levels, efforts to dictate the boundaries of its creativity according to the rhetoric of blues authenticity." Neff, *Let the World Listen Right*, 13.

22. Eagle, untitled video. Transcription by the author.

23. Komson Blues, "Blues Harmonica."

24. Gussow, "Sterling Magee and Adam Gussow."

25. Komson, "How to Sing Blues Songs."

26. "Komson Blues."

27. "About *Hindi Man Blues*."

28. Levesque, "Software Engineer Turned Bluesman."

29. Kumar, "Dilruba by Aki Kumar."

30. Kumar, "All Bark No Bite." I have modified these published lyrics slightly to reflect the way that Kumar actually sings them on the recording.

BIBLIOGRAPHY

Abbott, Lynn, and Doug Seroff. *Ragged but Right: Black Traveling Shows, "Coon Songs," and the Dark Pathway to Blues and Jazz*. Jackson: University Press of Mississippi, 2007.

———. *The Original Blues: The Emergence of the Blues in African American Vaudeville*. Jackson: University Press of Mississippi, 2017.

"About *Hindi Man Blues* (2018)." *Aki Kumar's Bollywood Blues*. https://www.akigoesto bollywood.com.

"About Sugar Brown." Sugarbrownmusic.com.

Albertson, Chris. *Bessie* (1972). Revised and expanded ed. New Haven, Conn.: Yale University Press, 2003.

Aldin, Mary Katherine. Review of *Weeds Like Us* by Janiva Magness. *Living Blues* 50, no. 4 (August 2019): 78–79.

Amini, Johari. "Books Noted." Review of *Can I Poet with You* by Sistr Mae Jackson. *Negro Digest*, September 1969, 51–52.

Ann Arbor Blues Festival program, 1969 and 1970. Blues Archive, University of Mississippi.

Antic, Predrag. "Predrag Antic Testimonial for Modern Blues Harmonica." YouTube video. Commentary by Predrag Antic. Adam Gussow, March 17, 2016. https://www.youtube.com/watch?v=kZCAWxuYHyY.

"Award Winners and Nominees." *Blues Foundation*. https://blues.org/awards/. Accessed August 17, 2018.

Bailey, Brandon O., and Adam Gussow. "Superstition." YouTube video. Brandon O. Bailey—Topic, August 22, 2018. https://www.youtube.com/watch?v=I7HU6Yojmz8.

Baker, Houston A., Jr. *Blues, Ideology, and Afro-American Literature: A Vernacular Theory*. Chicago: University of Chicago Press, 1984.

———. "Critical Change and Blues Continuity: An Essay on the Criticism of Larry Neal." Larry Neal: A Special Issue, *Callaloo*, no. 23 (Winter 1985): 70–84.

———. *Turning South Again: Re-thinking Modernism / Re-reading Booker T.* Durham, N.C.: Duke University Press, 2001.

Baraka, Amiri. Foreword to John Sinclair, *Fattening Frogs for Snakes: Delta Sound Suite*, 7–11. New Orleans: Surregional, 2002.

Barlow, William. *"Looking Up at Down": The Emergence of Blues Culture*. Philadelphia: Temple University Press, 1989.

Barrett, David. "About David Barrett." *David Barrett's BluesHarmonica.com*. https://www.bluesharmonica.com/about_dave. Accessed December 4, 2019.

Beaumont, Daniel E. *Preachin' the Blues: The Life and Times of Son House*. New York: Oxford University Press, 2011.

Benston, Kimberly. "Renovating Blackness: Remembrance and Revolution in the Coltrane Poem." In *Performing Blackness: Enactments of African-American Modernism*, 145–86. New York: Routledge, 2000.

Berlin, Irving. "If You Don't Want My Peaches, You'd Better Stop Shaking My Tree"
(1914). In *The Complete Lyrics of Irving Berlin*, edited by Robert Kimball and Linda
Emmet, 89. New York: Applause Cinema & Theatre Books, 2001.

Bims, Hamilton. "Blues City." *Ebony*, March 1972, 76–82, 84, 86.

Blackmon, Douglas. *Slavery by Another Name: The Re-enslavement of Black Americans from
the Civil War to World War II*. New York: Anchor, 2008.

"Blind Lemon Brothers: Travelin' Blues World." *Wandering Life* blog. http://yakume
.sakura.ne.jp/album/BLB/blbo1.html. Accessed September 10, 2018.

"BluesFirst." Internet Archive Wayback Machine. April 5, 2001. https://web.archive.org
/web/20010405093441/http://www.blues.org/bluesfirst/index.html.

Blues Foundation. "2019 Blues and Race Panel, Part 1." YouTube, July 11, 2019, https://
www.youtube.com/watch?v=EBEUyyy92wo.

"bluesman." In *Oxford English Dictionary*. https://www-oed-com.umiss.idm.oclc.org
/view/Entry/262441?redirectedFrom=bluesman#eid. Accessed September 7, 2018.

"Blues Talk: Conversations about the History, Culture, and Meanings of the Music."
Modern Blues Harmonica with Adam Gussow. https://www.modernbluesharmonica
.com/blues-talk.html.

"The Blues Were Born: Reverend Matthews." Vimeo video. Uploaded September 3, 2012.
https://vimeo.com/48746030.

Boyd, Valerie. *Wrapped in Rainbows: The Life of Zora Neale Hurston*. New York: Scribner,
2003.

Brackett, David. *Categorizing Sound: Genre and Twentieth-Century Popular Music*. Berkeley:
University of California Press, 2016.

"Bridging the Blues: Feeling the Music Where Its Roots Formed." https://www.visittheusa
.com/trip/bridging-blues.

Briggs, Kara. "Exploring Native American Influence on the Blues." *Tanka*, n.d. http://
www.tankabar.com/cgi-bin/nanf/public/viewStoryLeftRightImages.cvw?storyid
=101330&sectionname=Blog:%20In%20our%20View&commentbox=Y. Accessed
August 14, 2018.

Brown, Sterling. *Southern Road*. New York: Harcourt, Brace, 1932.

———. "The Blues as Folk Poetry" (1930). In *The Jazz Cadence of American Culture*,
edited by Robert G. O'Meally, 540–51. New York: Columbia University Press, 1998.

"Businessman Tries to End Mississippi's Bad Rap." Associated Press, December 4, 2006.
http://www.nbcnews.com/id/16043409/ns/us_news-life/t/businessman-tries-end
-mississippis-bad-rap/.

Calt, Stephen. *Barrelhouse Words: A Blues Dialect Dictionary*. Urbana: University of Illinois
Press, 2009.

———. *I'd Rather Be the Devil: Skip James and the Blues*. Chicago: Chicago Review Press,
1994.

Campbell, Joseph. *The Hero with a Thousand Faces* (1949). 2nd ed. Princeton, N.J.:
Princeton University Press, 1973.

Cartwright, Katherine. "'Guess These People Wonder What I'm Singing': Quotation
and Reference in Ella Fitzgerald's 'St. Louis Blues.'" In *Ramblin' on My Mind: New
Perspectives on the Blues*, edited by David Evans, 281–327. Urbana: University of Illinois
Press, 2008.

Charters, Samuel. *The Country Blues* (1959). New York: DaCapo, 1975.

Charters, Samuel B., and Leonard Kunstadt. *Jazz: A History of the New York Scene* (1962). New York: Da Capo, 1981.

Clar, Mimi. "Sammelreferat: Negro Blues Singers." *Western Folklore* 20, no. 3 (July 1961): 221–27.

"Clarksdale, Mississippi: Travel and Visitor Info—Where the Blues Were Born." https:// www.clarksdaletourism.com. Accessed August 21, 2018.

Cobb, James C. *The Most Southern Place on Earth: The Mississippi Delta and the Roots of Regional Identity.* New York: Oxford University Press, 1994.

Cone, James H. "The Blues: A Secular Spiritual." In *Write Me a Few of Your Lines: A Blues Reader,* edited by Steven C. Tracy, 231–51. Amherst: University of Massachusetts Press, 1999.

———. *The Spirituals and the Blues* (1972). Maryknoll, N.Y.: Orbis, 1992.

Cortez, Jayne. "Dinah's Back in Town." In *Pissstained Stairs and the Monkey Man's Wares,* n.p. New York: Phrase Text, 1969.

———. "Lead." *Negro Digest,* September 1969.

———. "You Know." In *Coagulations: New and Selected Poems,* 41–43. New York: Thunder's Mouth, 1984.

Crouch, Stanley. "Howlin' Wolf: A Blues Lesson Book." In *Ain't No Ambulances for No Nigguhs Tonight,* n.p. New York: R. W. Baron, 1972.

———. "The Big Feeling." *Negro Digest,* July 1969, 45–48.

Davis, Angela Y. *Blues Legacies and Black Feminism: Gertrude "Ma" Rainey, Bessie Smith, and Billie Holiday.* New York: Pantheon, 1998.

Davis, Francis. *The History of the Blues.* New York: Hyperion, 1995.

Dent, Tom. "For Walter Washington." In *New Black Voices: An Anthology of Contemporary Afro-American Literature,* edited by Abraham Chapman, 372–73. New York: New American Library, 1972.

DeSalvo, Debra. *The Language of the Blues: From Alcorub to Zuzu.* New York: Billboard, 2006.

Dickerson, James. *Goin' Back to Memphis: A Century of Blues, Rock 'n' Roll, and Glorious Soul.* New York: Schirmer Trade, 1996.

Dittmer, John. *Local People: The Struggle for Civil Rights in Mississippi.* Urbana: University of Illinois Press, 1995.

Dixon, Willie, with Don Snowden. *I Am the Blues: The Willie Dixon Story.* New York: Da Capo, 1989.

Dollard, John. *Caste and Class in a Southern Town* (1937). Madison: University of Wisconsin Press, 1988.

"Don L. Lee Interviews Stokely Carmichael." Special Issue, *Journal of Black Poetry* 1, no. 14 (1970–71): 70–81.

"Down Home and Dirty." *Time,* August 9, 1971.

Du Bois, W. E. B. *The Souls of Black Folk* (1903). New York: New American Library, 1982.

———. "Of the Sorrow Songs." In *The Souls of Black Folk,* 264–77. 1903. New York: New American Library, 1982.

Dumas, Henry. "Keep the Faith Blues." In *Understanding the New Black Poetry: Black Speech and Black Music as Poetic References,* by Stephen Henderson, 370. 1972. New York: William Morrow, 1973.

Durman, Chris L. H. "African American Old-Time String Band Music: A Selective

Discography." Music Publications and Other Works. Knoxville: Trace (Tennessee Research and Creative Exchange), 2008. http://trace.tennessee.edu/utk_musipubs/5.

Eagle, Joe. "Untitled video." Facebook. October 2, 2017. https://www.facebook.com/eagleacademy/videos/vb.701509113/10155831475224114/.

"Edmonton's Labatt Blues Festival." *2018 Edmonton Attractions Pass.* Accessed September 10, 2018.

"Edmonton's Labatt Blues Festival 2011: Festival Lineup." *YEGlive.ca.* https://yeglive.ca/groups/edmontons-labatt-blues-festival-2011.

Edwards, David Honeyboy. As told to Janis Martinson and Michael Robert Frank. *The World Don't Owe Me Nothing: The Life and Times of Delta Bluesman Honeyboy Edwards.* Chicago: Chicago Review Press, 1997.

Ellison, Ralph. "An Extravagance of Laughter." In *Going to the Territory,* 145–97. New York: Vintage, 1987.

———. *Invisible Man* (1952). New York: Vintage, 1972.

———. "'My Strength Comes from Louis Armstrong': Interview with Robert G. O'Meally, 1976." In *Living with Music: Ralph Ellison's Jazz Writings,* edited by Robert G. O'Meally, 265–88. New York: Modern Library, 2001.

———. "A Party Down at the Square." In *Flying Home and Other Stories,* 3–11. New York: Vintage, 1996.

———. "Remembering Richard Wright." In *Going to the Territory,* 198–216. New York: Vintage, 1987.

———. "Richard Wright's Blues." In *Shadow and Act,* 89–104. New York: New American Library, 1966.

"The Enlightenment of W. C. Handy." *Mississippi Blues Trail.* http://msbluestrail.org/blues-trail-markers/the-enlightenment-of-w-c-handy. Accessed September 11, 2018.

Evans, David. "Charley Patton: The Conscience of the Delta" (1987). In *Charley Patton: Voice of the Mississippi Delta,* edited by Robert Sacré, 23–138. Jackson: University Press of Mississippi, 2018.

"Examined Life—Cornell West." From *Examined Life,* 2008, directed by Astra Taylor. YouTube video, 13:31. March 22, 2013. https://www.youtube.com/watch?v=xfD3X3f5C_w.

Fabre, Michel. *The Unfinished Quest of Richard Wright* (1973). Translated by Isabel Barzun. 2nd ed. Urbana: University of Illinois Press, 1993.

Fanon, Franz. *Toward the African Revolution.* New York: Grove, 1967.

Ferdinand, Val (Kalamu ya Salaam). "The Blues (in two parts)." In *New Black Voices: An Anthology of Contemporary Afro-American Literature,* edited by Abraham Chapman, 375–77. New York: New American Library, 1972.

Ferguson, Josh-Wade. "Perpetual Reckoning: An Interview with Kiese Laymon." *New Ohio Review,* Summer 2019. https://newohioreview.org/2019/04/16/an-interview-with-kiese-laymon.

Ferris, William. *Blues from the Delta* (1978). Reprinted with a new introduction by Billy Taylor. New York: Da Capo, 1984.

———. *Give My Poor Heart Ease: Voices of the Mississippi Blues.* Chapel Hill: University of North Carolina Press, 2009.

———. "Richard Wright and the Blues." *Mississippi Quarterly* 61, no. 4 (Fall 2008): 539–52.

Field, Kim. *Harmonicas, Harps, and Heavy Breathers: The Evolution of the People's Instrument.* New York: Simon & Schuster, 1993.

"Five Stages of Grief by Elisabeth Kubler-Ross & David Kessler." https://grief.com/the
-five-stages-of-grief/. Accessed August 19, 2018.

Foster, Frances Smith. 'Til Death or Distance Do Us Part: Love and Marriage in African
America. New York: Oxford University Press, 2011.

Frede, Ari. "Words Sound Power: The Blues Vision of Corey Harris." Living Blues 126
(March/April 1996): 22–33.

Freeman, Roland L. "Don't Forget the Blues." Obsidian II: Black Literature in Review 13,
no. 1–2 (Spring/Summer 1998–Fall/Winter 1998–99): 63–65.

Garon, Paul. "White Blues." Race Traitor 4 (Winter 1995): 57–66.

Garon, Paul, and Beth Garon. Woman with Guitar: Memphis Minnie's Blues. New York:
Da Capo, 1992.

Gates, Henry Louis, Jr. "Black Creativity: On the Cutting Edge." Time, October 10, 1994.

———. The Signifying Monkey: A Theory of African American Literary Criticism. New York:
Oxford University Press, 1989.

———. "Why Richard Wright Hated Zora Neale Hurston." The Root, March 18, 2013.
https://www.theroot.com/why-richard-wright-hated-zora-neale-hurston-1790895606.

Gayle, Addison, Jr., ed. The Black Aesthetic. Garden City, N.Y.: Doubleday, 1971.

Gilmore, Martha Sanders. "Washington Blues Festival '70: A Benefit for Blacks in Blues."
Jazz Journal, February 1971, 18–29.

Gindick, Jon. Country & Blues Harmonica for the Absolute Beginner. 1987. VHS tape. 60
minutes.

———. Country & Blues Harmonica for the Musically Hopeless. Palo Alto, Calif.: Klutz, 1984.

———. "Jon's Mail-Order Store." https://gindick.myshopify.com/collections/cds.
Accessed December 4, 2019.

Gioia, Joe. The Guitar and the New World: A Fugitive History. Albany: State University of
New York Press, 2013.

Giovanni, Nikki. "Poem for Aretha" (1970) and "Master Charge Blues" (1970). In The
Selected Poems of Nikki Giovanni, 75–78, 87. New York: William Morrow, 1996.

Glover, Tony "Little Sun." Blues Harp: An Instruction Method for Playing the Blues
Harmonica (1965). New York: Oak, 1984.

Goins, Wayne Everett. Blues All Day Long: The Jimmy Rogers Story. Urbana: University of
Illinois Press, 2014.

Goldman, Albert. "Why Do Whites Sing Black?" New York Times, December 14, 1969.

Grazian, David. Blue Chicago: The Search for Authenticity in Urban Blues Clubs. Chicago:
University of Chicago Press, 2005.

Groom, Bob. The Blues Revival. London: Studio Vista, 1971.

Gussow, Adam. "Blues Heard 'Round the World: An International Perspective on
America's Down-Home Music." Presentation at the Liberal Arts Faculty Forum,
University of Mississippi. February 17, 2004.

———. " 'If Bessie Smith Had Killed Some White People': Racial Legacies, the Blues
Revival, and the Black Arts Movement." In New Thoughts on the Black Arts Movement,
edited by Lisa Gail Collins and Margo Natalie Crawford, 227–52. New Brunswick, N.J.:
Rutgers University Press, 2006.

———. Journeyman's Road: Modern Blues Lives from Faulkner's Mississippi to Post-9/11
New York. Knoxville: University of Tennessee Press, 2007.

———. Mister Satan's Apprentice: A Blues Memoir. New York: Pantheon, 1998.

———. "Modern Blues Harmonica — Harp Websites (Gussow.038)." YouTube video.

Commentary by Adam Gussow. Modern Blues Harmonica, April 3, 2007. https://www
.youtube.com/watch?v=Qf5LqdNOduY.

———. *Seems Like Murder Here: Southern Violence and the Blues Tradition*. Chicago:
University of Chicago Press, 2002.

———. "Sterling Magee and Adam Gussow — Swatch Watch Ad, Late 1980s (full
quality)." YouTube video. Modern Blues Harmonica, January 31, 2014. https://www
.youtube.com/watch?v=asEE5LriQks.

———. "Teaching the Blues: A Few Useful Concepts." *Blues Talk Documents: Syllabi,
Handouts, and More.* https://www.modernbluesharmonica.com/blues-talk-documents
.html. Accessed August 17, 2018.

———. "Where Is the Love? Racial Wounds, Racial Healing, and Blues Communities."
Southern Cultures 12, no. 4 (Winter 2006): 33–54.

Handy, W. C. *Father of the Blues: An Autobiography* (1941). New York: Da Capo, 1991.

———, ed. *Blues: An Anthology* (1926). Reprinted with a new introduction by William
Ferris. New York: Da Capo, 1990.

Haralambos, Michael. *Soul Music: The Birth of a Sound in Black America* (1974). New York:
Da Capo, 1985.

"Harmonica Blues with a 'Brand' New Beat." *Music Interviews, NPR Music,* July 31, 2011.

Harris, Corey. "Can White People Play the Blues?" *Blues Is Black Music!* blog, May 10, 2015.
http://bluesisblackmusic.blogspot.com/2015/05/can-white-people-play-blues.html.

Harris, Trudier. *Exorcising Blackness: Historical and Literary Lynching and Burning Rituals.*
Bloomington: Indiana University Press, 1984.

———. "No Outlet for the Blues: Silla Boyce's Plight in *Brown Girl, Brownstones.*"
Callaloo 18, no. 2 (Spring–Summer 1983): 57–67.

———. Untitled referee's report on *Seems Like Murder Here,* for University of Chicago
Press, 1998.

Harrison, Daphne Duval. *Black Pearls: Blues Queens of the 1920s.* New Brunswick, N.J.:
Rutgers University Press, 1990.

Harrison, Paul Carter. "Larry Neal: The Genesis of Vision." *Callaloo* 23. Larry Neal:
A Special Issue (Winter 1985): 170–94.

Hazzard-Gordon, Katrina. *Jookin': The Rise of Social Dance Formations in African-American
Culture.* Philadelphia: Temple University Press, 1990.

Hemenway, Robert E. *Zora Neale Hurston: A Literary Biography.* Urbana: University of
Illinois Press, 1980.

Henderson, Stephen. "Blues, Soul, and Black Identity: The Forms of Things Unknown."
Black Books Bulletin 1, no. 1 (Fall 1971): 11–15, 36–38.

———. *Understanding the New Black Poetry: Black Speech and Black Music as Poetic
References.* New York: William Morrow, 1973.

Hernton, Calvin C. "Dynamite Growing Out of Their Skulls." In *Black Fire: An Anthology
of Afro-American Writing,* edited by LeRoi Jones (Amiri Baraka) and Larry Neal, 81.
New York: William Morrow, 1969.

Herrick, Susan Oehler. "Performing Blues and Navigating Race in Transcultural
Contexts." *Issues in African American Music: Power, Gender, Race, Representation,* edited
by Portia K. Maultsby and Mellonee V. Burnim, 3–29. New York: Routledge, 2017.

Higginbotham, Evelyn Brooks. "African-American Women's History and the
Metalanguage of Race." *Signs* 17, no. 2 (Winter 1992): 251–74.

Hughes, Langston. "Bad Luck Card" (1927). In *Selected Poems,* 41.

————. "Bad Man" (1927). In *The Collected Poems*, 112.

————. *The Big Sea* (1940). New York: Hill and Wang, 1993.

————. *The Collected Poems of Langston Hughes*. Edited by Arnold Rampersad and David Roessel. New York: Vintage Classics, 1995.

————. *Fine Clothes to the Jew*. New York: Alfred A. Knopf, 1927.

————. "Ma Man." In *The Collected Poems*, 66–67.

————. "My Adventures as a Social Poet." *Phylon* 8, no. 3 (1947): 205–12.

————. "The Negro Artist and the Racial Mountain." *The Nation*, June 23, 1926, 692–94. http://www.modernamericanpoetry.org/content/langston-hughes-negro-artist-and -racial-mountain-1926.

————. "Note on Commercial Theatre" (1940). In *Selected Poems*, 190.

————. *Selected Poems of Langston Hughes* (1959). New York: Vintage Classics, 1990.

————. "Songs Called the Blues." *Phylon* 2, no. 2 (1941): 144–45.

————. "The Weary Blues" (1925). In *Selected Poems*, 33–34.

Hurston, Zora Neale. "Characteristics of Negro Expression" (1934). *The Sanctified Church: The Folklore Writings of Zora Neale Hurston*, 49–68. Berkeley: Turtle Island Foundation, 1981.

————. *Dust Tracks on a Road: An Autobiography* (1942). 2nd ed. Urbana: University of Illinois Press, 1984.

————. "How It Feels to Be Colored Me" (1928). In Hurston, *Folklore, Memoirs, and Other Writings*, 826–29. New York: Library of America, 1995.

————. *Mules and Men* (1935). New York: Perennial Library, 1990.

————. "The Ocoee Riot." In *Go Gator and Muddy the Water: Writings by Zora Neale Hurston from the Federal Writers Project*, edited by Pamela Bordelon, 146–51. New York: W. W. Norton, 1999.

————. *Their Eyes Were Watching God* (1937). New York: Perennial Library, 1990.

————. *Zora Neale Hurston: A Life in Letters*. Edited by Carla Kaplan. New York: Doubleday, 2001.

Husock, Habel. Untitled essay. Ann Arbor Blues Festival program, 1969. Blues Archive, University of Mississippi.

Hyde, Lewis. *The Gift: Imagination and the Erotic Life of Property*. New York: Vintage, 1983.

"ITTA BENA: BB King Day at MVSU Symposium 2018." Mississippi Blues Trail. http:// msbluestrail.org/announcements/itta-bena-bb-king-day-at-mvsu-symposium-2018.

"I've Got the 'Yes, We Have No Bananas BLUES! — Billy Jones, 1923." YouTube video. foxtrotgin, February 25, 2013. https://www.youtube.com/watch?v=Z16dzV6POPA.

Jahn, Janheinz. *Muntu: African Culture in the Western World* (1961). 2nd ed. New York: Grove, 1990.

Jess, Tyehimba. *leadbelly*. Seattle: Wave Books, 2005.

Johnson, Maria V. "'The World in a Jug and the Stopper in [Her] Hand': *Their Eyes* as Blues Performance." *African American Review* 32, no. 3 (Fall 1998): 401–14.

Johnson, Walter. *Soul by Soul: Life inside the Antebellum Slave Market*. Cambridge, Mass.: Harvard University Press, 1999.

Jones, Gayl. *Eva's Man*. New York: Random House, 1976.

Jones, LeRoi. *Blues People: The Negro Experience in White America and the Music That Developed from It*. New York: William Morrow, 1963.

————. "The Changing Same (R&B and the New Black Music)" (1967). In Jones, *Black Music*, 180–211. New York: Da Capo, 1980.

―――. *"Dutchman" and "The Slave"* (1964). New York: Perennial, 2001.

Karenga, Ron. "Black Art: A Rhythmic Reality of Revolution." *Negro Digest*, January 1968, 9.

Keil, Charles. *Urban Blues* (1966). Rev. ed. Chicago: University of Chicago Press, 1992.

King, B. B., with David Ritz. *Blues All around Me: The Autobiography of B. B. King.* New York: Avon, 1996.

King, Martin Luther, Jr. "The American Dream." *Negro History Bulletin* 31, no. 5 (May 1968): 22.

Knight, Etheridge. "Haiku" (1968). In *The Black Poets*, edited by Dudley Randall, 203. New York: Bantam, 1971.

Komson. "How to Sing Blues Songs." Personal email to Adam Gussow asking three questions. December 14, 2015.

"Komson Blues." YouTube video, n.d. https://www.youtube.com/channel/UCZjI03L9 qztYsAH4MxDT3bg/videos?view=0&sort=da&flow=grid.

Komson Blues. "Blues Harmonica: Adam Gussow Solo Cover." YouTube video. October 18, 2015. https://www.youtube.com/watch?v=e8vuim8fflQ.

Kubik, Gerhard. *Africa and the Blues.* Jackson: University Press of Mississippi, 1999.

Kumar, Aki. "All Bark No Bite―Hindi Man Blues―Track 6." *Aki Kumar's Bollywood Blues*, August 5, 2018. https://akikumar.com/lyrics/blog/all-bark-no-bite-hindi-man-blues -track-6.

―――. "Dilruba by Aki Kumar | Latest Song 2019." YouTube video. Sony Music India. August 15, 2019. https://www.youtube.com/watch?v=Q7_UHt_tqmk.

Laird, Ross. *Moanin' Low: A Discography of Female Popular Vocal Recordings, 1920–1933.* Westport, Conn.: Greenwood, 1996.

Lee, Justin. "Sugar Brown: The Shade of Blues." Vimeo. Justin Lee, April 12, 2016, vimeo .com/162549969.

Leitch, Vincent B. "Blues Southwestern Style." In *Theory Matters*, 137–64. New York: Routledge, 2003.

Lemann, Nicholas. *The Promised Land: The Great Black Migration and How It Changed America.* New York: Vintage, 1992.

Levesque, Roger. "Blues Fest Cooks Up Tasty Combos." *Edmonton Journal*, April 29, 2011. https://www.pressreader.com/canada/edmonton-journal/20110429/284846527337444.

―――. "Guitar Shorty Stands Tall at Blues Fest." *Edmonton Journal*, August 11, 2011. https://www.pressreader.com/canada/edmonton-journal/20110819/287664026013451.

―――. "Software Engineer Turned Bluesman Goes Back to Bollywood for New Inspiration." *Edmonton Journal*, May 17, 2018. https://edmontonjournal.com /entertainment/music/software-engineer-turned-bluesman-goes-back-to-bollywood -for-new-inspiration.

Levine, Lawrence W. *Black Culture and Black Consciousness: Afro-American Folk Thought from Slavery to Freedom.* New York: Oxford University Press, 1978.

Lomax, Alan. *Blues in the Mississippi Night* (1959). Sound recording with liner notes. Salem, Mass.: Ryko, 1990.

Love, G. "Down and Dirty with G. Love: The Gentle Blues of Mississippi John Hurt." *Guitar World*, January 25, 2012. https://www.guitarworld.com/blogs/down-and-dirty -g-love-gentle-blues-mississippi-john-hurt.

Macaluso, Scott. "The Best Modern Female Blues Musicians." *Joe Bonamassa*, Joe

Bonamassa, December 8, 2017. https://jbonamassa.com/best-new-female-blues
-musicians/.

Madhubuti, Haki (Don L. Lee). *Don't Cry, Scream*. Detroit: Broadside, 1969.

———. *We Walk the Way of the New World*. Detroit: Broadside, 1970.

"Mahindra Blues Festival 2018." Mahindrablues.com. Accessed September 11, 2018.

Mahon, Maureen. *Right to Rock: The Black Rock Coalition and the Cultural Politics of Race*.
Durham, N.C.: Duke University Press, 2004.

Matheis, Frank. "Favored Son." *Blues Access* 45 (Spring 2001): 16–18.

McGinley, Paige. *Staging the Blues: From Tent Shows to Tourism*. Durham, N.C.: Duke
University Press, 2014.

McKay, Claude. *Home to Harlem*. 1928. Boston: Northeastern University Press, 1987.

McTurk, Craig. *Tokyo Blues: Jazz and Blues in Japan*. VHS video. Santa Monica, Calif.:
Santa Monica Video, 1999.

Melnick, Jeffrey. *A Right to Sing the Blues: African Americans, Jews, and American Popular
Song*. Cambridge, Mass.: Harvard University Press, 1999.

"M1 The Call Performed by Monster." Featuring Taro Senga and Monster. Worldapart
ltd./apart.RECORDS, September 9, 2013. https://www.youtube.com/watch?v
=XzncQZbomZY.

Miller, Karl Hagstrom. *Segregating Sound: Inventing Folk and Pop Music in the Age of Jim
Crow*. Durham, N.C.: Duke University Press, 2010.

Millen, Gilmore. *Sweet Man*. New York: Viking, 1930.

"The Mississippi Blues Fest." YouTube video. Beauty by Sweet Angel, January 19, 2017.
https://www.youtube.com/watch?v=fqIvMRwaUJY.

Morton, Jelly Roll. "I Created Jazz in 1902, Not W. C. Handy." *Down Beat*, August 1938.
http://www.doctorjazz.co.uk/page10bc.html.

Mosley, Walter. *R. L.'s Dream*. New York: W. W. Norton, 1995.

Muir, Peter C. *Long Lost Blues: Popular Blues in America, 1850–1920*. Urbana: University of
Illinois Press, 2010.

Murphy, Jeannette Robinson. "The Survival of African Music in America." *Appletons'
Popular Science Monthly* 55 (1899). Edited by William Jay Youmans. Project Gutenberg,
2004.

Murray, Albert. *Stomping the Blues* (1976). New York: Da Capo, 1986.

———. *Train Whistle Guitar* (1974). Boston: Northeastern University Press, 1988.

Neal, Larry. "Any Day Now: Black Art and Black Liberation" (1972). In *Write Me a Few of
Your Lines: A Blues Reader*, edited by Steven C. Tracy, 422–33. Amherst: University of
Massachusetts Press, 1999.

———. "The Black Arts Movement." *Drama Review* 12, no. 4 (Summer 1968): 28–39.

———. "Can You Dig It?" In *Hoodoo Hollerin' Bebop Ghosts*, 71–72. Washington, D.C.:
Howard University Press, 1974.

———. "The Ethos of the Blues." *Black Scholar* 3 (Summer 1972): 42–48.

———. "For Our Women." In *Hoodoo Hollerin' Bebop Ghosts*, 55. Washington, D.C.:
Howard University Press, 1974.

———. "The Sound of Soul." Review of *The Sound of Soul* by Phyl Garland. *Negro Digest*,
January 1970, 43–47.

Neff, Ali Colleen. *Let the World Listen Right: The Mississippi Delta Hip-Hop Story*. Jackson:
University Press of Mississippi, 2009.

Oakley, Giles. *The Devil's Music: A History of the Blues* (1976). 2nd ed. New York: Da Capo, 1997.

Odum, Howard W. "Folk-Song and Folk-Poetry as Found in the Secular Songs of the Southern Negroes" (1911). In *Write Me a Few of Your Lines: A Blues Reader*, edited by Steven C. Tracy, 133–71. Amherst: University of Massachusetts Press, 1999.

———. *Social and Mental Traits of the Negro: Research into the Conditions of the Negro Race in Southern Towns; A Study in Race Traits, Tendencies and Prospects*. New York: Columbia University, 1910. https://archive.org/details/socialmentalooodumrich/page /n8/mode/2up.

Oliver, Paul. *Blues Fell This Morning: Meaning in the Blues* (1960). 2nd ed. Cambridge: Cambridge University Press, 1990.

———. *Screening the Blues: Aspects of the Blues Tradition* (1968). New York: Da Capo, 1989.

———. *Songsters and Saints: Vocal Traditions on Race Records*. Cambridge: Cambridge University Press, 1984.

O'Neal, Jim. "Junior Wells: Living Blues Interview." *Living Blues*, no. 119 (January/ February 1995): 8–29.

O'Neal, Jim, and Amy van Singel. *The Voice of the Blues: Classic Interviews from Living Blues Magazine*. New York: Routledge, 2001.

"Opening Plenary: Blues Summit on the State of the Music Today." YouTube video. Bluesandthespirit, July 13, 2012. https://www.youtube.com/watch?v=fE2FJEx1SAU.

Ottenheimer, Harriet. "Blues in the Heartland: African-American Music and Culture in the Middle West." In *Black Heartland: African American Life, the Middle West, and the Meaning of American Regionalism*, edited by Gerald Early, 16–36. St. Louis: Washington University African and Afro-American Studies Program, 1997.

———. "Comoro Crossroads: African Bardic Traditions and the Origins of the Blues." *Human Mosaic* 26, no. 2 (1993): 32–38.

Palmer, Robert. *Deep Blues*. New York: Viking, 1981.

Patterson, Orlando. *Slavery and Social Death: A Comparative Study*. Cambridge, Mass: Harvard University Press, 1982.

Peabody, Charles. "Notes on Negro Music." *Journal of American Folk-Lore* 16 (July– September 1903): 148–52.

Powell, Azizi, ed. "The Diddley Bow (Musical Instrument), Information and Videos." *Pancocojams* (blog). June 23, 2014. http://pancocojams.blogspot.com/2014/06/the -diddley-bow-musical-instrument.html.

"Prince McCoy." Mississippi Blues Trail marker. *Mississippi Blues Trail*. http://www .msbluestrail.org/blues-trail-markers/prince-mccoy.

"*Publishers Weekly* List of Bestselling Novels in the United States in the 1930s." https:// en.wikipedia.org/wiki/Publishers_Weekly_list_of_bestselling_novels_in_the _United_States_in_the_1930s.

Rampersad, Arnold. Introduction to Hughes, *The Big Sea*, iii–xxvi.

———. *The Life of Langston Hughes, 1902–1941*. Vol. 1, *I, Too, Sing America* (1986). New York: Oxford University Press, 2002.

Redmond, Eugene. "Double Clutch Lover." In *The Eye in the Ceiling*, 171–73. New York: Harlem River, 1991.

Reich, Howard. "Sugar Blue a Soaring Voice for the Blues." *Chicago Tribune*, October 23,

2012. https://www.chicagotribune.com/entertainment/ct-xpm-2012-10-23-ct-ent
-1024-jazz-sugar-blue-20121024-story.html.

Robertson, David. *W. C. Handy: The Life and Times of the Man Who Made the Blues.*
Tuscaloosa: University of Alabama Press, 2011.

Robinson, Zandria F. "Listening for the Country." *Oxford American*, no. 95 (Winter 2016).
https://www.oxfordamerican.org/magazine/item/1052-listening-for-the-country.

Rogin, Michael. *Blackface, White Noise: Jewish Immigrants in the Hollywood Melting Pot.*
Berkeley: University of California Press, 1998.

Rollins, Kenneth. "Festival to Celebrate Blues Roots; Women Artists, Past and Present,
Will Be in Spotlight." *Atlanta Journal-Constitution*, July 31, 1997.

Rowe, Mike. *Chicago Blues: The City and the Music.* New York: Da Capo, 1975.

Rowell, Charles H. "An Interview with Larry Neal." Taped in 1974. *Callaloo* 23. Larry Neal:
A Special Issue (Winter 1985): 11–35.

Rowley, Hazel. *Richard Wright: The Life and Times.* New York: Henry Holt, 2001.

"Ruth Etting—Shaking the Blues Away 1927—Irving Berlin Songs." YouTube video.
Warholsoup 100, May 15, 2011. https://www.youtube.com/watch?v=6z50-QHzM_c.

Sackheim, Eric, ed. *The Blues Line: A Collection of Blues Lyrics from Leadbelly to Muddy
Waters* (1969). Hopewell, N.J.: Ecco, 1993.

Salaam, Kalamu ya. "the blues aesthetic." In *What Is Life? Reclaiming the Black Blues Self*,
7–20. Chicago: Third World, 1994.

"Samm Bennett Interviews Sugar Brown." February 15, 2014. http://sugarbrownmusic
.com/press-and-reviews/extensive-interview-with-sugar-brown.

Sanchez, Sonia. "liberation / poem." In *We a BadddDDD People*, 54. Detroit: Broadside,
1970.

Schuyler, George. *Black No More: Being an Account of the Strange and Wonderful Workings
of Science in the Land of the Free, A.D. 1933–1940.* 1931. Boston: Northeastern University
Press, 1989.

"Selected Statistics on Slavery in the United States." Accessed August 17, 2018. https://
civilwarcauses.org/stat.htm.

Semuels, Alana. "The Racist History of Portland, the Whitest City in America." *The
Atlantic*, July 22, 2016. https://www.theatlantic.com/business/archive/2016/07/racist
-history-portland/492035/.

Sharpe, Christina. *In the Wake: On Blackness and Being.* Durham, N.C.: Duke University
Press, 2016.

Shaw, Arnold. *The Jazz Age: Popular Music in the 1920s.* New York: Oxford University Press,
1989.

"Stackolee." In *The Norton Anthology of African American Literature*, edited by Henry Louis
Gates Jr. and Nellie Y. McKay, 50. New York: W. W. Norton, 1997.

Steptoe, Tyina L. "Big Mama Thornton, Little Richard, and the Queer Roots of Rock 'n'
Roll." *American Quarterly* 70, no. 1 (March 2018): 55–77.

———. *Houston Bound: Culture and Color in a Jim Crow City.* Oakland: University of
California Press, 2016.

———. "'Jody's Got Your Girl and Gone': Gender, Folklore, and the Black Working
Class." *Journal of African American History* 99, no. 3 (Summer 2014): 251–74.

Stuckey, Sterling. *Slave Culture: Nationalist Theory and the Foundations of Black America.*
New York: Oxford University Press, 1987.

"Sugar Brown, blues singer_songwriter." August 2, [no year]. Proarts. https://www
.proartssociety.ca/sugar-brown-blues-singer_songwriter/.

Sweney, Mark. "First Ads Appear on YouTube Clips." *The Guardian*, August 17, 2007.
https://www.theguardian.com/media/2007/aug/22/advertising.digitalmedia.

Tate, Greg, ed. *Everything but the Burden: What White People Are Taking from Black Culture*.
New York: Broadway, 2003.

Thompson, James. "Media Means." *Negro Digest*, September 1969, 86–87.

Thompson, Robert Farris. "The 'Get-Down' Quality: Descending Direction in Melody,
Sculpture, Dance." In *African Art in Motion: Icon and Act*, 13–14. Berkeley: University of
California Press, 1974.

Titon, Jeff Todd. *Early Downhome Blues: A Musical and Cultural Analysis* (1977). 2nd ed.
Chapel Hill: University of North Carolina Press, 1994.

Toll, Robert. *Blacking Up: The Minstrel Show in Nineteenth-Century America*. New York:
Oxford University Press, 1977.

"Top 30 Southern Soul, Rhythm & Blues Albums." *Blues Critic: Soul Blues Music*. https://
www.soulbluesmusic.com/southernsoulbluescharts.htm. Accessed August 5, 2019.

Townsend, Henry, as told to Bill Greensmith. *A Blues Life*. Urbana: University of Illinois
Press, 1999.

Tracy, Steven C. *Langston Hughes and the Blues*. Urbana: University of Illinois Press, 1988.

Tran, E. M. "Obsession, Desperation, and Curiosity: A Conversation on the Poetics
of Blues with Tyehimba Jess and Derrick Harriell." *New Ohio Review*. Summer 2019.
https://newohioreview.org/2019/03/15/obsession-desperation-and-curiosity-a
-conversation-on-the-poetics-of-blues-with-tyehimba-jess-and-derrick-harriell/.

Troupe, Quincy. "Impressions / of Chicago; for Howlin Wolf." In *New Black Voices: An
Anthology of Contemporary Afro-American Literature*, edited by Abraham Chapman, 348.
New York: New American Library, 1972.

Troutman, John W. *Kika Kila: How the Hawaiian Steel Guitar Changed the Sound of Modern
Music*. Chapel Hill: University of North Carolina Press, 2016.

Upholt, Boyce. "Up All Night on Farish Street." *The Bitter Southerner* blog. https://
bittersoutherner.com/up-all-night-on-farish-street.

Wagner, Bryan. *Disturbing the Peace: Black Culture and the Police Power after Slavery*.
Cambridge, Mass.: Harvard University Press, 2009.

Wald, Elijah. *Escaping the Delta: Robert Johnson and the Invention of the Blues*. New York:
Amistad, 2004.

Welburn, Ron. "The Black Aesthetic Imperative." In Gayle, *The Black Aesthetic*, 132–49.

Werner, Craig. "Bigger's Blues: *Native Son* and the Articulation of Afro-American
Modernism." In *New Essays on "Native Son,"* edited by Kenneth Kinnamon, 117–52.
New York: Cambridge University Press, 1990.

Whiteis, David. "At 40 Years Old, Alligator Records Continues to Evolve." *Chicago
Reader*, May 11, 2011. https://www.chicagoreader.com/chicago/alligator-records
-40th-anniversary/Content?oid=3834565.

―――. *Blues Legacy: Tradition and Innovation in Chicago*. Photographs by Peter M.
Hurley. Urbana: University of Illinois Press, 2019.

"Why I'll Always Sing the Blues." ("Singing Since He Was Five, B. B. King Feels That Old
Songs Serve Social Purpose"). *Ebony*, April 1962: 94–96, 98.

Wilgus, D. K. "The Blues." *Journal of American Folklore* 78, no. 308 (April–June 1965):
183–88.

———. "From the Record Review Editor." *Journal of American Folklore* 74, no. 293 (July–September 1961): 282–86.

Williams, Sherley Anne. "The Blues Roots of Contemporary Afro-American Poetry" (1979). In *Write Me a Few of Your Lines: A Blues Reader*, edited by Steven C. Tracy, 445–55. Amherst: University of Massachusetts Press, 1999.

Wilson, August. *Ma Rainey's Black Bottom*. New York: Plume, 1985.

———. "Preface to Three Plays." In *The Jazz Cadence of American Culture*, edited by Robert G. O'Meally, 563–68. New York: Columbia University Press, 1998.

———. *Seven Guitars*. New York: Samuel French, 1996.

Wood, Berta. "Are Negroes Ashamed of the Blues? (White Critic Says They Scorn Tradition That Produced Jazz, Prefer White Culture)." *Ebony*, May 1957.

Work, John W., Jr. *American Negro Songs and Spirituals: A Comprehensive Collection of 230 Folk Songs, Religious and Secular*. New York: Bonanza, 1941.

Wright, Richard. "Between the World and Me" (1935). EdHelper.com. https://www.edhelper.com/poetry/Between_the_World_and_Me_by_Richard_Wright.htm.

———. "Big Boy Leaves Home." In *Uncle Tom's Children*, by Richard Wright. (1938). New York: Harper Perennial, 1993.

———. *Black Boy (American Hunger)* (1945). New York: Harper Perennial, 1993.

Young, Al. "A Dance for Ma Rainey." In *New Black Voices: An Anthology of Contemporary Afro-American Literature*, edited by Abraham Chapman, 366. New York: New American Library, 1972.

zur Heide, Karl Gert. *Deep South Piano: The Story of Little Brother Montgomery*. London: Studio Vista, 1970.

SELECTED DISCOGRAPHY

Aki Goes to Bollywood. Aki Kumar. 2016. Little Village Foundation.
"All Bark No Bite." Aki Kumar. 2018. UPC 814519024378.
Blues Mix 28: Dance Party Soul. Various artists. 2019. Ecko ECD2032.
"Bridging the Gap." Nas featuring Olu Dara. 2004. Ill Will / Columbia.
"Bumble Bee #2." Memphis Minnie. 1930. Vocalion 1556.
"Crazy Blues." Mamie Smith. 1920. Okeh 4169.
"Cry No More." Danielle Nicole. 2018. Concord CRE00629l (LP).
"Down Home Blues." Z. Z. Hill. 1982. Malaco 7406 (LP).
"Empty Bed Blues." Bessie Smith. 1928. Columbia 14312.
"Every Day I Have the Blues." Pinetop Sparks and Henry Townsend.
    1935. Bluebird 6125.
"The First Time I Met You." Little Brother Montgomery.
    1936. Bluebird B6766.
"Five Long Years." Eddie Boyd. 1952. J.O.B. 1007.
"Gone to Main Street." McKinley Morganfield (Muddy Waters).
    1952. Chess 1526.
Hindi Man Blues. Aki Kumar. 2019. Little Village Foundation.
"I Ain't Got Nobody." Bessie Smith. 1925. Columbia 14095.
"I Want My Mama." Salty Holmes. 1933. Bluebird B-5303.
"I've Got the Yes! We Have No Bananas Blues." Billy Jones.
    1923. Vocalion 14579.
"Killing Floor." Howlin' Wolf. 1964. Chess 1923.
Kick and Stomp. Adam Gussow. 2010. Modern Blues Harmonica.
"Luther's Blues." Luther Allison. 1974. Motown G 967V1.
"Mad Mama's Blues." Josie Miles. 1924. Document DOCD5467.
"Me and the Devil Blues." Robert Johnson. 1938. Vocalion 04108.
Memphis Grooves. Brandon O. Bailey. 2011. Modern Blues Harmonica.
"My Babe." Little Walter Jacobs. 1955. Checker 811.
"My Mind Is Trying to Leave Me." Albert Collins. 1983. Alligator 4730.
"My Own Fault, Darlin'." B. B. King. 1952. RPM 355.
New Cool Old School. Shoji Naito. 2016. Ogden Records ORCD 380.
"Oh Yeah." Muddy Waters. 1954. Chess 1571.
"Peach Orchard Mama." Blind Lemon Jefferson. 1929. Paramount 12801.

"See See Rider Blues." Ma Rainey. 1925. Paramount 12252.

"Shaking the Blues Away." Ruth Etting. 1927. Columbia 1113.

"She's Making Whoopee in Hell Tonight." Lonnie Johnson. 1930. Okeh 8768.

"Southern Blues." Roosevelt Sykes. 1948. RCA Victor 50–0040.

"Stay Out of the South." Sophie Tucker with Ted Dixon and His Orchestra. 1928. Composed by Harold Dixon. CO 4941.

"Talking Harmonica Blues." Sonny Terry and Brownie McGhee. 1960. Columbia DB 4433.

"That Black Snake Moan." Blind Lemon Jefferson. 1927. Paramount 12407.

"The Blues Is Alright." Little Milton. 1984. Malaco 2104.

"Trouble In Mind." Big Walter Horton with Carey Bell. 1973. Alligator 4702 (LP).

"Uncle Tom Is Dead (milk 'n cookies remix)." Guy Davis. 2006. Red House. RHR CD 192.

"Walking thru the Park." Muddy Waters. 1959. Chess 1718.

"Why I Sing the Blues." B. B. King. 1969. ABC/Bluesway 6.

INDEX

Abbott, Lynn, and Doug Seroff, 69, 106–7, 110–11, 112, 284n16, 285n14 (bar 6)

Africa, 25–26, 27, 31, 141, 166, 228; cultural inheritance from, 13–14, 20, 22, 32, 90, 92, 139, 213, 223; Senegal, 26; West Africa, 25, 91, 93, 114, 123, 166, 223. *See also* call-and-response

Alli, Andrew, 247, 268

Alligator Records, 6, 258, 281n5

Allison, Luther, 93, 211, 223

Ann Arbor Blues Festival, 44–45, 211, 212–13, 221–23

appropriation, cultural, 62, 120, 128, 130–32, 135, 208–9, 219, 224–25, 230

Armstrong, Howard "Louie Bluie," 63

Arnold, Billy Boy, 262, 263, 272

Atlanta, Ga., 263–64

Bailey, Brandon, 18, 248–51

Baraka, Amiri (LeRoi Jones), 105, 200–201, 203, 204, 207, 225, 282n12

Barrett, David, 241–42, 244, 272, 291n18

Beauchamp, Lincoln T. "Chicago Beau," 6–7, 252

Bell, Carey, 240, 242, 254, 263

beloved community, 198, 221, 283n1

Berlin, Irving, 42–43, 96, 134, 282n3

Berry, Chuck, 42

black aesthetic, the, 209, 214, 216, 219, 220–21, 222, 285n15 (bar 6); *The Black Aesthetic*, 200, 209

Black Arts Movement, 2, 211–14, 219, 223, 285n15 (bar 6); alliance with Blues Revival, 219, 224–25; attempt to reconcile blues origins and white audiences, 217, 220–23, 226; blues festival shaped by, 223–24; condemnation of white appropriation of blues, 208–9, 210, 213–14, 219, 230; conflict with Blues Revival,

216; and connection of artist to black community, 218, 222; and desire to isolate black art from white America, 201, 209, 216–17, 244–45, 285n15 (bar 6); impact on African American literature, 200–201; and jazz, 200; legacy of, 224–26; reclamation and embrace of blues, 137–38, 200, 204, 206–8, 209, 210, 213, 219–20; rejection of blues, 204, 206–7, 220. *See also* Baraka, Amiri; Blues Revival; Karenga, Ron; Lee, Don L.; Neal, Larry

black community, the, 21–22, 32, 44, 58, 128, 155, 187, 209–10, 214, 218, 222–23, 226, 231, 238

black dialect, 6, 117, 120. *See also* minstrels/minstrelsy

black elite (Talented Tenth), 139, 153

black history, 4, 30, 32–34, 36–37, 39, 56, 76, 84, 100, 112, 123, 143, 197, 212–13, 220–21, 230–31, 234, 253

Black Lives Matter, 59, 74, 198, 199, 265

black music, 65, 88, 119, 136, 229, 252; as agency, 145–46; and black memory, 219–20; blues as, 2, 6–7, 11, 13–14, 19, 25, 27, 38, 62, 82, 240, 253, 272; and Blues Revival, 217; consumers of, 66; "New Black Music," 207; rock and roll as, 283n4; white exploitation of, 82–83, 209, 213, 215, 223. *See also* slogans

Black Power, 203–4, 216–17; blues as, 207; era of, 221–22

black press, the, 16, 106–7, 142–43, 152, 153

black youth, 1, 11, 18, 22, 33, 41, 44, 47, 73, 118, 155, 162, 172, 184, 188, 198, 202–3, 210, 217, 219, 222–25, 229, 238, 264, 267–68, 270

Bland, Bobby "Blue," 44, 198–99, 220

bluegrass, black contributions to, 282n7

blues: and black audiences, 63, 65–66, 77,

126, 201, 203, 214, 219, 224, 239, 255, 259, 265–67; and black bluesism, 7, 12, 19–23, 25, 27, 61–62, 67, 71, 78, 82, 198, 219, 235, 247, 256, 261, 283n4; as black cultural inheritance and/or racial legacy, 7, 13–14, 35, 41, 71–72, 74, 91, 112, 199, 204–5, 207, 209, 225, 231, 239–40, 247, 261, 264, 292n17; black displacement from, 19–20, 27, 45, 112, 132, 214–15; as black history, 32–33, 39–40, 76, 84, 230–31, 234; and black mentors, 219, 232–35, 240, 246; black rejection of, 197, 203–4, 206–7, 214, 219–20, 224, 289n13; blues community as transracial and/or multicultural, 18, 27, 29, 45, 60–61, 126, 128, 136, 216–17, 230–31, 234–35, 253–58, 261, 291n7, 292n17; blues dialectic, 11, 15, 46–48, 78, 84, 92, 100, 147, 171, 172, 175, 180–81, 191; blues scale, 93, 114, 121; blues societies, 6, 25, 45, 61, 201–3, 225, 263; blues tourism, 20, 23–24, 105–6, 112, 255; blues universalism, 2, 4, 15, 23, 25–27, 60–62, 78, 211–12, 221, 238; country, 16, 42, 44, 64, 66, 69; creole origins of, 13, 41, 114; as devil's music, 117, 142, 146, 167, 253; as escape, 13, 56, 168, 184; fans/fandom of, 6, 15, 35, 67, 75, 86, 201, 216, 219, 224–25, 234, 268; fundamentalist framings of, 14, 245, 253–54; and fusion with Bollywood, 273–76; hillbilly, 15–16, 43–44, 65; history of, 67–68, 107, 114, 128, 267; as locus of ideological struggle between black bluesism and blues universalism, 2, 4, 15, 24–25, 38–40, 60–62, 221–22; as lyrical form, 90, 120, 151, 158–59, 180, 196, 221; Mississippi, 5, 15, 23–24, 121–22, 265, 268; Native American contributions to, 13, 281n9; performance and performers of, 5–6, 8–9, 14, 24, 35, 44–45, 54, 60, 63–64, 67, 72, 74, 76, 78, 81, 84, 91, 95–96, 107, 110, 132, 139, 144–50, 164, 166, 183, 201, 207, 210–12, 214–15, 221, 229, 232, 248–51, 253–54, 259–62, 264, 267–68, 288n7, 292n17; rural, 113, 222; and sexuality, 16, 42, 52, 80, 94–98, 128, 130, 139, 153–54, 170–71, 174–75, 184, 200–201, 211, 265; as white culture, 112, 201; and white

mentors, 18, 236–38, 240–41, 245. *See also* appropriation, cultural; blues in global context; call-and-response; Chicago blues; contemporary blues; Delta blues; juke joint(s); postmodernity; soul blues; white blues

Blues Coalition, 258–63

blues conditions, 15, 41, 49–59, 66, 86–87, 101

blues conferences: "Blues and the Spirit" symposium (Dominican University), 5, 9, 71, 258, 289n8; International Conference on the Blues, 267; "Race, Gender, and the Blues" conference (Dominican University), 230

blues cruises, 21, 259

blues culture, 26, 225, 254; black southern, 167, 182, 194; contemporary, 7, 10–11, 18, 60–61, 201, 247, 283n1, 292n17; Ellison and, 194–95; Hurston and, 169, 177; Wright's erasure of, 181, 190. *See also* soul blues; violence

blues ethos, 15, 49–50, 87–88, 98–104, 147, 149–50, 158, 181, 238

blues feelings, 15, 38, 46–47, 49–50, 52–53, 66, 71, 74–75, 77–78, 80–85, 86, 88, 122, 183, 184, 191, 199, 222, 224–25

blues festivals, 7, 18, 19, 44–45, 214, 223, 224–25, 247, 258–63; Ann Arbor, 211–12, 221–23; *Blues Festival Guide*/ BluesFestivalGuide.com, 214, 265; Edmonton Labatt, 259–62, 292n12; Santa Cruz, 290n42. *See also* Chicago, Ill.; Washington, D.C.

blues form, 145–47, 149, 200; AAB stanzaic pattern, 14, 16, 26, 88–91, 93–94, 98, 108, 113, 123–24, 145, 147–48, 166–67, 170; blues idiomatic language, 94, 98. *See also* call-and-response; signifying; vocalizations

Blues Foundation, 202, 258, 289n10; as placeholder for blues universalism, 25; and Howard Stovall, 1. *See also* Blues Music Awards; International Blues Challenge, Keeping the Blues Alive Awards

Blues God, 14, 200, 219–23

blues harmonica. *See* harmonica

Blues Harp. See Glover, Tony "Little Sun"

blues in global context, 25, 51, 197, 227, 229–30, 231, 245, 272, 291n7; Argentina (Buenos Aires), 119; Asia, 18, 45, 240, 254, 256; Australia, 25, 103–4; Bosnia-Herzegovina, 229; Brazil, 272; Cambodia, 252, 272; Canada, 25, 256, 258, 263; China, 18, 119, 229, 271–72; Europe, 13, 81, 119, 210, 213–14, 227, 240; France, 25, 119, 272, 283n6; Germany, 13, 25, 113, 119, 242, 272; Global South, 166; Guam, 26–27, 282n6; India, 18, 254, 262–63, 272–74; Japan, 18, 239, 254–55, 256–58, 292n3; Mexico, 240–41; South America, 240; Spain, 25, 272; Switzerland, 252, 272; United Kingdom, 248, 272, 291n18, 291n20; Vietnam, 230. *See also* Africa; blues; British blues invasion; Kawashima, Ken "Sugar Brown"; Kumar, Aki; Naito, Shoji; postmodernity; Senga, Taro

blues literature, 2, 88, 145, 153, 167, 181, 185, 190, 194, 201; autobiography, 16, 17, 33, 36, 44, 61, 75–78, 88, 91, 106, 114, 116–20, 141, 152, 153–54, 159, 162, 180–82, 187–88, 194, 201, 205, 245–46. *See also* Ellison, Ralph; Handy, W. C.; Hughes, Langston; Hurston, Zora Neale; Sharpe, Christina; Wilson, August; Wright, Richard

blues literary tradition, 16, 56, 133, 145–46, 151, 180, 187

bluesman, 27, 33, 41, 55, 58, 66, 75, 100–101, 129, 178, 184, 188, 194, 219, 234, 249; association with freedom of movement, 34, 47; and call-and-response, 91; country, 44, 69, 110, 217; Delta, 19, 69–70, 79, 208; as marker of authenticity, 66, 69; outside U.S., 18, 252, 258; as problematic term, 15–16, 63–65, 283n6; in *Their Eyes Were Watching God*, 17, 154, 169, 170, 176–77, 178–79; in "The Weary Blues," 144–45, 149–50; urban, 41, 210–11; Handy as not, 114

Blues Music Awards, 5–6, 25, 258, 263, 264. *See also* Blues Foundation; Jus' Blues (Music) Awards

blues musician(s), 1, 5–6, 11, 18, 23, 36, 38, 39, 44, 45, 51, 60, 61, 63–65, 67–68, 72, 74, 76–78, 80–81, 84, 93, 104, 110, 124, 132–33, 144–45, 148, 176, 181, 183, 201, 203, 210, 212–13, 219, 221, 225, 230, 232, 234, 236, 238, 253–56, 257, 259–60, 262–64, 267, 272, 288n7, 292n17; author as, 35, 83, 102–4, 237–39, 243, 245–46; in Deep South, 126, 164; in *Ma Rainey's Black Bottom*, 30, 59; rising, 273; young, 42, 211, 229, 231, 234, 240. *See also* blues: performance and performers; bluesman; blueswoman; white blues; *and specific musicians*

Blues Revival, 2, 11, 42–43, 64, 112, 127, 131, 201–2, 209, 211, 213–19, 221, 223–24, 226, 273. *See also* British blues invasion; Butterfield, Paul; Jones, Tom; Joplin, Janis; white blues

blueswoman, 12, 34, 69–70, 264, 284n16; country, 69; urban, 16, 113–14

Bollywood, 18, 275

Boyd, Eddie, 81

Boyd, Valerie, 17, 158, 161, 164, 167, 169, 173

Bradford, Perry, 69, 108, 133

Branch, Billy, 7–9, 11, 72, 289n8; accolades as harmonica player and teacher, 240–41; as bandleader, 254; as blues festival headliner, 5, 8–9, 247; as Blues Music Award nominee, 263; as critic of all-white blues festivals, 7, 262; "Son of Juke," 256; and The Blues Coalition, 258

British blues invasion, 42, 44, 127. *See also* blues in global context

Brooks, Lonnie, 1

Brooks, Ronnie Baker, 264

Brooks, Wayne Baker, 7

Broonzy, Big Bill, 74, 183

Brown, James, 203, 210–11, 220

Brown, Sterling, 88, 130–31, 153, 183

Burns, Jimmy, 254, 255

Butterfield, Paul, 44–45, 57, 209–10, 214–16, 228–30, 237

Cadillac Records (film), 42

call-and-response: audience engagement with, 166; in blues literature, 145, 175; as expression of dialogue between blues and hip-hop, 293n20; function of in

all-black settings, 266; as structuring
principle of blues, 45, 91–94, 98, 112, 126.
See also blues; blues form
Carr, Leroy, 41, 67–68
Charles, Ray, 211, 215
Charters, Samuel, 42, 64, 222
Chicago, Ill., 2, 28, 47, 71, 87, 103, 107, 118,
141, 195, 219, 226, 230, 235, 254–58; as
"birthplace" of the blues, 24; blues
community/culture in, 5, 231, 234, 254,
256, 257, 281n5, 292n3, 292n17; Blues
Hall of Fame in, 265; blues musicians
affiliated with, 1, 5, 6–7, 11, 101, 210–11,
233–34, 240, 244, 254, 261, 265–66;
blues performances in, 259; Chicago
Blues Festival, 259; movement of black
southerners to, 33, 41, 46, 81–82, 101, 233;
Obama in Grant Park in, 198; *Original
Chicago Blues Annual*, 6; as setting
of *Ma Rainey's Black Bottom*, 30, 56,
58–59. *See also* Alligator Records; blues
conferences; *Cadillac Record*; *Living
Blues*; Wilson, August
Chicago blues, 10–11, 210–11, 264, 273,
292n17
Chicago Defender, 107
Chicago Whip, The, 143
Chubby Carrier, 260–61
civil rights movement, 42, 234–35; National
Civil Rights Museum, 198
Clapton, Eric, 68–69, 217–18
Clarksdale, Miss., 21, 24, 69, 105–6, 122, 255,
268. *See also* Mississippi Delta
Collins, Albert, 82, 93
Cone, James H., 62, 71, 93, 190, 200, 206, 207
Connor, Joanna, 267, 292n17
contemporary blues, 2, 5, 7, 11, 15, 74,
291n20, 293n21; academic debates about,
14–15, 22–23, 24–25, 60–61; audience, 11,
22, 67, 201, 259; and black community/
experience, 28, 72, 230–31; criticism of,
5, 132; culture of, 7, 10–12, 18, 22–23, 253;
as escape, 13; festivals for, 7, 18, 214, 247,
255, 258–64; history's impact on, 41, 59,
197–98, 213; industry disputes about,
17; as locus of transracial community,

18, 60–61, 197, 254–56, 261, 283n1, 291n7,
292n3, 292n17; musicians, 107, 201, 203,
230, 240, 247, 254–56, 264, 272; paradoxes
of, 24, 292n17; racial politics of, 5, 40, 45,
71, 212–13, 240, 262, 292n17; scholarship
on, 13, 62. *See also* blues
Copeland, Shemekia, 214, 292–93n18
Cortez, Jayne, 200
cotton, 16, 20, 33, 39, 54–55, 106, 114, 120–21,
221; bluesmen and, 46, 102; and field
labor, including sharecropping, 13, 22–23,
47, 78, 113; cottonfields as source of the
blues, 23, 69, 70, 106; and slave labor, 32;
and vagrancy, 34–35, 54–55, 70. *See also*
Edwards, David Honeyboy; slavery
Cotton, James, 211, 213, 223, 237, 240, 242,
256, 262, 263, 272
"Crazy Blues." *See* Smith, Mamie
Crouch, Stanley, 200, 206–7, 211

Dan Lynch (blues bar), 85, 238
Davis, Angela Y., 52, 97–98, 170, 171, 172,
200
Deak Harp, 240, 241–42
Delta blues, 66, 70, 112–14, 126, 204. *See also*
bluesman
Dent, Tom, 200, 206, 211
devil, 66, 90, 116–17, 142, 146, 167, 253
Diddley, Bo, 42, 45, 248
Dixon, Willie, 47, 53, 75, 201, 246, 288n7
Dominican University. *See* blues
conferences
drums, 46, 91, 93–94, 139, 166, 214, 223, 261,
265
Du Bois, W. E. B., 123, 139, 159–60
Dumas, Henry, 200, 206

Edwards, David Honeyboy, 15, 64–66, 80,
126, 190, 195, 201, 246; apprenticeship
with Big Joe Williams, 232; association
with Harmonica Frank Floyd, 61; as
traveling bluesman, 47–49, 51–52, 56,
70; *The World Don't Owe Me Nothing*, 33,
34–35, 47, 61, 75, 78, 181–82, 185, 194
Ellison, Ralph, 17, 180–84, 185–87; and
Black Boy, 158–59, 185, 186–87; "An

Extravagance of Laughter," 191; *Invisible Man*, 17, 191, 193–96; "A Party Down at the Square," 191; "Richard Wright's Blues," 180–82, 184; and Wright, 158–59, 182–83, 191

Estrin, Rick, 234, 272

Fanon, Franz, 204
Faulkner, William, 68, 198
Ferris, William, 37, 79–80, 283n13, 288n7
Fish, Samantha, 6, 214, 265, 292–93n18
Floyd, Harmonica Frank, 61
Foxfire Ranch, 7–8
Freeman, Roland L., 19–22, 27, 28–29, 132

Garon, Paul, "White Blues," 219, 255
Gates, Henry Louis, Jr., 155, 157, 200
Gindick, Jon, 241–42, 243
Giovanni, Nikki, 200, 206
globalization and blues. *See* blues in global context
Global South, 166
Glover, Tony "Little Sun," 18, 236–38, 243
Gold, Scott, 26
Goldman, Albert, 215–16
gospel music, 91, 105; and B. B. King, 25; and Sheryl Youngblood, 266
Great Migration, 33–34, 160. *See also* migration
Grainger, Porter, 135–36
guitar, 6, 12, 27, 46, 56, 70, 85, 110, 114, 129, 234, 289n8; and blues tonality, 121; and call-and-response, 91–93; in early blues, 91; as equivalent of drum, 94; Handy and, 90, 116–19, 121–26; in Hughes's poetry, 141; in Hurston's writings, 161, 163, 167, 168, 170, 174, 181, 148; as instrument of emotional release, 50; and Native American blues origins, 281n9; *Seven Guitars*, 185; slide, 13, 70, 90–91, 93, 114, 122–23; talking, 93; *Train Whistle Guitar*, 184–85, 194, 288n8; women who play, 6, 292–93n18
Gussow, Adam, 2–18 passim, 63, 82–83, 84–85, 98–99, 100–104, 227–29, 230, 235–50 passim; and Hill Country Harmonica,

5, 7, 9, 10, 227, 247, 278, 291n20; as member of Satan and Adam, 7, 15, 63, 98–99, 102–3, 248–49, 271; and Modern Blues Harmonica, 4, 21, 228–29, 247, 281–82n3, 290n1; as solo performer and recording artist, 103–4, 250–51; and son, 29. *See also* YouTube

Guy, Buddy, 83, 201, 213–14, 223, 268, 273

Handy, W. C., 2, 4, 18, 54, 66, 88, 107–8, 109, 139–40, 143–44, 147, 151, 160, 166, 180, 181, 247; and "Blue Note," 121; contested status as originator of blues, 114–16, 121; *Father of the Blues*, 90–91, 106, 114, 116–18, 121–27, 138, 152, 153; marker on Mississippi Blues Trail, 267; and minstrelsy, 16, 117–18, 119, 120, 122, 138; renaming of W. C. Handy Awards, 5–6; and sexuality, 153, 154; "St. Louis Blues," 16, 66, 70, 88–89, 108, 119–21, 130, 144, 254. *See also* guitar

Harlem, 63, 71, 133–34, 150; author as street musician in, 35, 83, 98, 102, 227, 238–39, 266; as haven for southern migrants, 133–34; as home to black artists and intellectuals, 136–37, 141, 143–44, 151, 160, 162, 169, 204; in "The Weary Blues," 16, 144–45, 150

Harlem Renaissance, 151, 155, 160, 199–200; and Alain Locke, 95

harmonica (harp), 5, 9, 18, 41, 229, 231–34, 240, 241–42, 254, 255, 256, 261–62, 263, 271, 273, 274–75, 291n18; author's experience with, 4, 10, 12, 14, 21, 29, 83, 98, 103, 227–29, 235–39, 242–45, 247–51, 268, 272; and call-and-response, 91, 148; and vocalizations, 93. *See also* Glover, Tony "Little Sun;" Hill Country Harmonica; "Juke"; *and specific musicians*

Harriell, Derrick, 198, 199
Harris, Corey, 2–3, 11, 62, 74, 132, 240, 289n8, 301n8
Harris, Marion, 108, 126
Harris, Trudier, 38, 39, 188
Henderson, Stephen, 200, 206, 208–9, 210, 213, 215–16, 224, 226

Keil, Charles, 44, 112, 204, 222, 282n5

King, Albert, 211, 216–17, 293n2

King, B. B., 3, 12, 41, 45, 84, 207, 219–20, 223, 241–42, 293n20; association of blues and racial terror in testimony of, 13, 37–38, 75–78; B. B. King Museum, 106; B. B. King's Blues Club, 189; and black audiences, 44–45, 77, 203, 211, 219, 229; *Blues All Around Me*, 75, 76–77, 201; and gospel music, 25; and white audiences, 44, 201, 209, 222, 229

King, Martin Luther, Jr., 18, 234–35

Knox, Marquise, 198, 214, 225, 267–71

Kubik, Gerhard, 25–26, 90, 114

Kumar, Akarsha "Aki," 18, 241, 247, 272–74, 293n30

LaSalle, Denise, 67, 265

Laymon, Kiese, 86, 198, 278

Lee, Don L. (Haki Madhubuti), 200, 204, 208, 209, 213, 292n3, 292n9

Lewis, Sharon, 6, 11

Lipscomb, Mance, 201, 223

Little Richard (Peniman), 95, 101, 211

Little Walter (Jacobs), 12, 41–42, 53, 56, 237, 244, 254, 256, 268, 272. *See also* "Juke"

Living Blues, 28, 203, 219, 226, 239, 264, 273

Locke, Alain, 95

Lomax, Alan, 65, 74, 75, 222

Louisiana, 25, 36, 260–61; New Orleans, 210, 221

lynching, 23, 36, 39–40, 51, 54, 81–83, 189–90, 221; in blues literature, 185–86, 191, 193, 195; connection to blues, 35–36, 38, 63, 76–77, 83, 118, 185; Hurston's historical essay on, 160; lynch law, 33, 47, 70, 78; threat of as form of social control, 13, 55, 82, 133, 184–85, 187. *See also* Jim Crow; slavery; violence

Magee, Sterling "Mr. Satan," 15, 98–99, 244, 249, 250–51; as author's mentor and partner, 7, 63, 98–99, 102–4, 237, 238–39, 242, 271

Magic Dick, 236, 250, 272; "Whammer Jammer," 236, 248

Magness, Janiva, 246

Ma Rainey's Black Bottom. See Wilson, August

Martin, Trayvon, 2, 12, 198

Massey, Mark "Muleman," 24, 39

May, Butler "String Beans," 110–12, 284n16

McCoy, Prince, 125–26, 267

McGinley, Paige, 15–16, 66–67, 96, 284n16

McKay, Claude, 88, 162, 169

Memphis, Tenn., 21, 28, 81, 122, 138, 161, 181, 182, 198, 199, 231, 234, 248–49, 251, 254, 255, 279, 281n6; Beale Street, 3, 119, 182, 202, 248, 249; as "birthplace" of the blues, 24; and Blues Hall of Fame, 253, 292n2; "Memphis Blues," 119, 120–21, 130; musicians from, 18, 152, 227, 248, 291n10. *See also* Blues Foundation; Blues Music Awards; International Blues Challenge

Memphis Minnie, 170–71, 180, 194

Memphis Slim, 74, 111, 189

migration, 81–82, 161, 177, 188; and August Wilson, 29; and U.S. South, 155. *See also* Great Migration

Miles, Josie, 186

Miles, Lizzie, 69

Miller, Karl Hagstrom, 15–16, 61, 65, 66, 256

minstrels/minstrelsy, 16, 69, 82–83, 94, 109–10, 112, 113, 208, 219; and blackface, 16, 60, 108, 110, 117, 120, 138; and "coon shouter," 43, 69–70; and "coon songs," 16, 119, 120, 129, 138, 168–69; Handy and, 117–18, 119, 120, 122, 138

Mississippi, 7, 9, 11, 22, 27, 29, 41, 103, 112, 129, 191, 194, 208, 228, 232, 247, 264, 271; and blues, 3, 16, 49, 65, 113–14, 127, 129, 181, 190, 226, 259, 269; blues tourism in, 23–24, 112–13; Clarksdale, 21, 24, 69, 105–6, 122, 255, 268; Freedom Summer, 204; Handy and, 90, 124–26; Jackson, 3, 65; and Jim Crow, 23, 33, 123, 198–99; B. B. King and, 37–58, 75–77, 106; in *Ma Rainey's Black Bottom*, 56–59, 194; *Mississippi Lockdown*, 24; Mississippi plan, 54; musicians from, 5, 7, 15, 24, 39, 46, 52, 61, 63, 75, 81, 83, 92, 98, 101, 134, 188, 239, 255, 261; and slavery, 33, 36, 54;

speaking about race, 12, 35–36; musicians, 5, 6, 11, 63, 72, 107–8, 229–30, 263, 268; tourists, 19–20, 23–24; "White Blues" (Paul Garon), 255

Whiteis, David, 264, 281n5

white man, 30, 81, 83, 116, 186, 234, 241, 245; author's perspective as, 82, 229, 245, 246; in blues literature, 193, 194–95; as "boss" who protects black man from other whites, 78; as profiting from black music, 23; and sharecropping system, 22–23, 48–49; and slavery, 36–37, 51; as "the" white man, 32, 39, 54–59, 83, 92, 117, 120–21, 130, 157, 165, 183. *See also* lynching; slavery; white supremacy

white supremacy, 13, 118, 122, 179

Wiggins, Phil, 5, 8, 247

Williams, Big Joe, 47, 232

Williams, Sherley Anne, 149, 183, 200

Williamson, Sonny Boy, 27, 74, 232–33, 237–38

Willis, Jontavious, 267–70

Wilson, August, 20–21, 29–30, 33, 61; *Ma Rainey's Black Bottom*, 30–34, 56–59, 194

Wilson, Kim, 228, 234–35, 241–42, 260–62

Wright, Louis, 118

Wright, Richard, 183, 185, 187, 188, 191, 193, 196, 198; *Black Boy*, 17, 181–82, 185–86, 189–91, 288n7; and Hurston, 153, 155–57, 158; *Uncle Tom's Children*, 157. *See also* blues culture; Ellison, Ralph; violence

Young, Al, 200, 206, 211

Young, Kevin, 198, 225

Youngblood, Sheryl, 265–67

YouTube, 4–5, 12, 18, 22, 227–30, 237, 238, 242–44, 247–49, 251, 255, 271, 281–82n3, 291n16

CPSIA information can be obtained
at www.ICGtesting.com
Printed in the USA
LVHW040505180920
666443LV00003B/103